Fruits Basket™

Volume 22

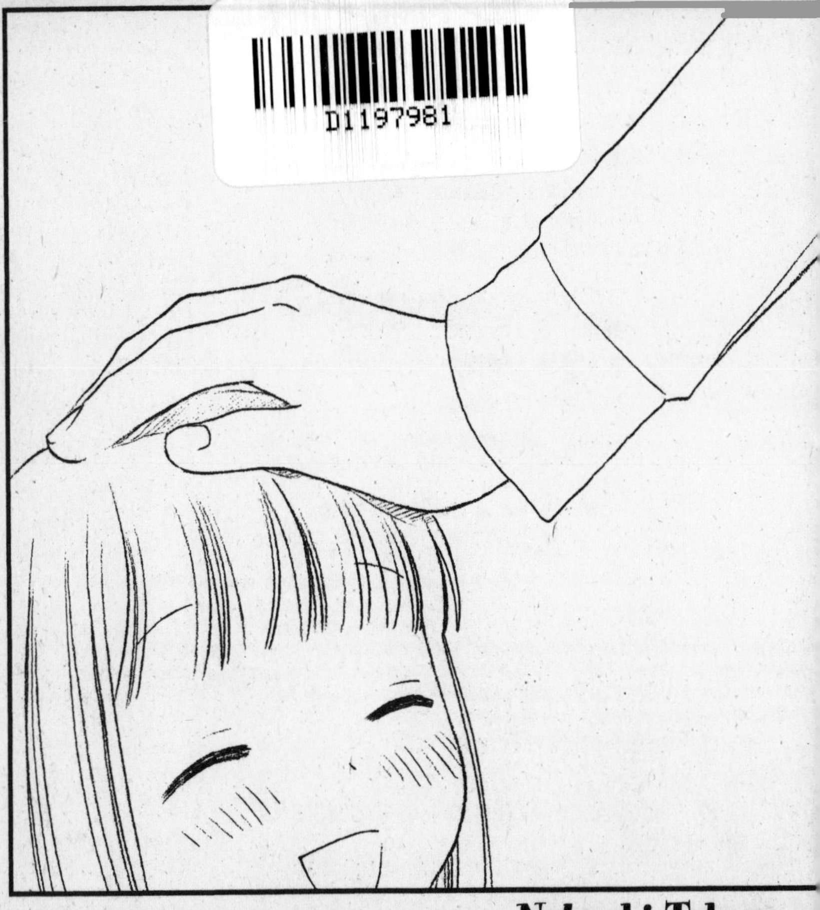

Natsuki Takaya

Fruits Basket Volume 22
Created by Natsuki Takaya

Translation - Alethea & Athena Nibley
English Adaptation - Lianne Sentar
Copy Editor - Stephanie Duchin
Retouch and Lettering - Star Print Brokers
Production Artist - Michael Paolilli
Graphic Designer - Tina Corrales

Editor - Alexis Kirsch
Pre-Production Supervisor - Vicente Rivera, Jr.
Print-Production Specialist - Lucas Rivera
Managing Editor - Vy Nguyen
Senior Designer - Louis Csontos
Senior Designer - James Lee
Senior Editor - Bryce P. Coleman
Senior Editor - Jenna Winterberg
Associate Publisher - Marco F. Pavia
President and C.O.O. - John Parker
C.E.O. and Chief Creative Officer - Stu Levy

A **TOKYOPOP** Manga

TOKYOPOP and 🐭 are trademarks or registered trademarks of TOKYOPOP Inc.

TOKYOPOP Inc.
5900 Wilshire Blvd. Suite 2000
Los Angeles, CA 90036

E-mail: info@TOKYOPOP.com
Come visit us online at www.TOKYOPOP.com

FRUITS BASKET by Natsuki Takaya   All rights reserved. No portion of this book may be
© 2007 Natsuki Takaya   reproduced or transmitted in any form or by any means
All rights reserved.   without written permission from the copyright holders.
First published in Japan in 2007 by HAKUSENSHA, INC., Tokyo   This manga is a work of fiction. Any resemblance to
English language translation rights in the United States of   actual events or locales or persons, living or dead, is
America, Canada and the United Kingdom arranged with   entirely coincidental.
HAKUSENSHA, INC., Tokyo through Tuttle-Mori Agency Inc.,
Tokyo English text copyright © 2009 TOKYOPOP Inc.

ISBN: 978-1-4278-0683-3

First TOKYOPOP printing: March 2009

10 9 8 7 6 5 4 3 2 1

Printed in the USA

Fruits Basket ™

Volume 22

By
Natsuki Takaya

HAMBURG // LONDON // LOS ANGELES // TOKYO

Fruits Basket ™

Table of Contents

STORY SO FAR...

Hello, I'm Tohru Honda, and I have come to know a terrible secret. After the death of my mother, I was living by myself in a tent, when the Sohma family took me in. I soon learned that the Sohma family lives with a curse! Each family member is possessed by the vengeful spirit of an animal from the Chinese Zodiac. Whenever one of them becomes weak or is hugged by a member of the opposite sex, that person changes into his or her Zodiac animal!

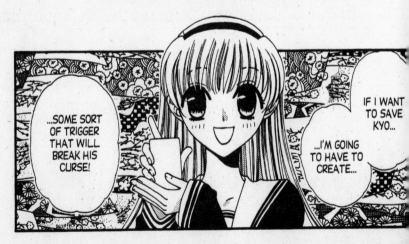

IF I WANT TO SAVE KYO...
...I'M GOING TO HAVE TO CREATE...
...SOME SORT OF TRIGGER THAT WILL BREAK HIS CURSE!

Tohru Honda

The ever-optimistic heroine of our story. An orphan, she now lives in Shigure's house, along with Yuki and Kyo, and is the only person outside of the family who knows the Sohma family's curse.

Yuki Sohma, the Rat

Soft-spoken. Self-esteem issues. At school, he's called "Prince Yuki."

Kyo Sohma, the Cat

The Cat who was left out of the Zodiac. Hates Yuki, leeks and miso. But mostly Yuki.

Kagura Sohma, the Boar

Bashful, yet headstrong. Determined to marry Kyo, even if it kills him.

Fruits Basket Characters

Mabudachi Trio

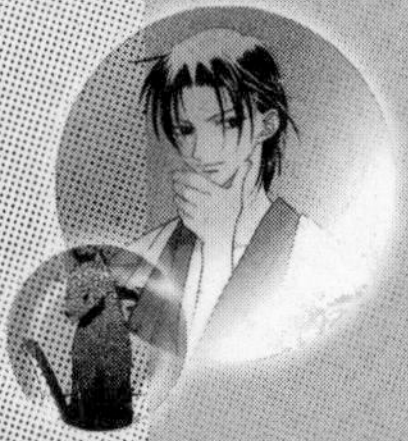

Shigure Sohma, the Dog

Enigmatic, mischievous and a little perverted. A popular novelist.

Hatori Sohma, the Dragon

Family doctor to the Sohmas. Only thing he can't cure is his broken heart.

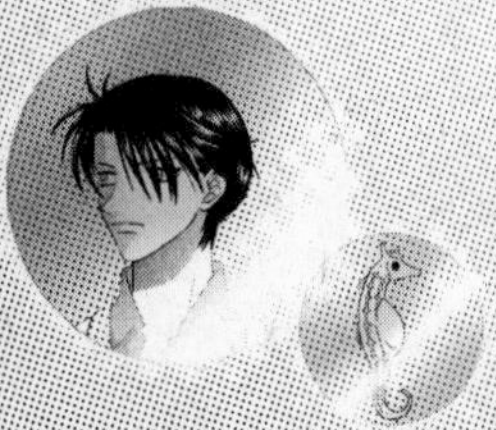

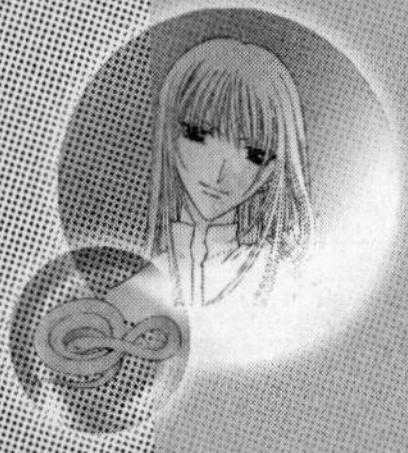

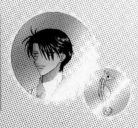

Ayame Sohma, the Snake

Yuki's older brother. A proud and playful drama queen…er, king. Runs a costume shop.

Saki Hanajima

"Hana-chan." Can sense people's "waves." Goth demeanor scares her classmates.

Arisa Uotani

"Uo-chan." A tough-talking "Yankee" who looks out for her friends.

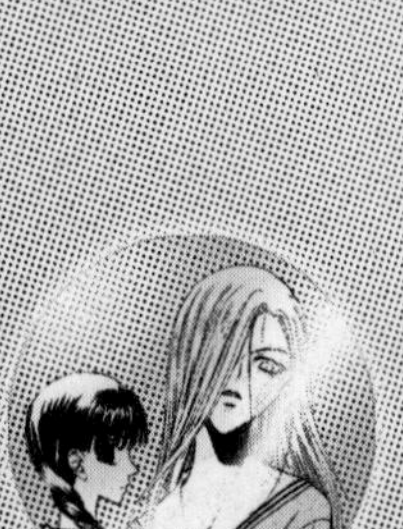

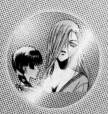

Tohru's Best Friend

Hiro Sohma, the Ram (or sheep)

This caustic tyke is skilled at throwing verbal barbs, but he has a soft spot for Kisa.

Momiji Sohma, the Rabbit

Half German. He's older than he looks. His mother rejected him because of the Sohma curse. His little sister, Momo, has been kept from him most of her life.

Hatsuharu Sohma, the Ox

The nicest of guys, except when he goes "Black." Then you'd better watch out. He was once in a relationship with Rin.

Kisa Sohma, the Tiger

Kisa became shy and self-conscious due to constant teasing by her classmates. Yuki, who has similar insecurities, feels particularly close to Kisa.

Fruits Basket Characters

Isuzu "Rin" Sohma, the Horse

She was once in a relationship with Hatsuharu (Haru)...and Tohru leaves her rather cold. Rin is full of pride, and she can't stand the amount of deference the other Sohma family members give Akito.

Ritsu Sohma, the Monkey

This shy, kimono-wearing member of the Sohma family is gorgeous. But this "she" is really a he!! Cross-dressing calms his nerves.

Kureno Sohma, the Rooster (or bird)

He is Akito's very favorite, and spends almost all of his time on the Sohma estate, tending to Akito's every desire. Kureno was born possessed by the spirit of the Bird, but his curse broke long ago...which means we've never seen him transformed. He pities Akito's loneliness, and can't bring himself to leave her.

"God"

Akito Sohma

The head of the Sohma clan. A dark figure of many secrets. Treated with fear and reverence. It has recently been revealed that Akito is actually a woman!

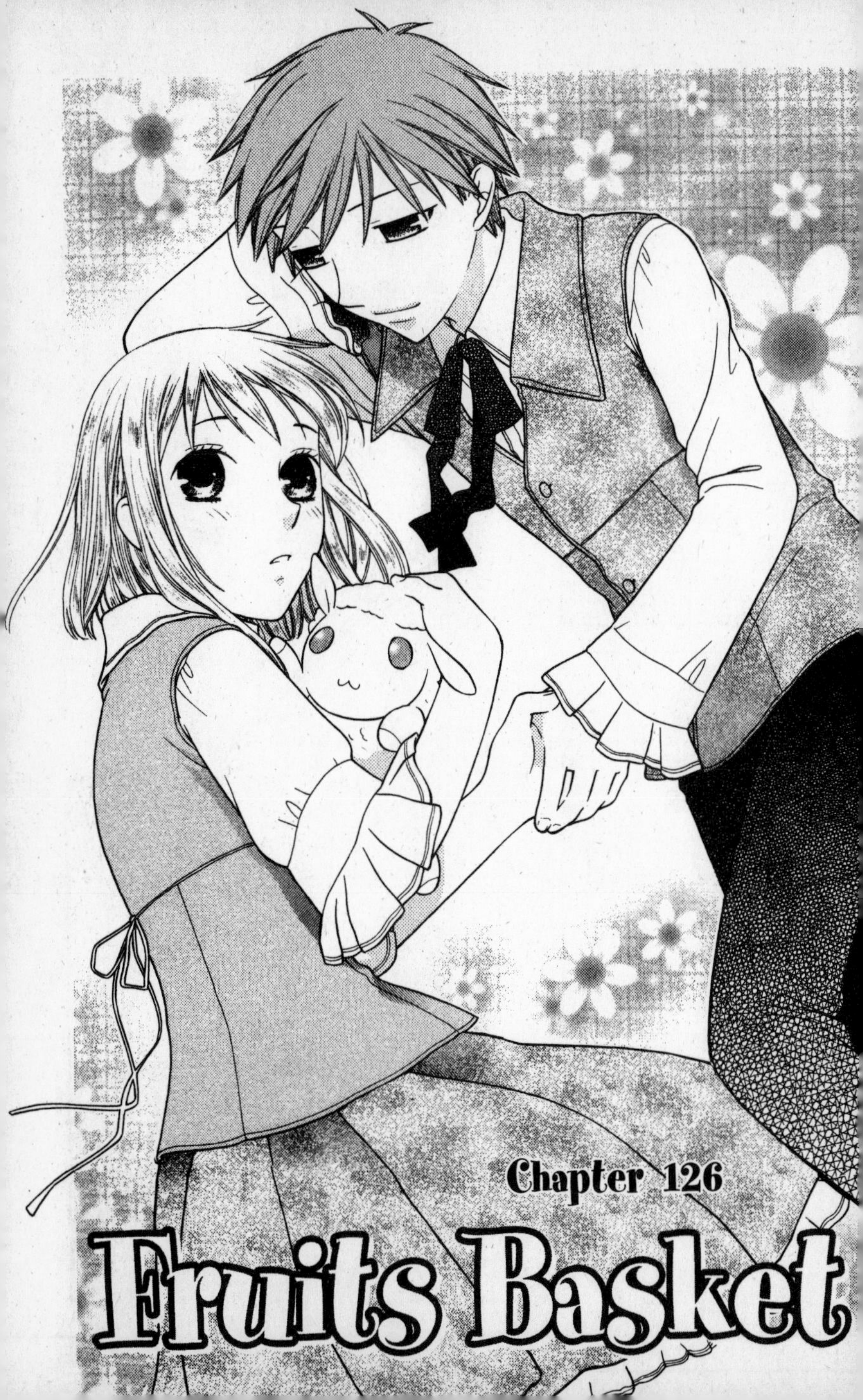
Chapter 126
Fruits Basket

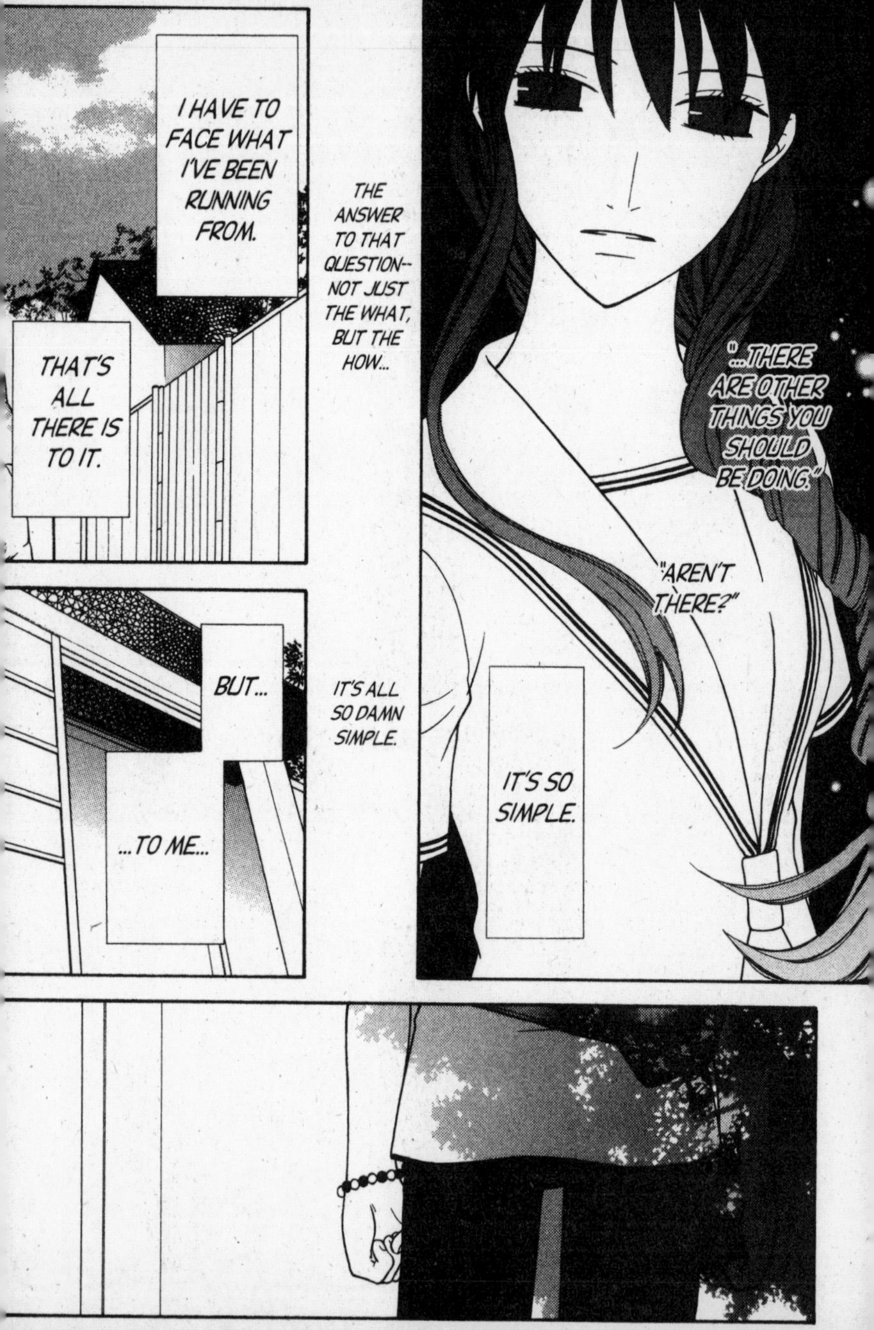
"...THERE ARE OTHER THINGS YOU SHOULD BE DOING."
"AREN'T THERE?"
IT'S SO SIMPLE.
THE ANSWER TO THAT QUESTION-- NOT JUST THE WHAT, BUT THE HOW...
IT'S ALL SO DAMN SIMPLE.
I HAVE TO FACE WHAT I'VE BEEN RUNNING FROM.
THAT'S ALL THERE IS TO IT.
BUT...
...TO ME...

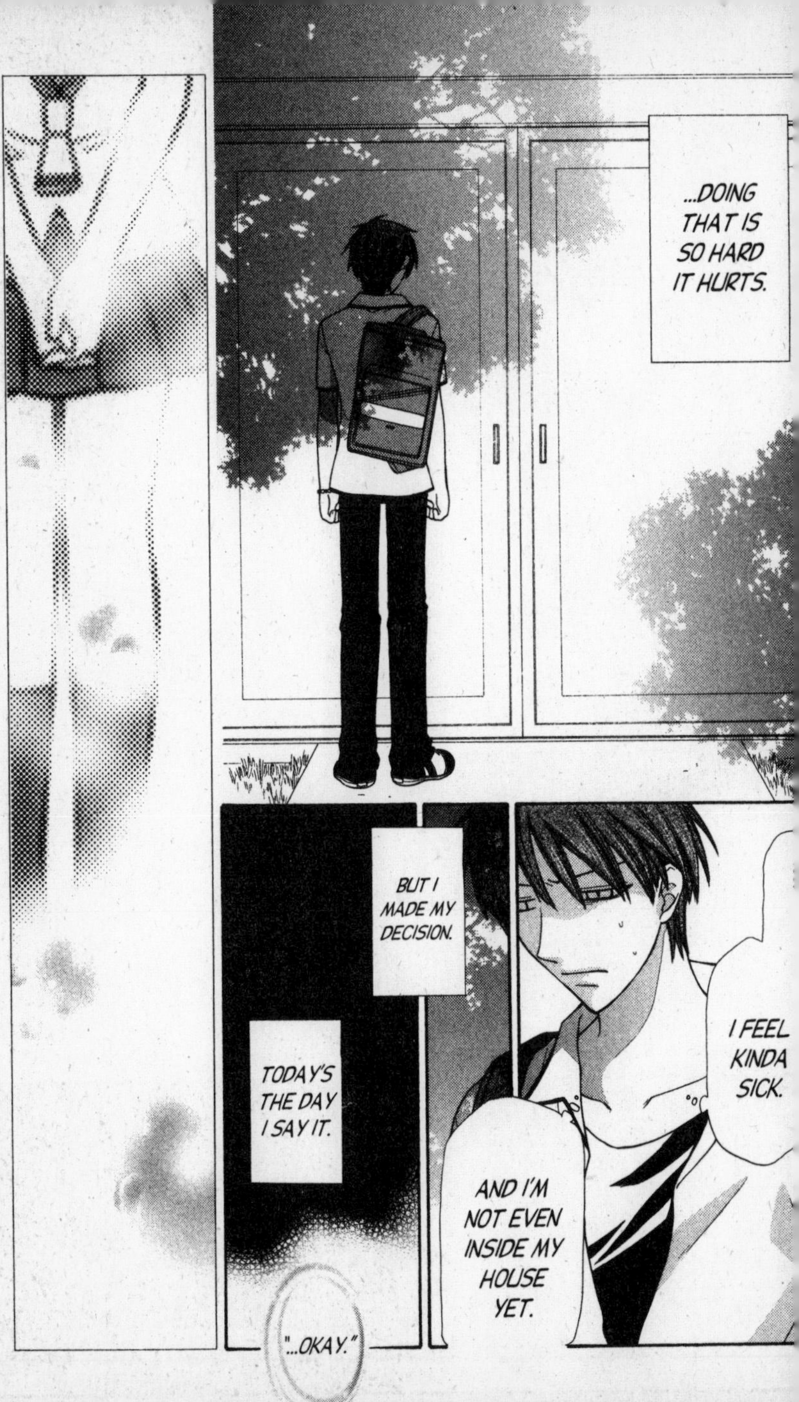
...DOING THAT IS SO HARD IT HURTS.
I FEEL KINDA SICK.
AND I'M NOT EVEN INSIDE MY HOUSE YET.
BUT I MADE MY DECISION.
TODAY'S THE DAY I SAY IT.
"...OKAY."

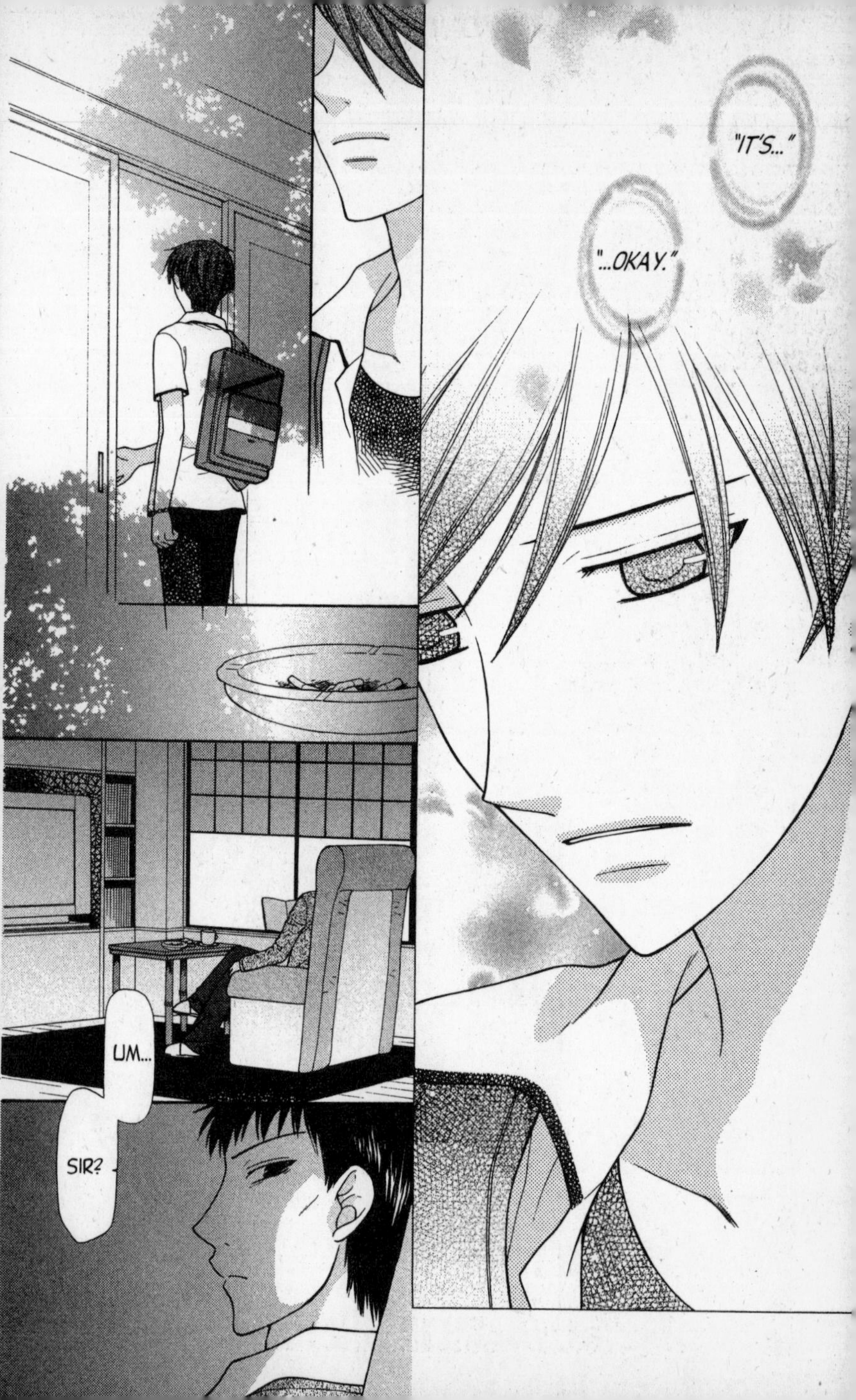
"IT'S..."
"...OKAY."
UM...
SIR?

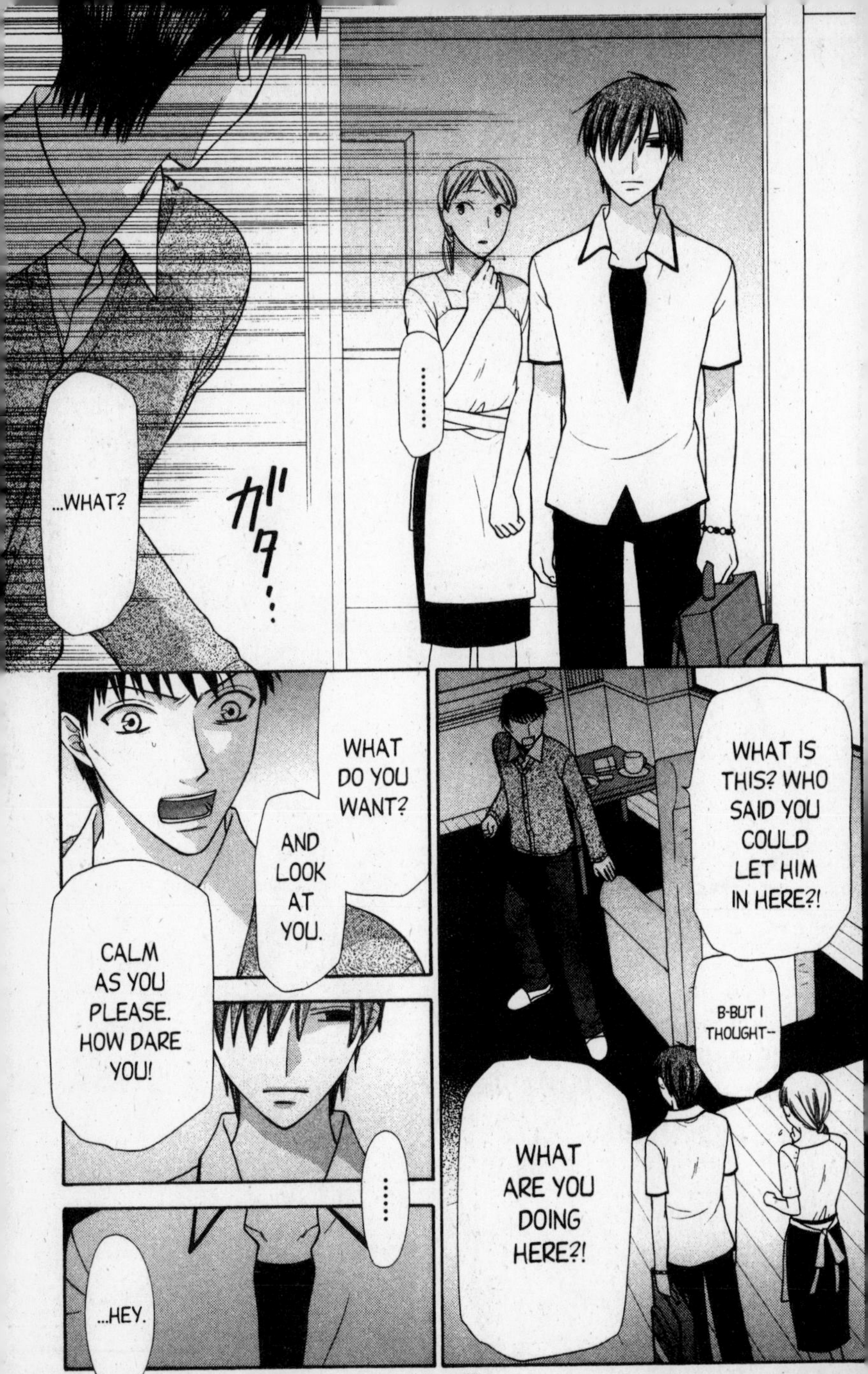
......
ガタ...
...WHAT?
WHAT IS THIS? WHO SAID YOU COULD LET HIM IN HERE?!
B-BUT I THOUGHT--
WHAT ARE YOU DOING HERE?!
WHAT DO YOU WANT?
AND LOOK AT YOU.
CALM AS YOU PLEASE. HOW DARE YOU!
......
...HEY.

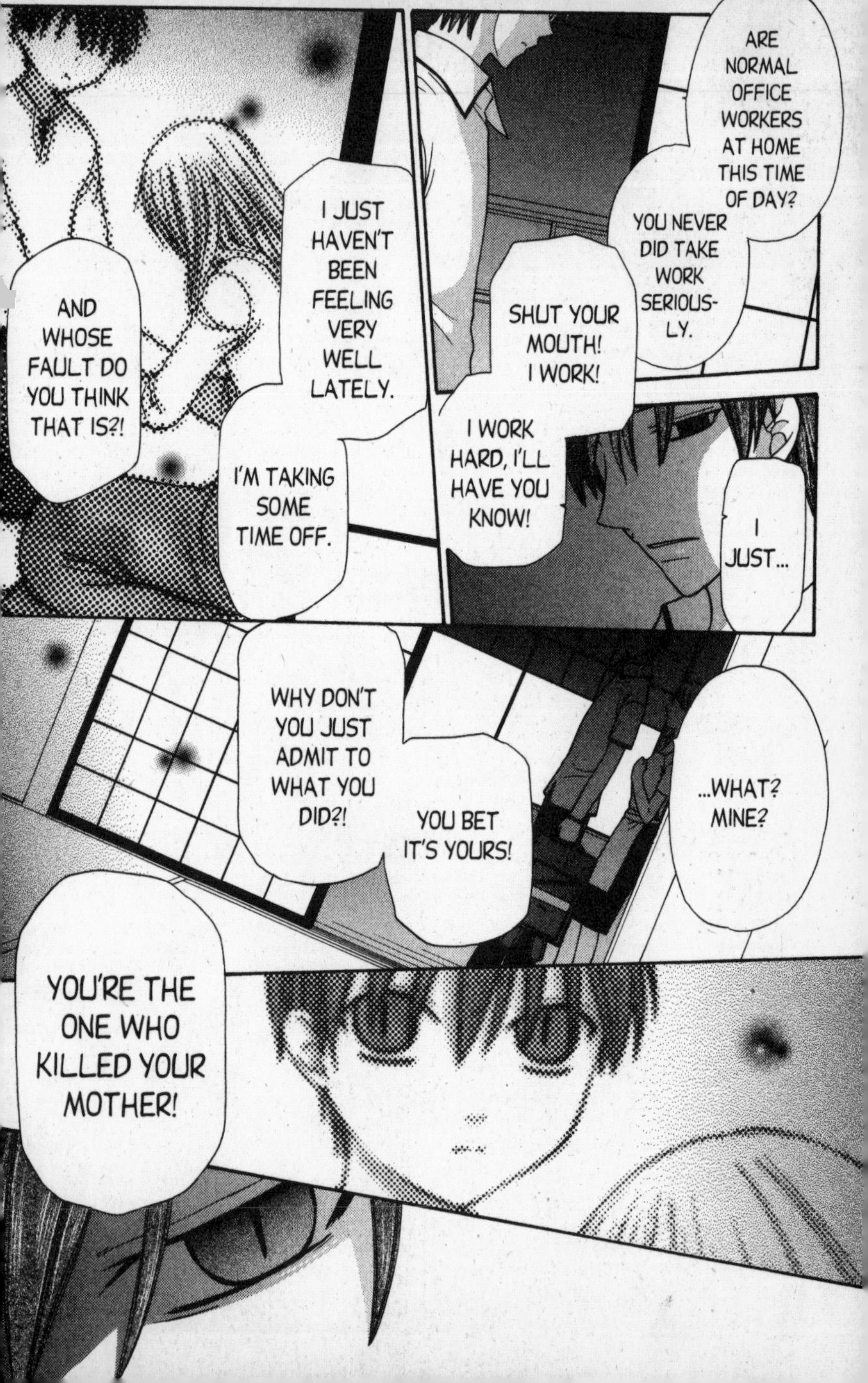
ARE NORMAL OFFICE WORKERS AT HOME THIS TIME OF DAY?
YOU NEVER DID TAKE WORK SERIOUS-LY.
SHUT YOUR MOUTH! I WORK!
I WORK HARD, I'LL HAVE YOU KNOW!
I JUST...
I JUST HAVEN'T BEEN FEELING VERY WELL LATELY.
I'M TAKING SOME TIME OFF.
AND WHOSE FAULT DO YOU THINK THAT IS?!
...WHAT? MINE?
YOU BET IT'S YOURS!
WHY DON'T YOU JUST ADMIT TO WHAT YOU DID?!
YOU'RE THE ONE WHO KILLED YOUR MOTHER!

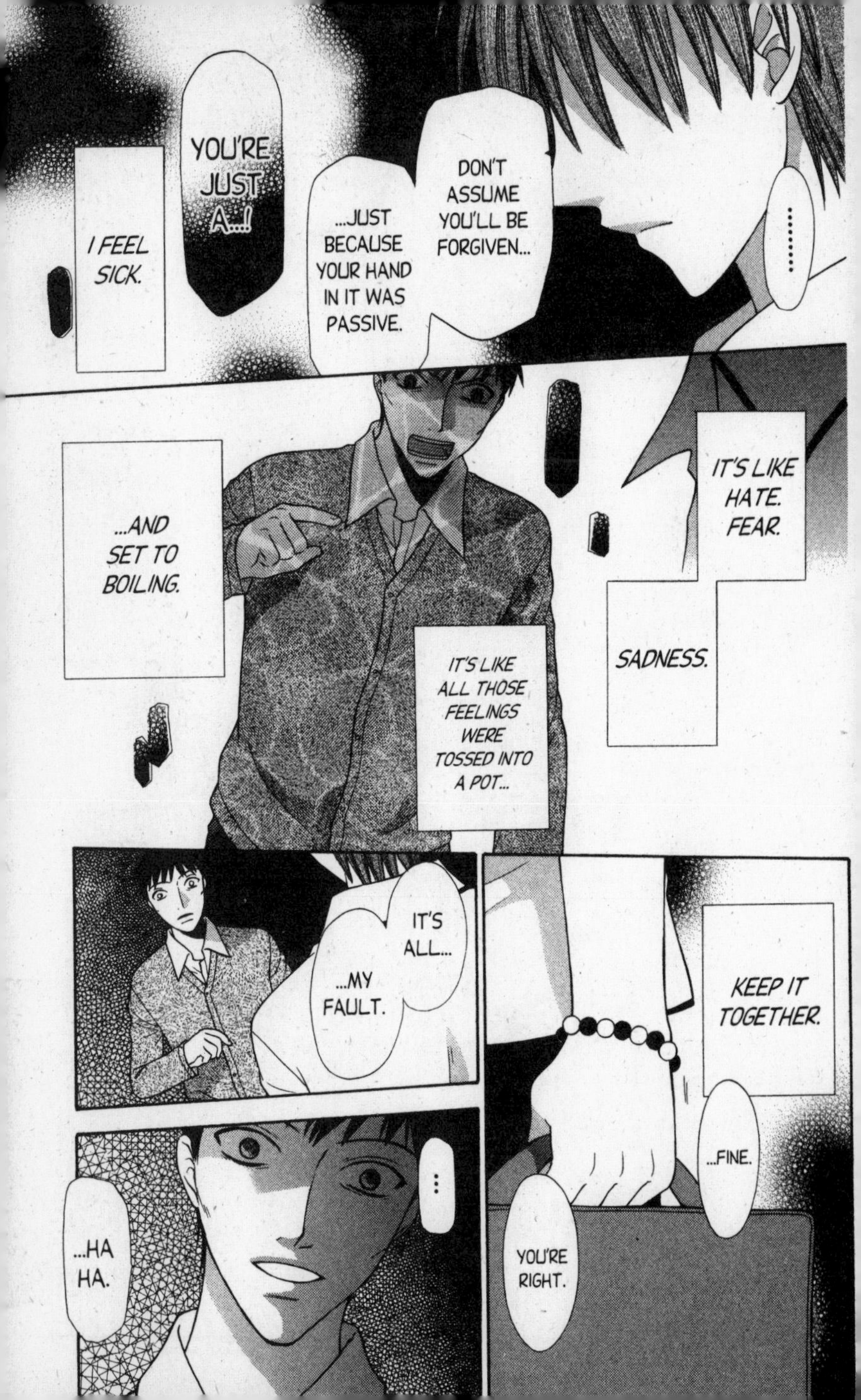

....
DON'T ASSUME YOU'LL BE FORGIVEN...
...JUST BECAUSE YOUR HAND IN IT WAS PASSIVE.
YOU'RE JUST A...!
I FEEL SICK.
IT'S LIKE HATE. FEAR.
SADNESS.
IT'S LIKE ALL THOSE FEELINGS WERE TOSSED INTO A POT...
...AND SET TO BOILING.
KEEP IT TOGETHER.
...FINE.
YOU'RE RIGHT.
IT'S ALL...
...MY FAULT.
...
...HA HA.

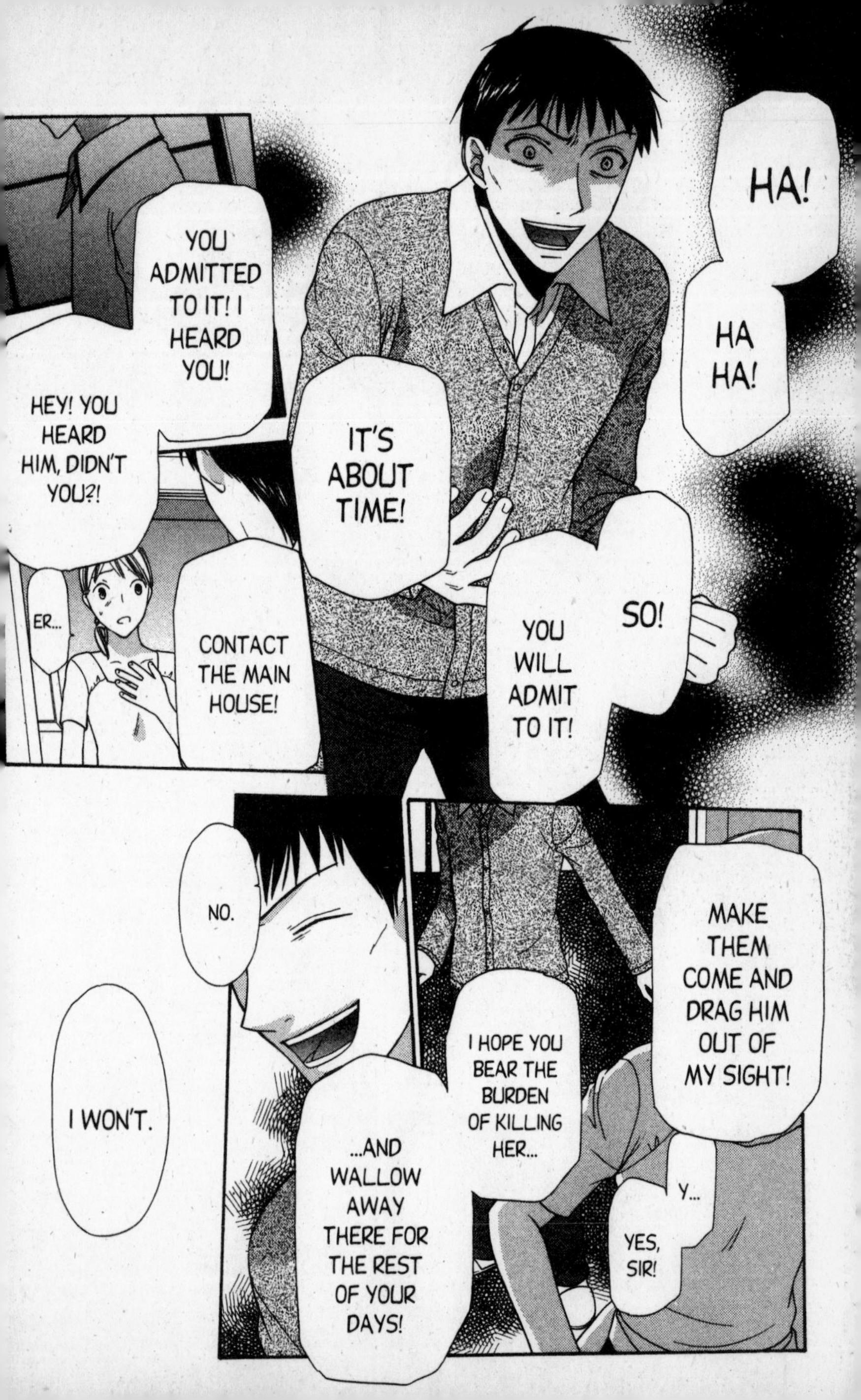
HA!
HA HA!
IT'S ABOUT TIME!
SO!
YOU WILL ADMIT TO IT!
YOU ADMITTED TO IT! I HEARD YOU!
HEY! YOU HEARD HIM, DIDN'T YOU?!
CONTACT THE MAIN HOUSE!
ER...
MAKE THEM COME AND DRAG HIM OUT OF MY SIGHT!
Y...
YES, SIR!
I HOPE YOU BEAR THE BURDEN OF KILLING HER...
...AND WALLOW AWAY THERE FOR THE REST OF YOUR DAYS!
NO.
I WON'T.

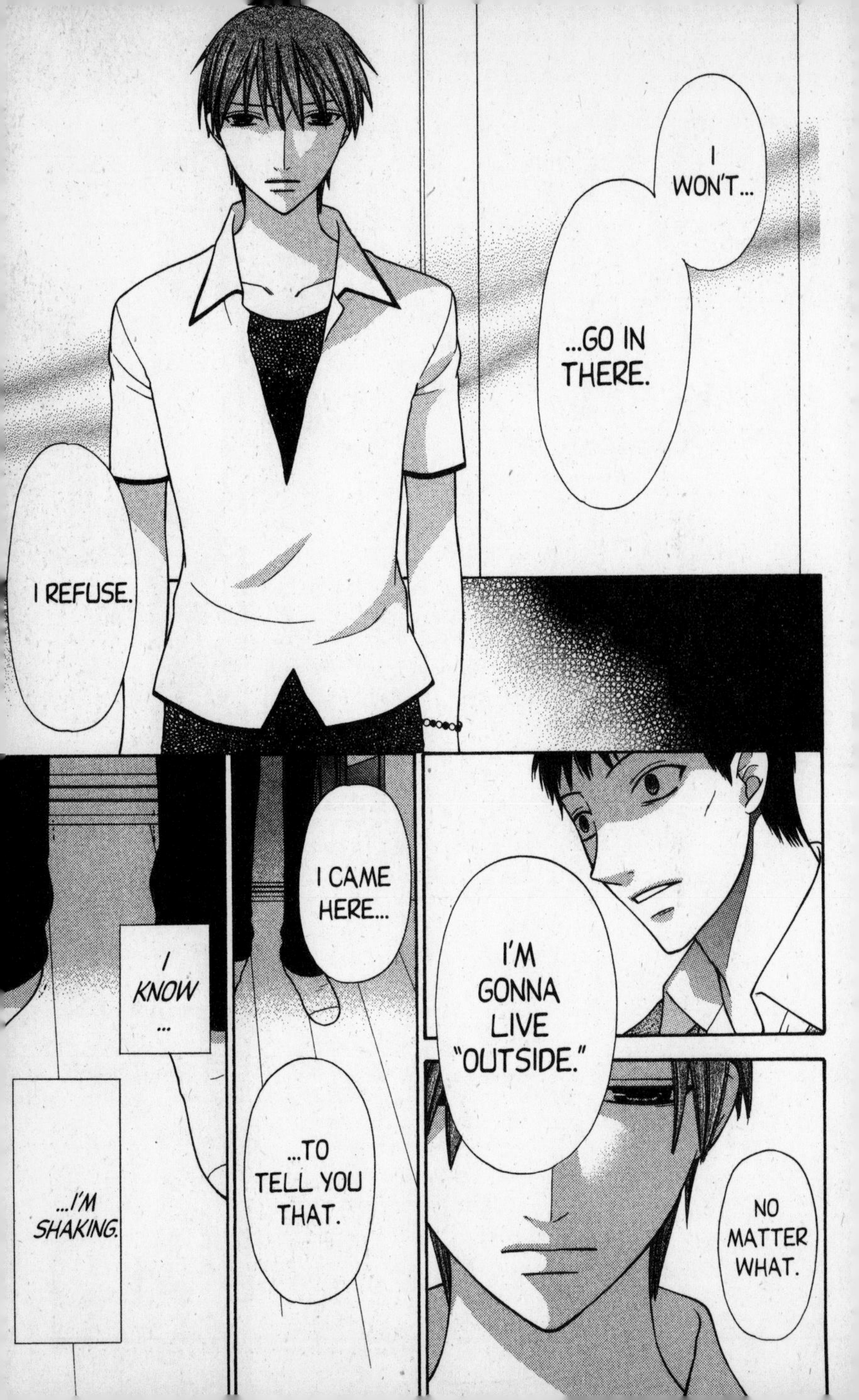
I WON'T...
...GO IN THERE.
I REFUSE.
I'M GONNA LIVE "OUTSIDE."
NO MATTER WHAT.
I CAME HERE...
...TO TELL YOU THAT.
I KNOW...
...I'M SHAKING.

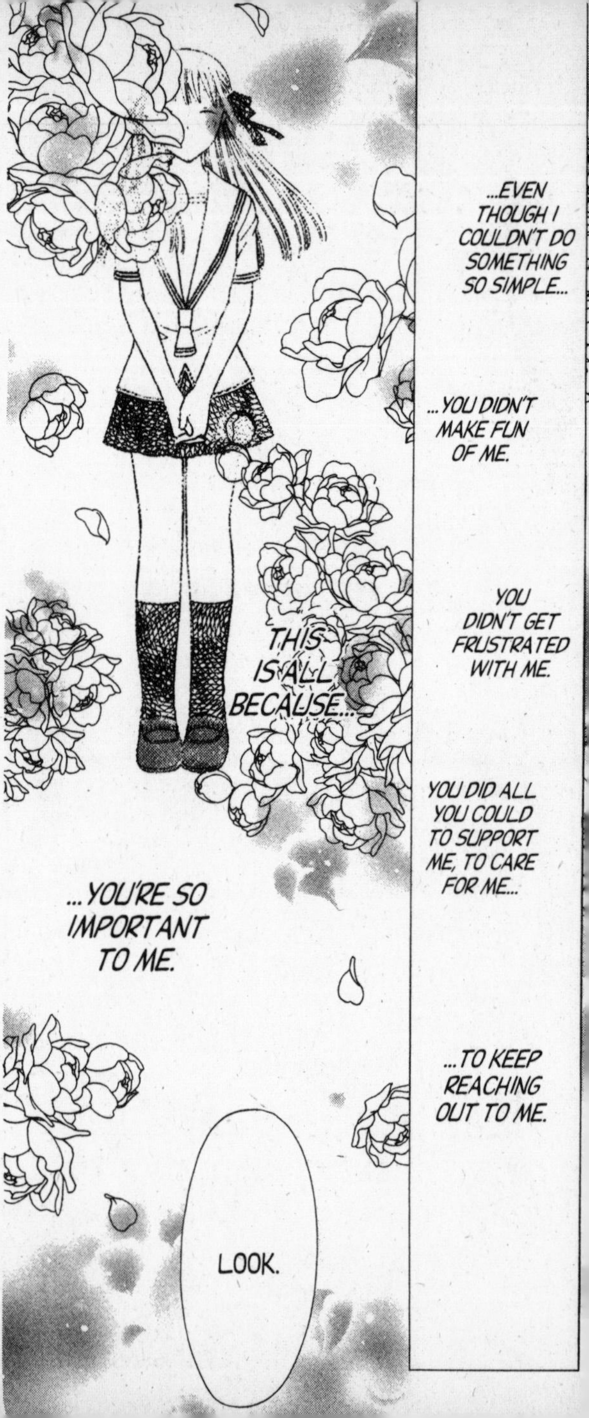
...EVEN THOUGH I COULDN'T DO SOMETHING SO SIMPLE...
...YOU DIDN'T MAKE FUN OF ME.
YOU DIDN'T GET FRUSTRATED WITH ME.
YOU DID ALL YOU COULD TO SUPPORT ME, TO CARE FOR ME...
...TO KEEP REACHING OUT TO ME.
THIS IS ALL BECAUSE...
...YOU'RE SO IMPORTANT TO ME.
LOOK.

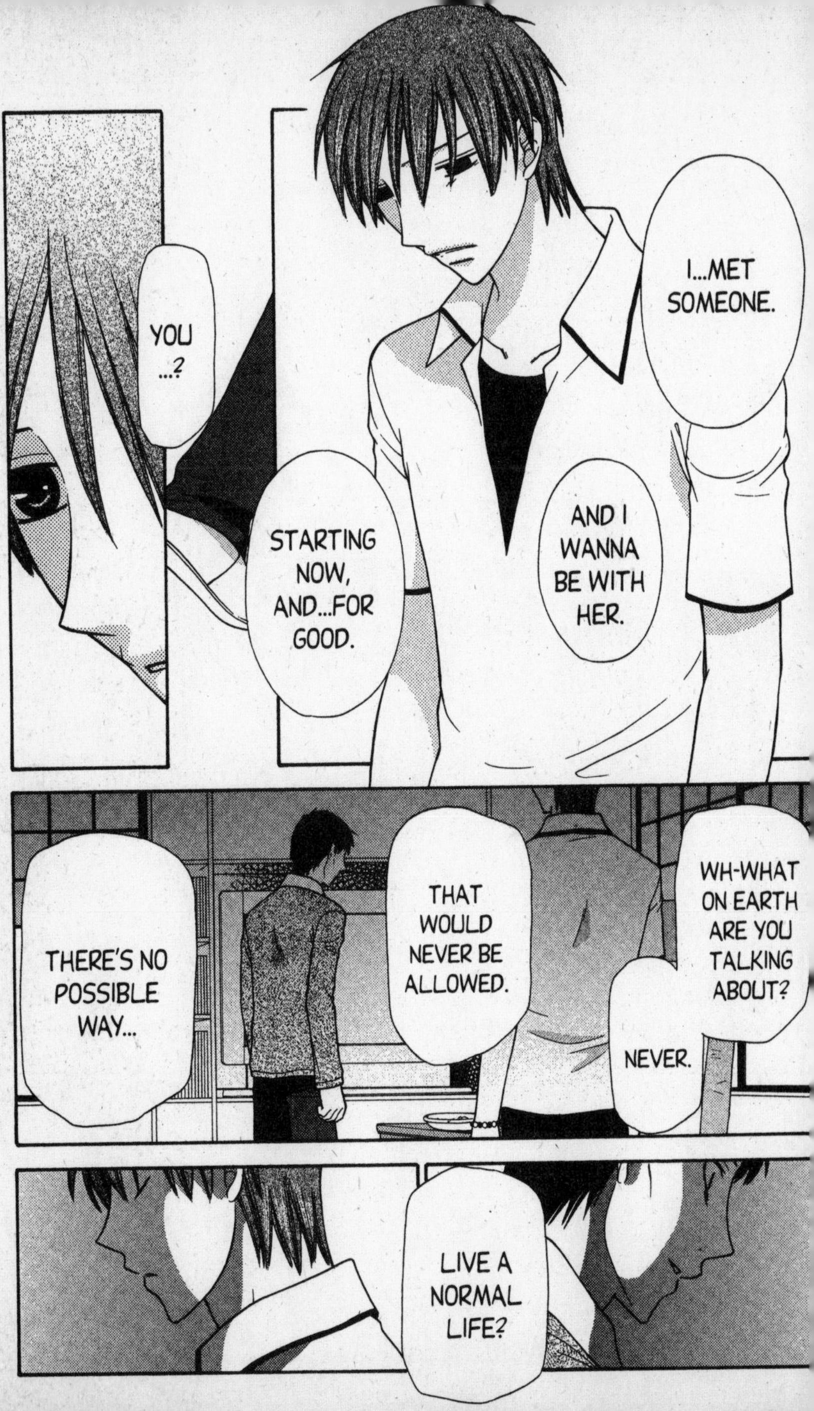
I...MET SOMEONE.
AND I WANNA BE WITH HER.
STARTING NOW, AND...FOR GOOD.
YOU ...?
WH-WHAT ON EARTH ARE YOU TALKING ABOUT?
NEVER.
THAT WOULD NEVER BE ALLOWED.
THERE'S NO POSSIBLE WAY...
LIVE A NORMAL LIFE?

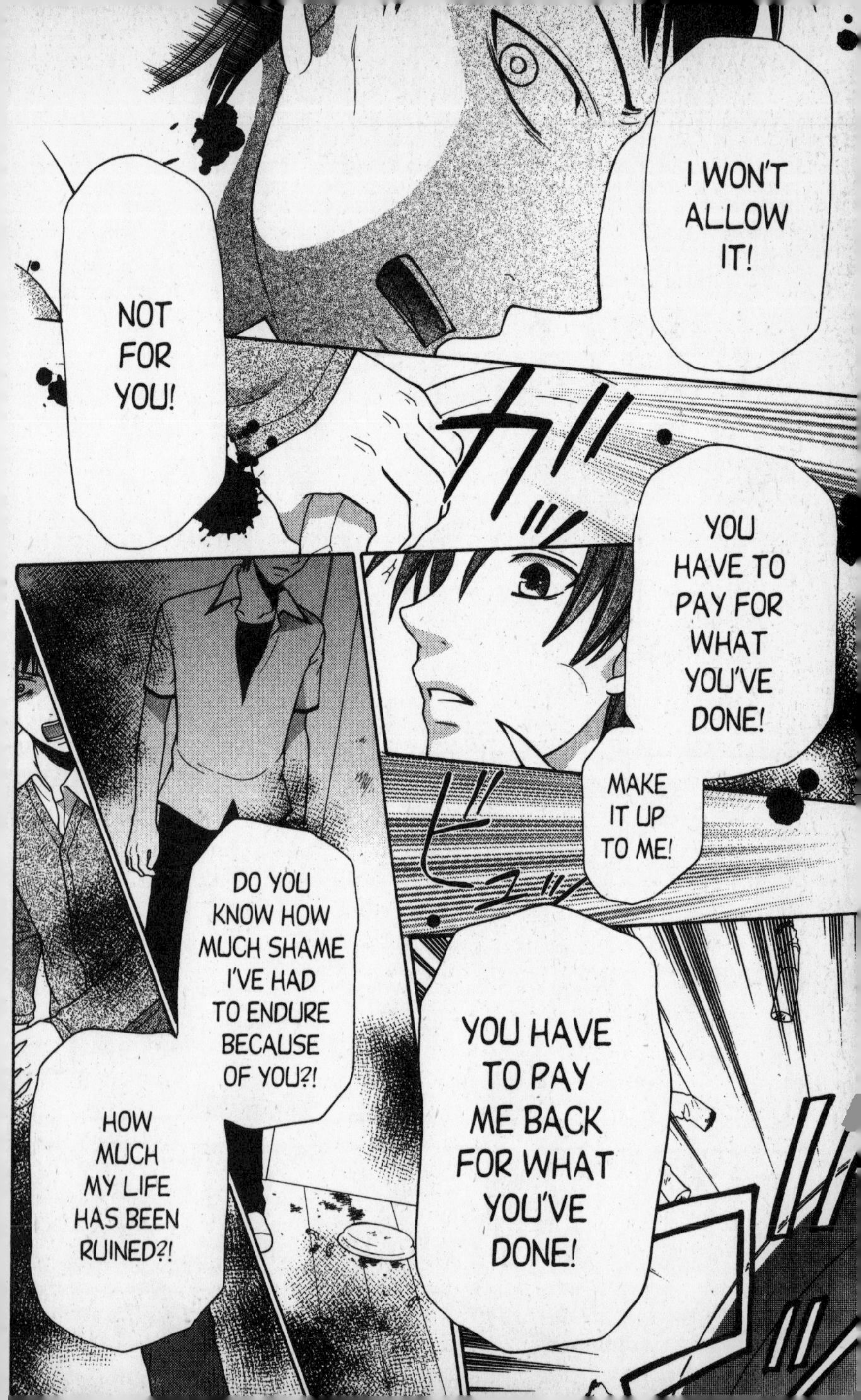
I WON'T ALLOW IT!
NOT FOR YOU!
ガッ
YOU HAVE TO PAY FOR WHAT YOU'VE DONE!
MAKE IT UP TO ME!
YOU HAVE TO PAY ME BACK FOR WHAT YOU'VE DONE!
DO YOU KNOW HOW MUCH SHAME I'VE HAD TO ENDURE BECAUSE OF YOU?!
HOW MUCH MY LIFE HAS BEEN RUINED?!

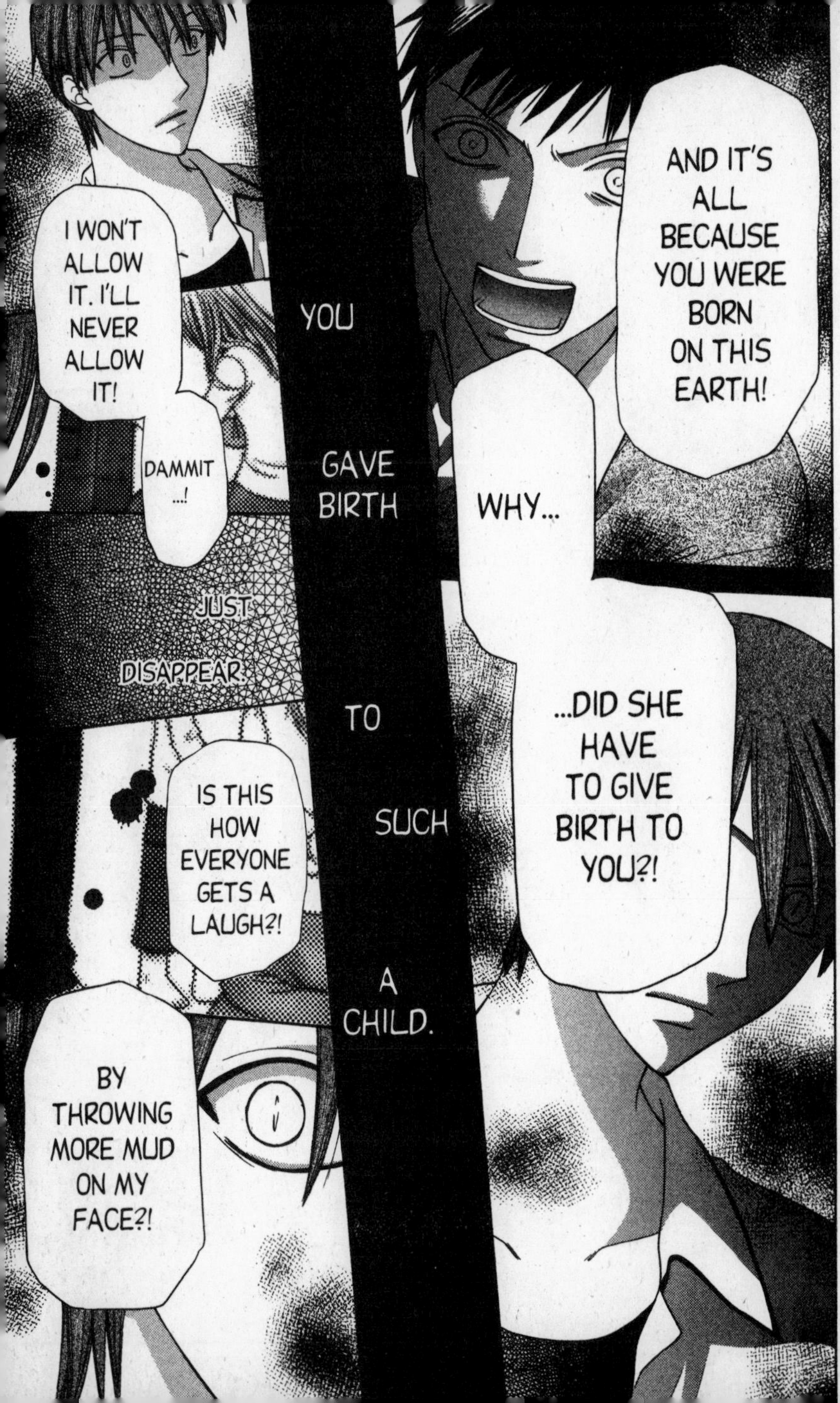
AND IT'S ALL BECAUSE YOU WERE BORN ON THIS EARTH!
WHY...
...DID SHE HAVE TO GIVE BIRTH TO YOU?!
YOU GAVE BIRTH TO SUCH A CHILD.
I WON'T ALLOW IT. I'LL NEVER ALLOW IT!
DAMMIT ...!
JUST DISAPPEAR.
IS THIS HOW EVERYONE GETS A LAUGH?!
BY THROWING MORE MUD ON MY FACE?!

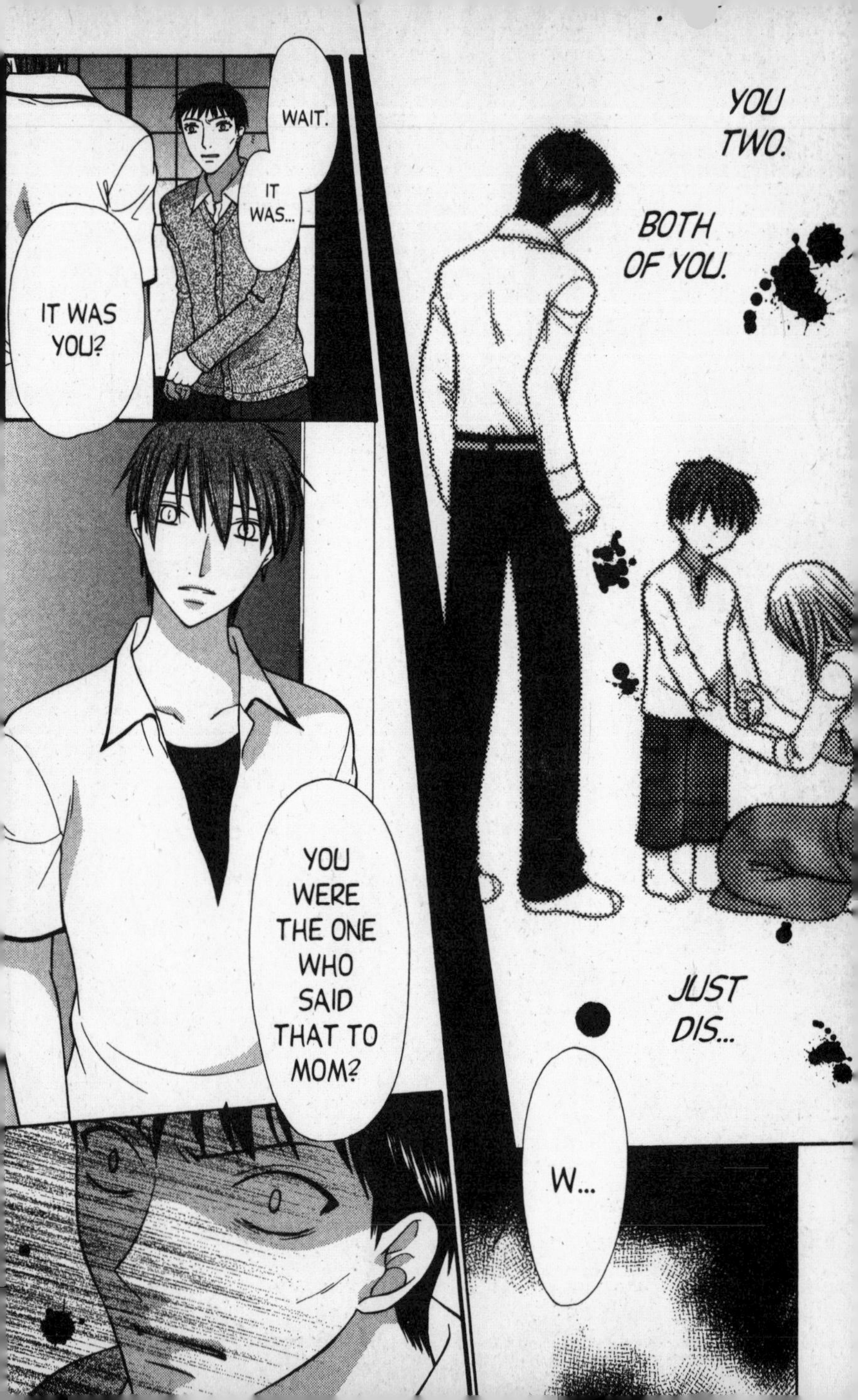
YOU TWO.
BOTH OF YOU.
JUST DIS...
W...
WAIT.
IT WAS...
IT WAS YOU?
YOU WERE THE ONE WHO SAID THAT TO MOM?

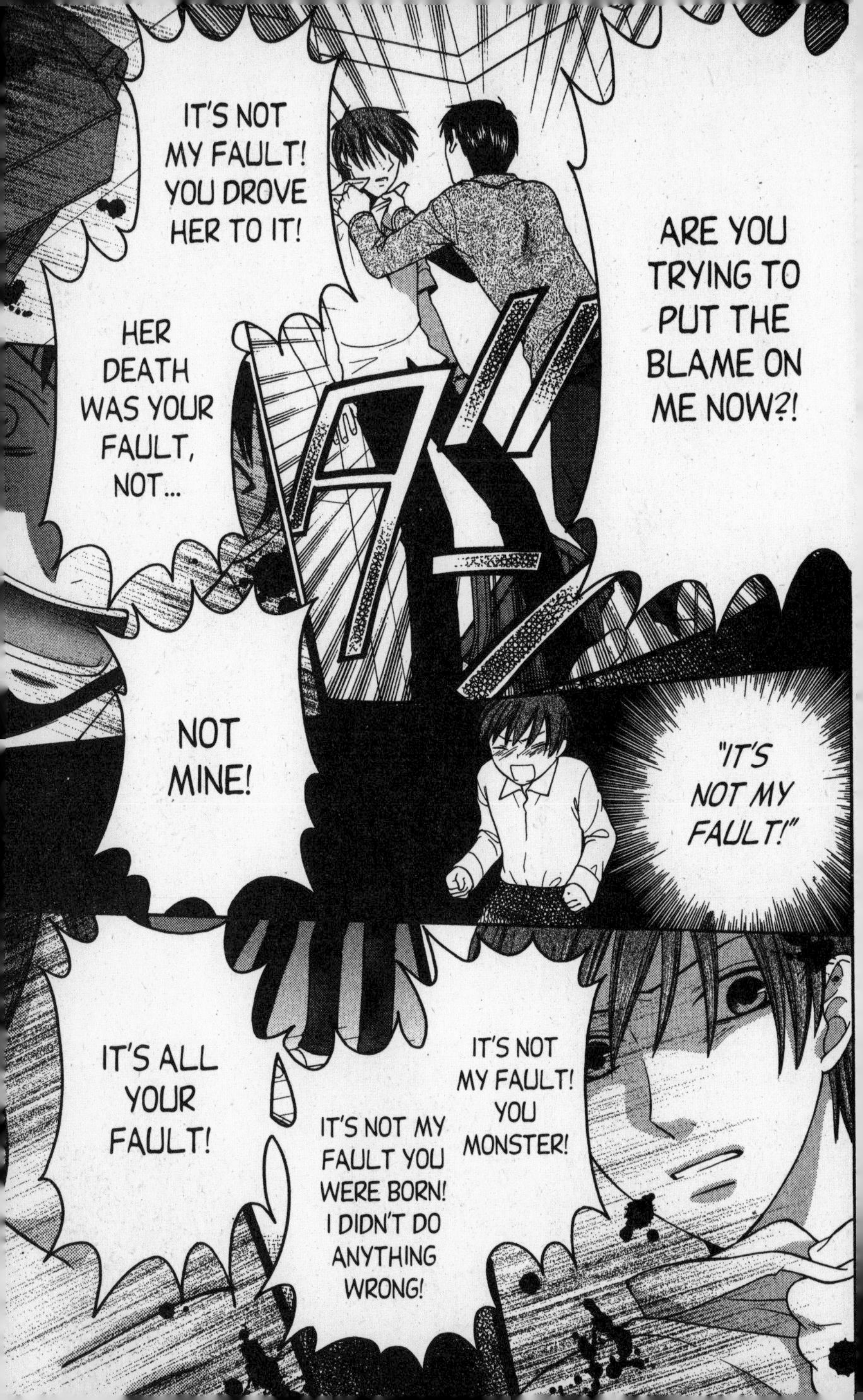
ARE YOU TRYING TO PUT THE BLAME ON ME NOW?!
IT'S NOT MY FAULT! YOU DROVE HER TO IT!
"IT'S NOT MY FAULT!"
HER DEATH WAS YOUR FAULT, NOT...
NOT MINE!
IT'S NOT MY FAULT! YOU MONSTER!
IT'S NOT MY FAULT YOU WERE BORN! I DIDN'T DO ANYTHING WRONG!
IT'S ALL YOUR FAULT!

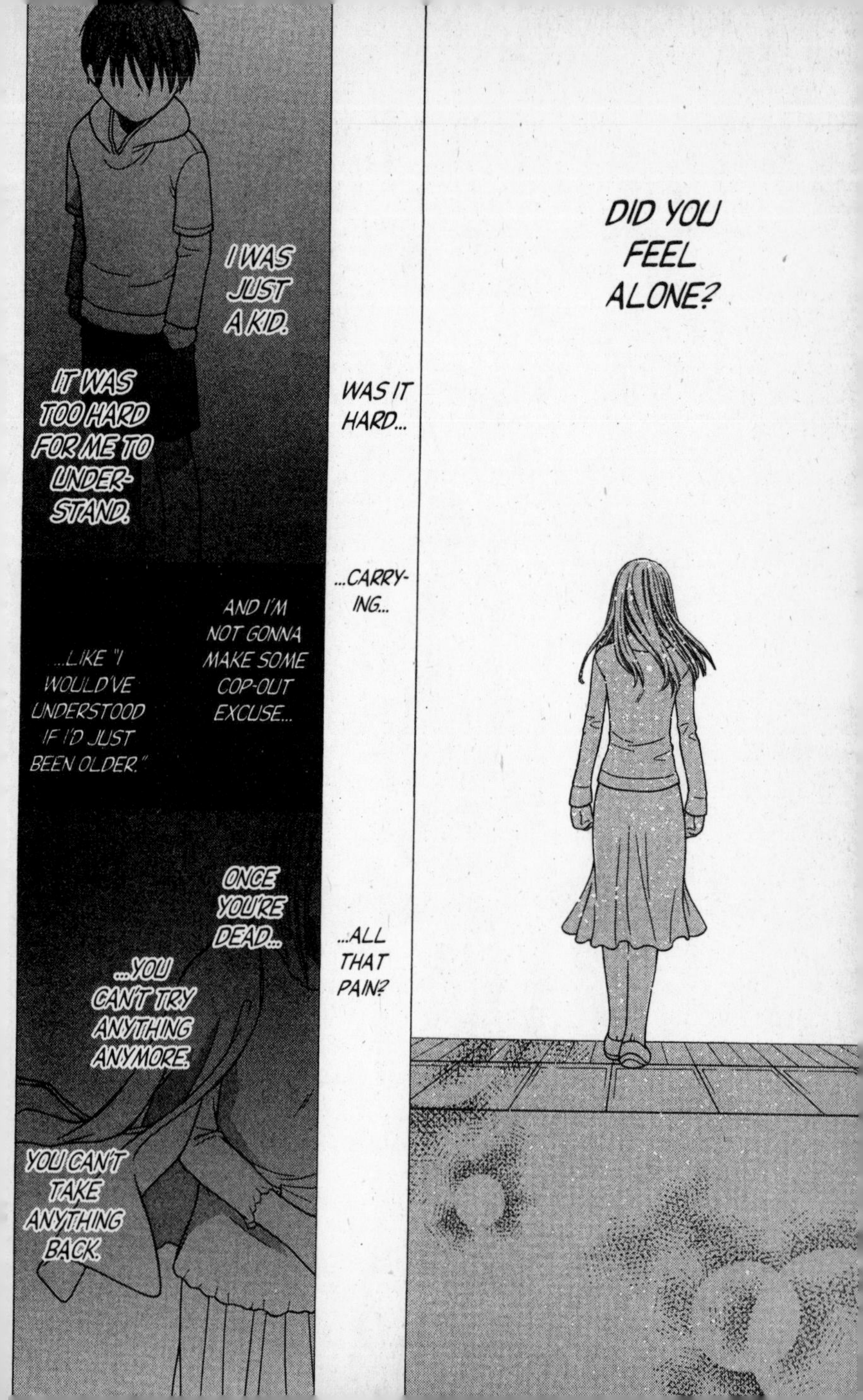
DID YOU FEEL ALONE?
WAS IT HARD...
...CARRYING...
...ALL THAT PAIN?
I WAS JUST A KID.
IT WAS TOO HARD FOR ME TO UNDER-STAND.
AND I'M NOT GONNA MAKE SOME COP-OUT EXCUSE...
...LIKE "I WOULD'VE UNDERSTOOD IF I'D JUST BEEN OLDER."
ONCE YOU'RE DEAD...
...YOU CAN'T TRY ANYTHING ANYMORE.
YOU CAN'T TAKE ANYTHING BACK.

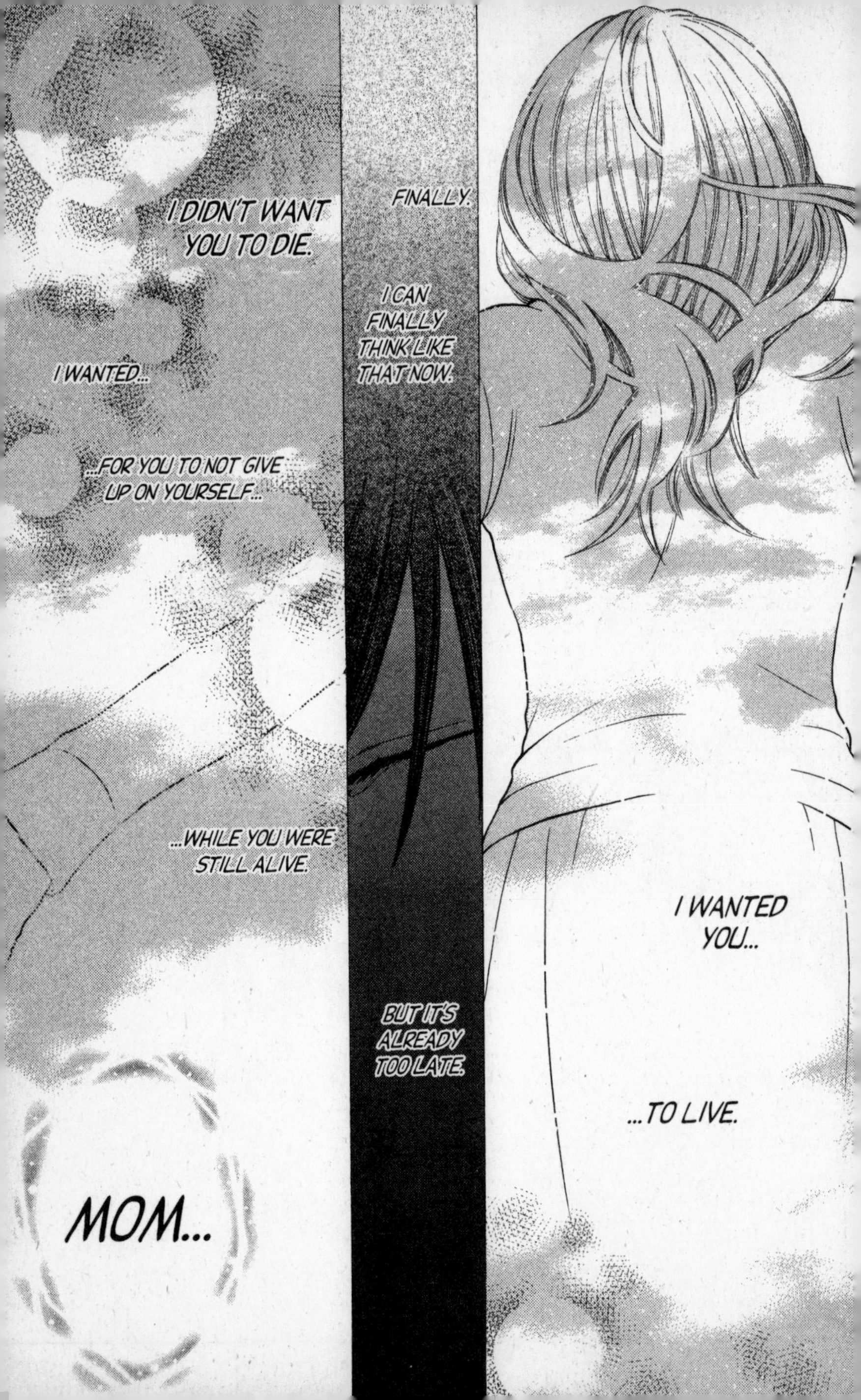
I WANTED YOU...
...TO LIVE.
FINALLY.
I CAN FINALLY THINK LIKE THAT NOW.
BUT IT'S ALREADY TOO LATE.
I DIDN'T WANT YOU TO DIE.
I WANTED...
...FOR YOU TO NOT GIVE UP ON YOURSELF...
...WHILE YOU WERE STILL ALIVE.
MOM...

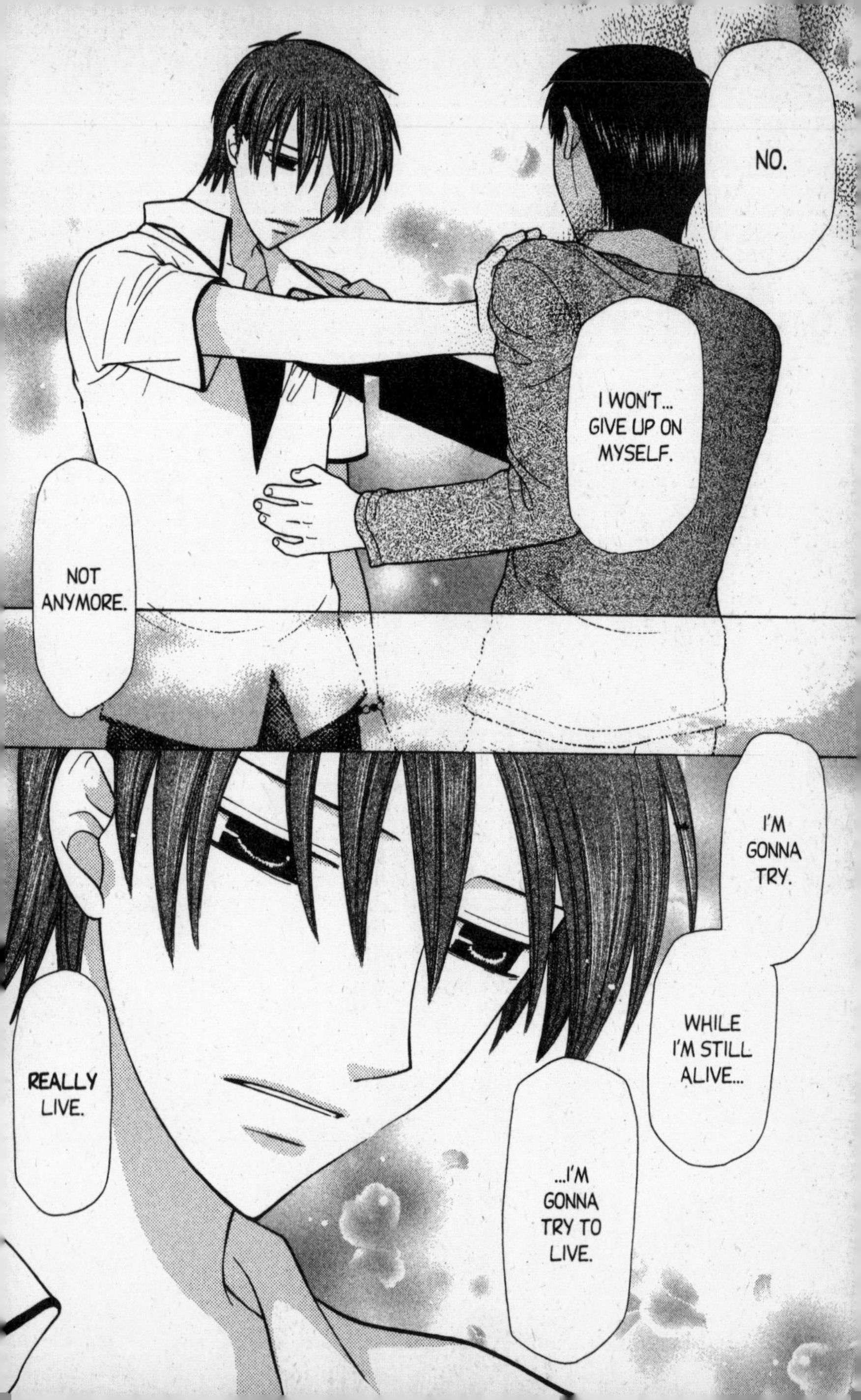
NO.
I WON'T... GIVE UP ON MYSELF.
NOT ANYMORE.
I'M GONNA TRY.
WHILE I'M STILL ALIVE...
...I'M GONNA TRY TO LIVE.
REALLY LIVE.

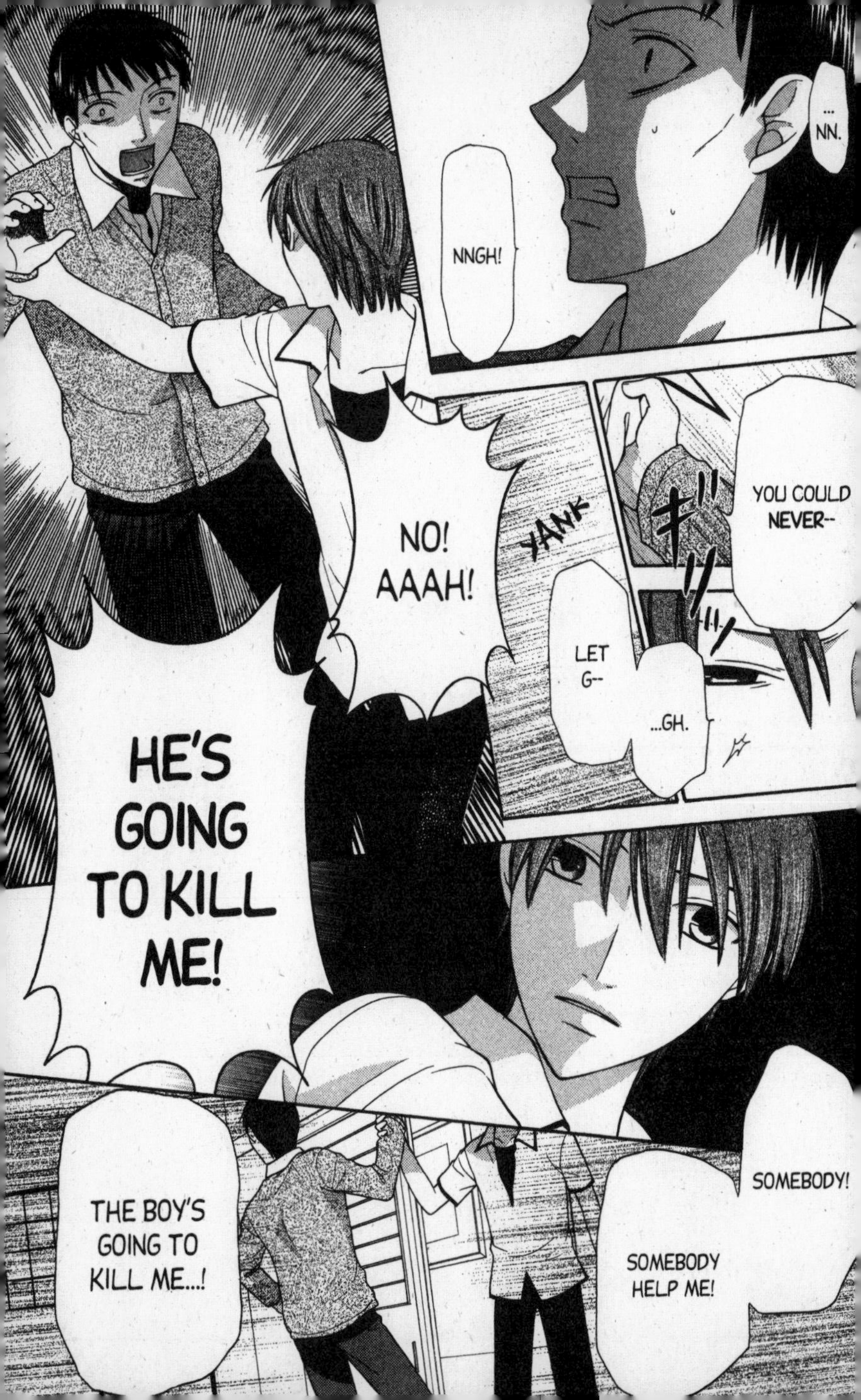

...NN.
NNGH!
YOU COULD NEVER--
YANK
LET G--
...GH.
NO! AAAH!
HE'S GOING TO KILL ME!
SOMEBODY!
SOMEBODY HELP ME!
THE BOY'S GOING TO KILL ME...!

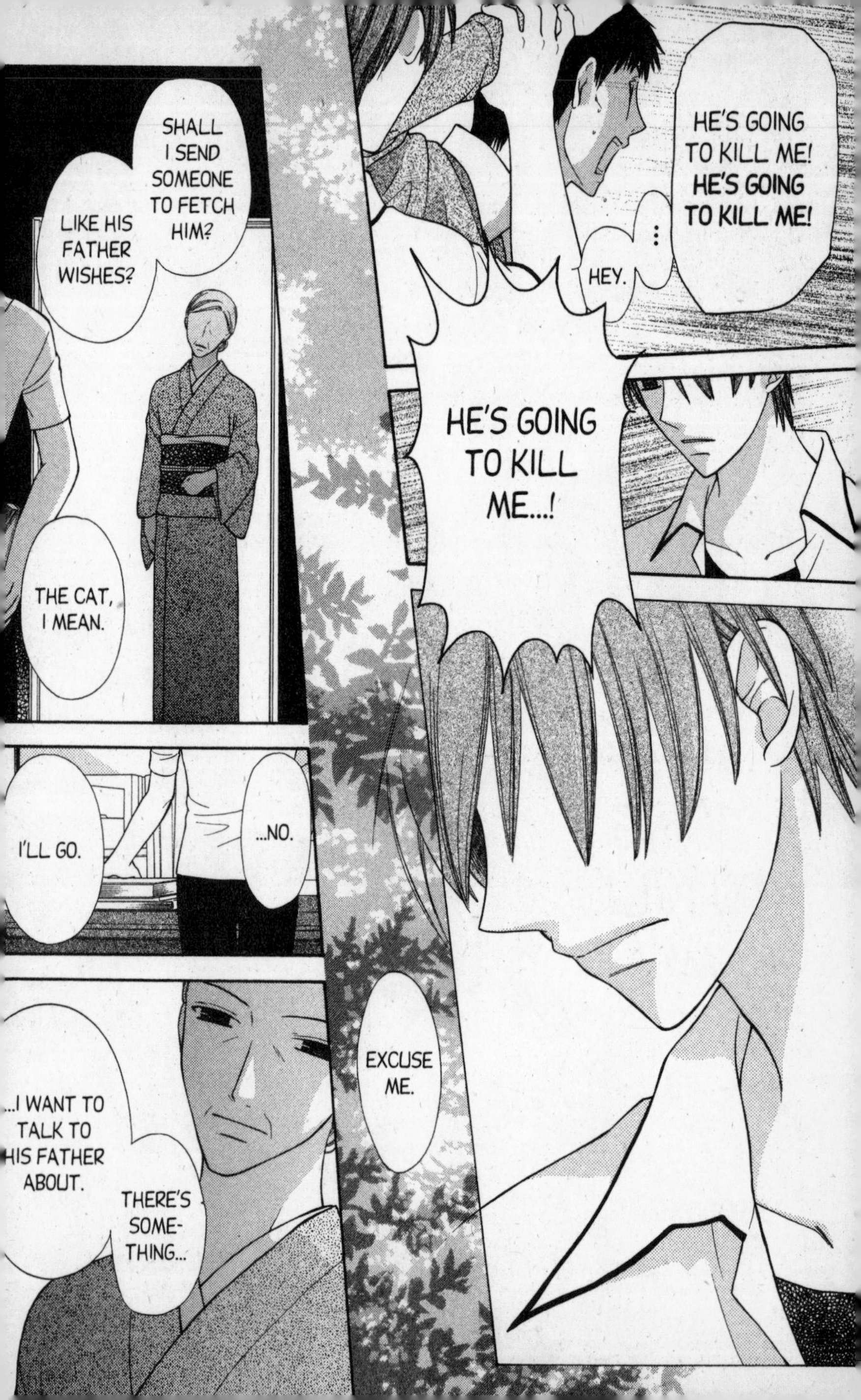
HE'S GOING TO KILL ME! HE'S GOING TO KILL ME!
...
HEY.
HE'S GOING TO KILL ME...!
EXCUSE ME.
SHALL I SEND SOMEONE TO FETCH HIM?
LIKE HIS FATHER WISHES?
THE CAT, I MEAN.
...NO.
I'LL GO.
THERE'S SOME-THING...
...I WANT TO TALK TO HIS FATHER ABOUT.

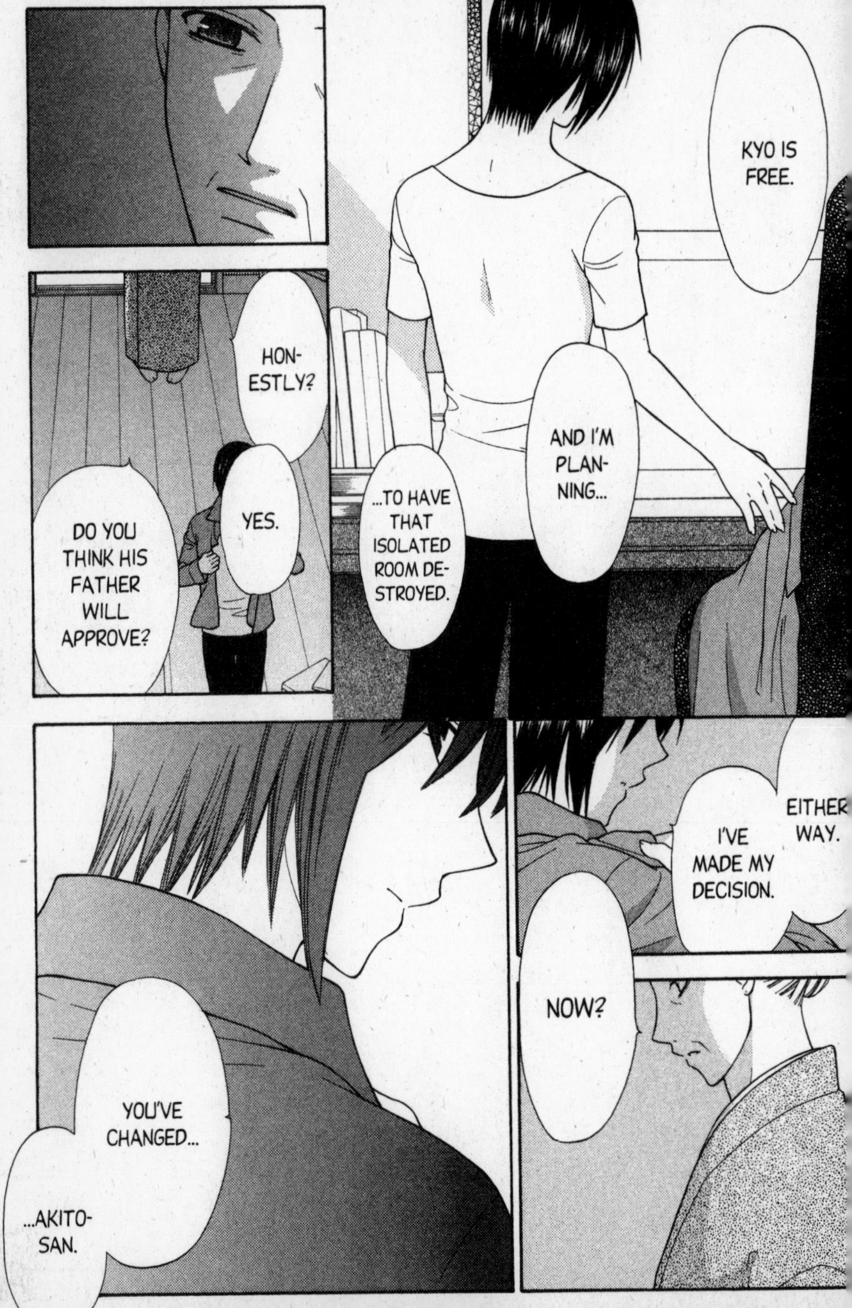
KYO IS FREE.
AND I'M PLAN-NING...
...TO HAVE THAT ISOLATED ROOM DE-STROYED.
HON-ESTLY?
YES.
DO YOU THINK HIS FATHER WILL APPROVE?
EITHER WAY.
I'VE MADE MY DECISION.
NOW?
YOU'VE CHANGED...
...AKITO-SAN.

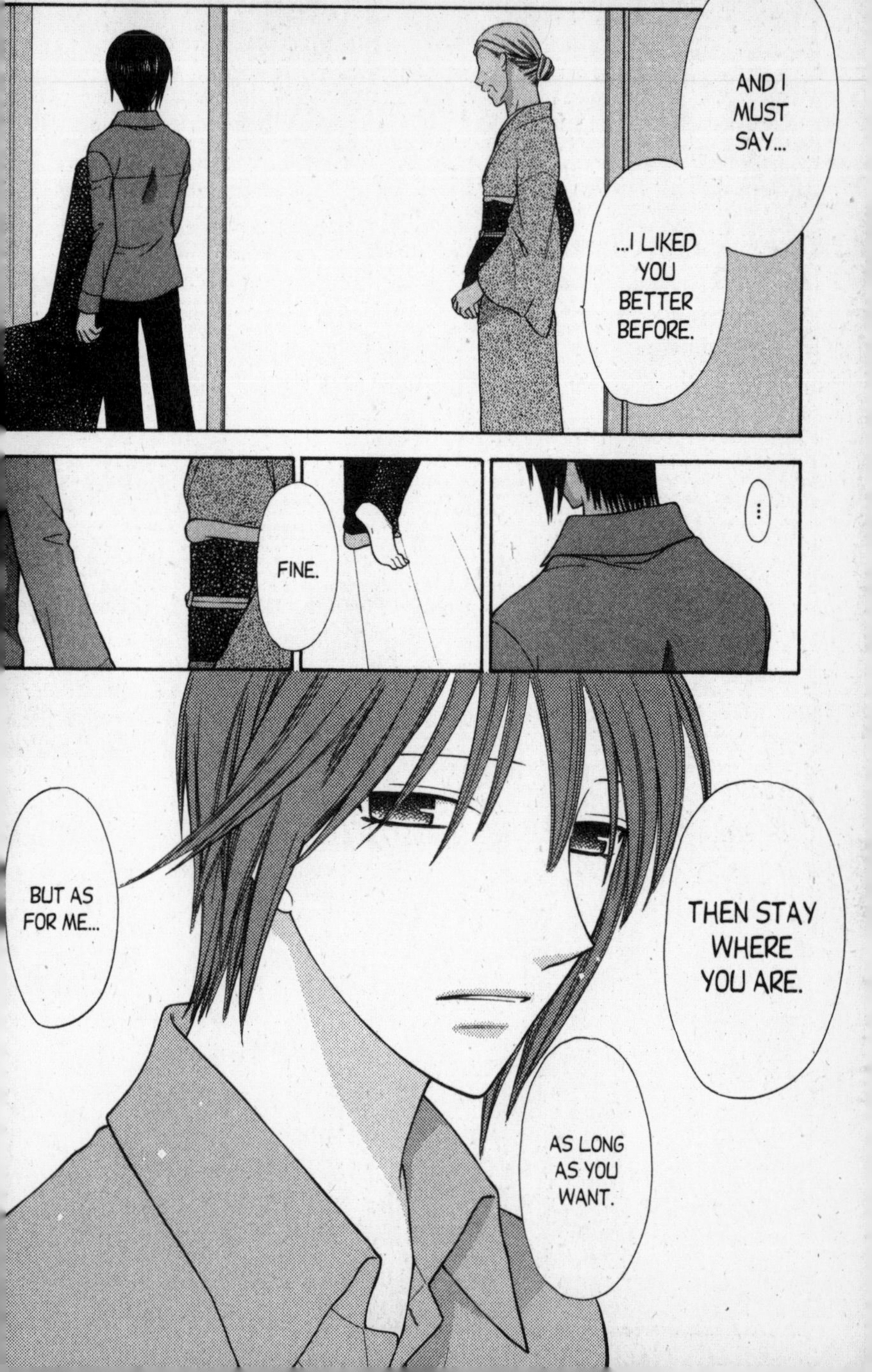
AND I MUST SAY...
...I LIKED YOU BETTER BEFORE.
...
FINE.
THEN STAY WHERE YOU ARE.
AS LONG AS YOU WANT.
BUT AS FOR ME...

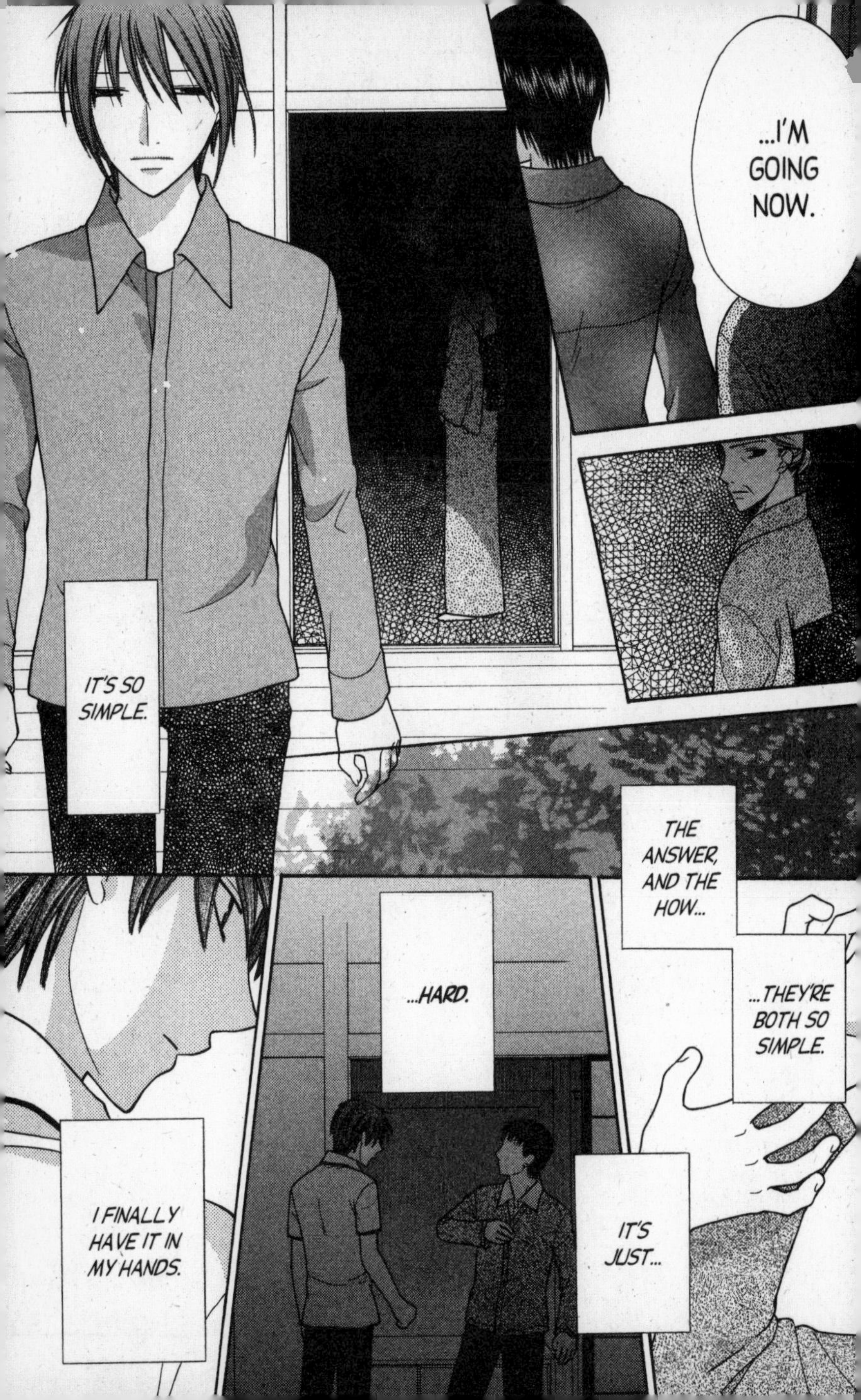
...I'M GOING NOW.
IT'S SO SIMPLE.
THE ANSWER, AND THE HOW...
...THEY'RE BOTH SO SIMPLE.
IT'S JUST...
...HARD.
I FINALLY HAVE IT IN MY HANDS.

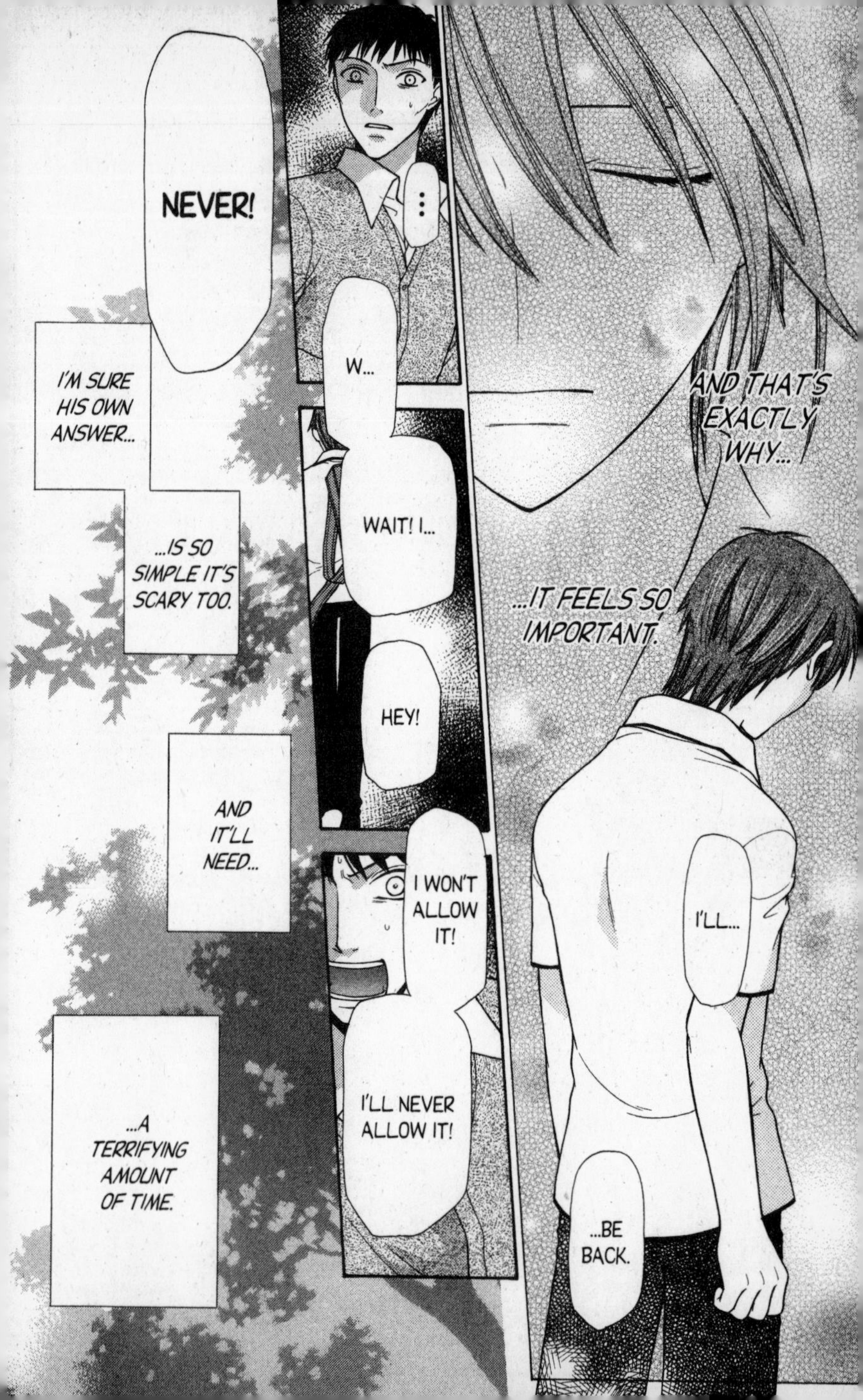
AND THAT'S EXACTLY WHY...
...IT FEELS SO IMPORTANT.
I'LL...
...BE BACK.
...
W...
WAIT! I...
HEY!
I WON'T ALLOW IT!
I'LL NEVER ALLOW IT!
NEVER!
I'M SURE HIS OWN ANSWER...
...IS SO SIMPLE IT'S SCARY TOO.
AND IT'LL NEED...
...A TERRIFYING AMOUNT OF TIME.

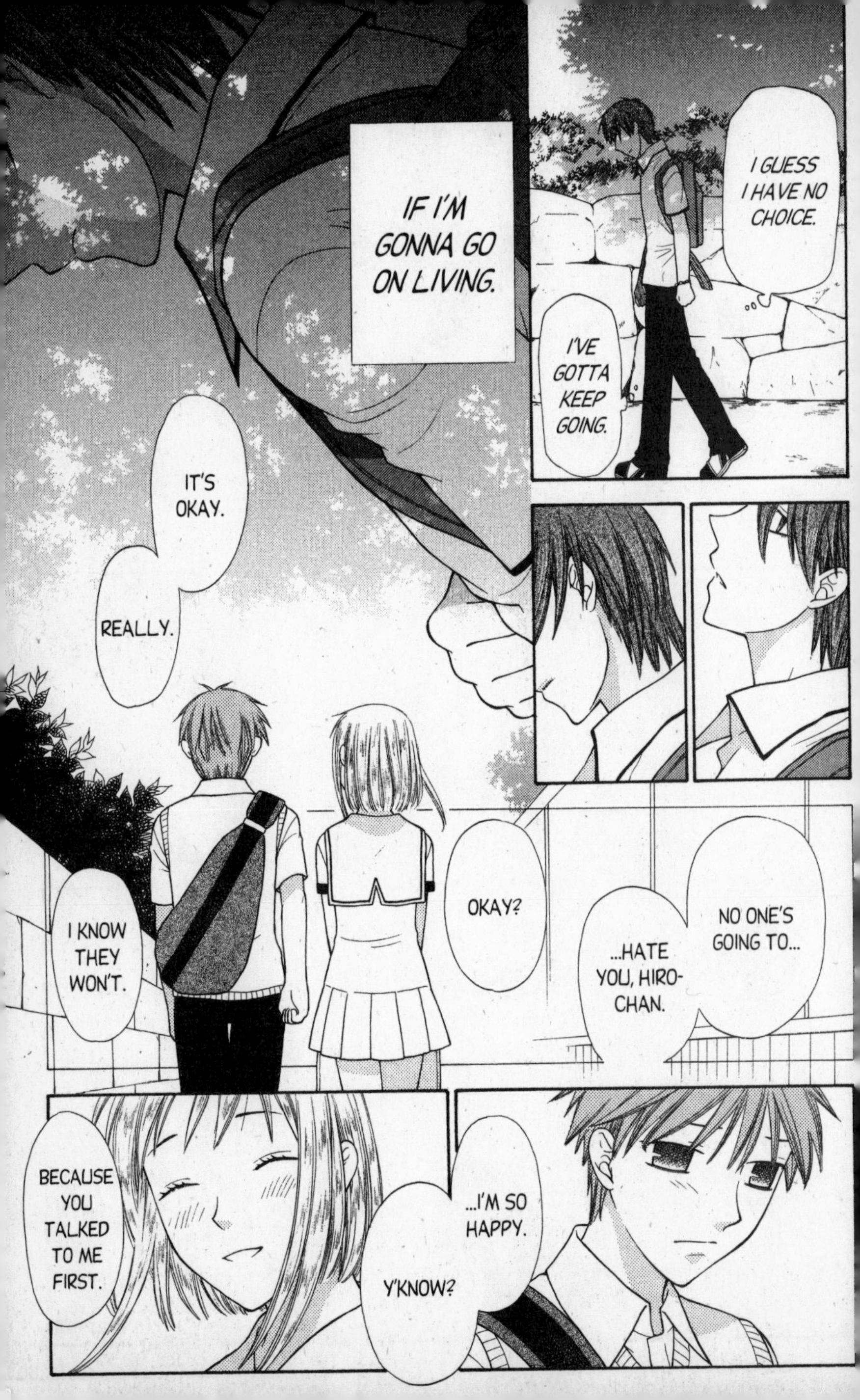
I GUESS I HAVE NO CHOICE.
I'VE GOTTA KEEP GOING.
IF I'M GONNA GO ON LIVING.
IT'S OKAY.
REALLY.
NO ONE'S GOING TO...
...HATE YOU, HIRO-CHAN.
OKAY?
I KNOW THEY WON'T.
...I'M SO HAPPY.
Y'KNOW?
BECAUSE YOU TALKED TO ME FIRST.

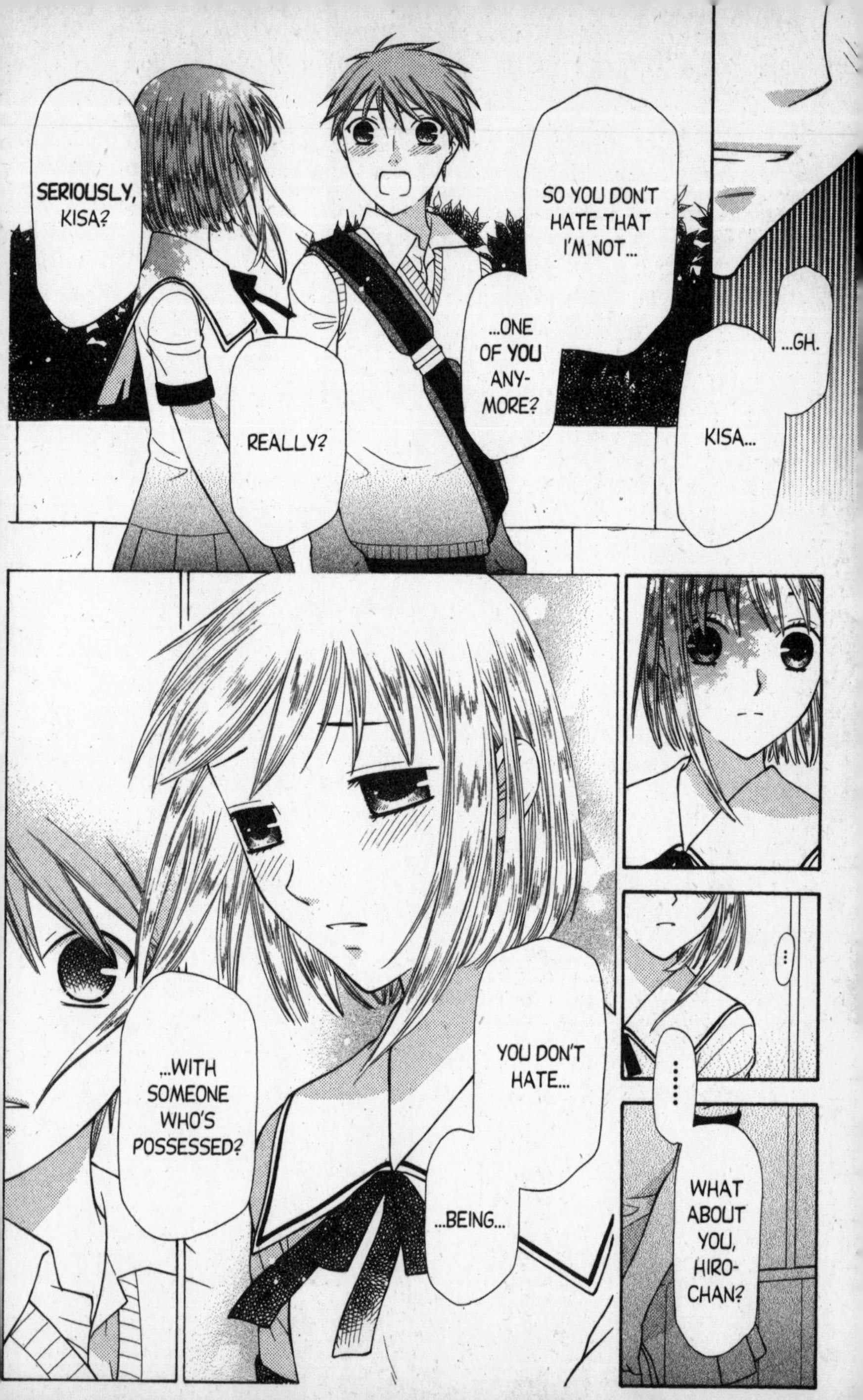
...GH.
KISA...
SO YOU DON'T HATE THAT I'M NOT...
...ONE OF YOU ANY-MORE?
REALLY?
SERIOUSLY, KISA?
...
......
WHAT ABOUT YOU, HIRO-CHAN?
YOU DON'T HATE...
...BEING...
...WITH SOMEONE WHO'S POSSESSED?

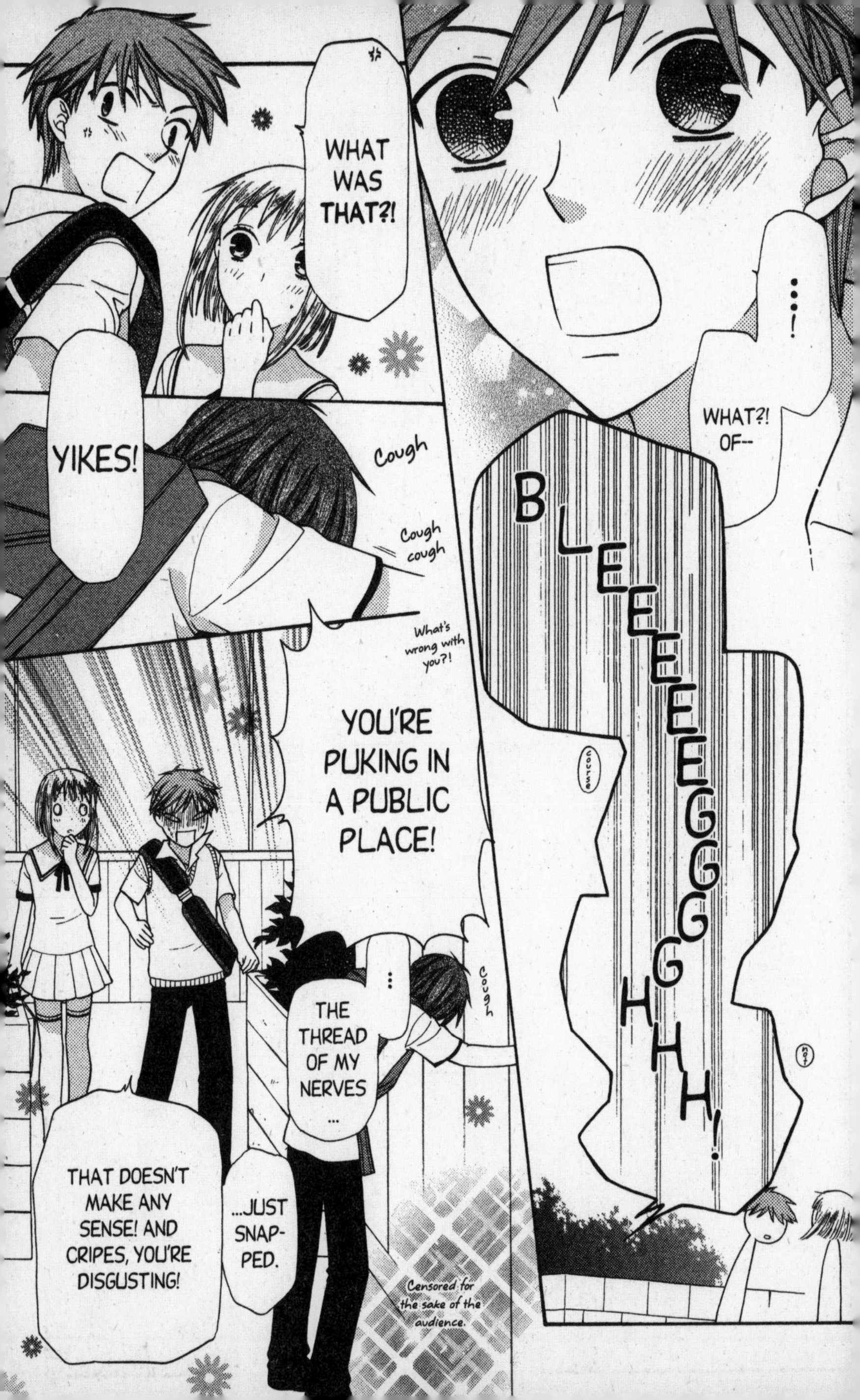
...!
WHAT?! OF--
BLEEEEEEGGGGHHHH!
course
not
WHAT WAS THAT?!
YIKES!
Cough
Cough cough
What's wrong with you?!
YOU'RE PUKING IN A PUBLIC PLACE!
Cough
...
THE THREAD OF MY NERVES...
...JUST SNAPPED.
THAT DOESN'T MAKE ANY SENSE! AND CRIPES, YOU'RE DISGUSTING!
Censored for the sake of the audience.

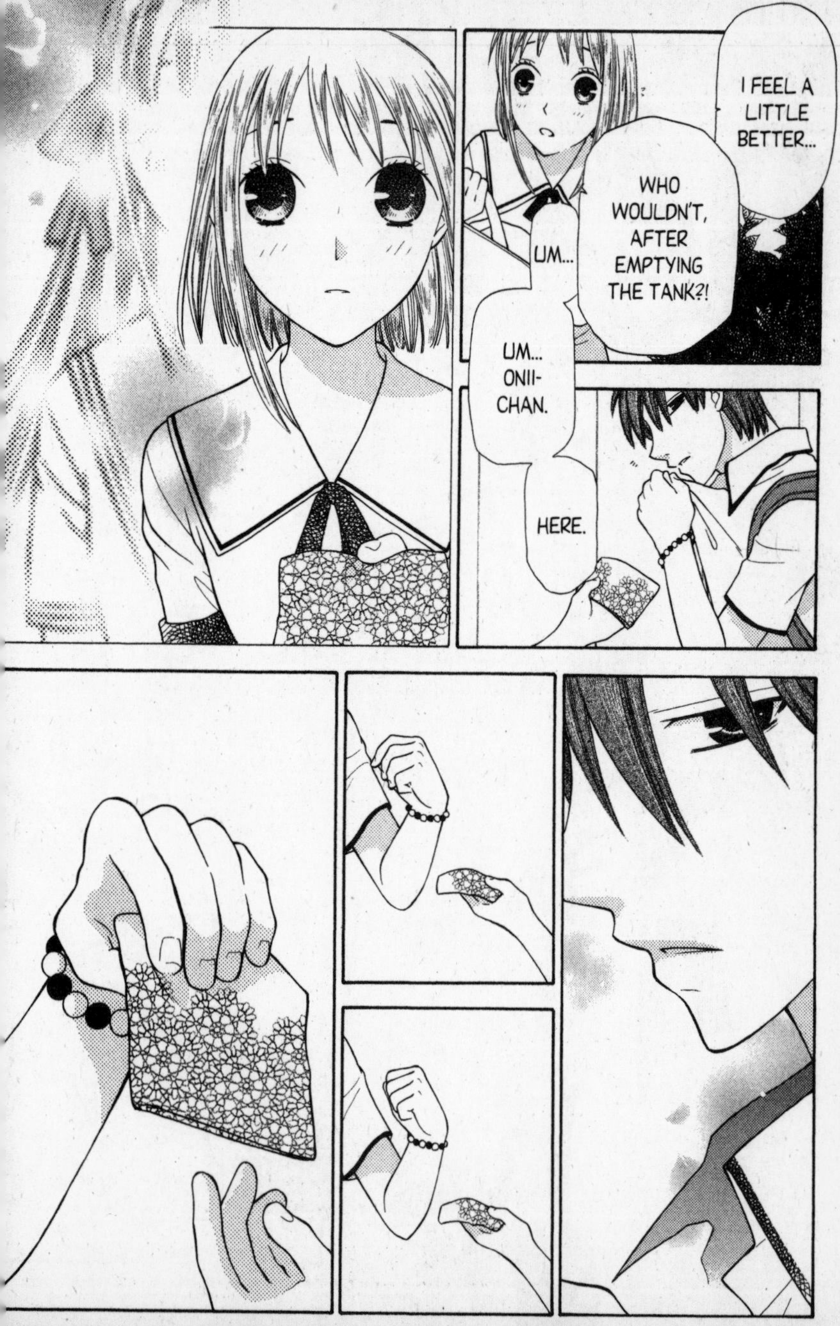
I FEEL A LITTLE BETTER...
WHO WOULDN'T, AFTER EMPTYING THE TANK?!
UM...
UM... ONII-CHAN.
HERE.

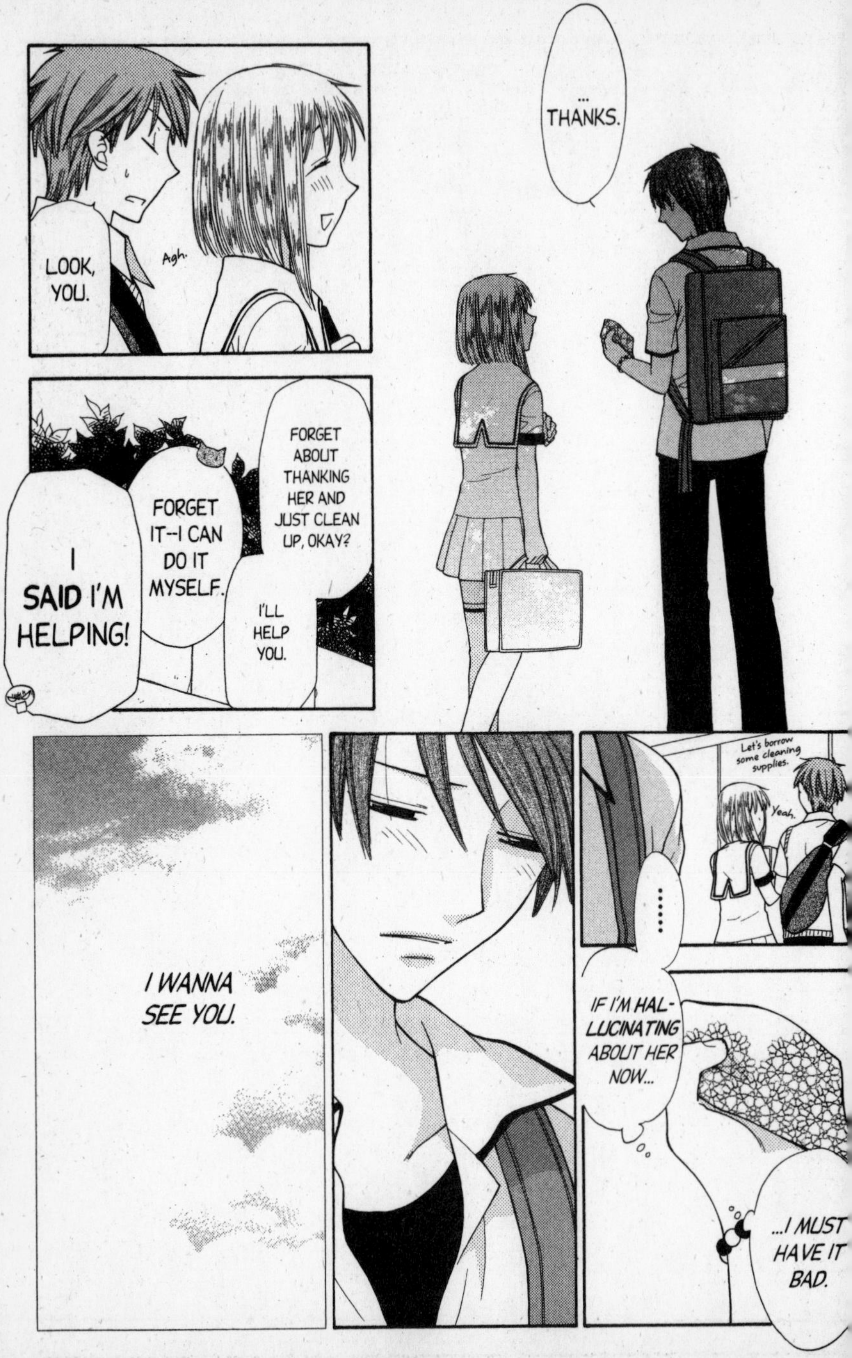
...THANKS.
LOOK, YOU.
Agh.
FORGET ABOUT THANKING HER AND JUST CLEAN UP, OKAY?
I'LL HELP YOU.
FORGET IT--I CAN DO IT MYSELF.
I SAID I'M HELPING!
Let's borrow some cleaning supplies.
Yeah.
......
IF I'M HAL-LUCINATING ABOUT HER NOW...
...I MUST HAVE IT BAD.
I WANNA SEE YOU.

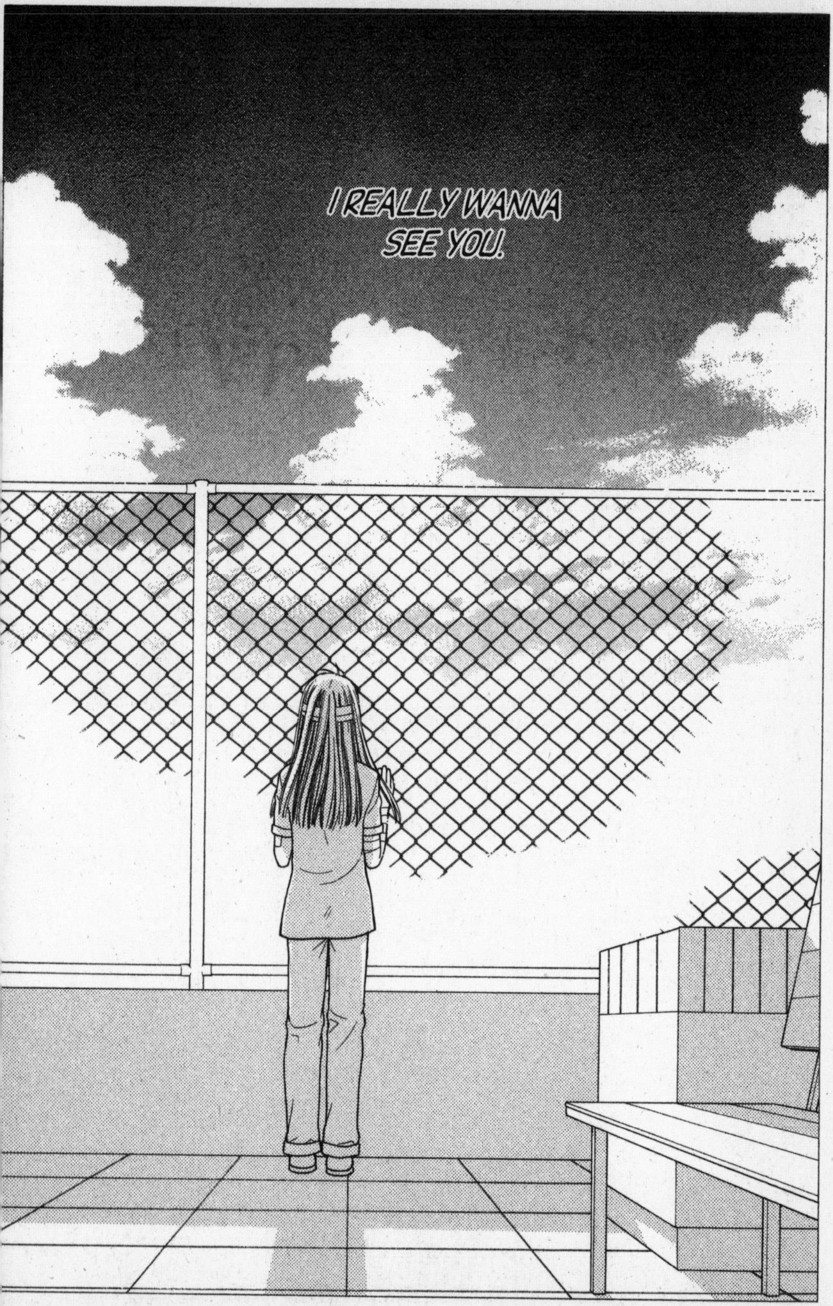
I REALLY WANNA SEE YOU.

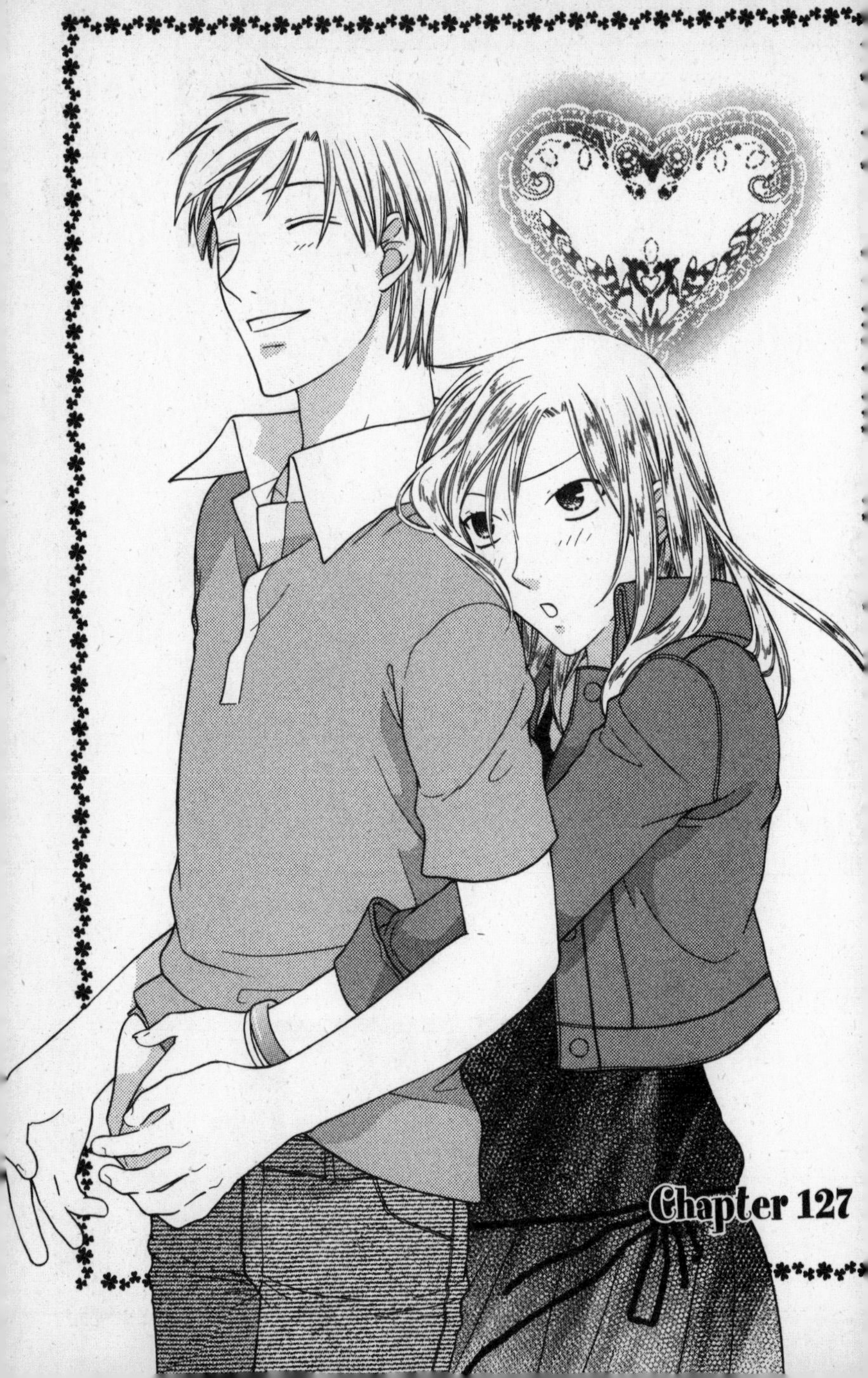
Chapter 127

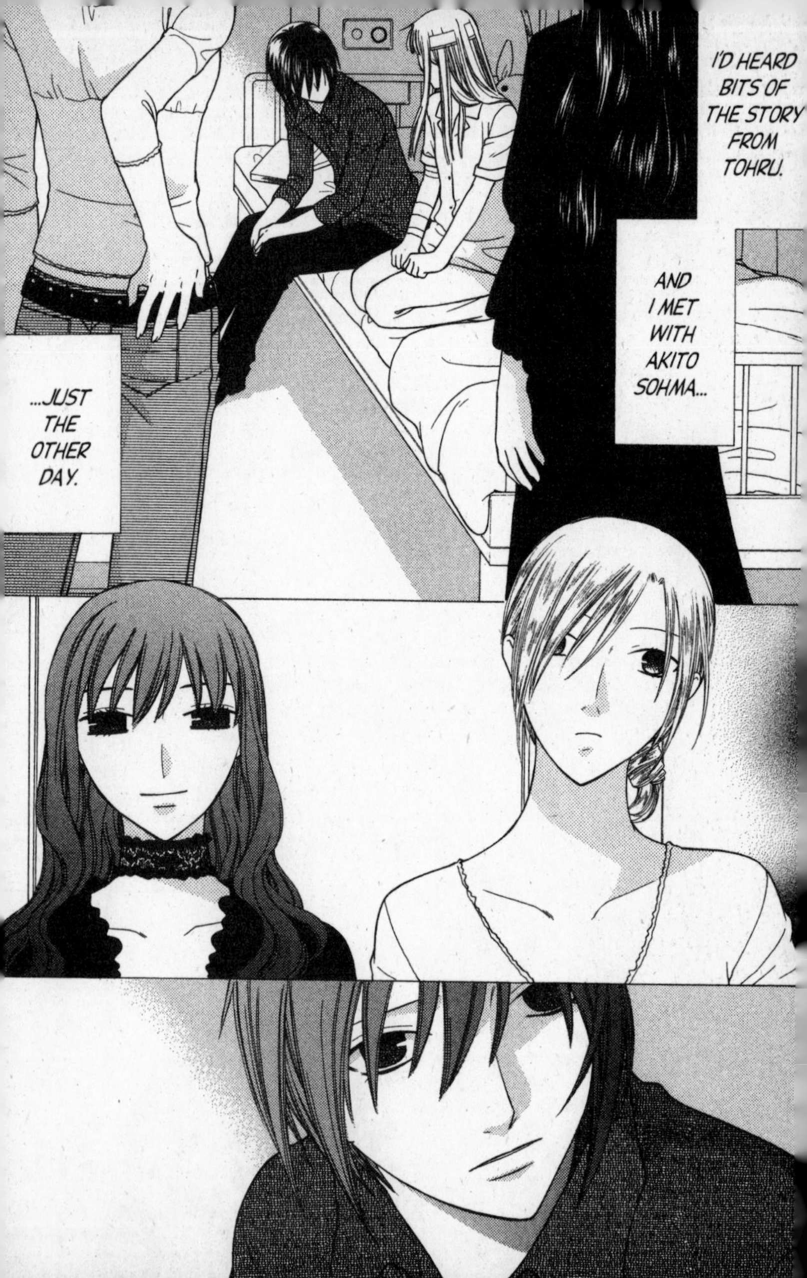
I'D HEARD BITS OF THE STORY FROM TOHRU.
AND I MET WITH AKITO SOHMA...
...JUST THE OTHER DAY.

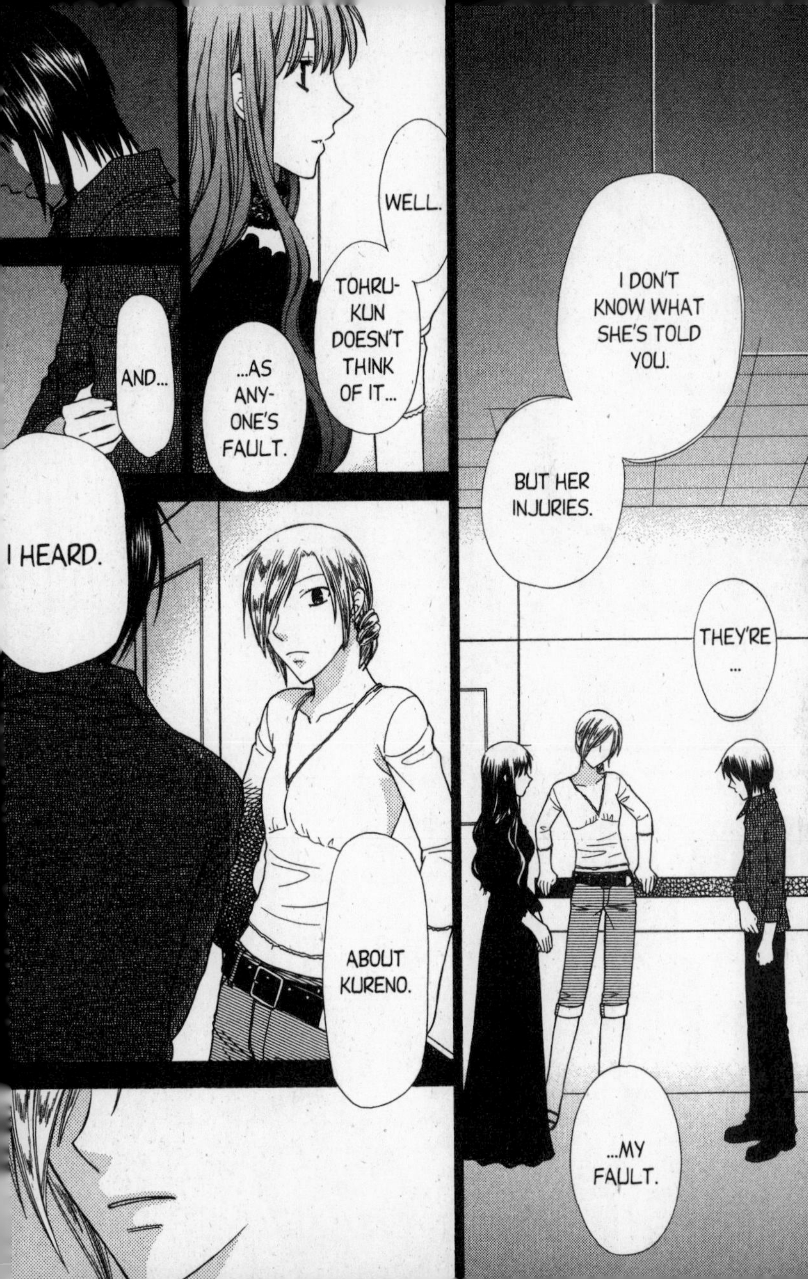
I DON'T KNOW WHAT SHE'S TOLD YOU.
BUT HER INJURIES.
THEY'RE ...
...MY FAULT.
WELL.
TOHRU-KUN DOESN'T THINK OF IT...
...AS ANY-ONE'S FAULT.
AND...
I HEARD.
ABOUT KURENO.

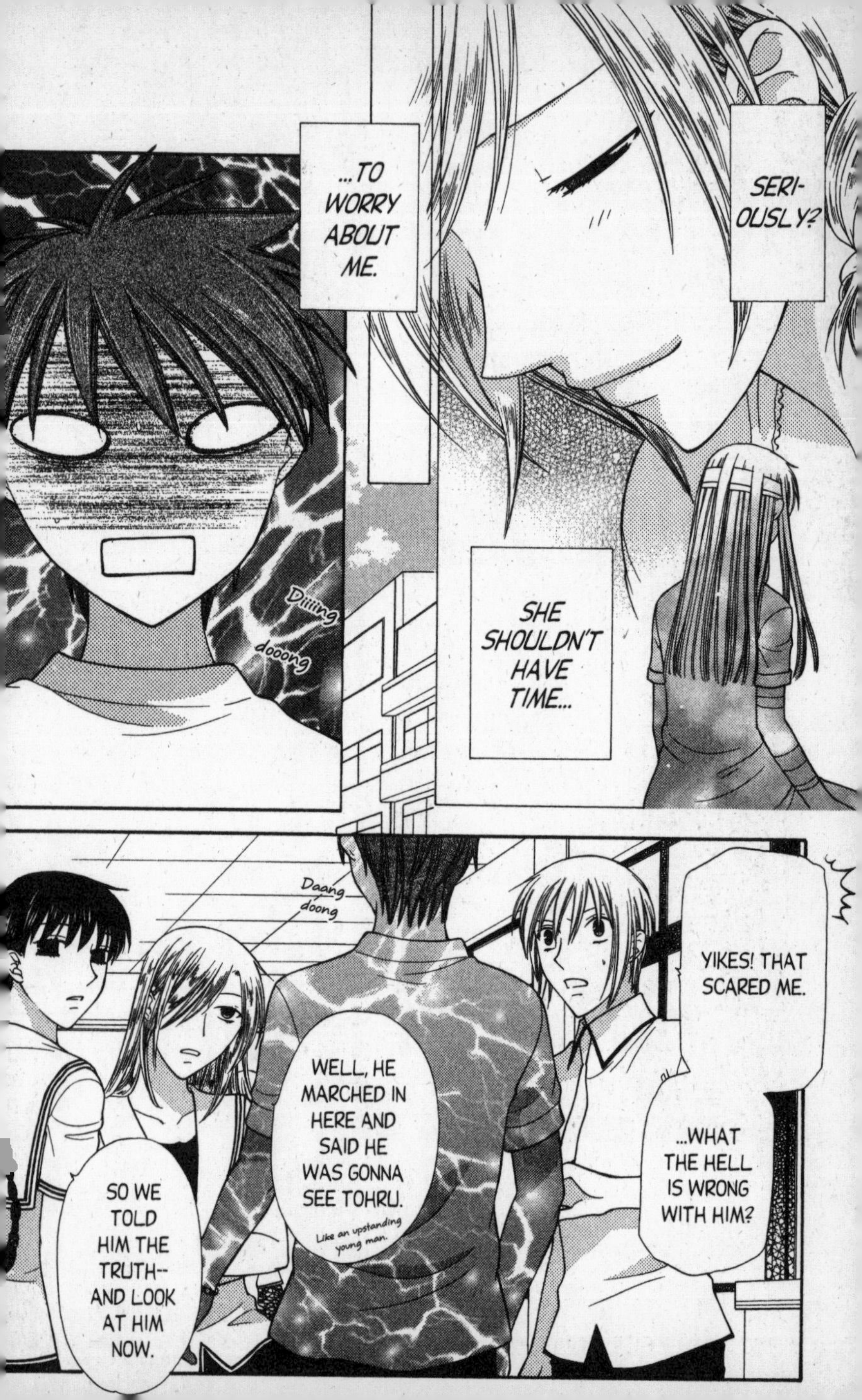
SERI-OUSLY?
SHE SHOULDN'T HAVE TIME...
...TO WORRY ABOUT ME.
Diiiing dooong
YIKES! THAT SCARED ME.
...WHAT THE HELL IS WRONG WITH HIM?
Daang doong
WELL, HE MARCHED IN HERE AND SAID HE WAS GONNA SEE TOHRU.
Like an upstanding young man.
SO WE TOLD HIM THE TRUTH--AND LOOK AT HIM NOW.

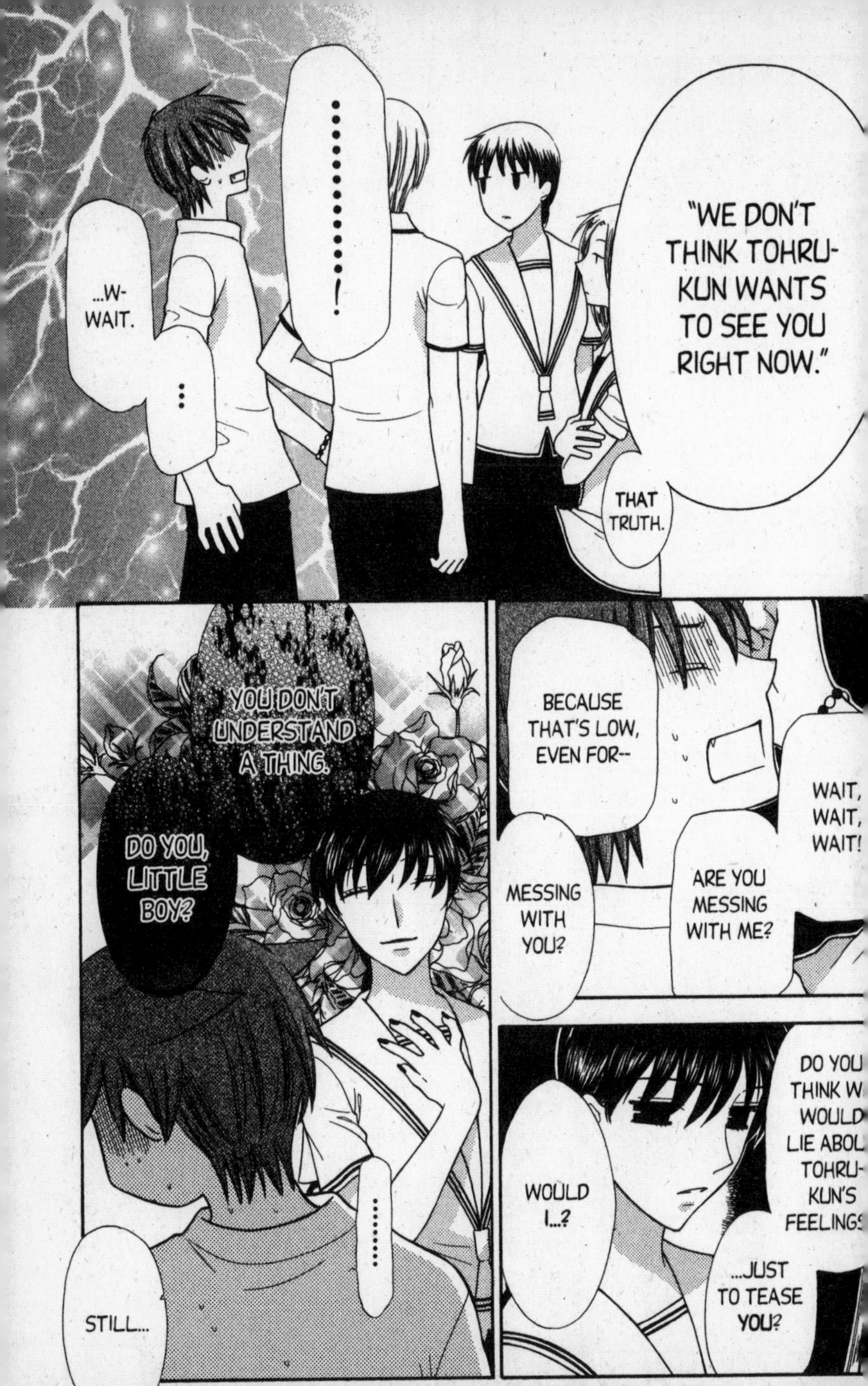
"WE DON'T THINK TOHRU-KUN WANTS TO SEE YOU RIGHT NOW."
THAT TRUTH.
..........!
...W-WAIT.
...
WAIT, WAIT, WAIT!
ARE YOU MESSING WITH ME?
BECAUSE THAT'S LOW, EVEN FOR--
MESSING WITH YOU?
DO YOU THINK W WOULD LIE ABOU TOHRU-KUN'S FEELINGS
...JUST TO TEASE YOU?
WOULD I...?
YOU DON'T UNDERSTAND A THING.
DO YOU, LITTLE BOY?
......
STILL...

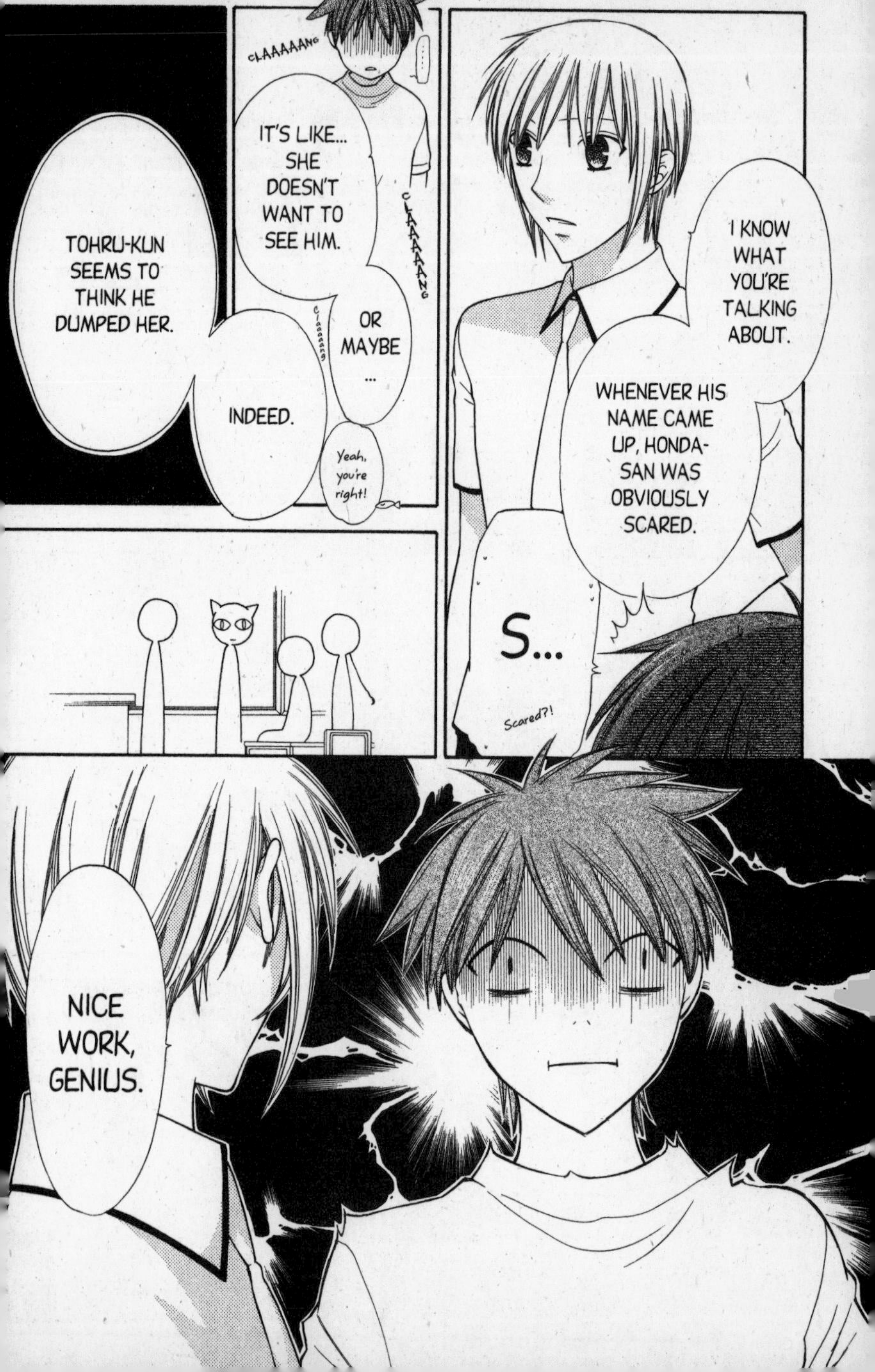

I KNOW WHAT YOU'RE TALKING ABOUT.
WHENEVER HIS NAME CAME UP, HONDA-SAN WAS OBVIOUSLY SCARED.
S...
Scared?!
CLAAAAAANG
...
IT'S LIKE... SHE DOESN'T WANT TO SEE HIM.
CLAAAAAANG
OR MAYBE ...
Yeah, you're right!
TOHRU-KUN SEEMS TO THINK HE DUMPED HER.
INDEED.
NICE WORK, GENIUS.

Fruits Basket

Nice to meet you and hello. I'm Takaya, presenting Volume 22. The cover has Tohru's Daddy on it this time around. I was going to make the color behind him white, but then he would end up looking like Akkii, so I changed it.

(It might not matter much, but in my head, Akkii has a white image.)

Now then. In the magazine, Furuba has safely reached its final chapter. The next volume will be the last graphic novel.

Sometimes people ask me if that makes me sad, but it doesn't--not really, anyway. An author never **actually** says goodbye to her works.

It's true that a manga ends, but it's something that will continue to exist inside me forever. Maybe I'm not explaining it very well? Basically, what I want to say is that I think the ones who will really be sad will be the people who have kept reading and loving Furuba.

Thank you very much. Now please enjoy Furuba Volume 22!

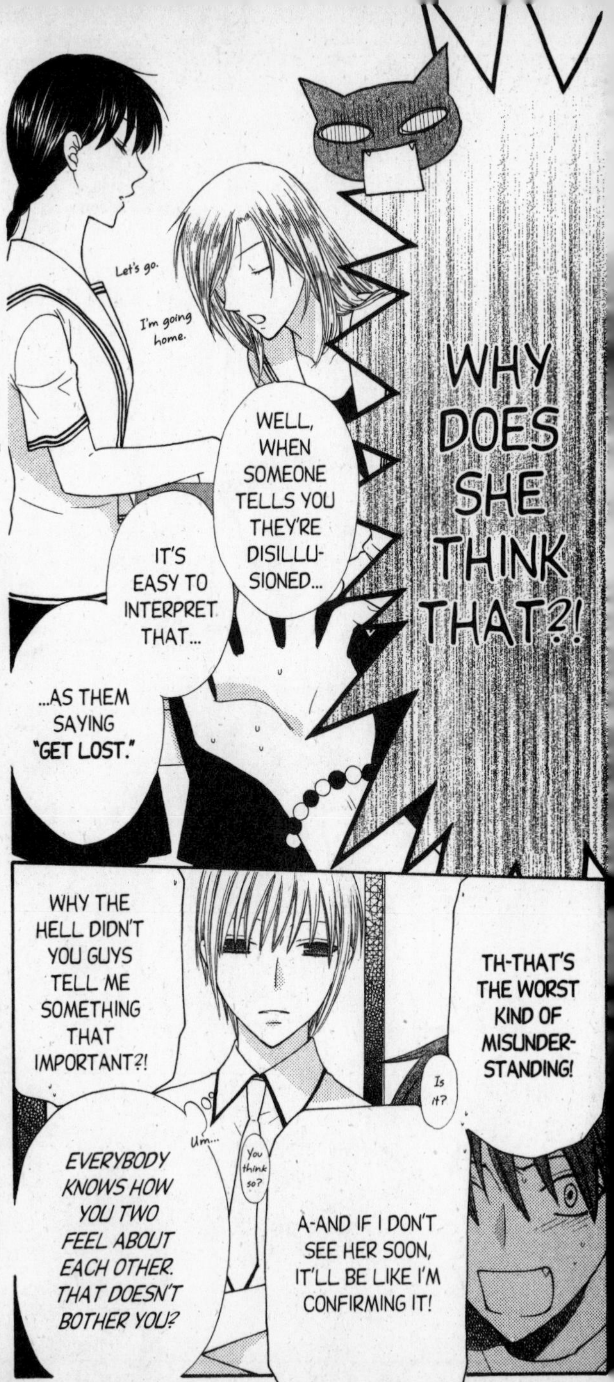
WHY DOES SHE THINK THAT?!
Let's go.
I'm going home.
WELL, WHEN SOMEONE TELLS YOU THEY'RE DISILLUSIONED...
IT'S EASY TO INTERPRET THAT...
...AS THEM SAYING "GET LOST."
TH-THAT'S THE WORST KIND OF MISUNDERSTANDING!
Is it?
A-AND IF I DON'T SEE HER SOON, IT'LL BE LIKE I'M CONFIRMING IT!
You think so?
WHY THE HELL DIDN'T YOU GUYS TELL ME SOMETHING THAT IMPORTANT?!
Um...
EVERYBODY KNOWS HOW YOU TWO FEEL ABOUT EACH OTHER. THAT DOESN'T BOTHER YOU?

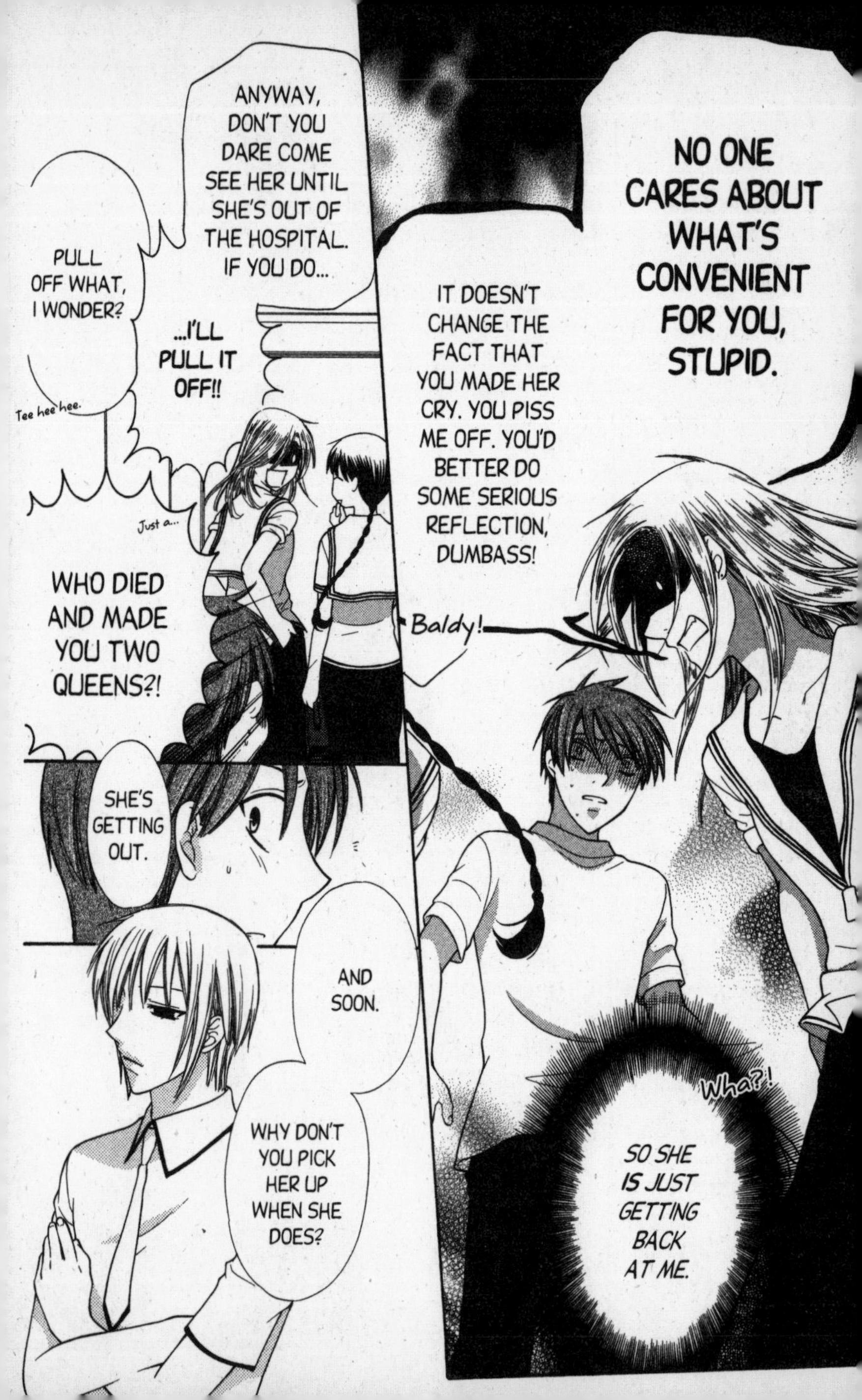
NO ONE CARES ABOUT WHAT'S CONVENIENT FOR YOU, STUPID.
IT DOESN'T CHANGE THE FACT THAT YOU MADE HER CRY. YOU PISS ME OFF. YOU'D BETTER DO SOME SERIOUS REFLECTION, DUMBASS!
Baldy!
Wha?!
SO SHE IS JUST GETTING BACK AT ME.
ANYWAY, DON'T YOU DARE COME SEE HER UNTIL SHE'S OUT OF THE HOSPITAL. IF YOU DO...
...I'LL PULL IT OFF!!
PULL OFF WHAT, I WONDER?
Tee hee hee.
Just a...
WHO DIED AND MADE YOU TWO QUEENS?!
SHE'S GETTING OUT.
AND SOON.
WHY DON'T YOU PICK HER UP WHEN SHE DOES?

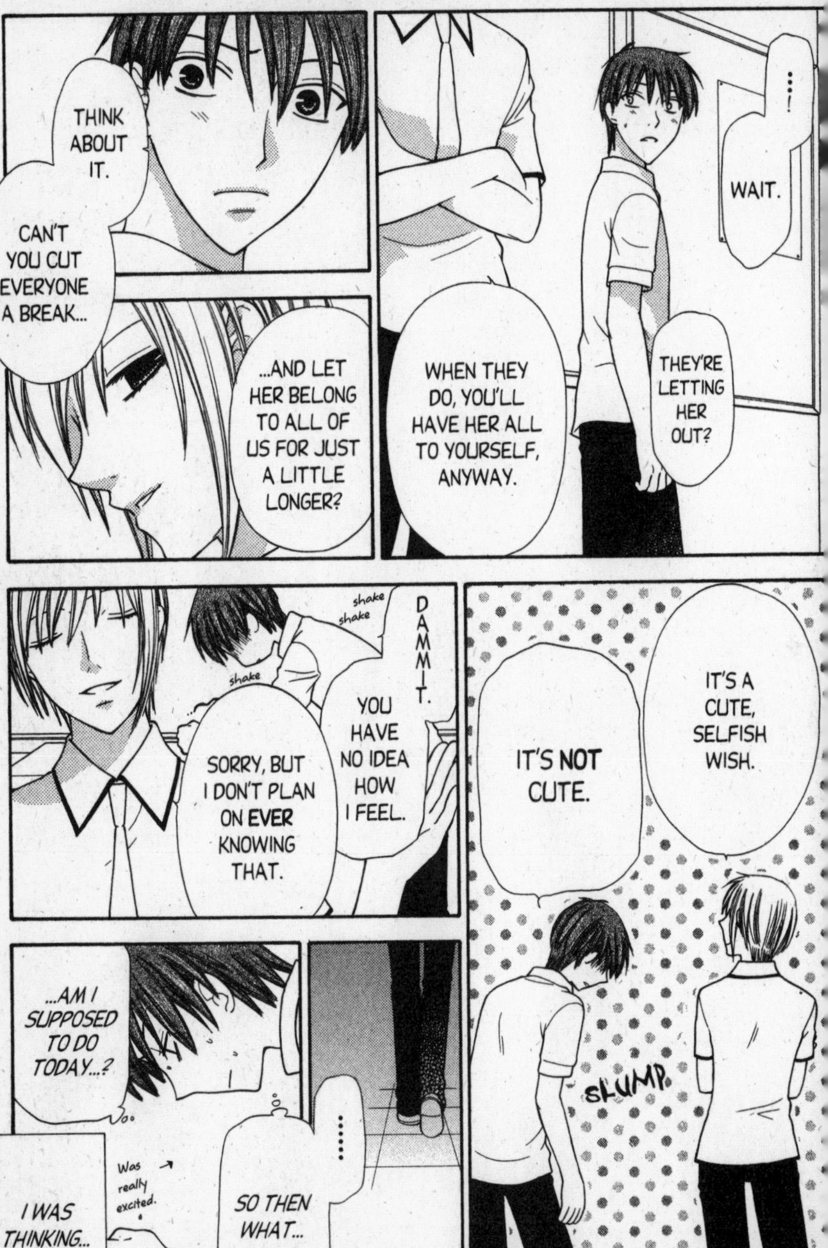
...!
WAIT.
THEY'RE LETTING HER OUT?
WHEN THEY DO, YOU'LL HAVE HER ALL TO YOURSELF, ANYWAY.
THINK ABOUT IT.
CAN'T YOU CUT EVERYONE A BREAK...
...AND LET HER BELONG TO ALL OF US FOR JUST A LITTLE LONGER?
IT'S A CUTE, SELFISH WISH.
IT'S **NOT** CUTE.
SLUMP
DAMMIT.
shake shake
YOU HAVE NO IDEA HOW I FEEL.
shake
SORRY, BUT I DON'T PLAN ON **EVER** KNOWING THAT.
......
SO THEN WHAT...
...AM I SUPPOSED TO DO TODAY...?
Was really excited.
I WAS THINKING...

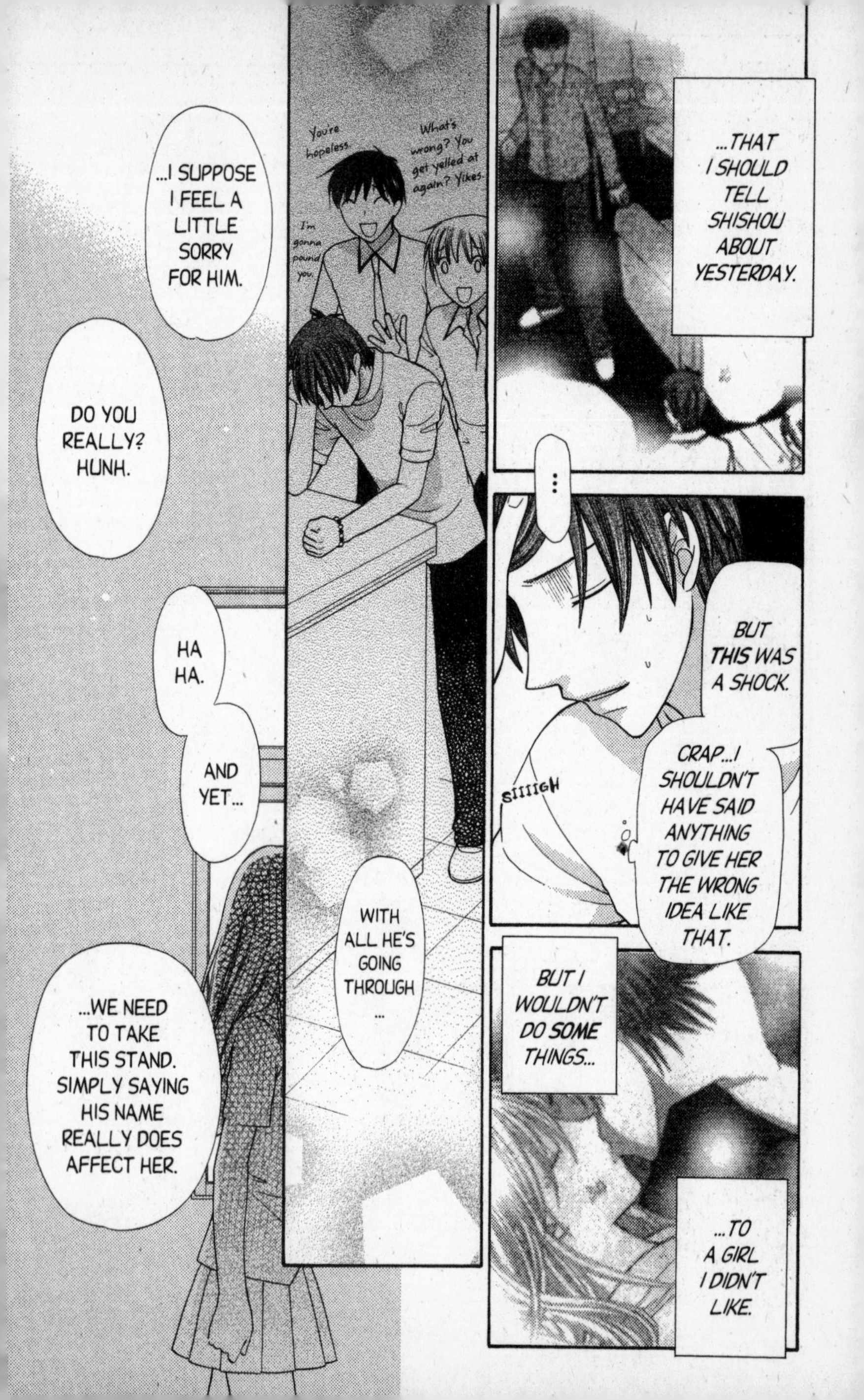
...THAT I SHOULD TELL SHISHOU ABOUT YESTERDAY.
...
BUT THIS WAS A SHOCK.
CRAP...I SHOULDN'T HAVE SAID ANYTHING TO GIVE HER THE WRONG IDEA LIKE THAT.
SIIIGH
BUT I WOULDN'T DO SOME THINGS...
...TO A GIRL I DIDN'T LIKE.
What's wrong? You get yelled at again? Yikes.
You're hopeless.
I'm gonna pound you.
WITH ALL HE'S GOING THROUGH...
...I SUPPOSE I FEEL A LITTLE SORRY FOR HIM.
DO YOU REALLY? HUNH.
HA HA.
AND YET...
...WE NEED TO TAKE THIS STAND. SIMPLY SAYING HIS NAME REALLY DOES AFFECT HER.

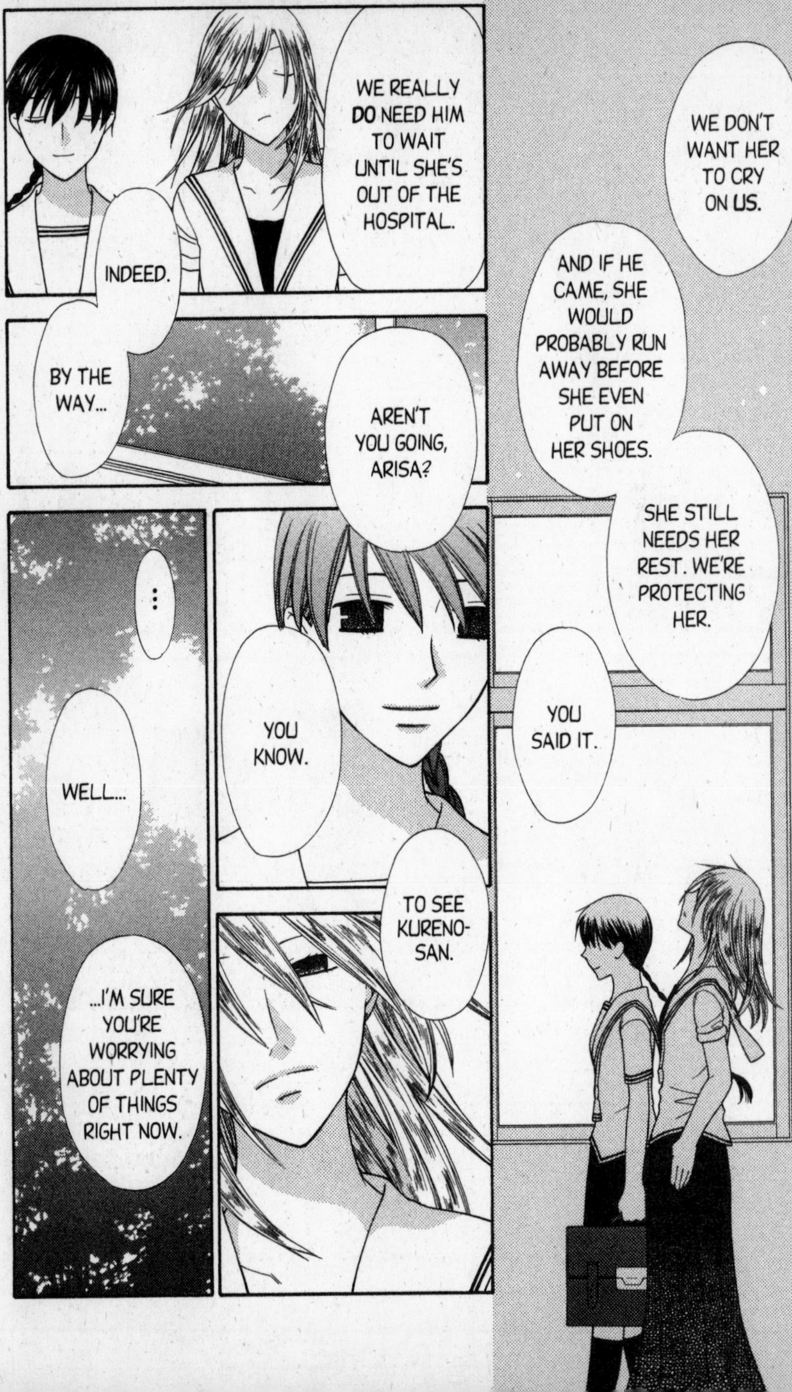
WE DON'T WANT HER TO CRY ON US.
AND IF HE CAME, SHE WOULD PROBABLY RUN AWAY BEFORE SHE EVEN PUT ON HER SHOES.
SHE STILL NEEDS HER REST. WE'RE PROTECTING HER.
YOU SAID IT.
WE REALLY DO NEED HIM TO WAIT UNTIL SHE'S OUT OF THE HOSPITAL.
INDEED.
BY THE WAY...
AREN'T YOU GOING, ARISA?
YOU KNOW.
TO SEE KURENO-SAN.
...
WELL...
...I'M SURE YOU'RE WORRYING ABOUT PLENTY OF THINGS RIGHT NOW.

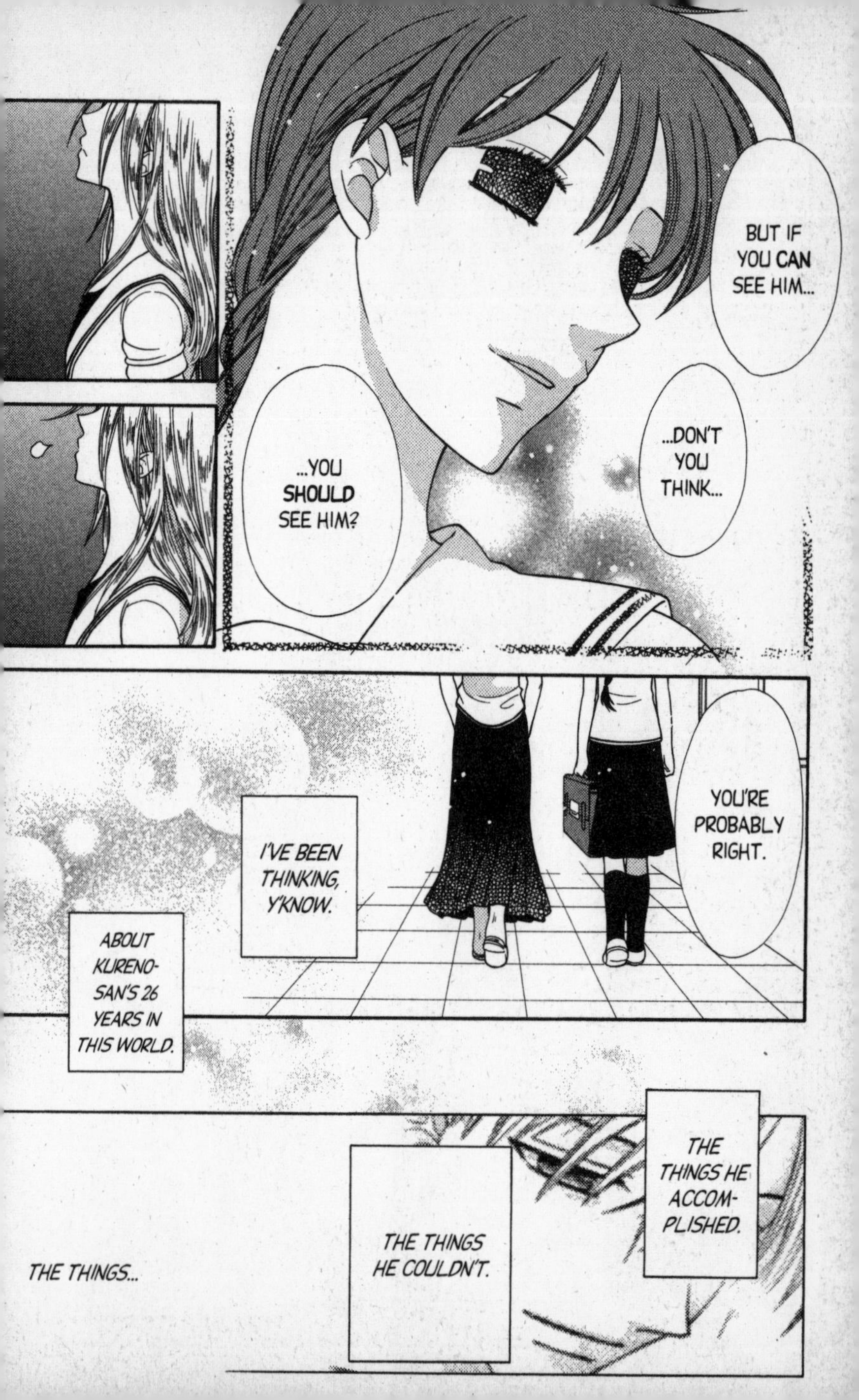
BUT IF YOU CAN SEE HIM...
...DON'T YOU THINK...
...YOU SHOULD SEE HIM?
YOU'RE PROBABLY RIGHT.
I'VE BEEN THINKING, Y'KNOW.
ABOUT KURENO-SAN'S 26 YEARS IN THIS WORLD.
THE THINGS HE ACCOMPLISHED.
THE THINGS HE COULDN'T.
THE THINGS...

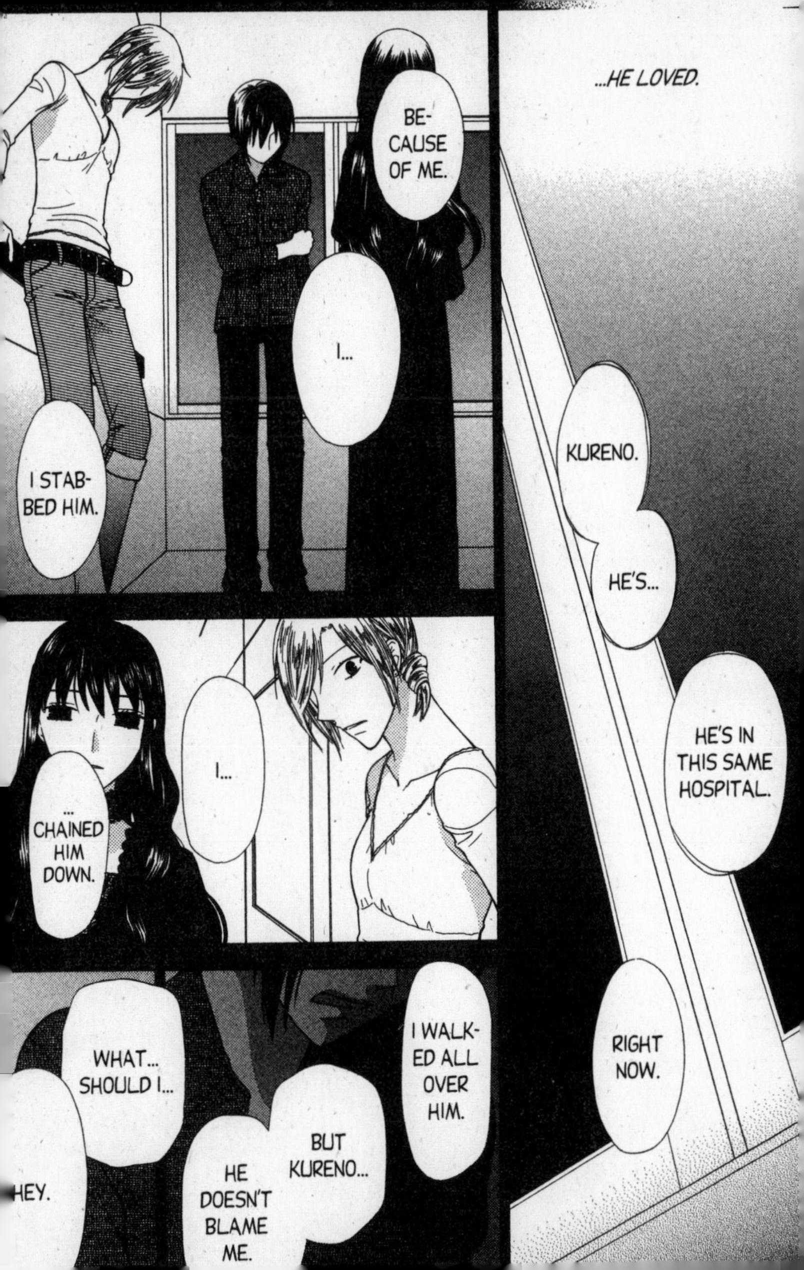
...HE LOVED.
KURENO.
HE'S...
HE'S IN THIS SAME HOSPITAL.
RIGHT NOW.
BE-CAUSE OF ME.
I...
I STAB-BED HIM.
I...
...CHAINED HIM DOWN.
I WALK-ED ALL OVER HIM.
BUT KURENO...
HE DOESN'T BLAME ME.
WHAT... SHOULD I...
HEY.

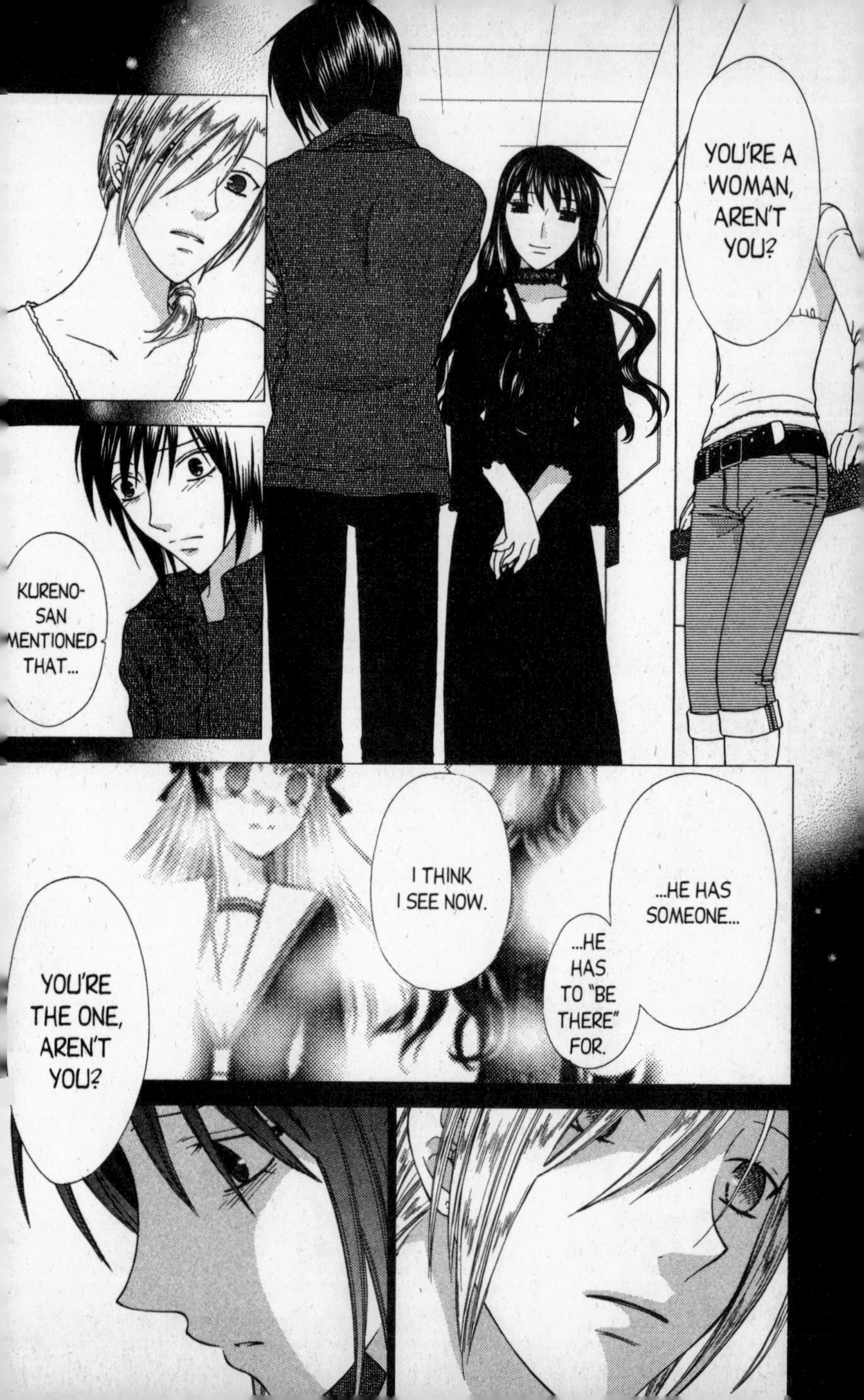
YOU'RE A WOMAN, AREN'T YOU?
KURENO-SAN MENTIONED THAT...
...HE HAS SOMEONE...
...HE HAS TO "BE THERE" FOR.
I THINK I SEE NOW.
YOU'RE THE ONE, AREN'T YOU?

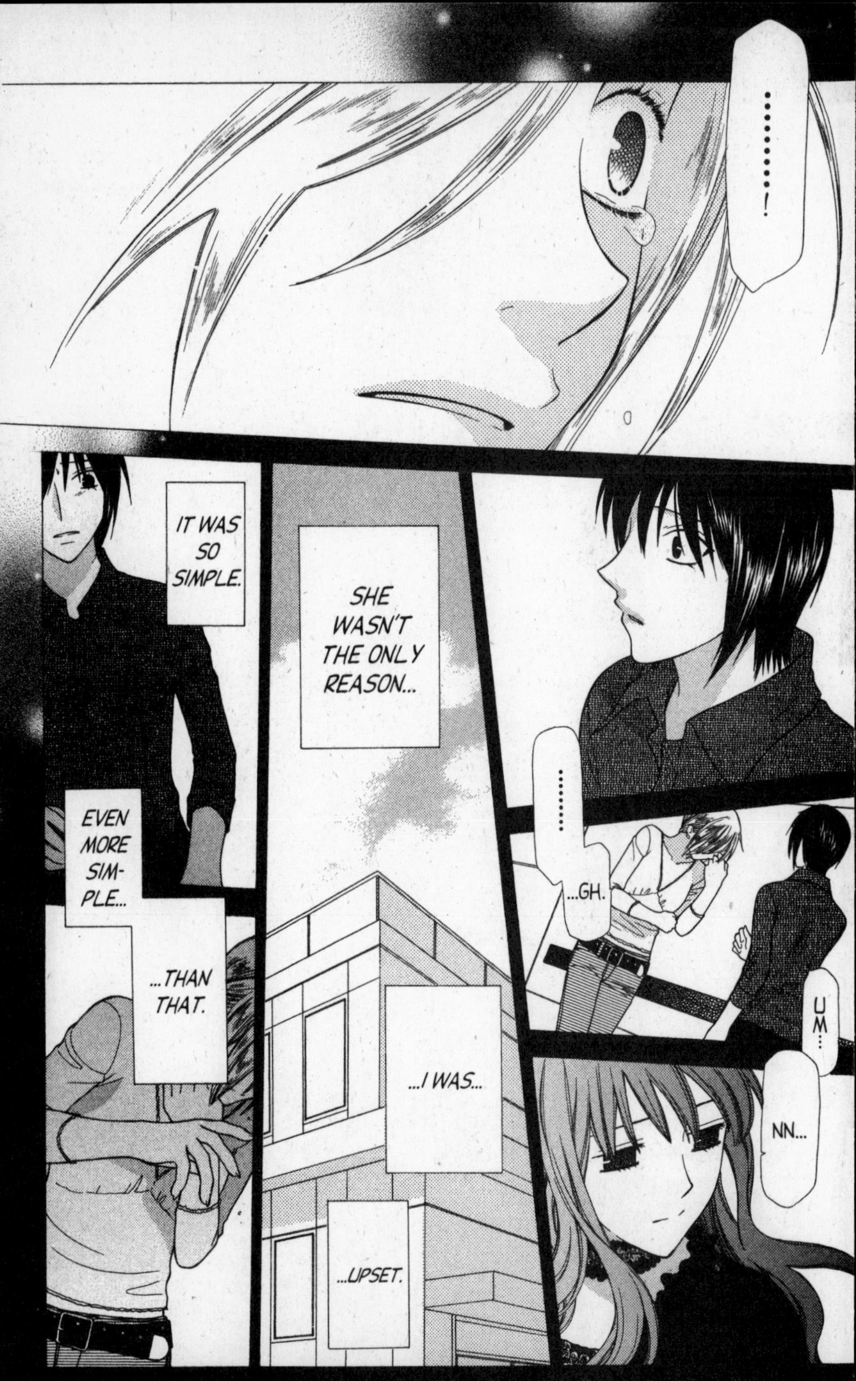
......!
......
...GH.
UM...
NN...
SHE WASN'T THE ONLY REASON...
...I WAS...
...UPSET.
IT WAS SO SIMPLE.
EVEN MORE SIM-PLE...
...THAN THAT.

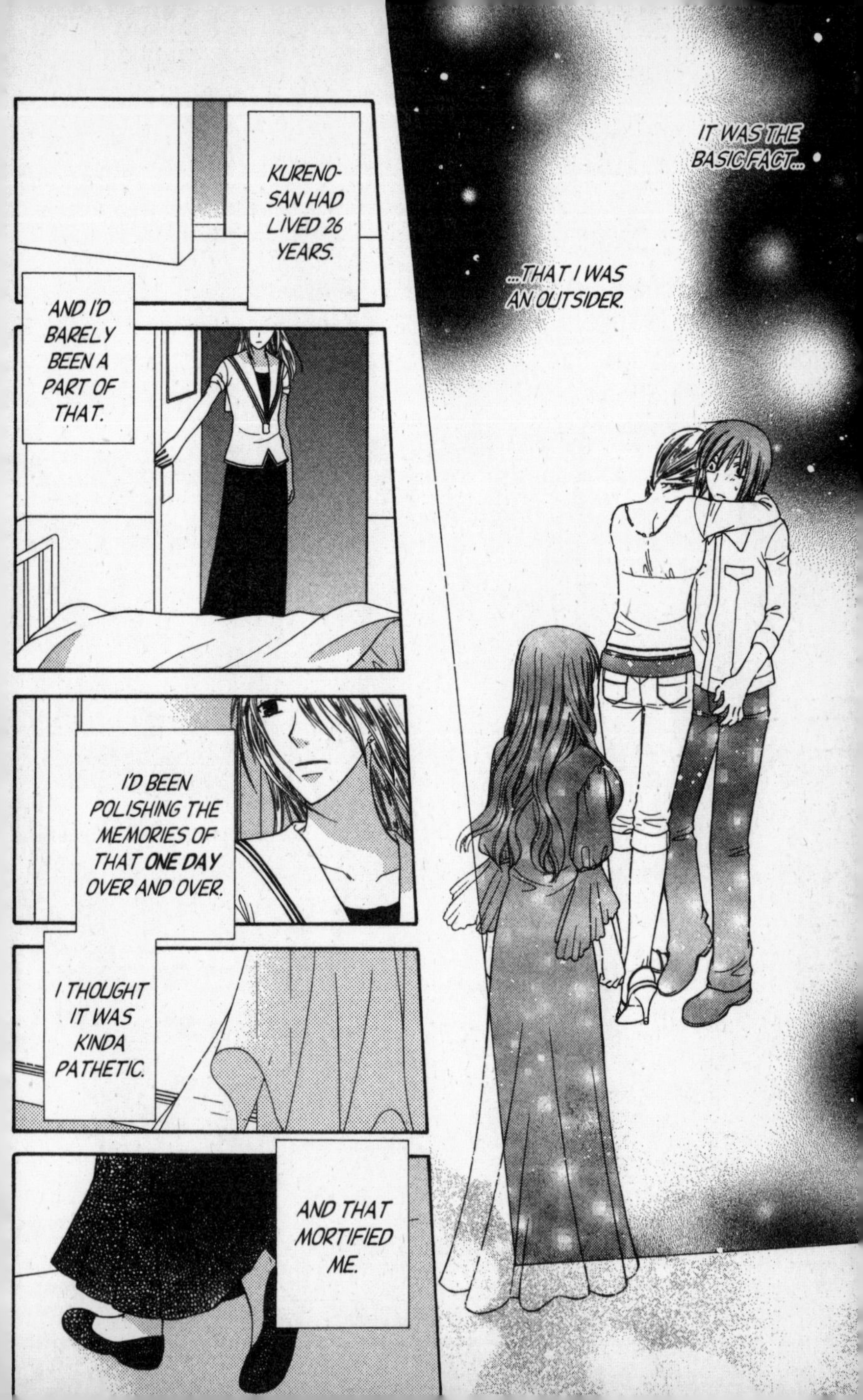
IT WAS THE BASIC FACT...
...THAT I WAS AN OUTSIDER.
KURENO-SAN HAD LIVED 26 YEARS.
AND I'D BARELY BEEN A PART OF THAT.
I'D BEEN POLISHING THE MEMORIES OF THAT ONE DAY OVER AND OVER.
I THOUGHT IT WAS KINDA PATHETIC.
AND THAT MORTIFIED ME.

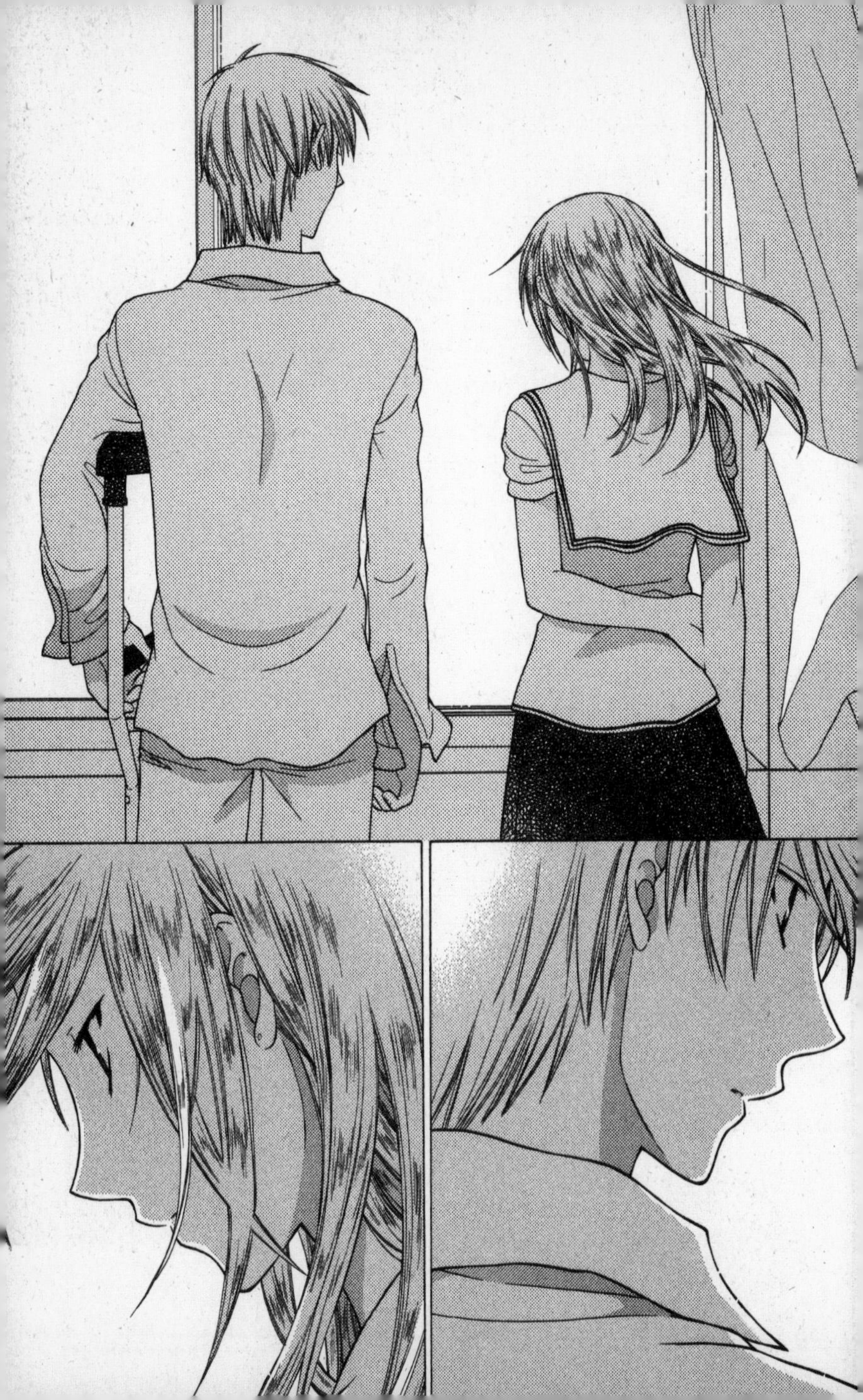

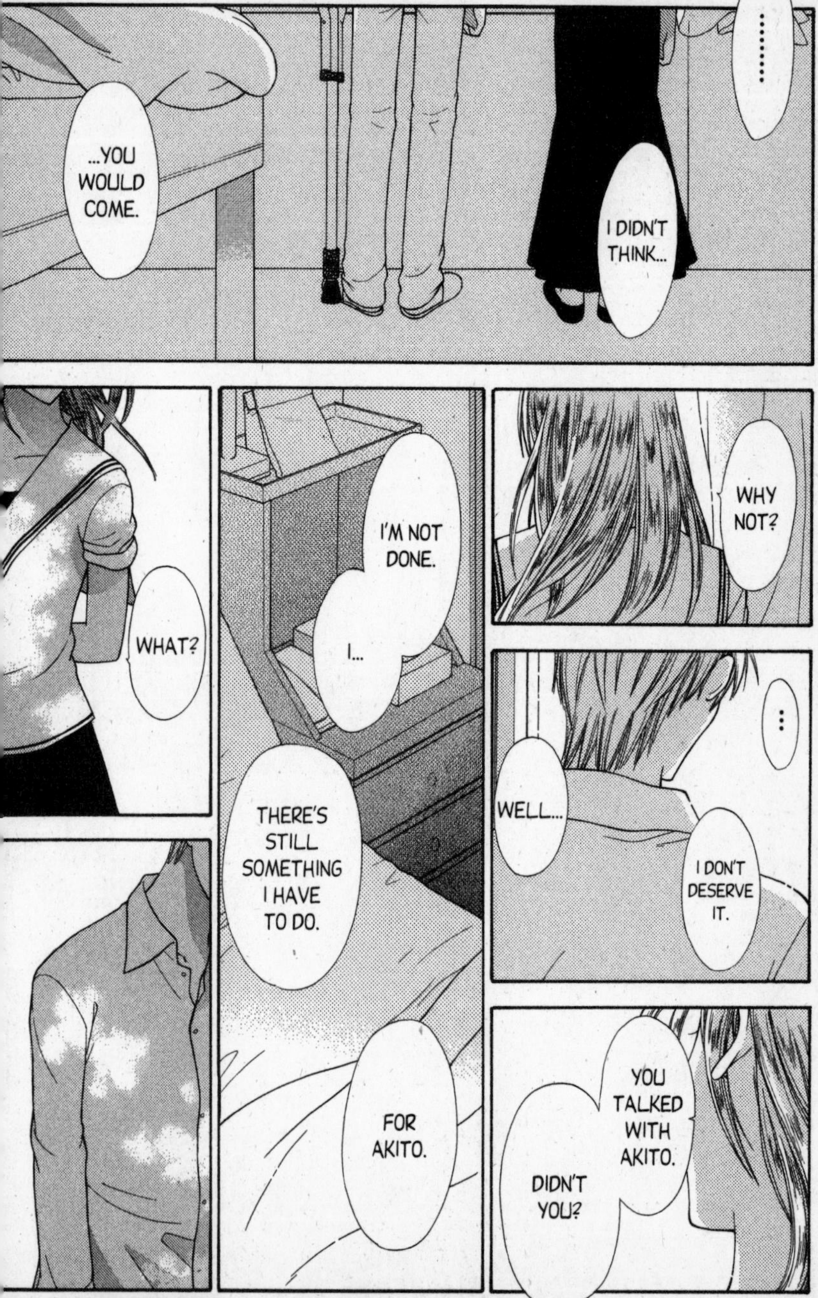
......
I DIDN'T THINK...
...YOU WOULD COME.
WHY NOT?
...
WELL...
I DON'T DESERVE IT.
YOU TALKED WITH AKITO.
DIDN'T YOU?
I'M NOT DONE.
I...
THERE'S STILL SOMETHING I HAVE TO DO.
FOR AKITO.
WHAT?

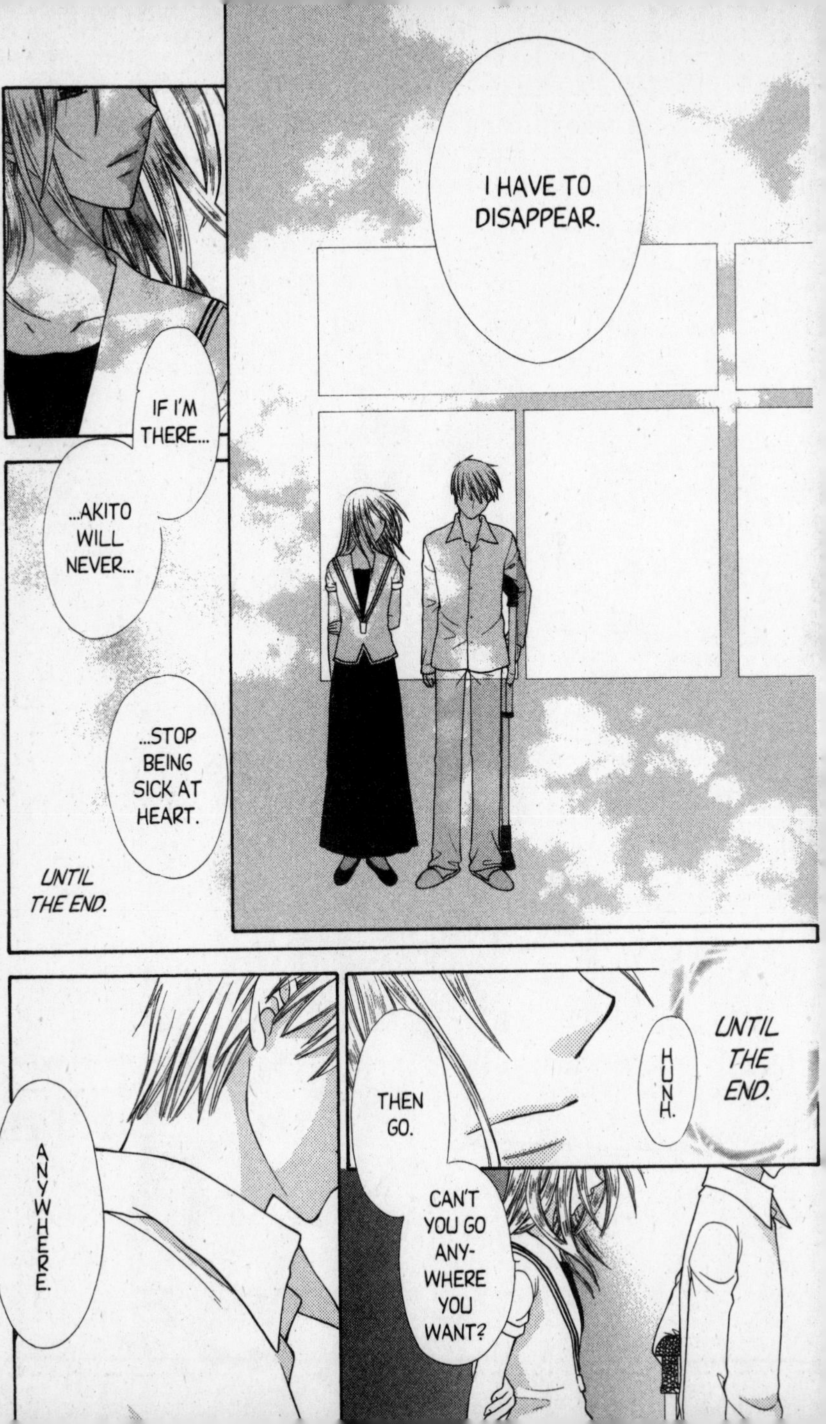
I HAVE TO DISAPPEAR.
IF I'M THERE...
...AKITO WILL NEVER...
...STOP BEING SICK AT HEART.
UNTIL THE END.
UNTIL THE END.
HUNH.
THEN GO.
CAN'T YOU GO ANY-WHERE YOU WANT?
ANYWHERE.

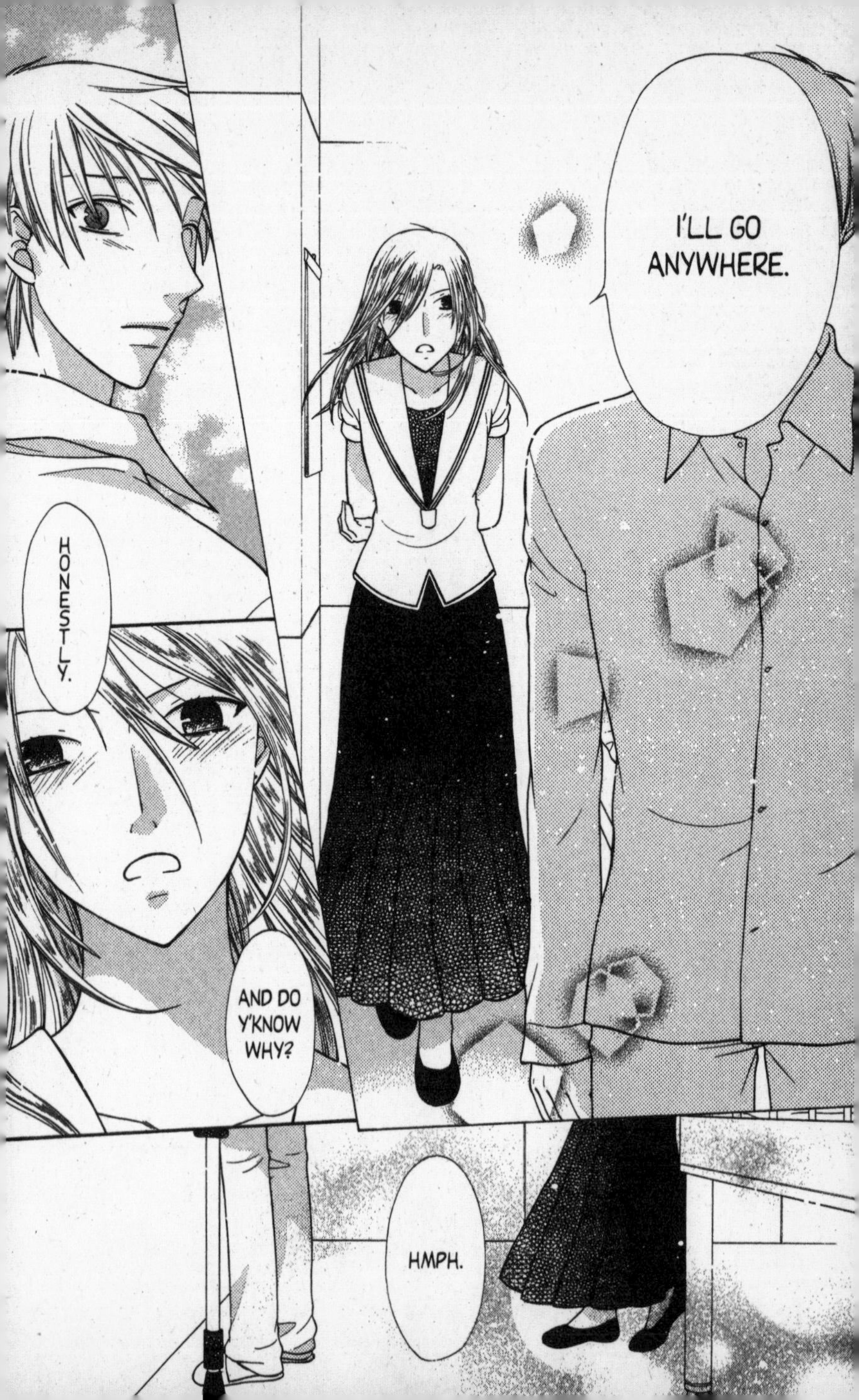
I'LL GO ANYWHERE.
HONESTLY.
AND DO Y'KNOW WHY?
HMPH.

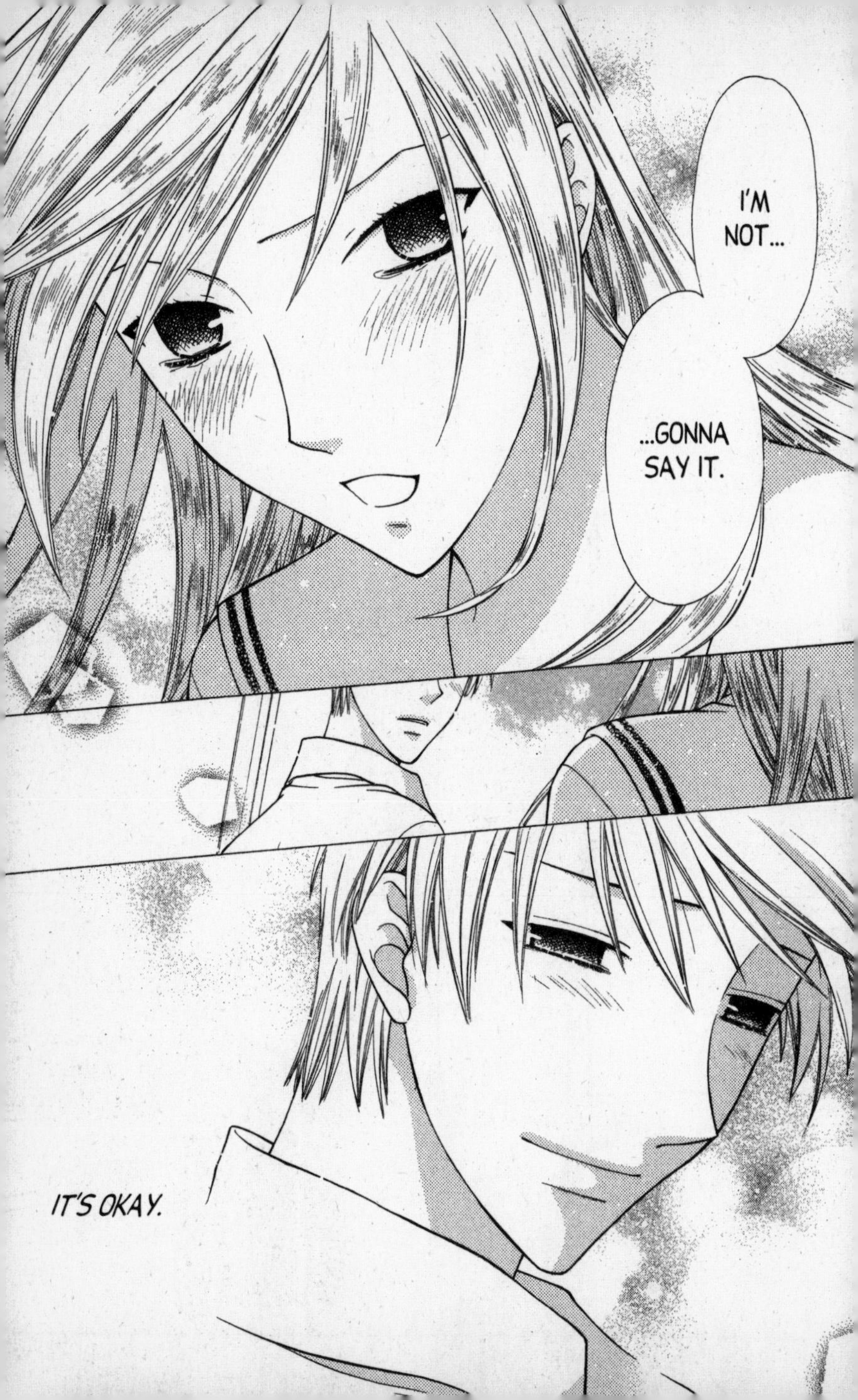
I'M NOT...
...GONNA SAY IT.
IT'S OKAY.

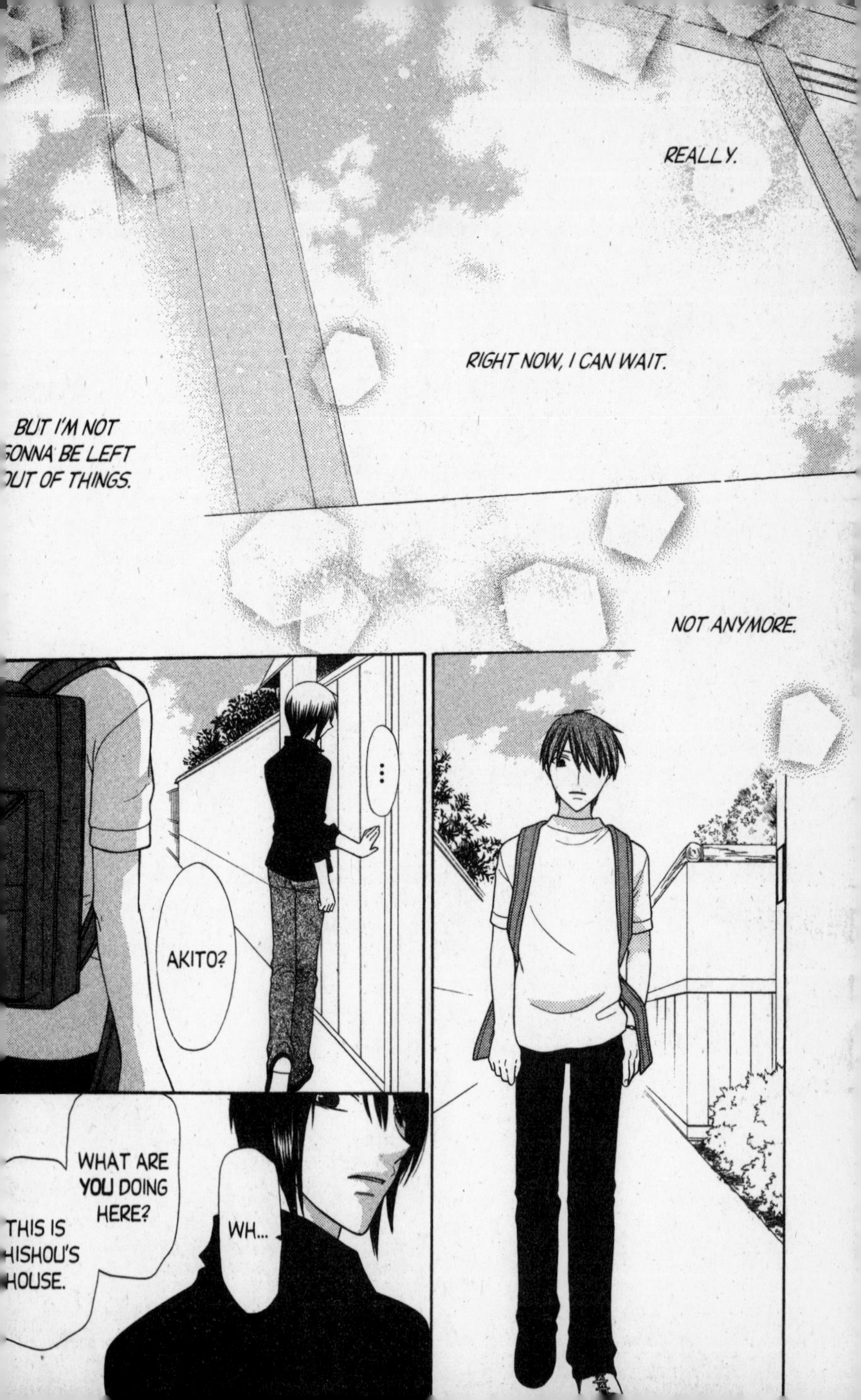
REALLY.
RIGHT NOW, I CAN WAIT.
BUT I'M NOT GONNA BE LEFT OUT OF THINGS.
NOT ANYMORE.
...
AKITO?
WH...
WHAT ARE YOU DOING HERE?
THIS IS HISHOU'S HOUSE.

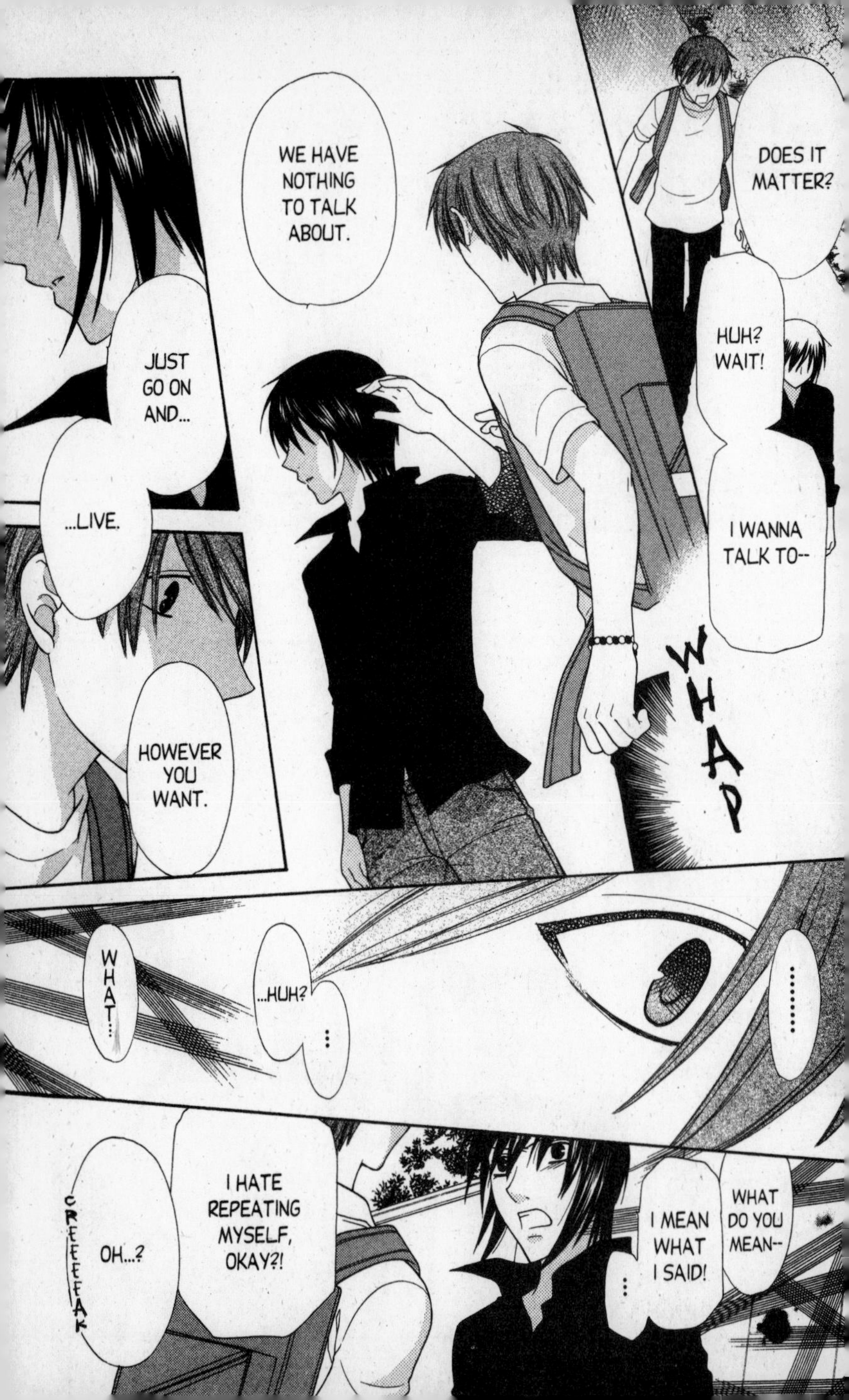
DOES IT MATTER?
HUH? WAIT!
I WANNA TALK TO--
WHAP
WE HAVE NOTHING TO TALK ABOUT.
JUST GO ON AND...
...LIVE.
HOWEVER YOU WANT.
......
...HUH? ...
WHAT...
WHAT DO YOU MEAN--
I MEAN WHAT I SAID! ...
I HATE REPEATING MYSELF, OKAY?!
OH...?
CREEEEAK

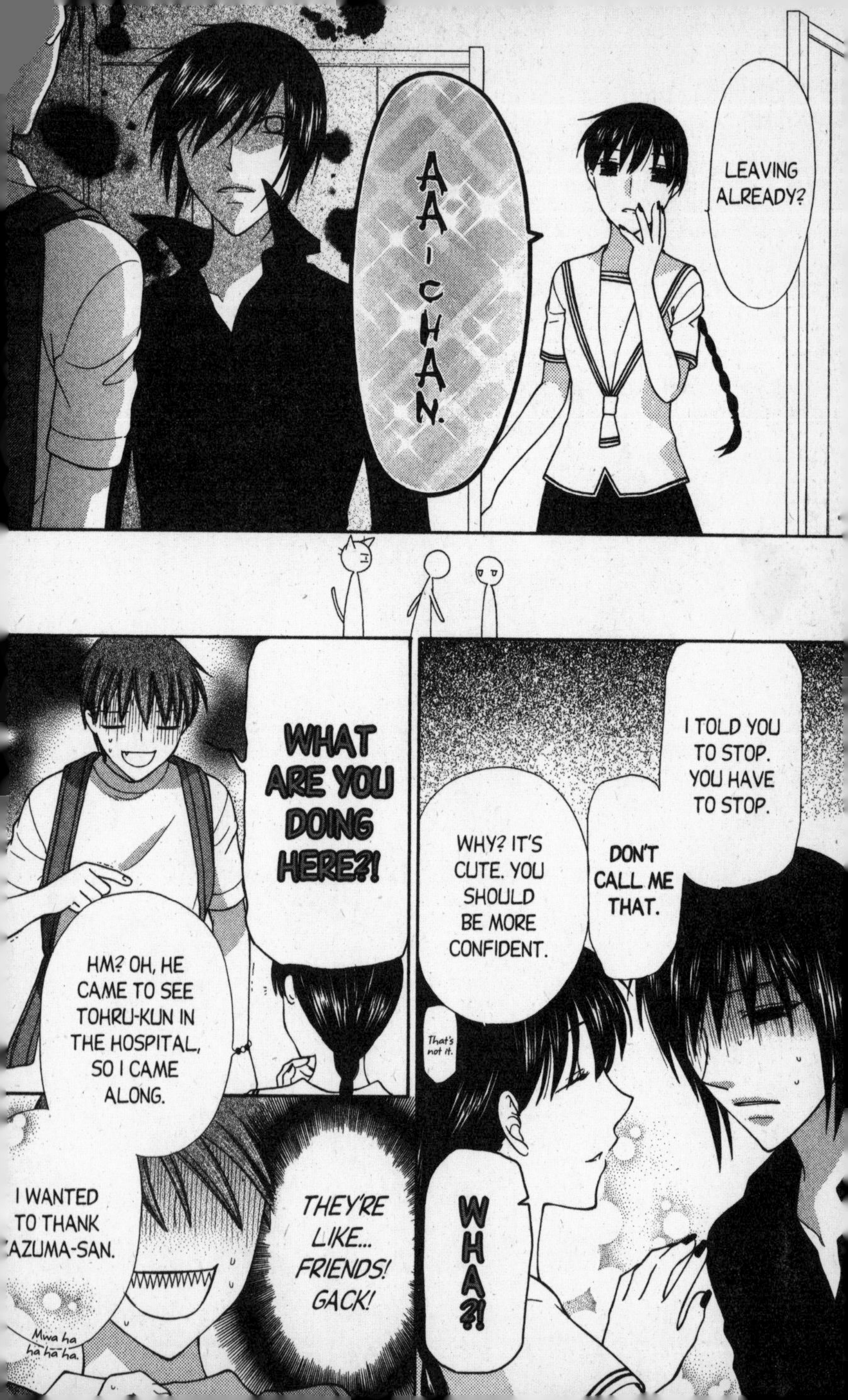

LEAVING ALREADY?
AA-CHAN.
I TOLD YOU TO STOP. YOU HAVE TO STOP.
DON'T CALL ME THAT.
WHY? IT'S CUTE. YOU SHOULD BE MORE CONFIDENT.
That's not it.
WHA?!
WHAT ARE YOU DOING HERE?!
HM? OH, HE CAME TO SEE TOHRU-KUN IN THE HOSPITAL, SO I CAME ALONG.
THEY'RE LIKE... FRIENDS! GACK!
I WANTED TO THANK AZUMA-SAN.
Mwa ha ha ha ha.

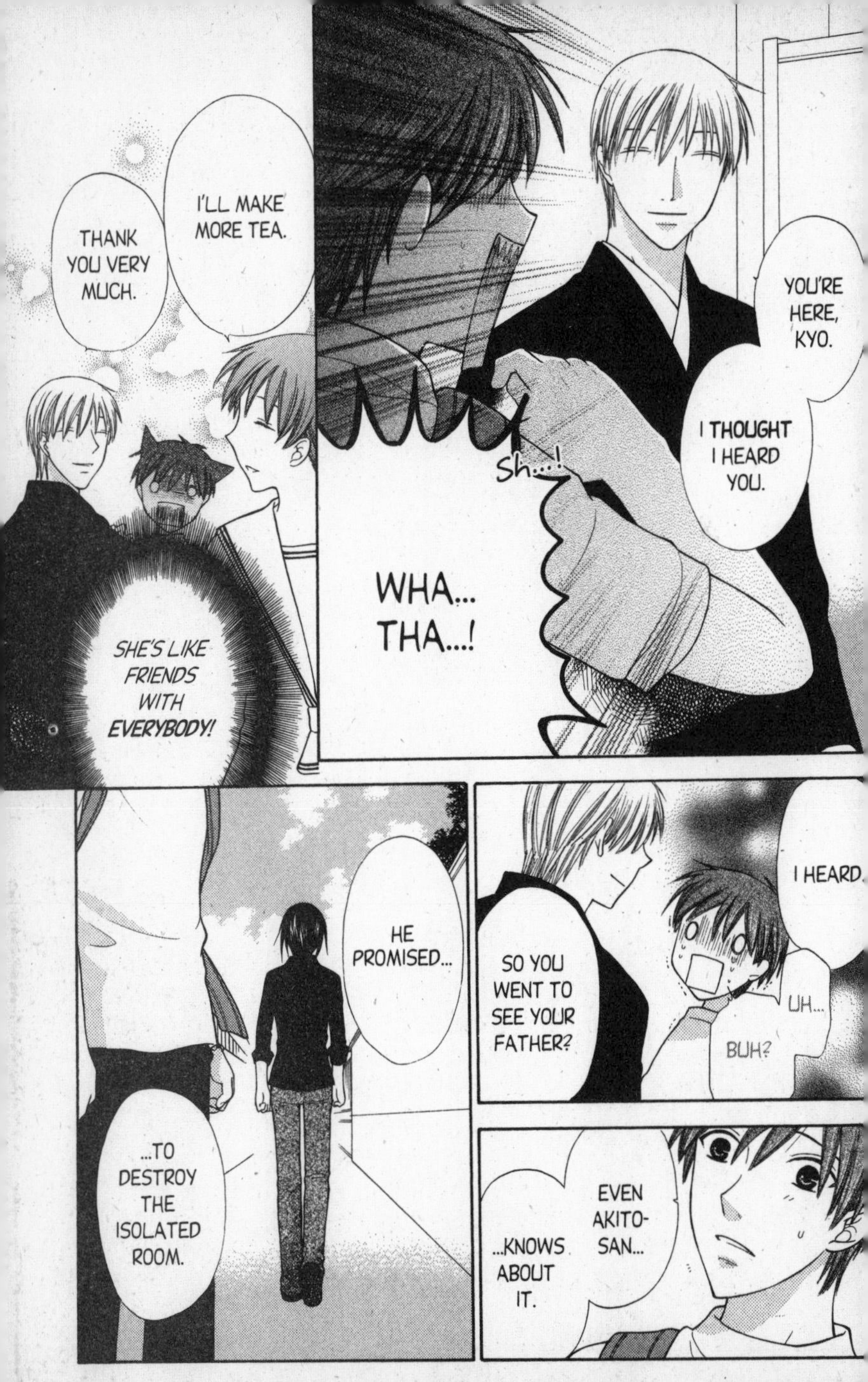
YOU'RE HERE, KYO.
I THOUGHT I HEARD YOU.
Sh...!
WHA... THA...!
I'LL MAKE MORE TEA.
THANK YOU VERY MUCH.
SHE'S LIKE FRIENDS WITH EVERYBODY!
I HEARD.
UH...
BUH?
SO YOU WENT TO SEE YOUR FATHER?
EVEN AKITO-SAN...
...KNOWS ABOUT IT.
HE PROMISED...
...TO DESTROY THE ISOLATED ROOM.

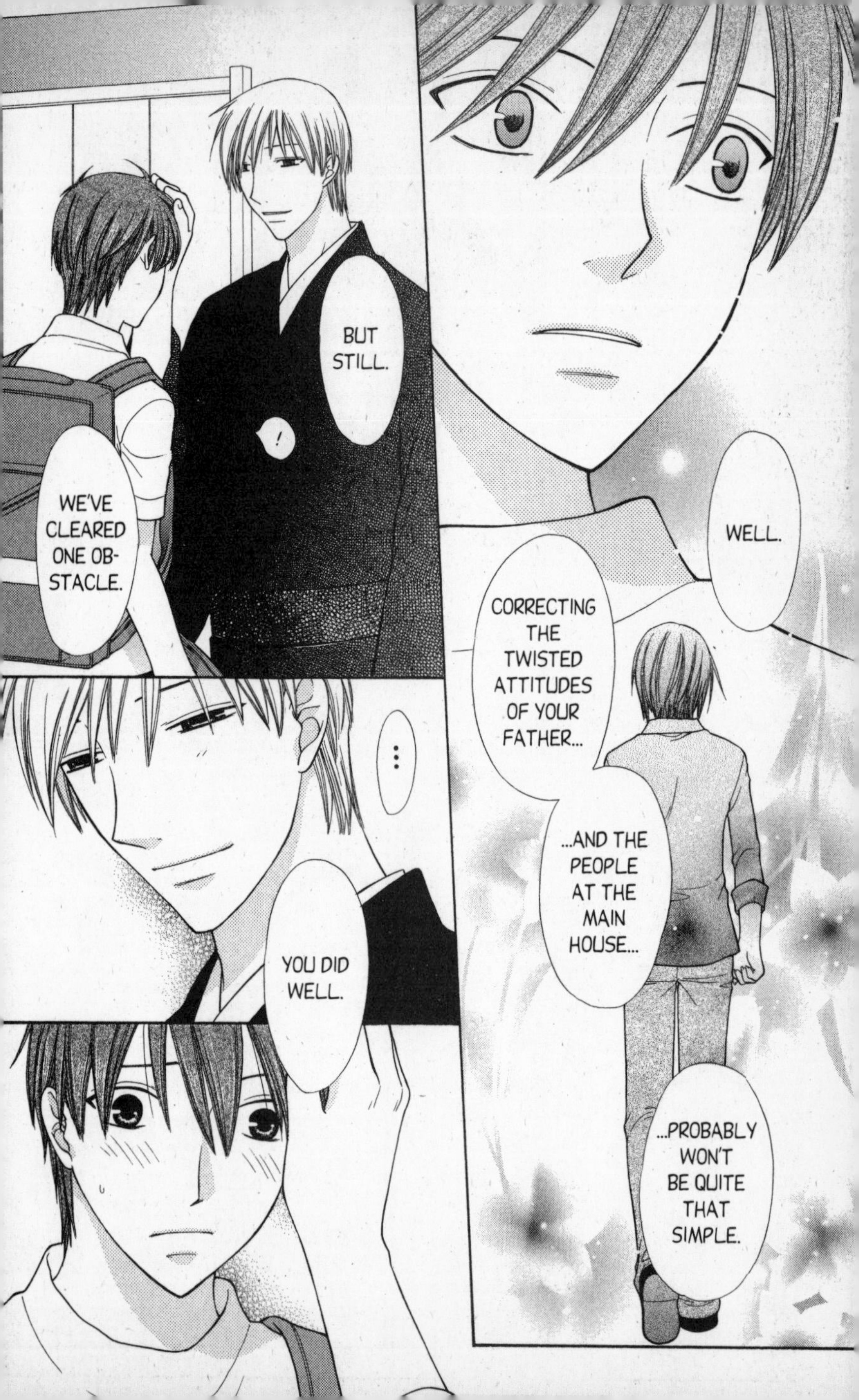
WELL.
CORRECTING THE TWISTED ATTITUDES OF YOUR FATHER...
...AND THE PEOPLE AT THE MAIN HOUSE...
...PROBABLY WON'T BE QUITE THAT SIMPLE.
BUT STILL.
WE'VE CLEARED ONE OB-STACLE.
!
...
YOU DID WELL.

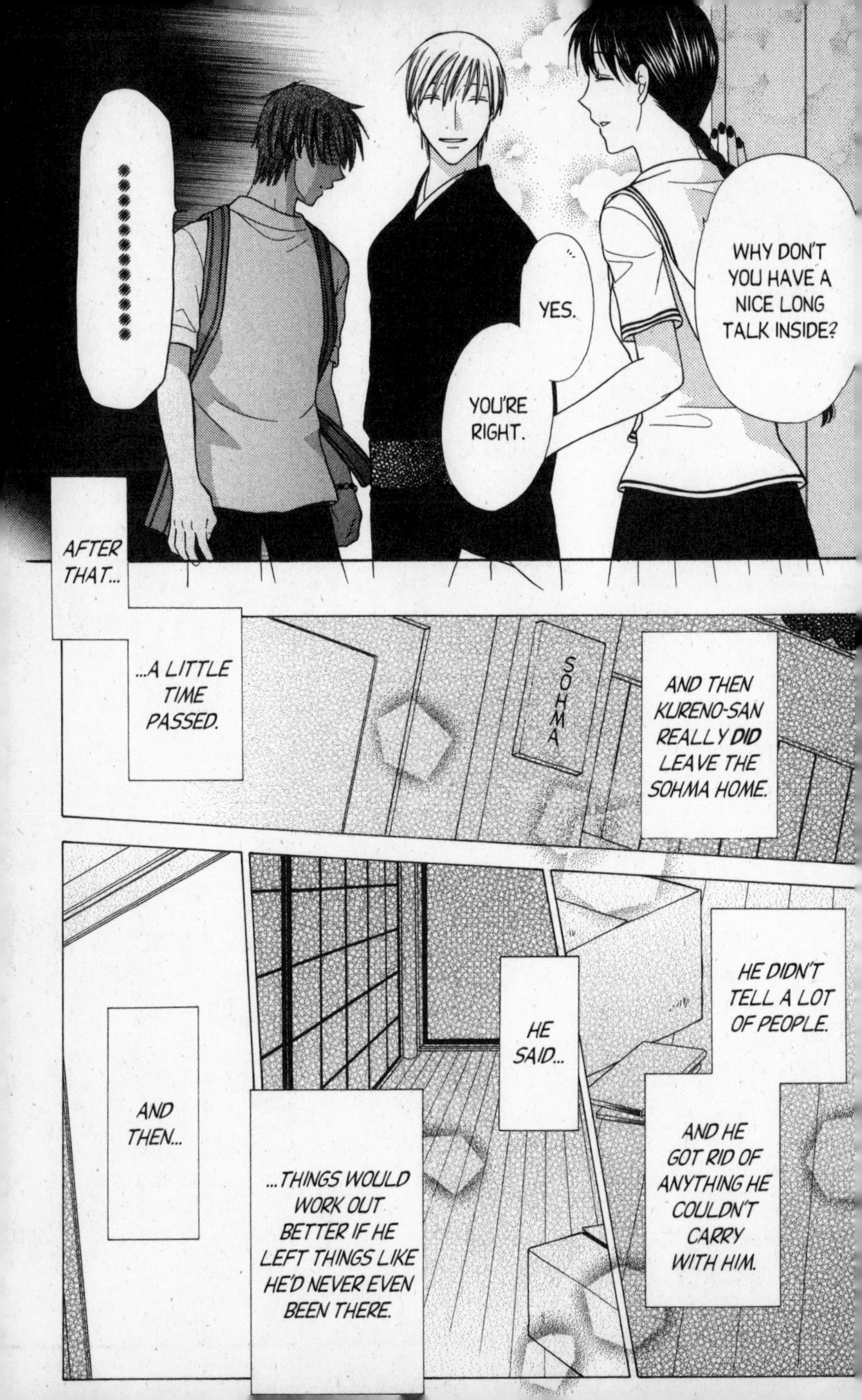
WHY DON'T YOU HAVE A NICE LONG TALK INSIDE?
...
YES.
YOU'RE RIGHT.
....
AFTER THAT...
...A LITTLE TIME PASSED.
AND THEN KURENO-SAN REALLY **DID** LEAVE THE SOHMA HOME.
SOHMA
HE DIDN'T TELL A LOT OF PEOPLE.
AND HE GOT RID OF ANYTHING HE COULDN'T CARRY WITH HIM.
HE SAID...
...THINGS WOULD WORK OUT BETTER IF HE LEFT THINGS LIKE HE'D NEVER EVEN BEEN THERE.
AND THEN...

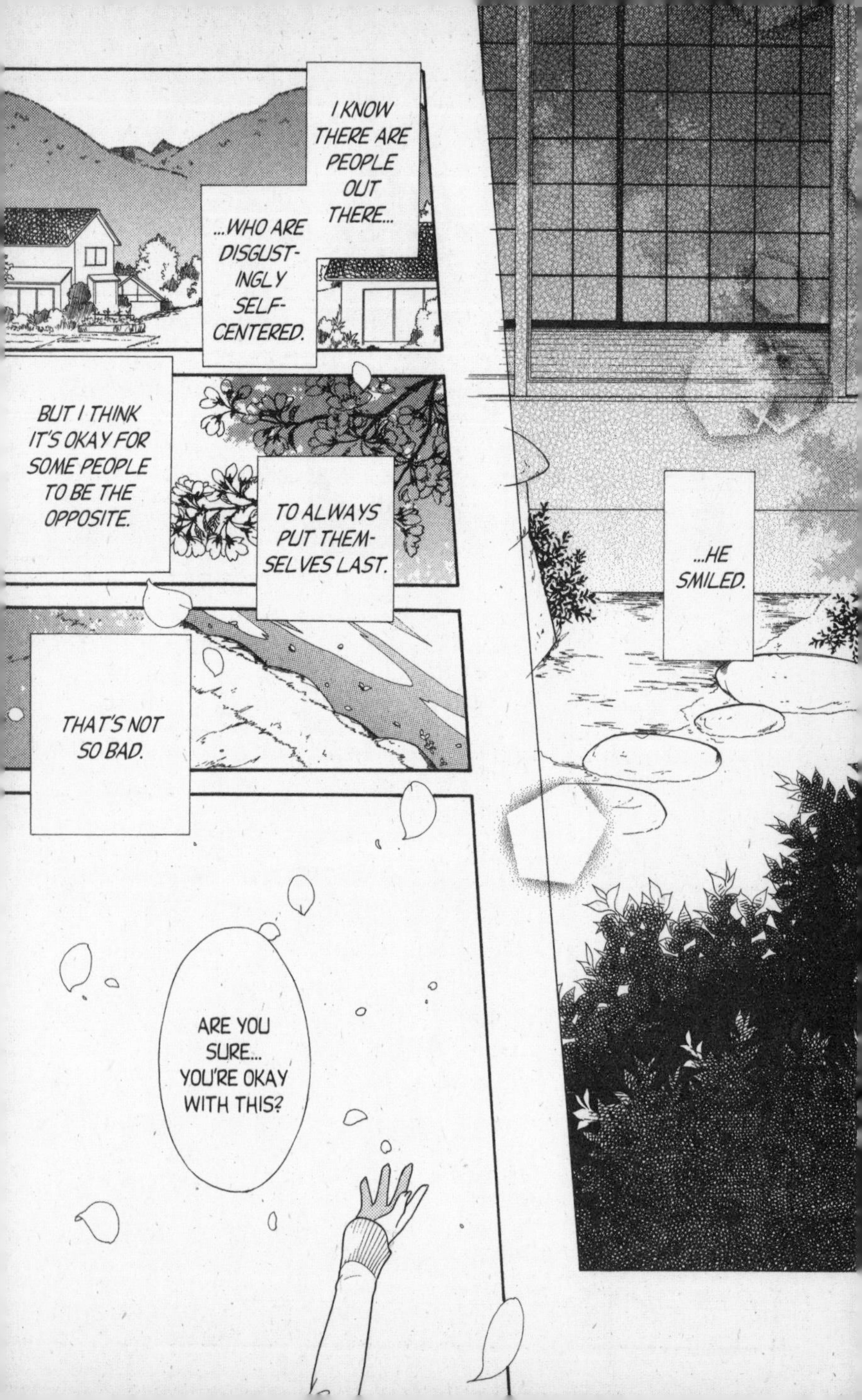
...HE SMILED.
I KNOW THERE ARE PEOPLE OUT THERE...
...WHO ARE DISGUST-INGLY SELF-CENTERED.
BUT I THINK IT'S OKAY FOR SOME PEOPLE TO BE THE OPPOSITE.
TO ALWAYS PUT THEM-SELVES LAST.
THAT'S NOT SO BAD.
ARE YOU SURE... YOU'RE OKAY WITH THIS?

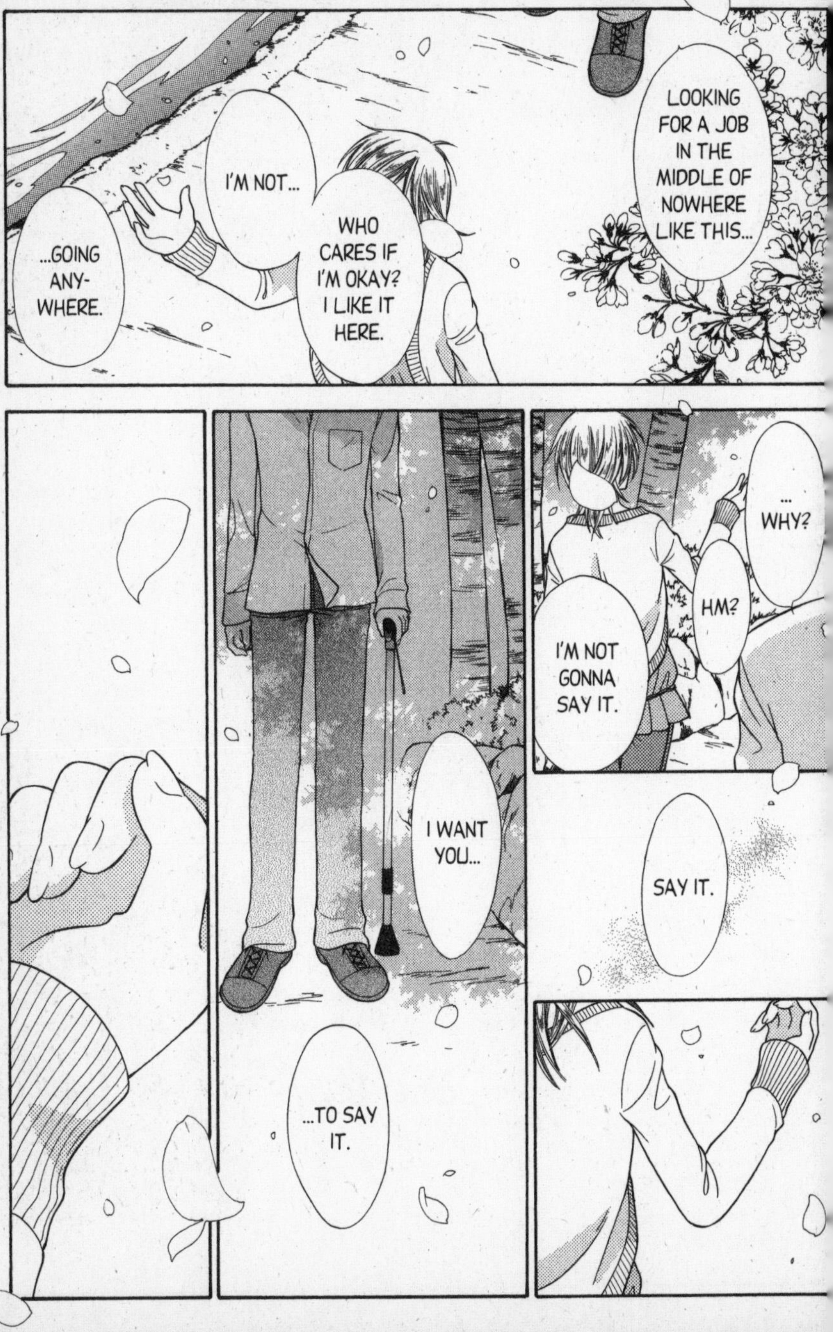
LOOKING FOR A JOB IN THE MIDDLE OF NOWHERE LIKE THIS...
WHO CARES IF I'M OKAY? I LIKE IT HERE.
I'M NOT...
...GOING ANY-WHERE.
...WHY?
HM?
I'M NOT GONNA SAY IT.
SAY IT.
I WANT YOU...
...TO SAY IT.

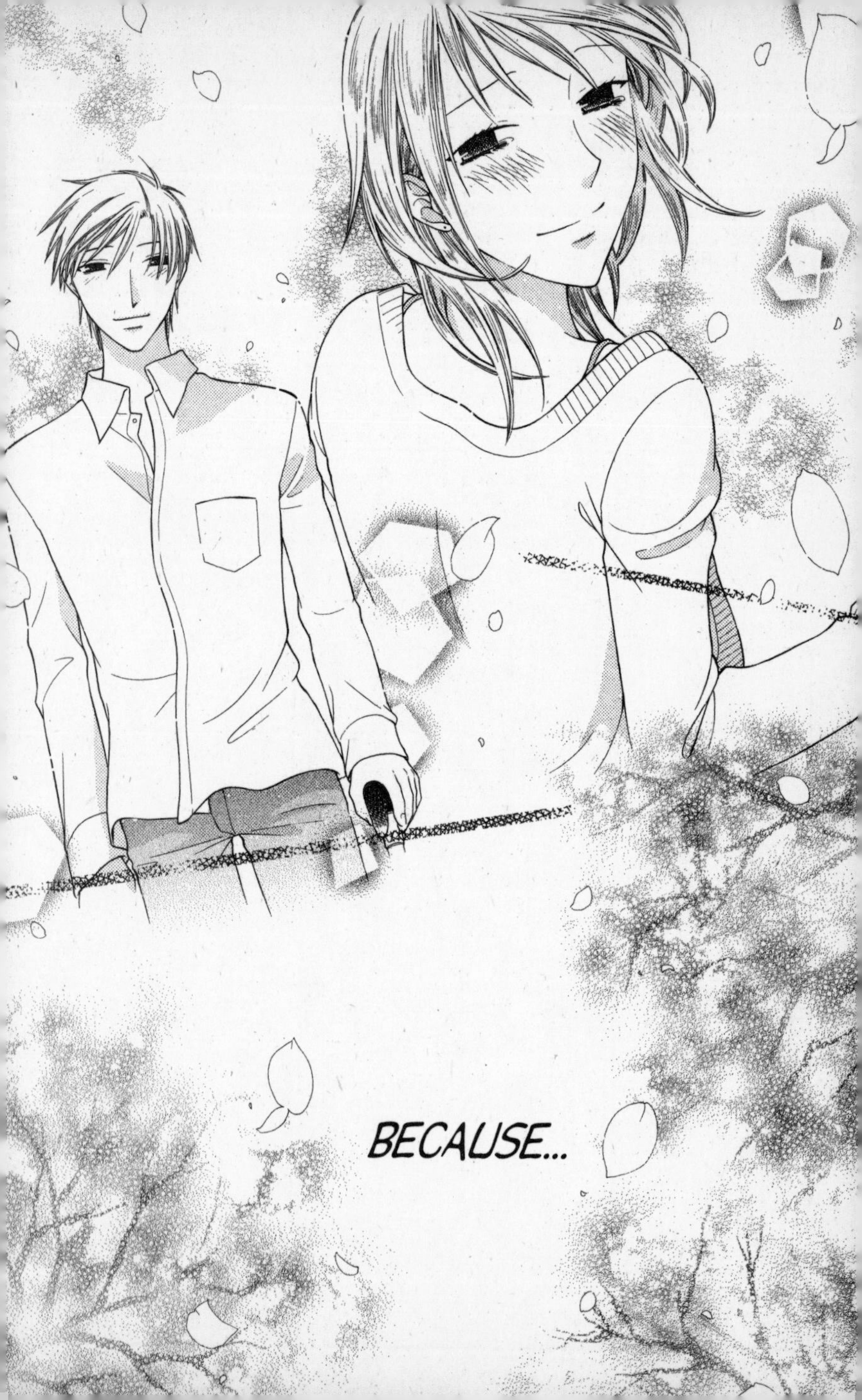
BECAUSE...

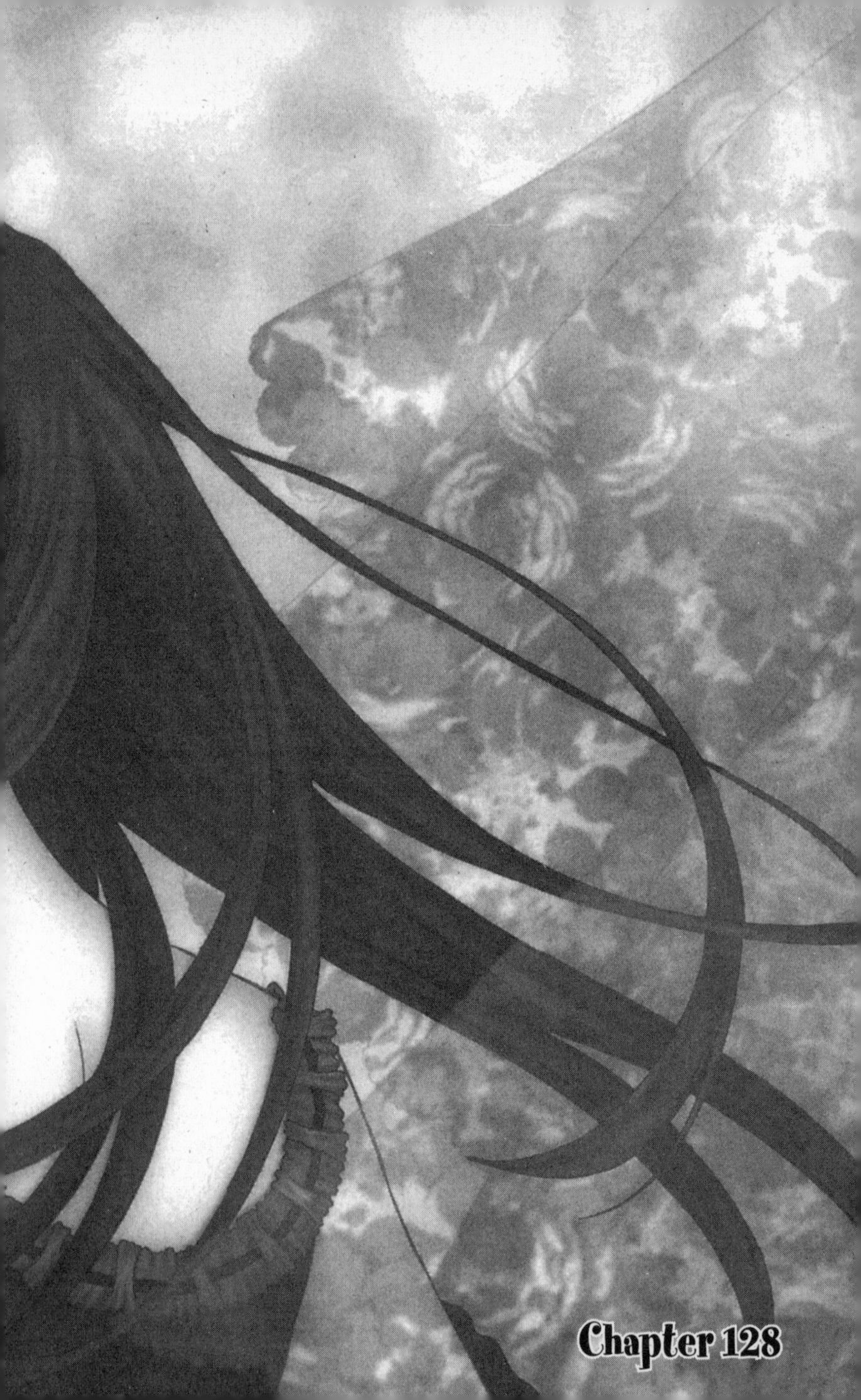
Chapter 128

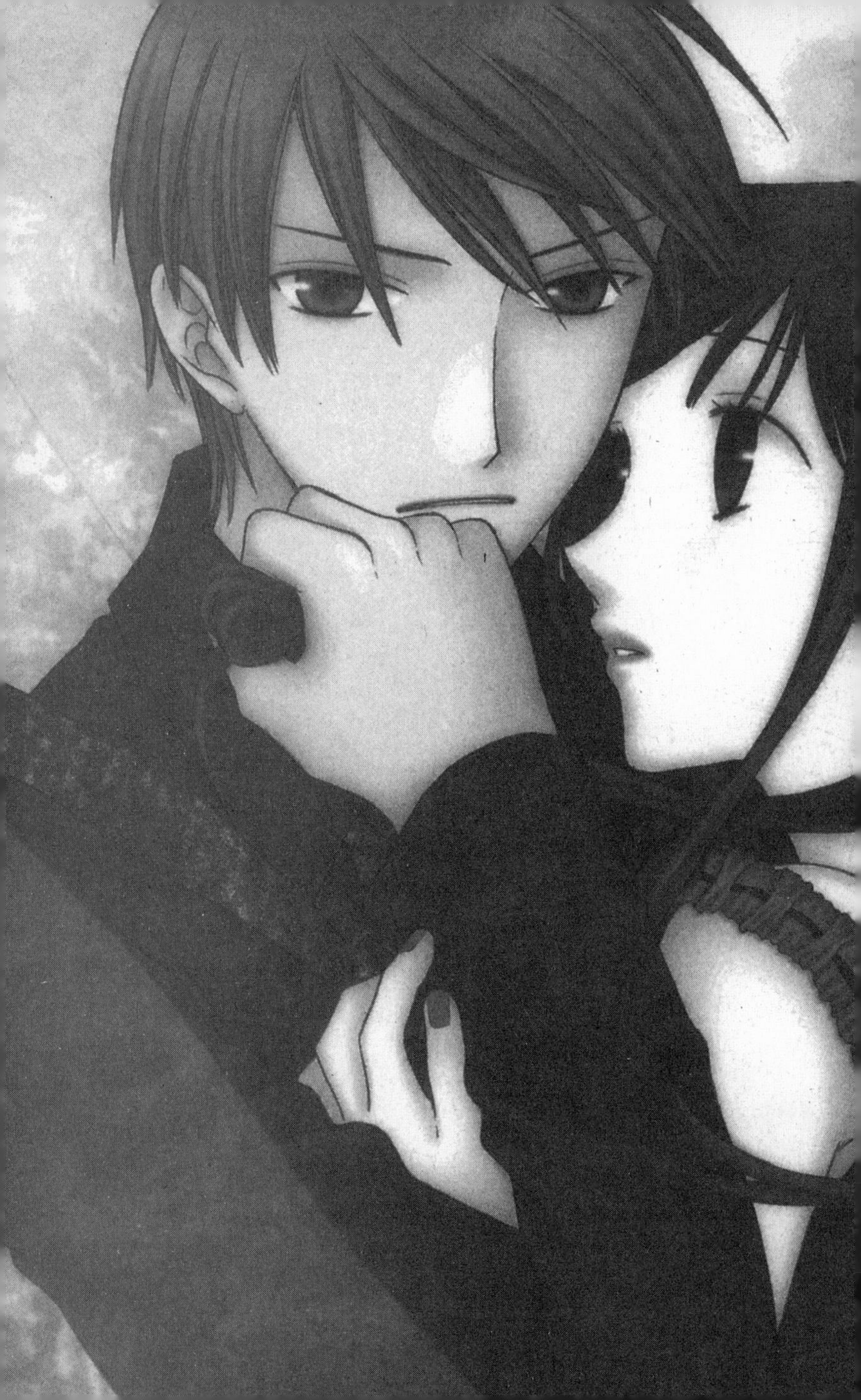

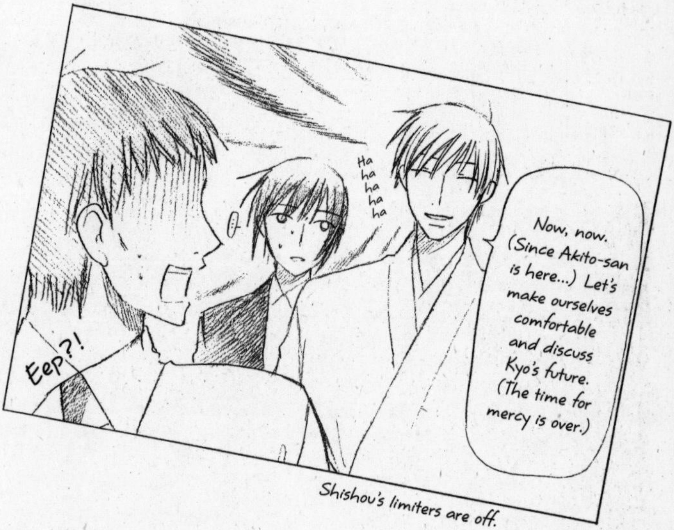
Now, now. (Since Akito-san is here...) Let's make ourselves comfortable and discuss Kyo's future. (The time for mercy is over.)
Ha ha ha ha ha
Eep?!
Shishou's limiters are off.

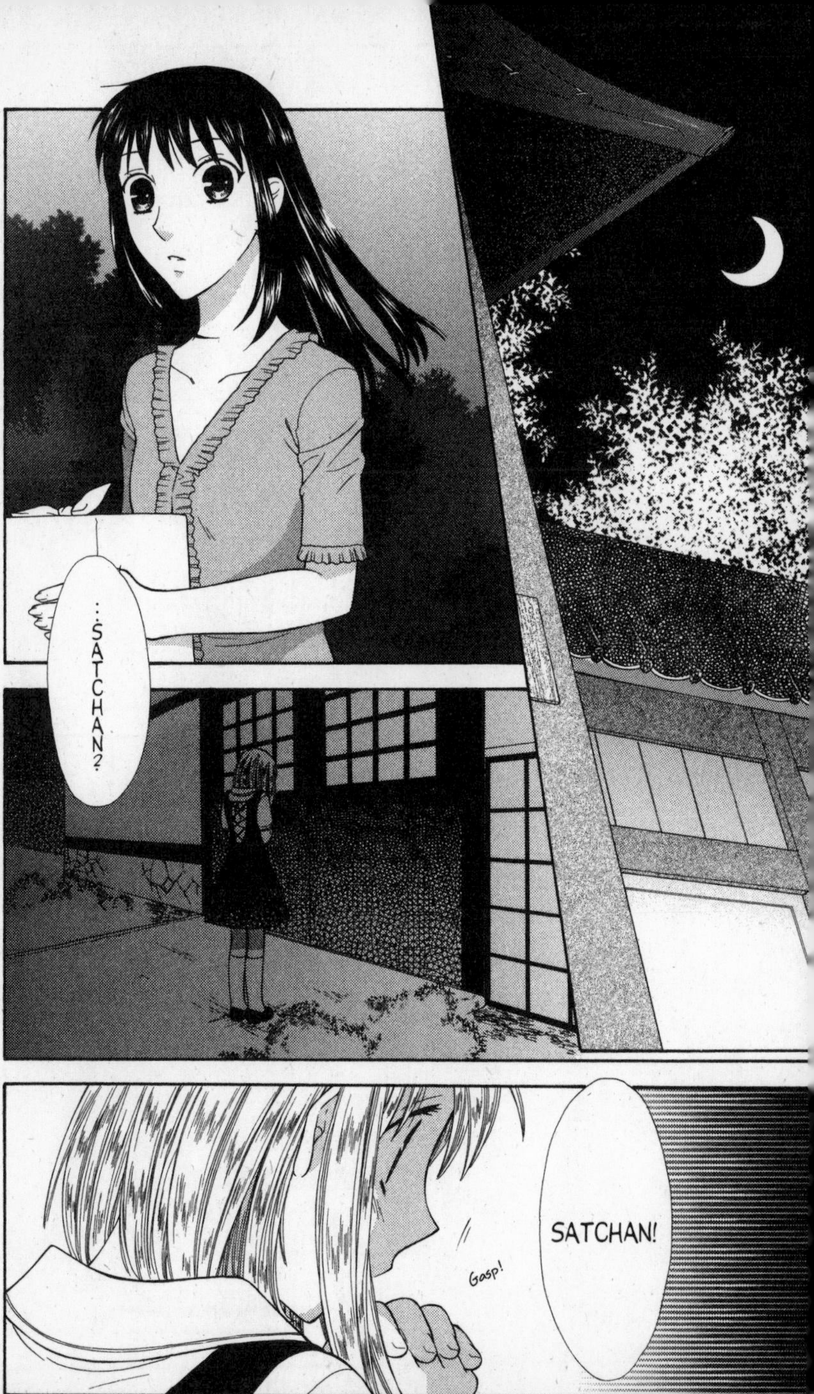
...SATCHAN?
SATCHAN!
Gasp!

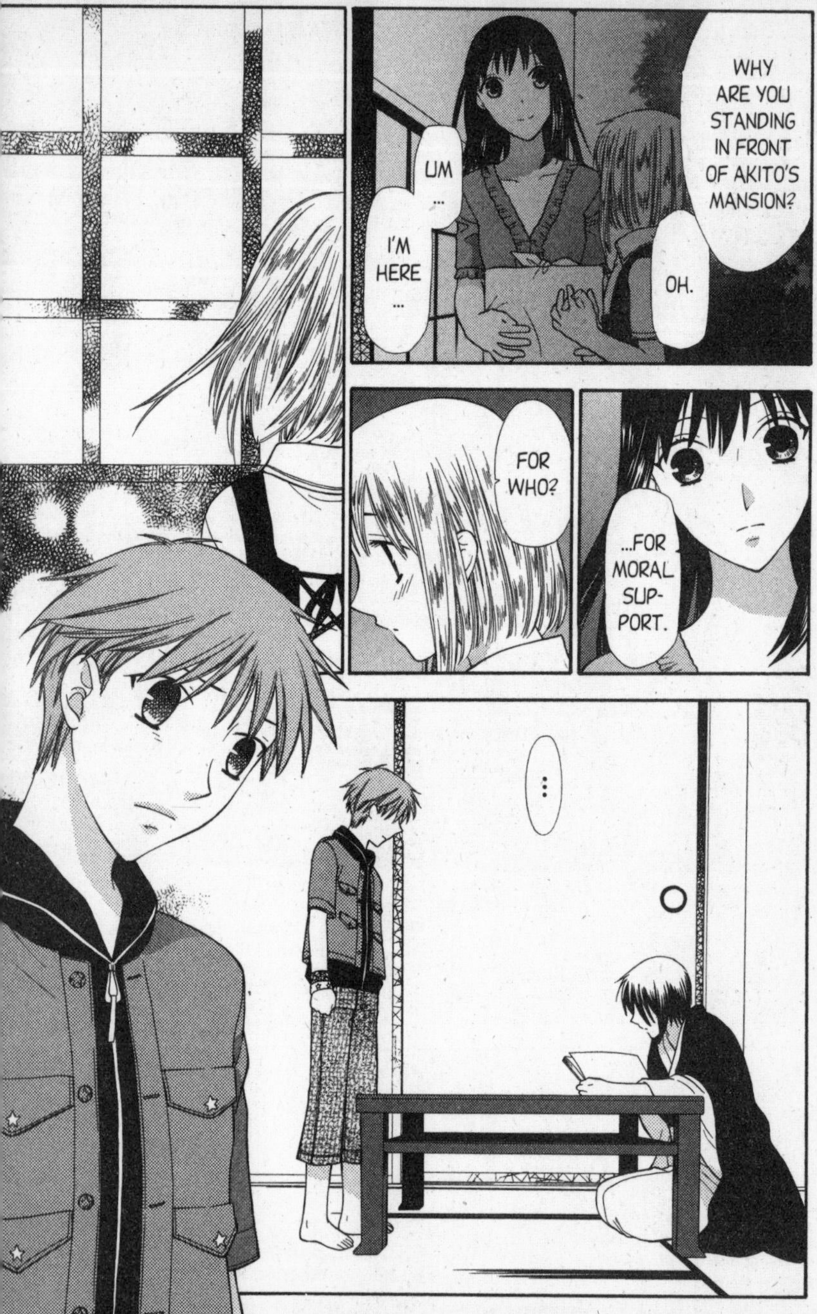
WHY ARE YOU STANDING IN FRONT OF AKITO'S MANSION?
OH.
UM ...
I'M HERE ...
...FOR MORAL SUP-PORT.
FOR WHO?
...

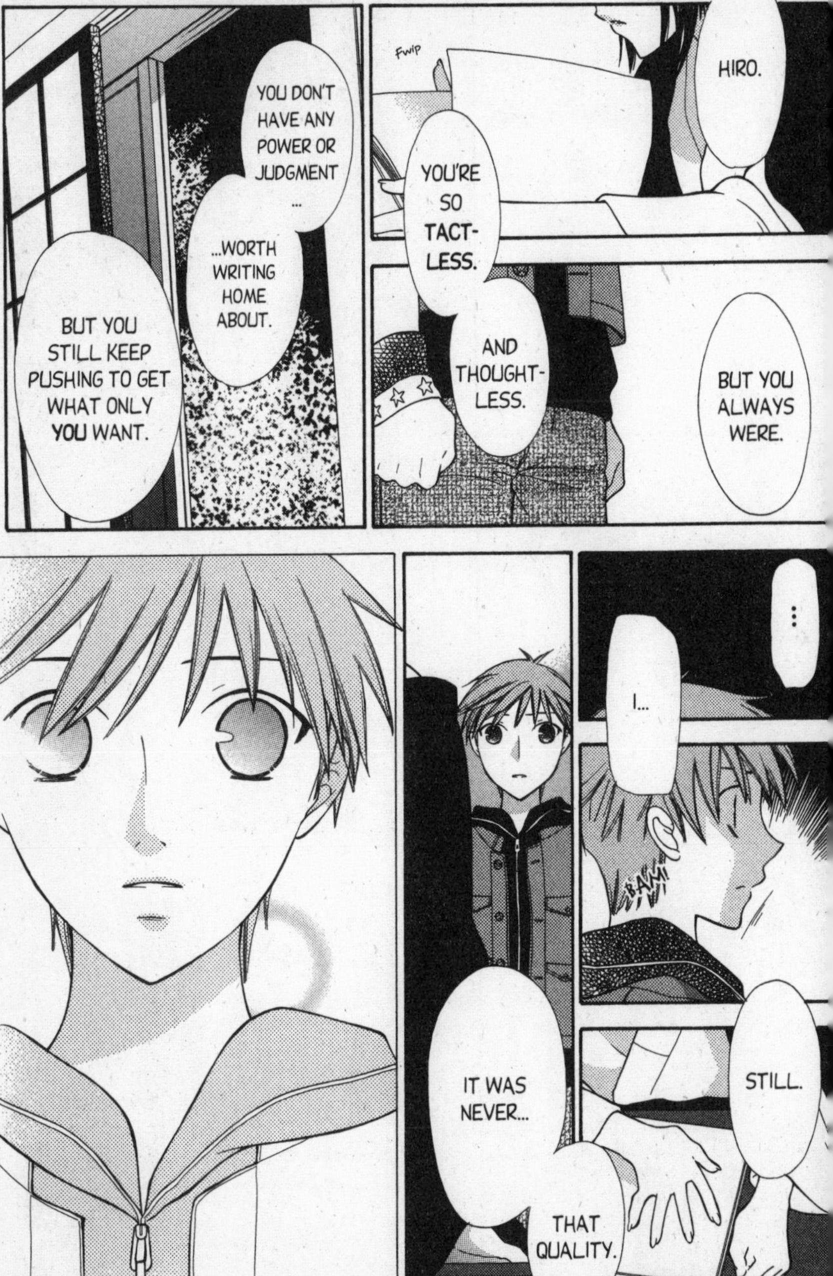
Fwip
HIRO.
YOU'RE SO TACT-LESS.
AND THOUGHT-LESS.
BUT YOU ALWAYS WERE.
YOU DON'T HAVE ANY POWER OR JUDGMENT ...
...WORTH WRITING HOME ABOUT.
BUT YOU STILL KEEP PUSHING TO GET WHAT ONLY YOU WANT.
...
I...
BAM!
STILL.
IT WAS NEVER...
THAT QUALITY.

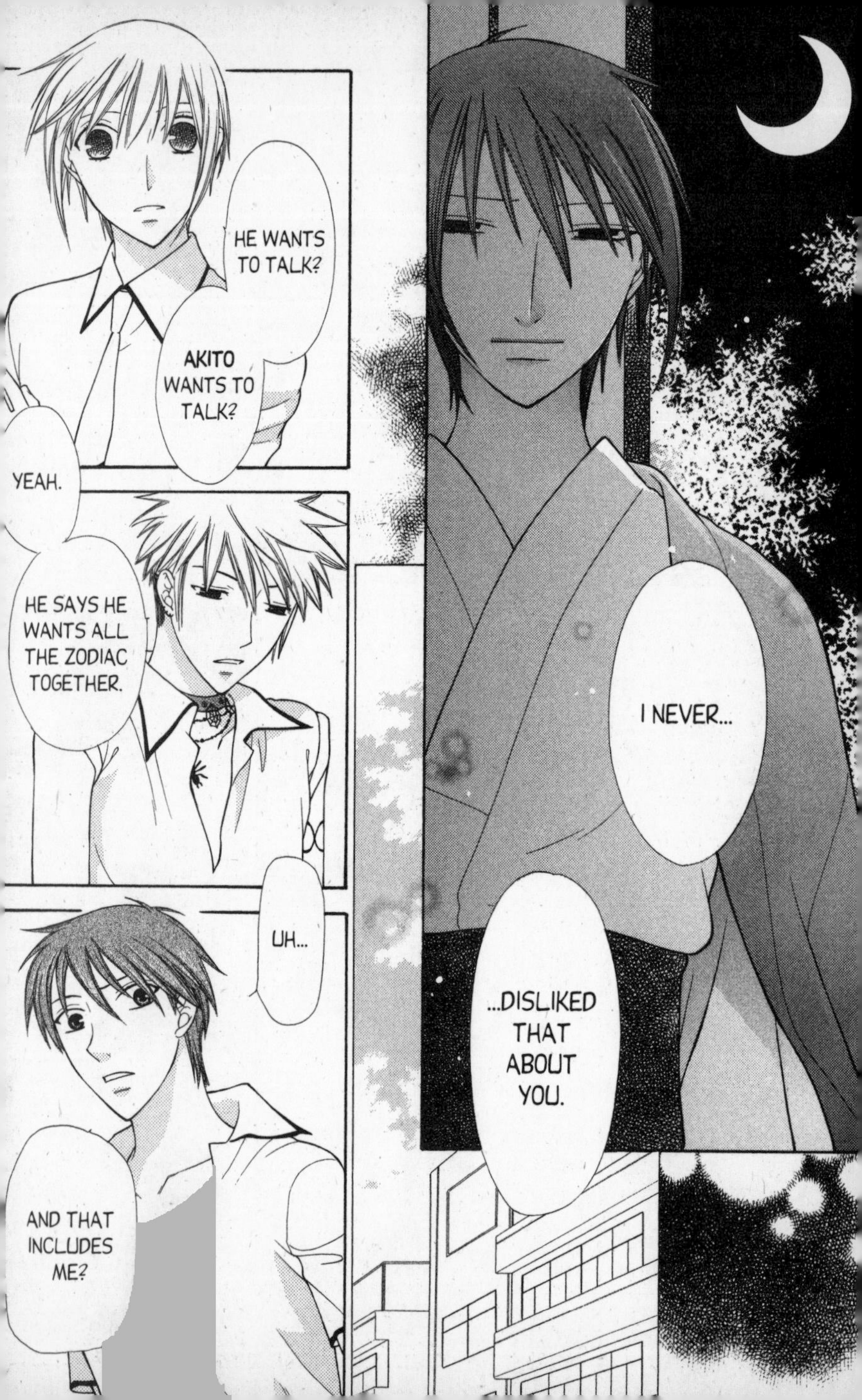
I NEVER...
...DISLIKED THAT ABOUT YOU.
HE WANTS TO TALK?
AKITO WANTS TO TALK?
YEAH.
HE SAYS HE WANTS ALL THE ZODIAC TOGETHER.
UH...
AND THAT INCLUDES ME?

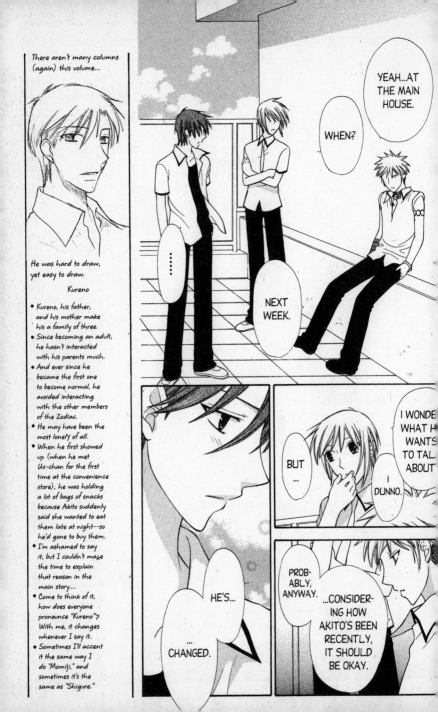

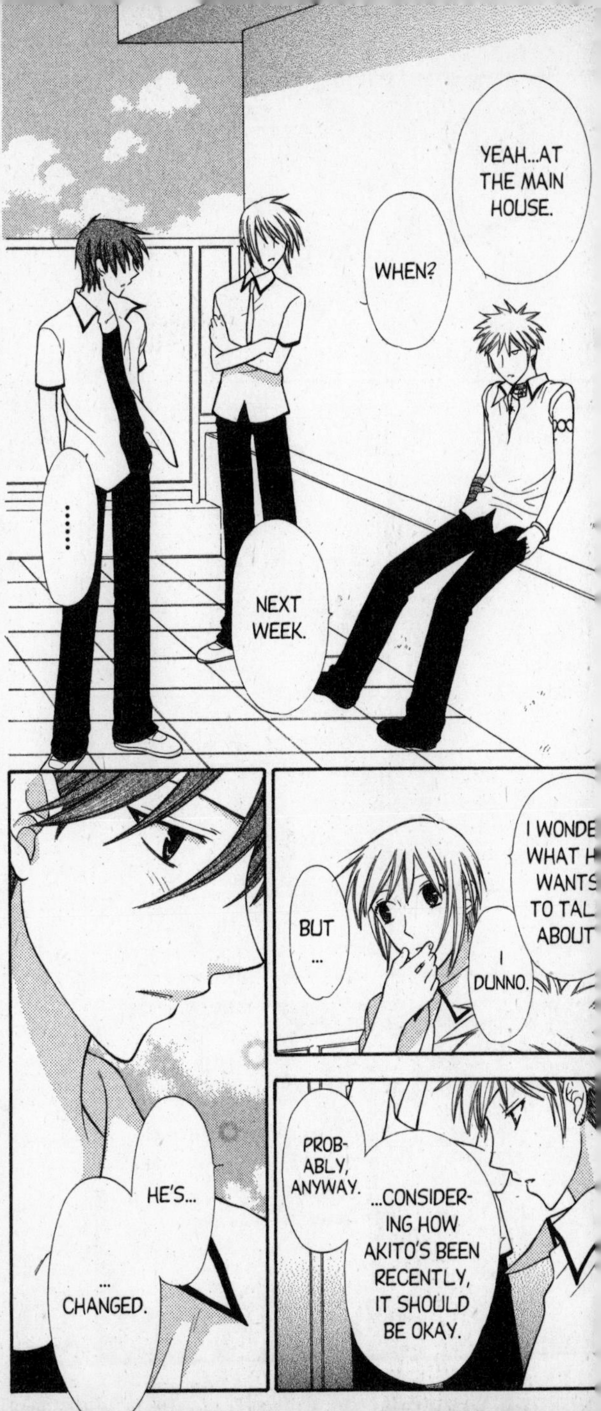
YEAH...AT THE MAIN HOUSE.
WHEN?
NEXT WEEK.
......
I WONDE WHAT H WANTS TO TAL ABOUT
I DUNNO.
BUT ...
PROB-ABLY, ANYWAY.
...CONSIDER-ING HOW AKITO'S BEEN RECENTLY, IT SHOULD BE OKAY.
HE'S...
... CHANGED.

There aren't many columns (again) this volume...

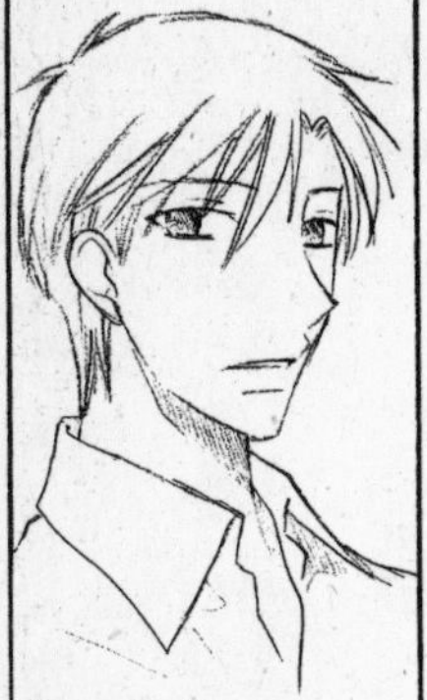

He was hard to draw, yet easy to draw.

Kureno

- Kureno, his father, and his mother make his a family of three.
- Since becoming an adult, he hasn't interacted with his parents much.
- And ever since he became the first one to become normal, he avoided interacting with the other members of the Zodiac.
- He may have been the most lonely of all.
- When he first showed up (when he met Uo-chan for the first time at the convenience store), he was holding a lot of bags of snacks because Akito suddenly said she wanted to eat them late at night--so he'd gone to buy them.
- I'm ashamed to say it, but I couldn't make the time to explain that reason in the main story....
- Come to think of it, how does everyone pronounce "Kureno"? With me, it changes whenever I say it.
- Sometimes I'll accent it the same way I do "Momiji," and sometimes it's the same as "Shigure."

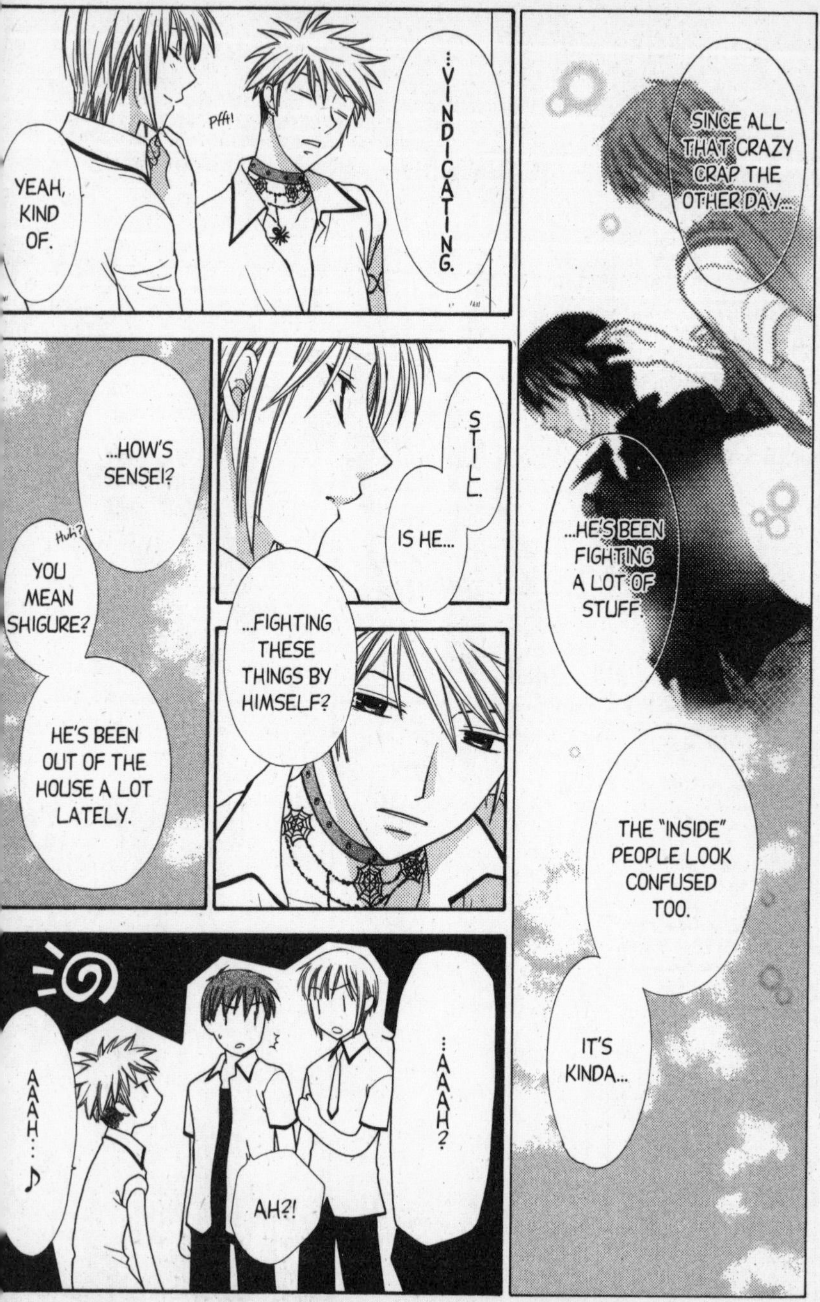
SINCE ALL THAT CRAZY CRAP THE OTHER DAY...
...HE'S BEEN FIGHTING A LOT OF STUFF.
THE "INSIDE" PEOPLE LOOK CONFUSED TOO.
IT'S KINDA...
...VINDICATING.
Pfft!
YEAH, KIND OF.
STILL.
IS HE...
...FIGHTING THESE THINGS BY HIMSELF?
...HOW'S SENSEI?
Huh?
YOU MEAN SHIGURE?
HE'S BEEN OUT OF THE HOUSE A LOT LATELY.
...AAAAH?
AH?!
AAAH...♪

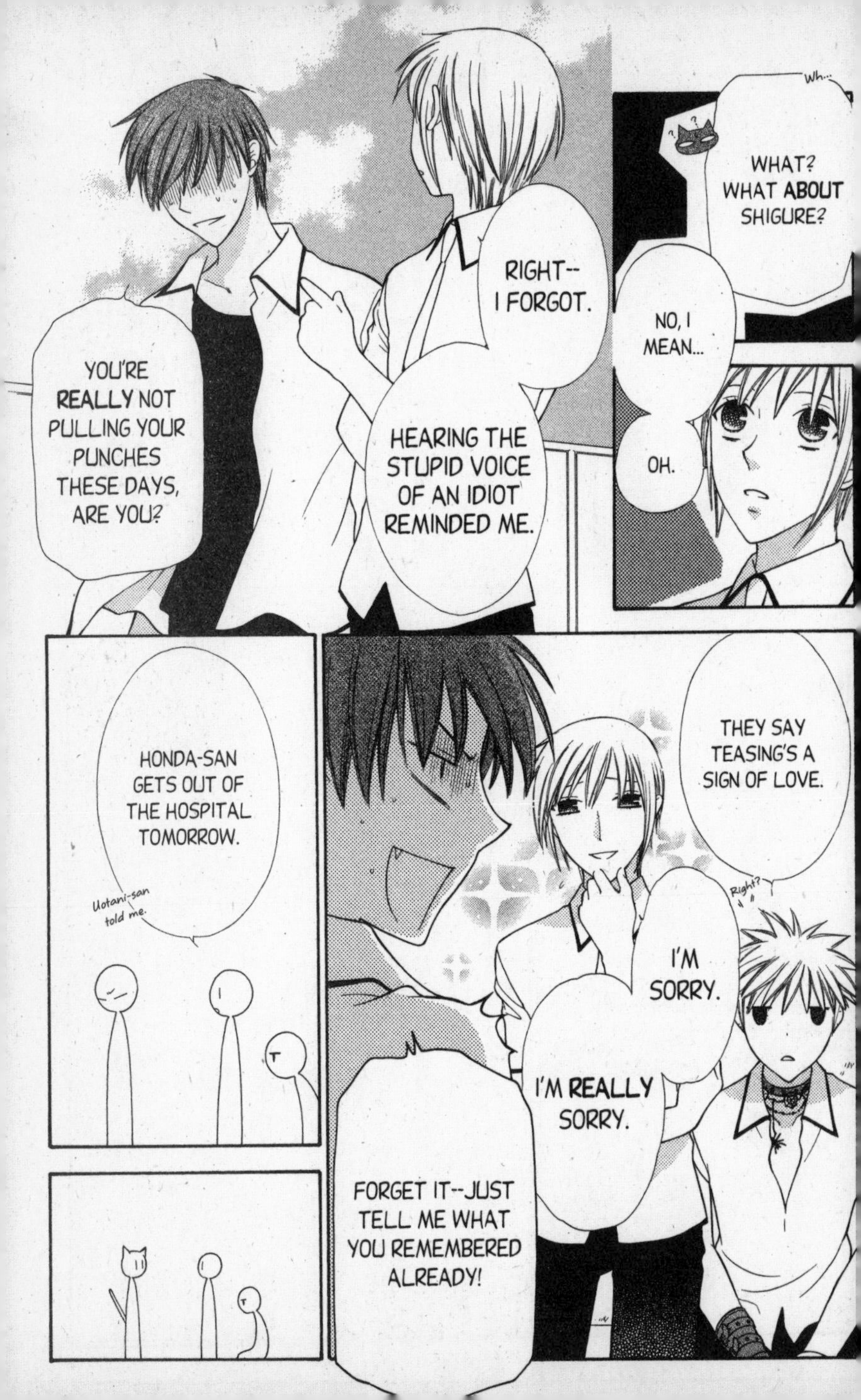
Wh...
WHAT? WHAT ABOUT SHIGURE?
NO, I MEAN...
OH.
RIGHT-- I FORGOT.
HEARING THE STUPID VOICE OF AN IDIOT REMINDED ME.
YOU'RE REALLY NOT PULLING YOUR PUNCHES THESE DAYS, ARE YOU?
THEY SAY TEASING'S A SIGN OF LOVE.
Right?
I'M SORRY.
I'M REALLY SORRY.
FORGET IT--JUST TELL ME WHAT YOU REMEMBERED ALREADY!
HONDA-SAN GETS OUT OF THE HOSPITAL TOMORROW.
Uotani-san told me.

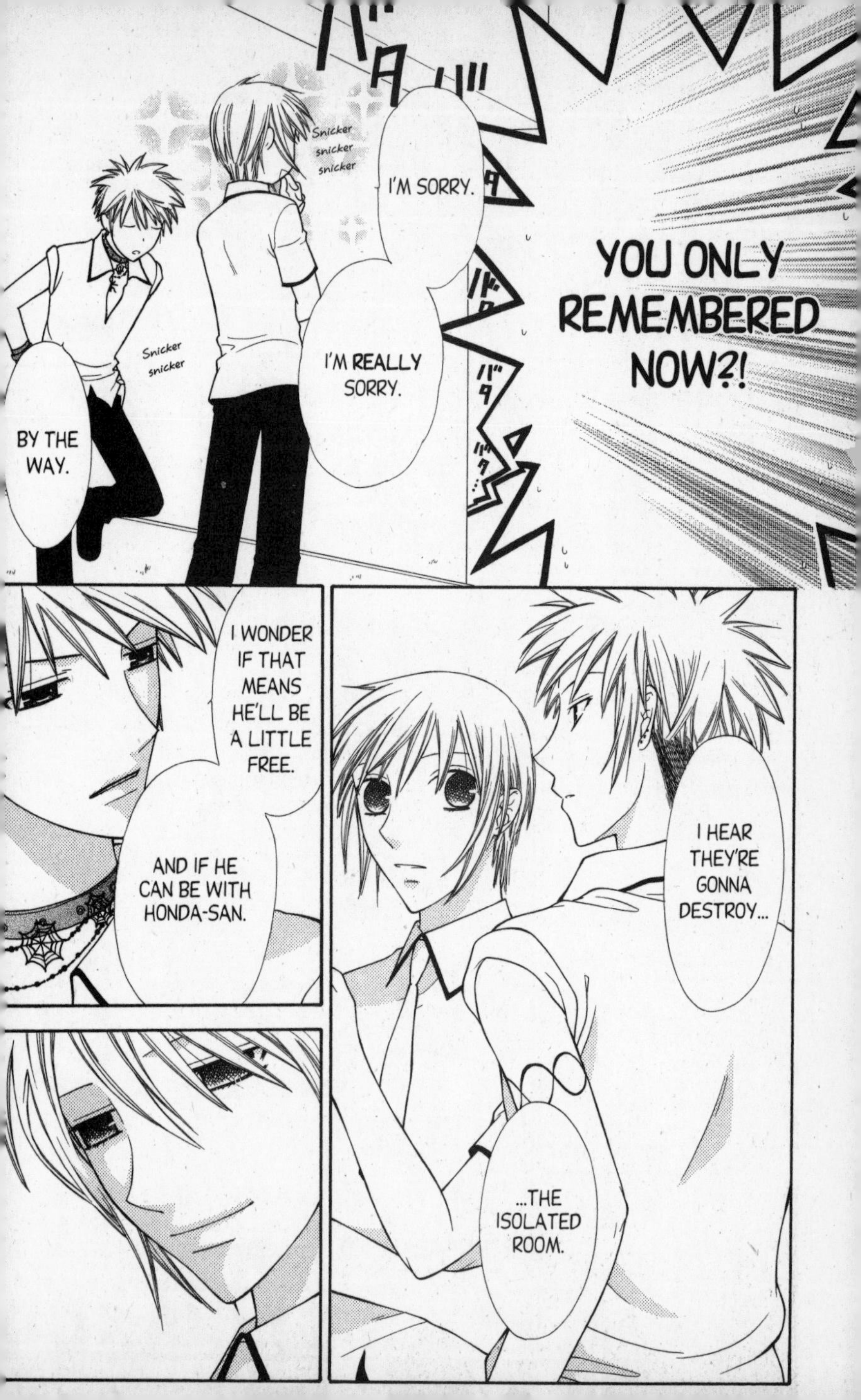
YOU ONLY REMEMBERED NOW?!
I'M SORRY.
I'M REALLY SORRY.
Snicker snicker snicker
Snicker snicker
BY THE WAY.
I HEAR THEY'RE GONNA DESTROY...
...THE ISOLATED ROOM.
I WONDER IF THAT MEANS HE'LL BE A LITTLE FREE.
AND IF HE CAN BE WITH HONDA-SAN.

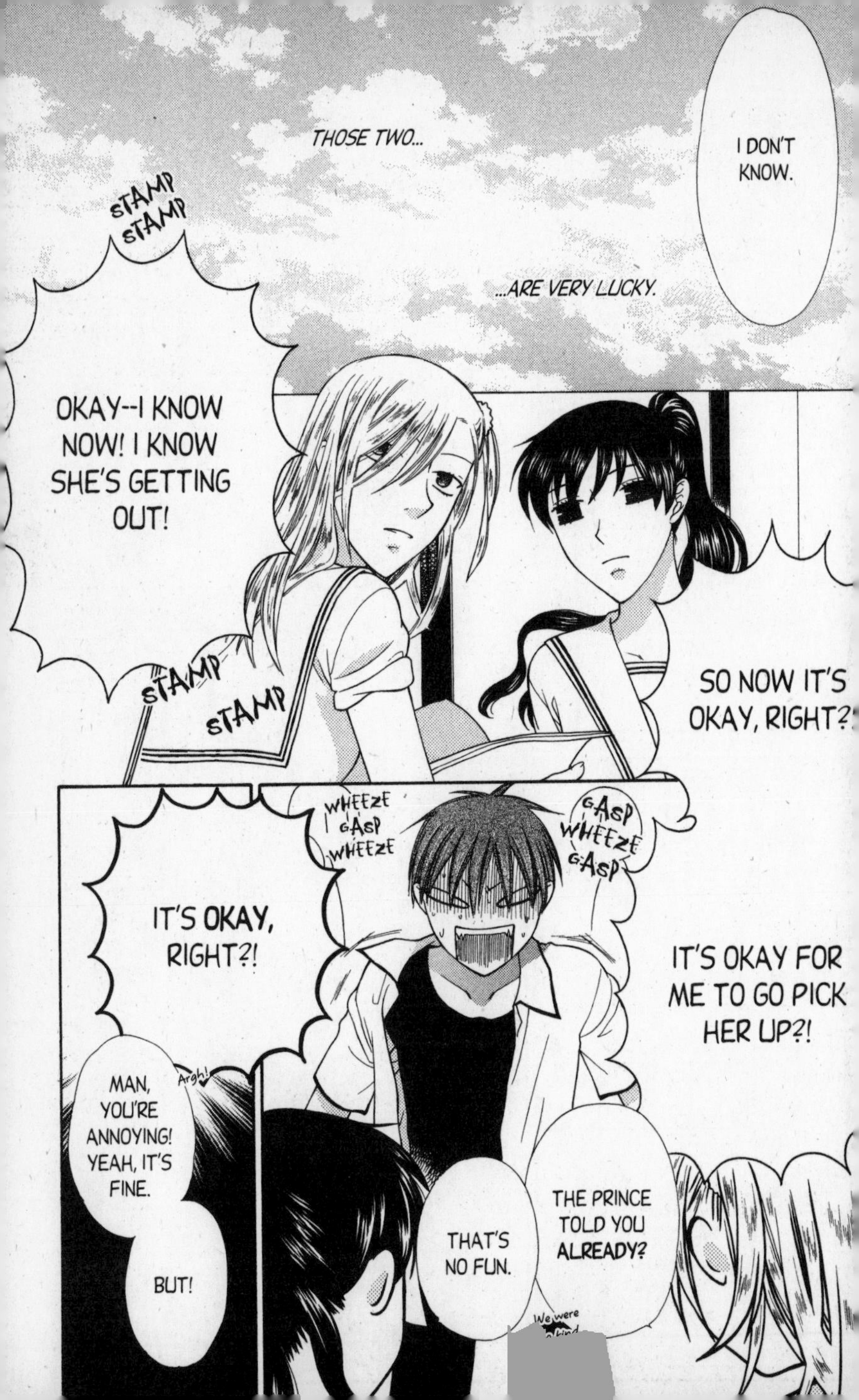
I DON'T KNOW.
THOSE TWO...
...ARE VERY LUCKY.
STAMP STAMP
OKAY--I KNOW NOW! I KNOW SHE'S GETTING OUT!
STAMP STAMP
SO NOW IT'S OKAY, RIGHT?!
IT'S OKAY FOR ME TO GO PICK HER UP?!
GASP WHEEZE GASP
WHEEZE GASP WHEEZE
IT'S OKAY, RIGHT?!
THE PRINCE TOLD YOU ALREADY?
We were
THAT'S NO FUN.
MAN, YOU'RE ANNOYING! YEAH, IT'S FINE.
Argh!
BUT!

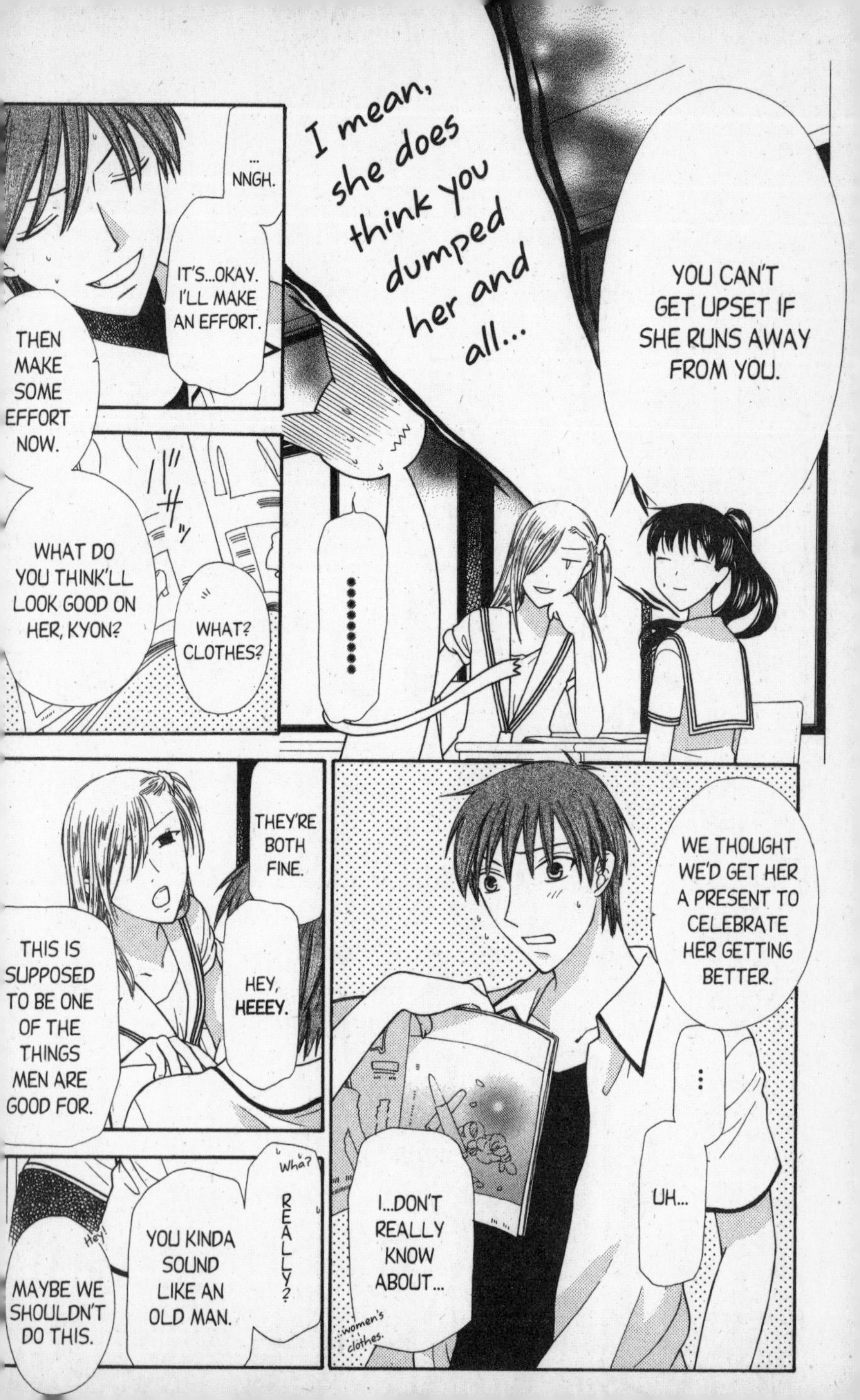
YOU CAN'T GET UPSET IF SHE RUNS AWAY FROM YOU.
I mean, she does think you dumped her and all...
....
... NNGH.
IT'S...OKAY. I'LL MAKE AN EFFORT.
THEN MAKE SOME EFFORT NOW.
WHAT DO YOU THINK'LL LOOK GOOD ON HER, KYON?
WHAT? CLOTHES?
WE THOUGHT WE'D GET HER A PRESENT TO CELEBRATE HER GETTING BETTER.
...
UH...
I...DON'T REALLY KNOW ABOUT...
...women's clothes.
THEY'RE BOTH FINE.
HEY, HEEEY.
THIS IS SUPPOSED TO BE ONE OF THE THINGS MEN ARE GOOD FOR.
Wha?
REALLY?
YOU KINDA SOUND LIKE AN OLD MAN.
Hey!
MAYBE WE SHOULDN'T DO THIS.

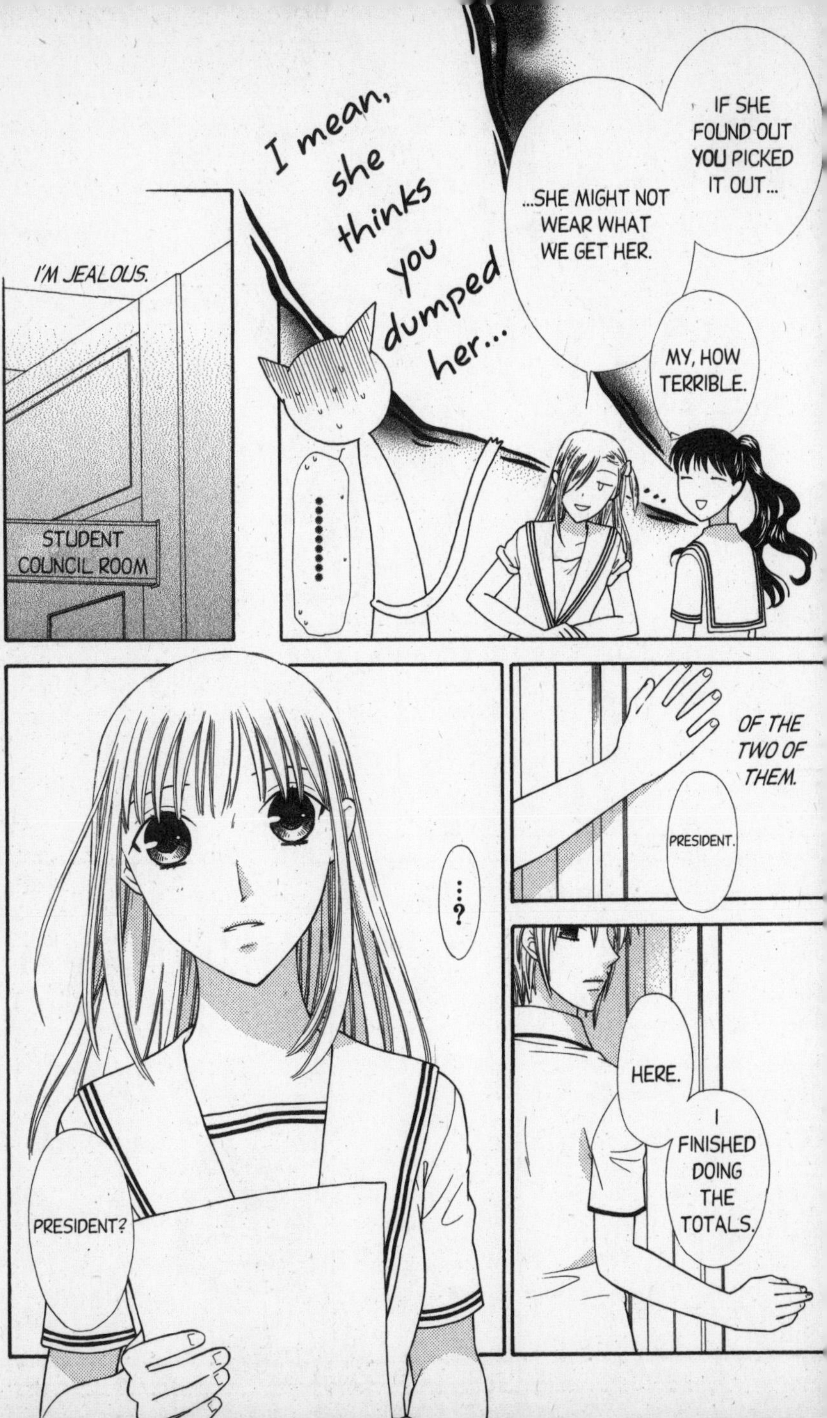
IF SHE FOUND OUT YOU PICKED IT OUT...
...SHE MIGHT NOT WEAR WHAT WE GET HER.
I mean, she thinks you dumped her...
MY, HOW TERRIBLE.
...
......
I'M JEALOUS.
STUDENT COUNCIL ROOM
OF THE TWO OF THEM.
PRESIDENT.
HERE.
I FINISHED DOING THE TOTALS.
...?
PRESIDENT?

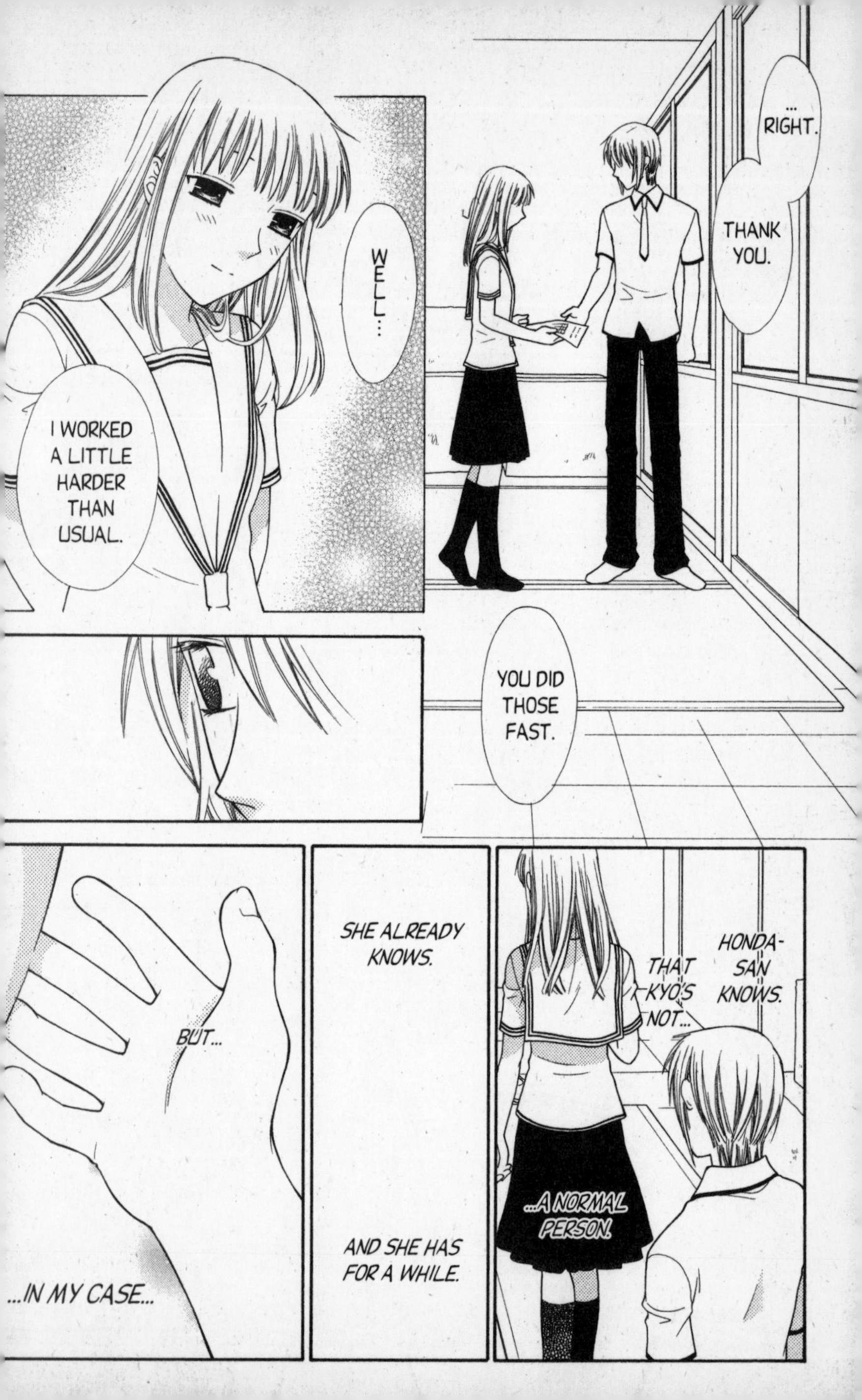
...RIGHT.
THANK YOU.
YOU DID THOSE FAST.
WELL...
I WORKED A LITTLE HARDER THAN USUAL.
HONDA-SAN KNOWS.
THAT KYO'S NOT...
...A NORMAL PERSON.
SHE ALREADY KNOWS.
AND SHE HAS FOR A WHILE.
BUT...
...IN MY CASE...

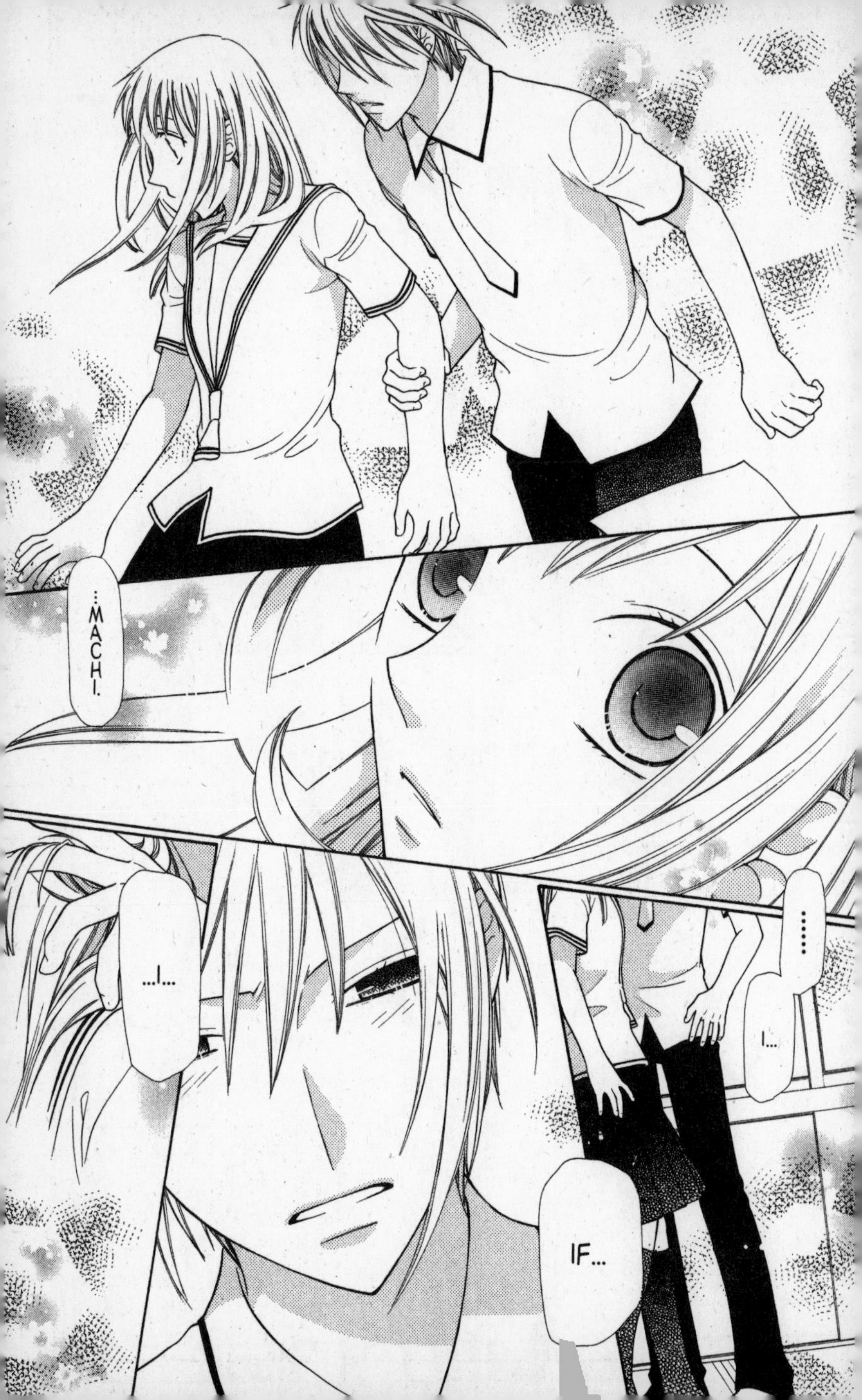

...MACHI.
......
I...
IF...
...I...

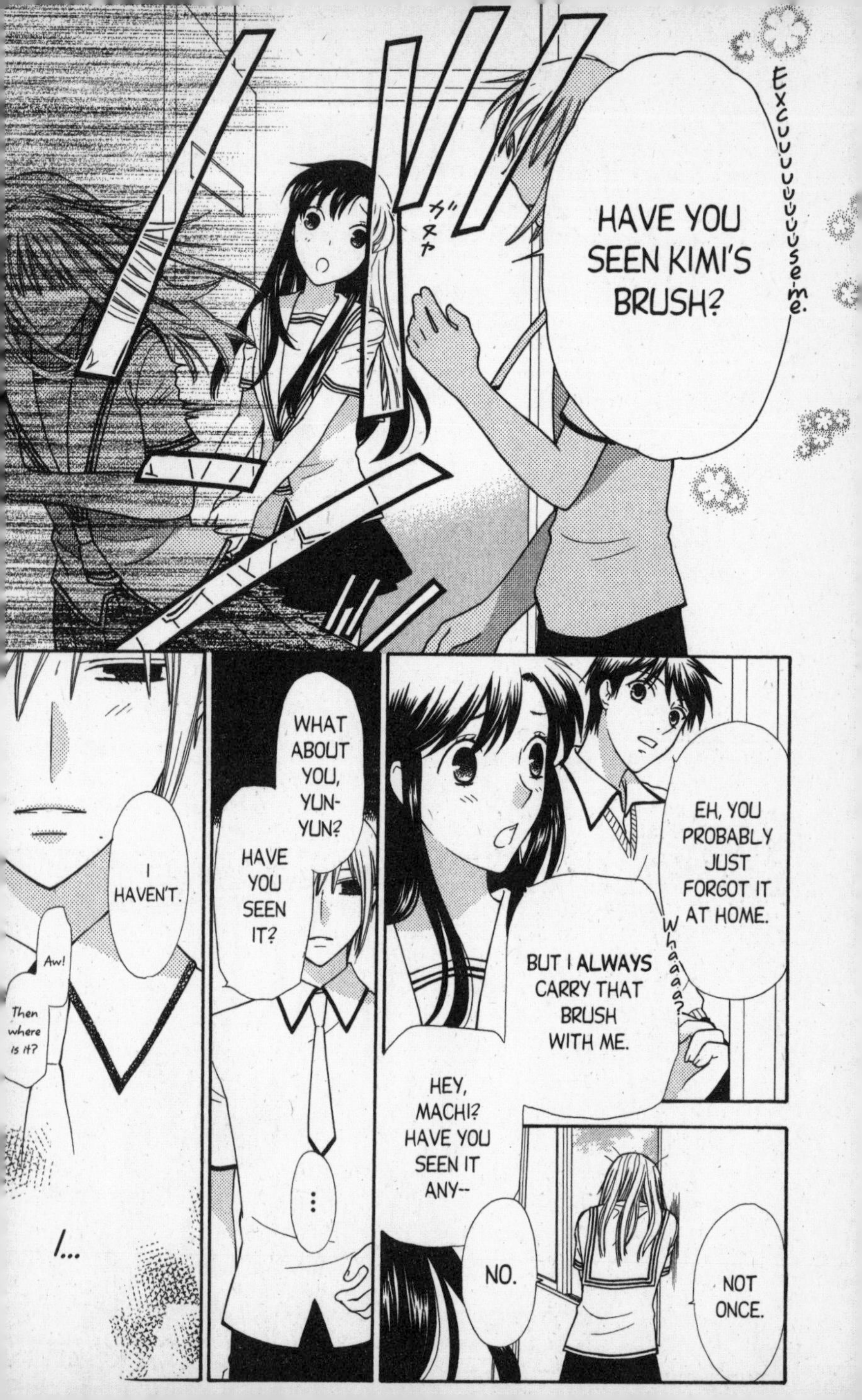
Excuuuuuuuuse-me.
HAVE YOU SEEN KIMI'S BRUSH?
ガタッ
EH, YOU PROBABLY JUST FORGOT IT AT HOME.
Whaaaa?
BUT I ALWAYS CARRY THAT BRUSH WITH ME.
HEY, MACHI? HAVE YOU SEEN IT ANY--
NO.
NOT ONCE.
WHAT ABOUT YOU, YUN-YUN?
HAVE YOU SEEN IT?
...
I HAVEN'T.
Aw!
Then where is it?
I...

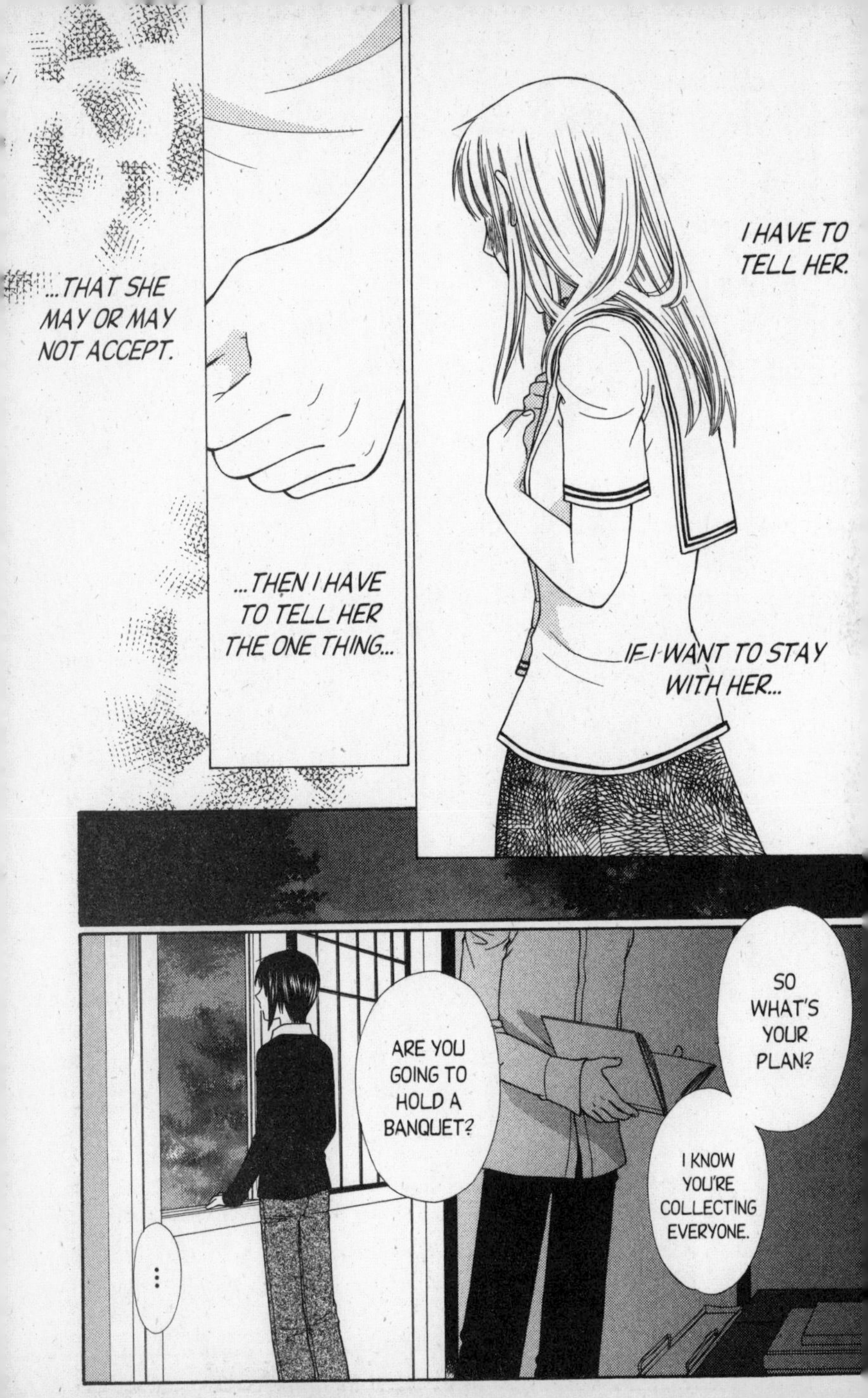
I HAVE TO TELL HER.
IF I WANT TO STAY WITH HER...
...THEN I HAVE TO TELL HER THE ONE THING...
...THAT SHE MAY OR MAY NOT ACCEPT.
SO WHAT'S YOUR PLAN?
I KNOW YOU'RE COLLECTING EVERYONE.
ARE YOU GOING TO HOLD A BANQUET?
...

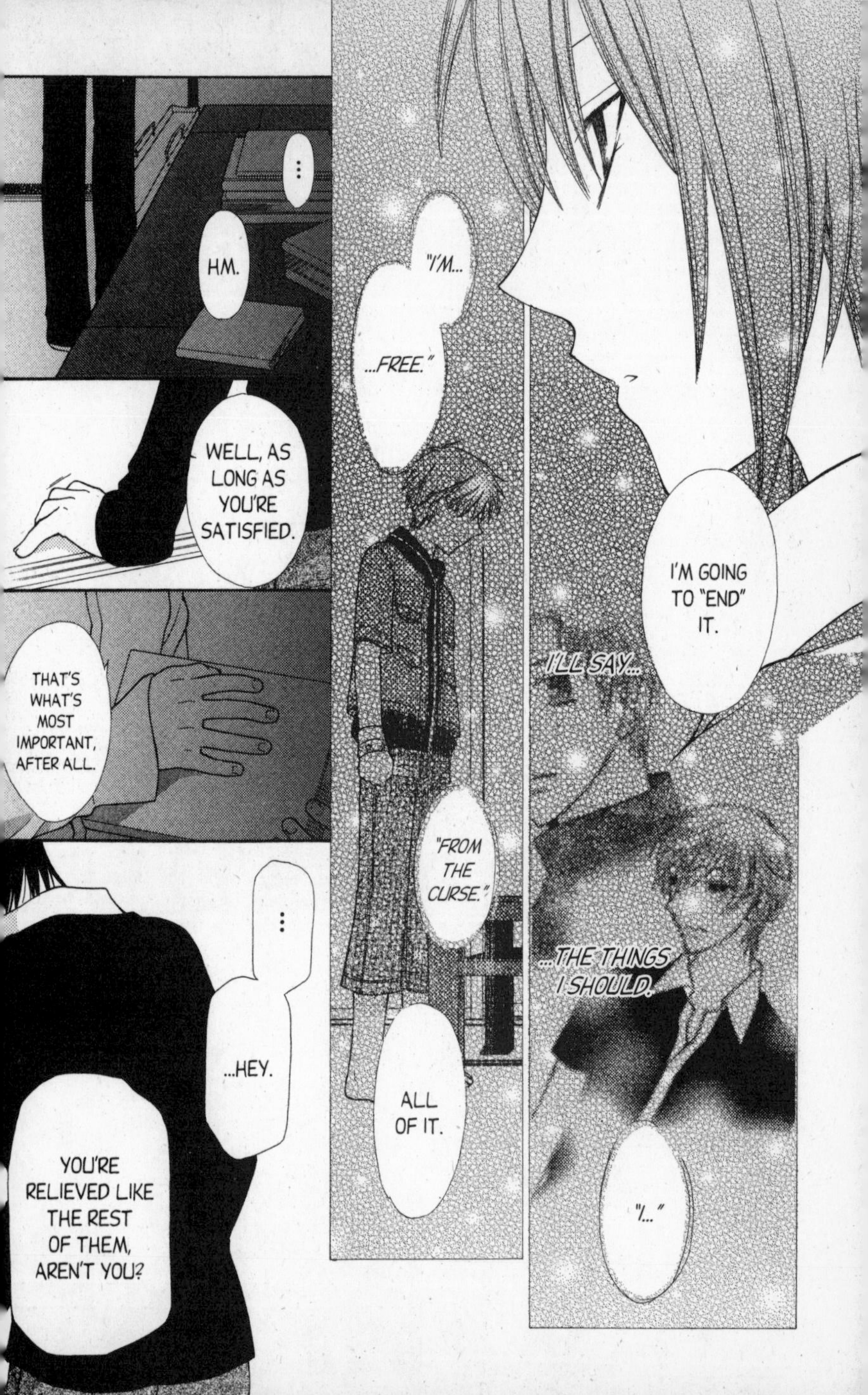
I'M GOING TO "END" IT.
I'LL SAY...
...THE THINGS I SHOULD.
"I..."
"I'M...
...FREE."
"FROM THE CURSE."
ALL OF IT.
...
HM.
WELL, AS LONG AS YOU'RE SATISFIED.
THAT'S WHAT'S MOST IMPORTANT, AFTER ALL.
...
...HEY.
YOU'RE RELIEVED LIKE THE REST OF THEM, AREN'T YOU?

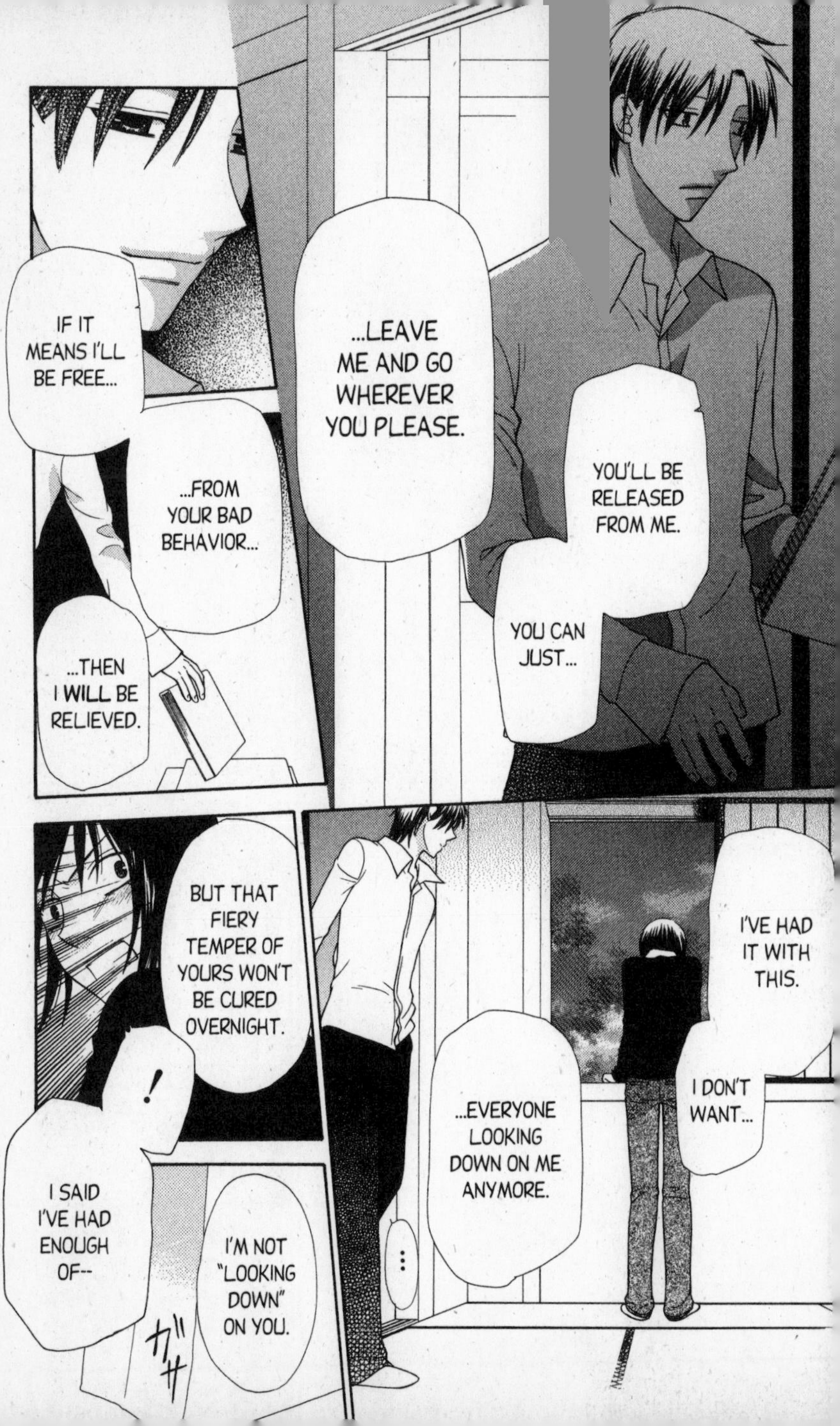
YOU'LL BE RELEASED FROM ME.
YOU CAN JUST...
...LEAVE ME AND GO WHEREVER YOU PLEASE.
IF IT MEANS I'LL BE FREE...
...FROM YOUR BAD BEHAVIOR...
...THEN I WILL BE RELIEVED.
I'VE HAD IT WITH THIS.
I DON'T WANT...
...EVERYONE LOOKING DOWN ON ME ANYMORE.
...
BUT THAT FIERY TEMPER OF YOURS WON'T BE CURED OVERNIGHT.
!
I'M NOT "LOOKING DOWN" ON YOU.
I SAID I'VE HAD ENOUGH OF--

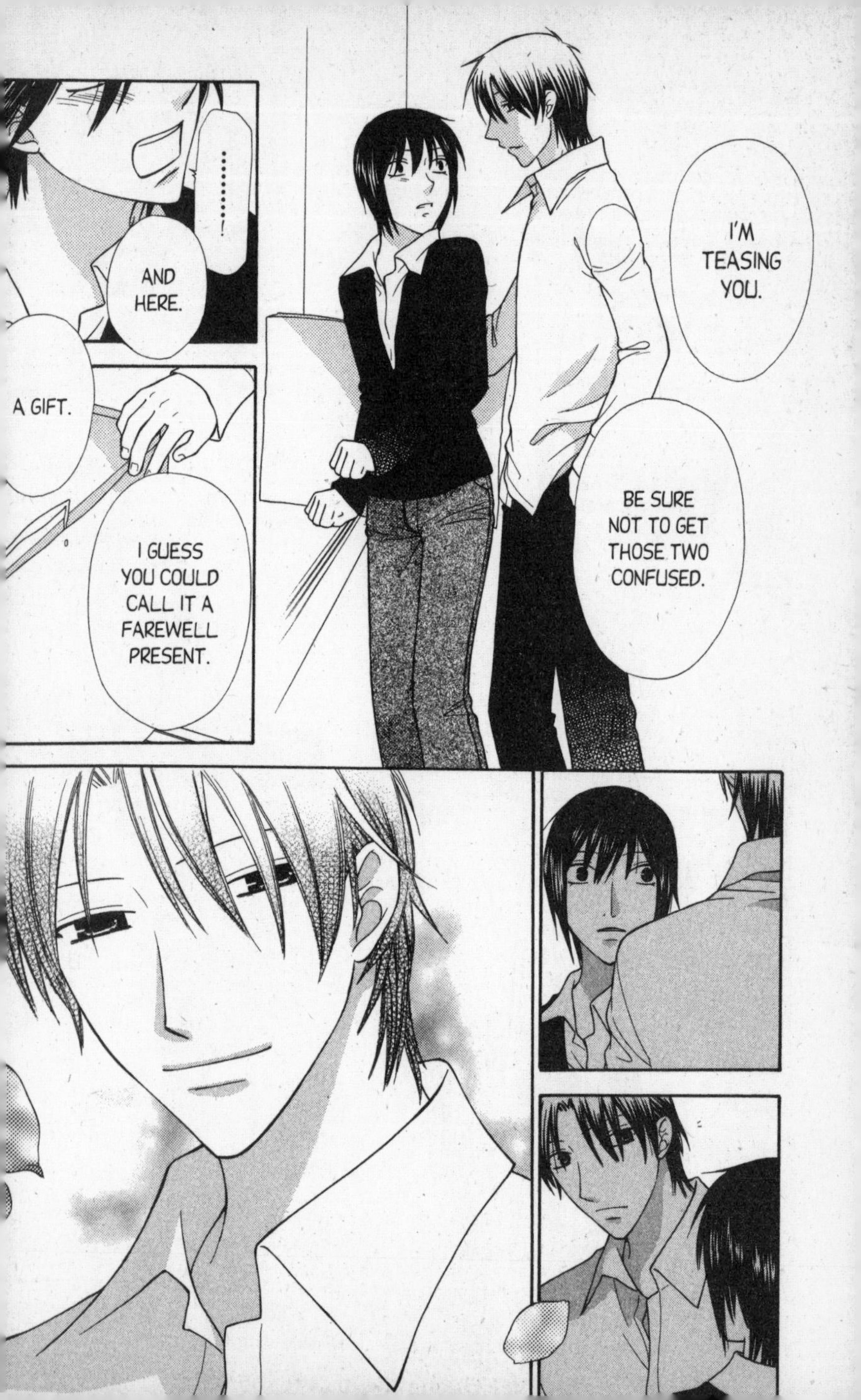
I'M TEASING YOU.
BE SURE NOT TO GET THOSE TWO CONFUSED.
.......!
AND HERE.
A GIFT.
I GUESS YOU COULD CALL IT A FAREWELL PRESENT.

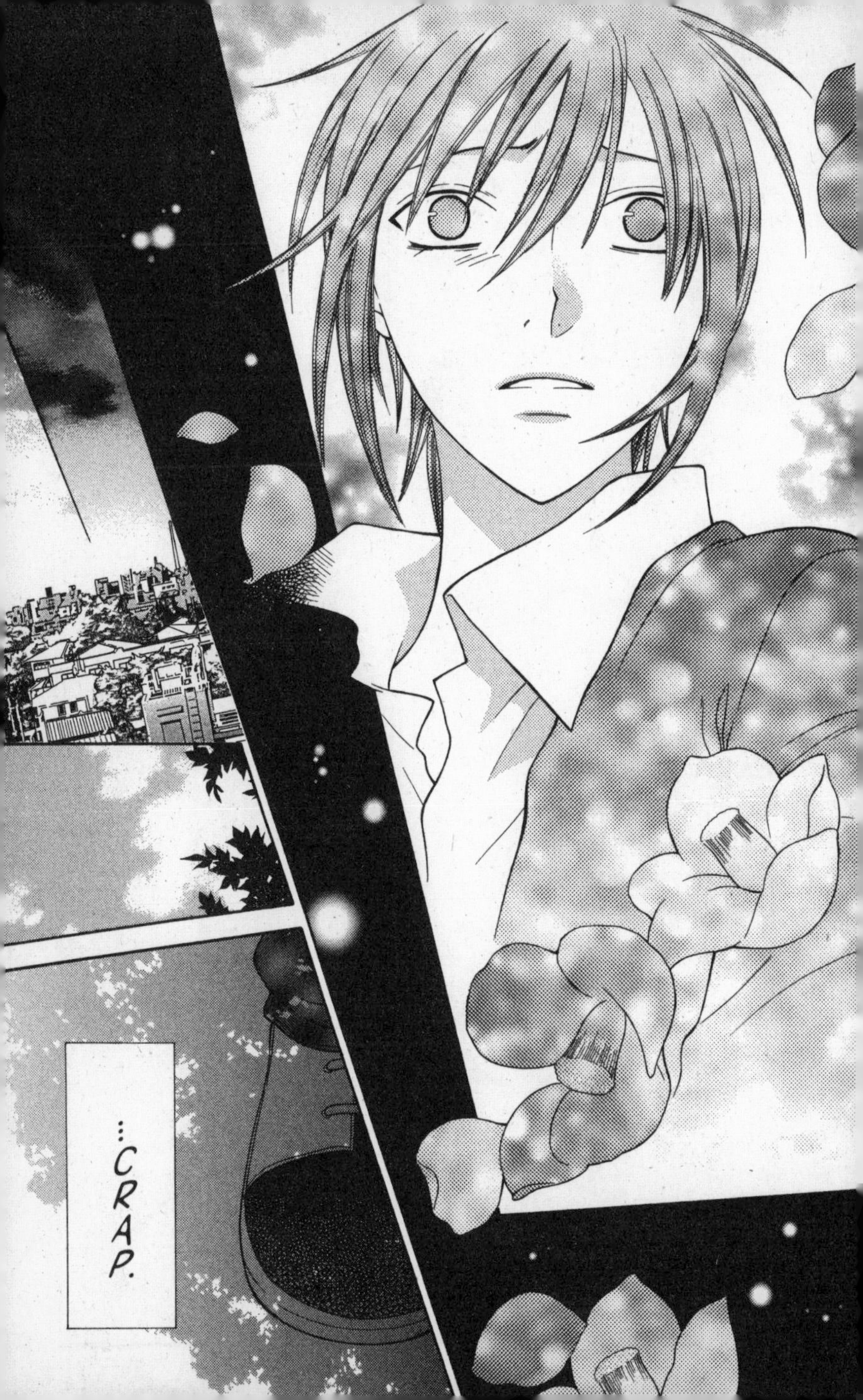
...CRAP.

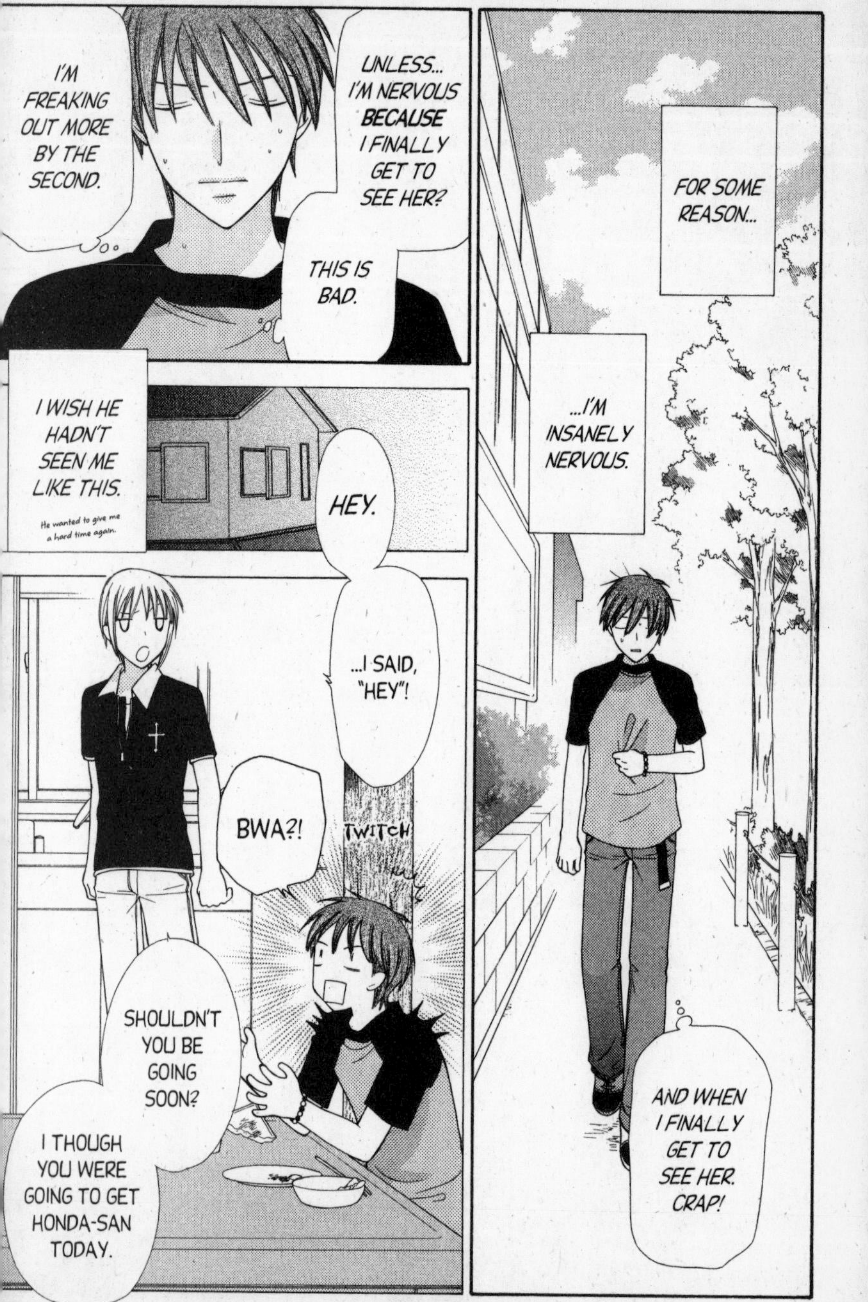
FOR SOME REASON...
...I'M INSANELY NERVOUS.
AND WHEN I FINALLY GET TO SEE HER. CRAP!
UNLESS... I'M NERVOUS BECAUSE I FINALLY GET TO SEE HER?
I'M FREAKING OUT MORE BY THE SECOND.
THIS IS BAD.
HEY.
I WISH HE HADN'T SEEN ME LIKE THIS.
He wanted to give me a hard time again.
...I SAID, "HEY"!
TWITCH
BWA?!
SHOULDN'T YOU BE GOING SOON?
I THOUGH YOU WERE GOING TO GET HONDA-SAN TODAY.

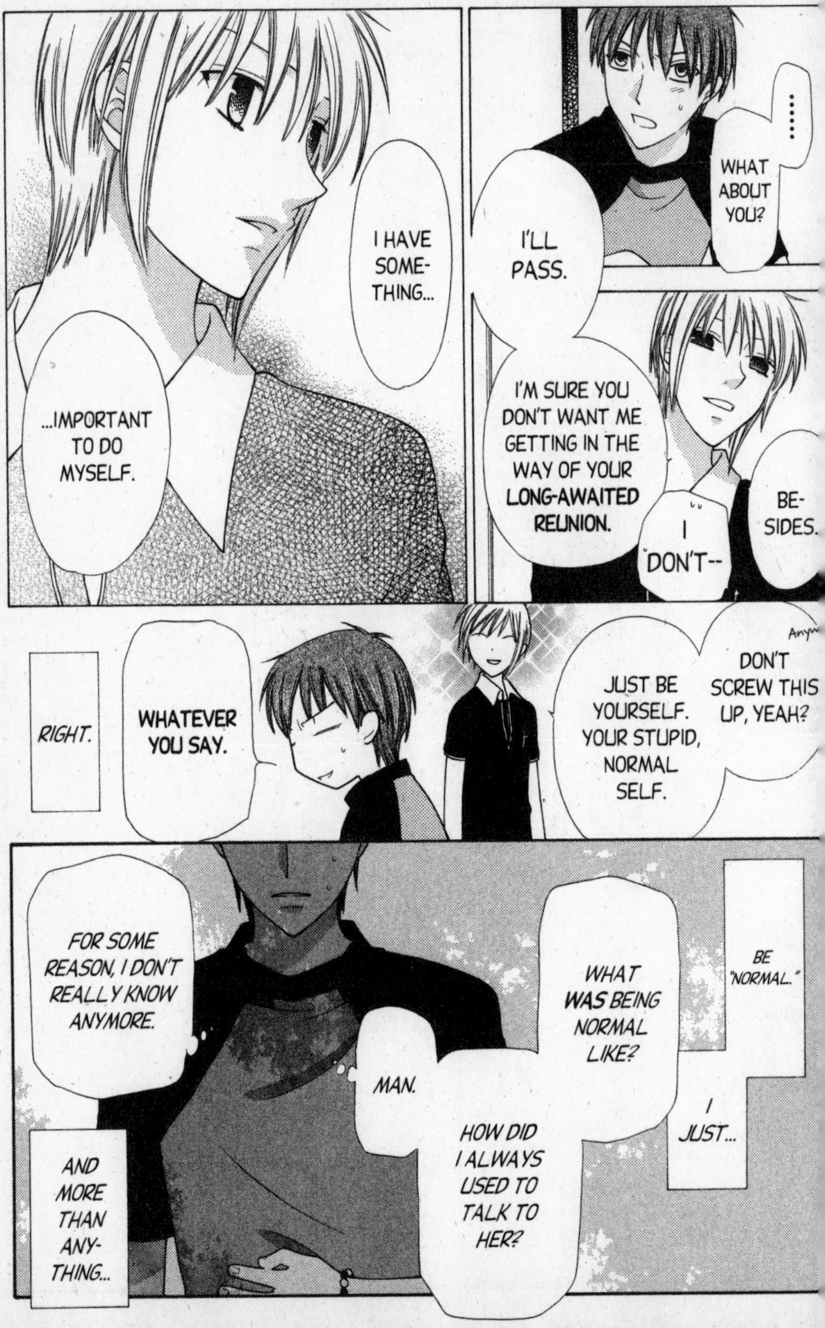
......
WHAT ABOUT YOU?
I'LL PASS.
I'M SURE YOU DON'T WANT ME GETTING IN THE WAY OF YOUR **LONG-AWAITED REUNION.**
BE-SIDES.
I DON'T--
I HAVE SOME-THING...
...IMPORTANT TO DO MYSELF.
DON'T SCREW THIS UP, YEAH?
JUST BE YOURSELF. YOUR STUPID, NORMAL SELF.
WHATEVER YOU SAY.
RIGHT.
BE "NORMAL."
I JUST...
WHAT WAS BEING NORMAL LIKE?
MAN.
HOW DID I ALWAYS USED TO TALK TO HER?
FOR SOME REASON, I DON'T REALLY KNOW ANYMORE.
AND MORE THAN ANY-THING...

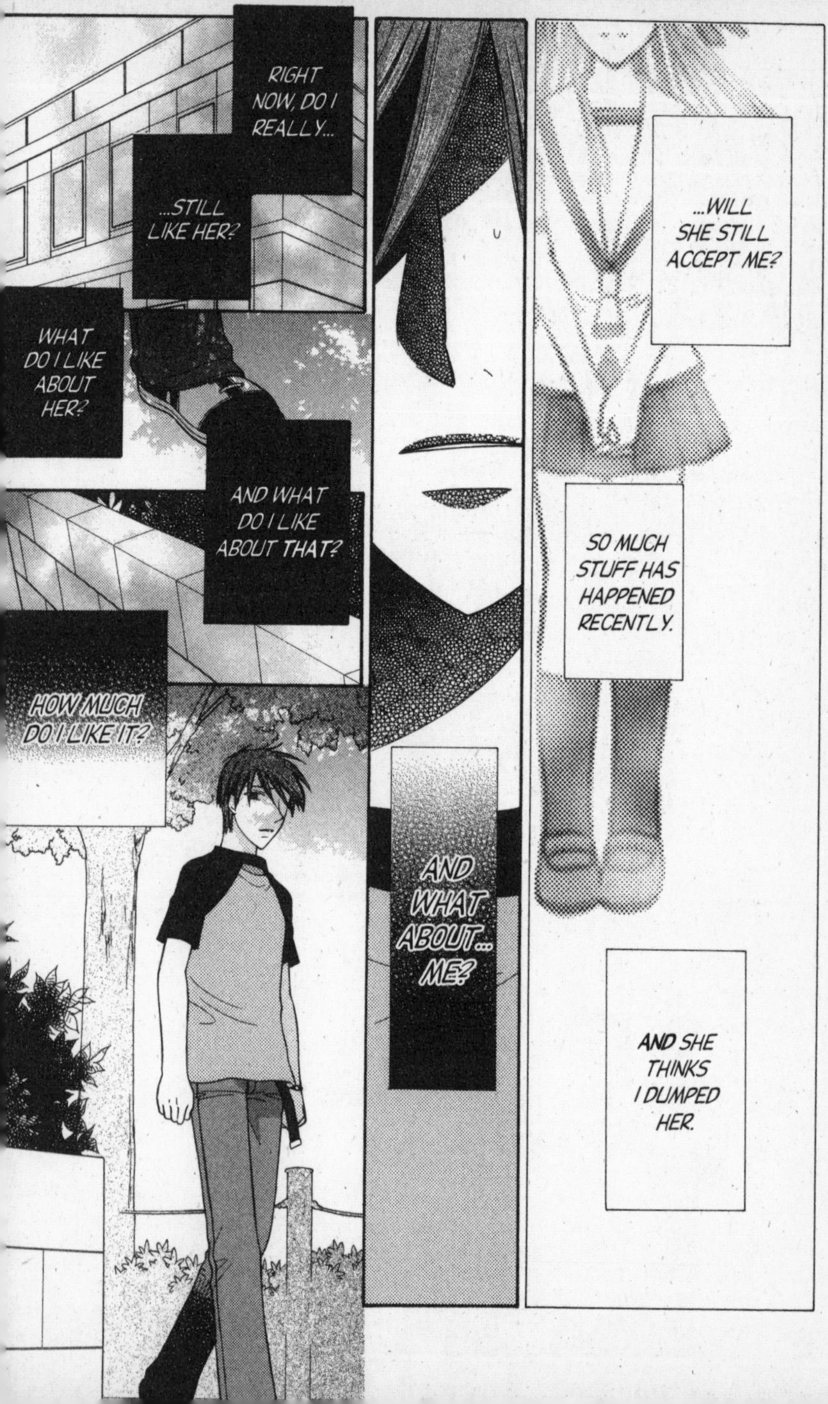
...WILL SHE STILL ACCEPT ME?
SO MUCH STUFF HAS HAPPENED RECENTLY.
AND SHE THINKS I DUMPED HER.
AND WHAT ABOUT... ME?
RIGHT NOW, DO I REALLY...
...STILL LIKE HER?
WHAT DO I LIKE ABOUT HER?
AND WHAT DO I LIKE ABOUT THAT?
HOW MUCH DO I LIKE IT?

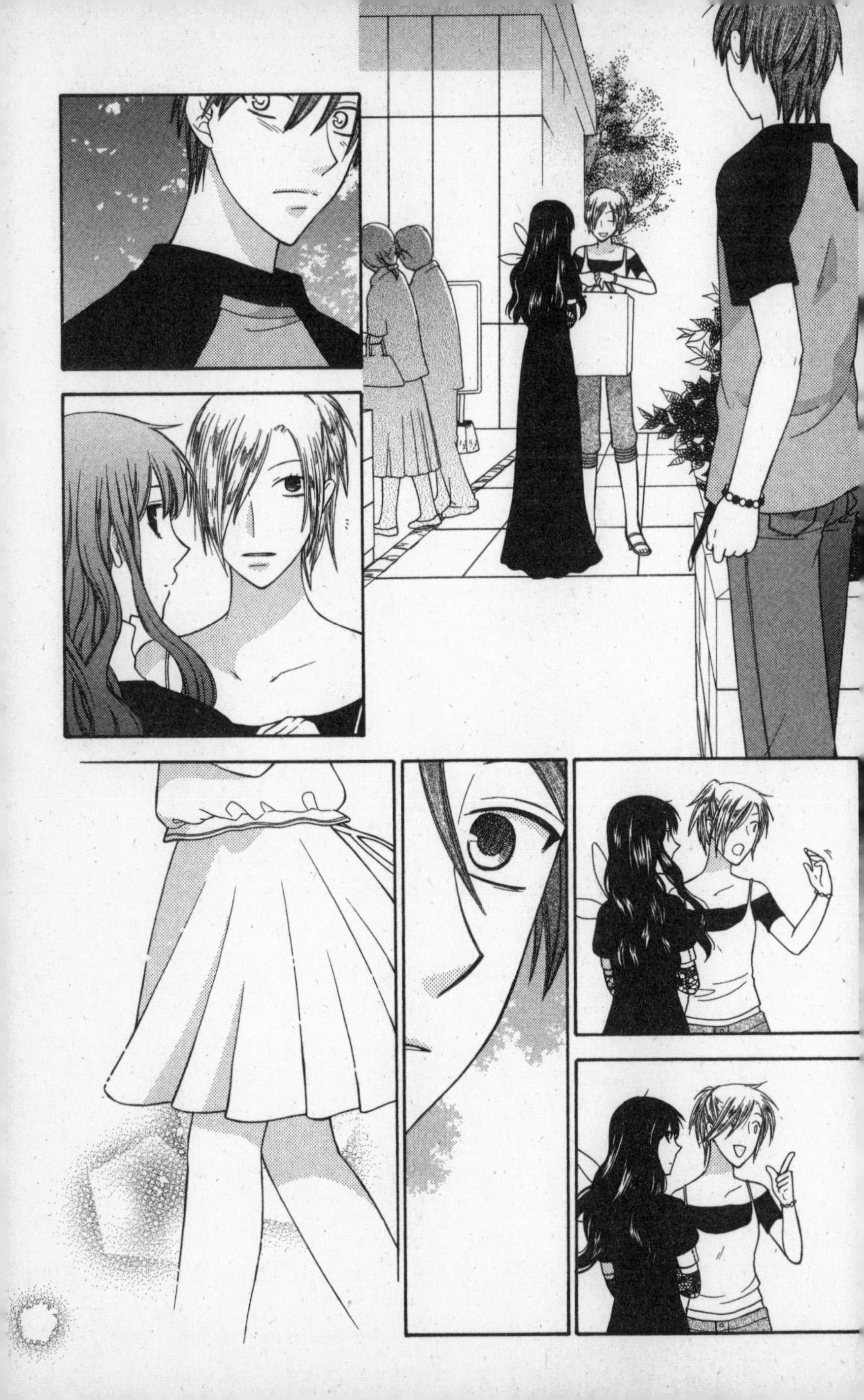

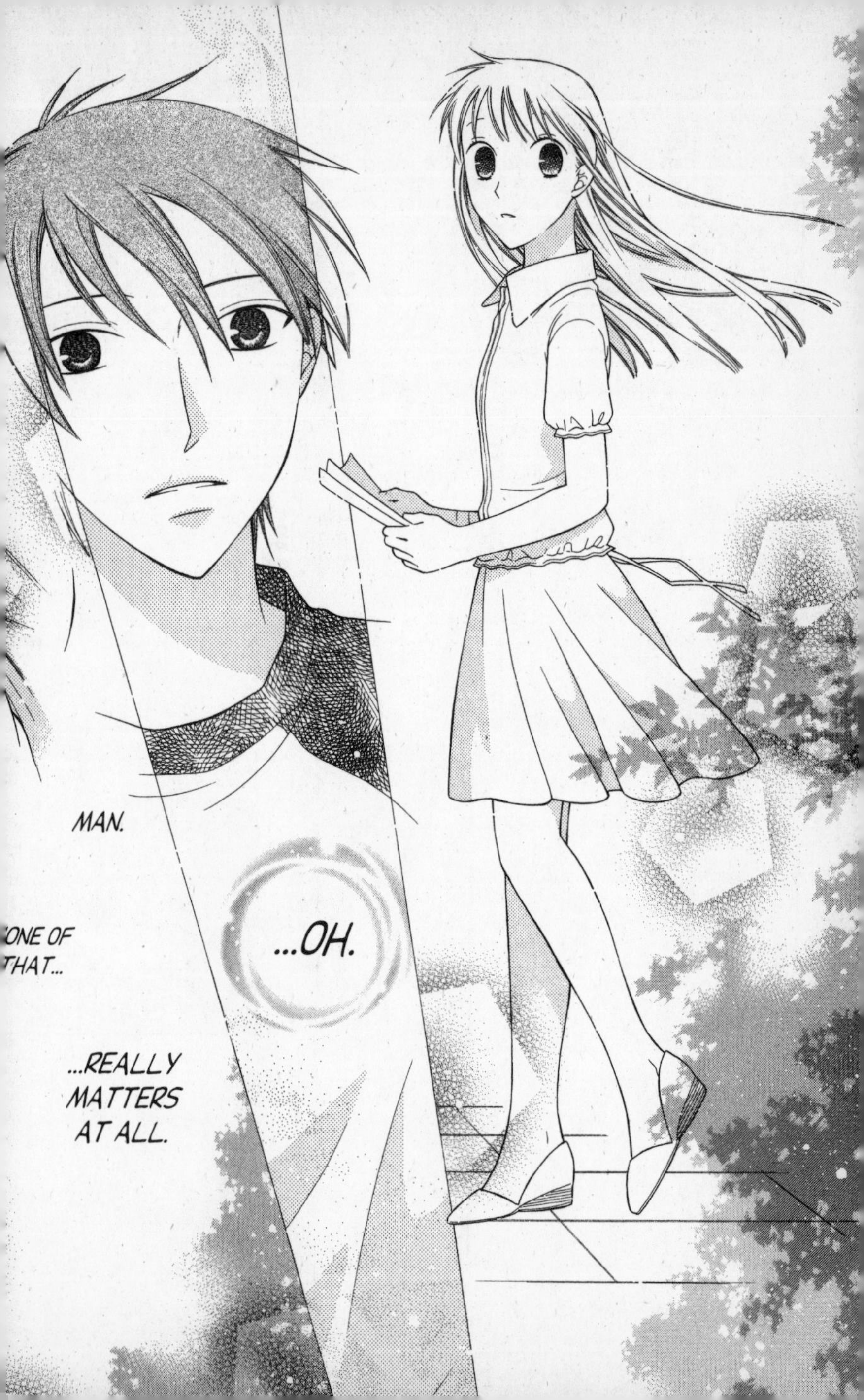
MAN.
...OH.
ONE OF
THAT...
...REALLY
MATTERS
AT ALL.

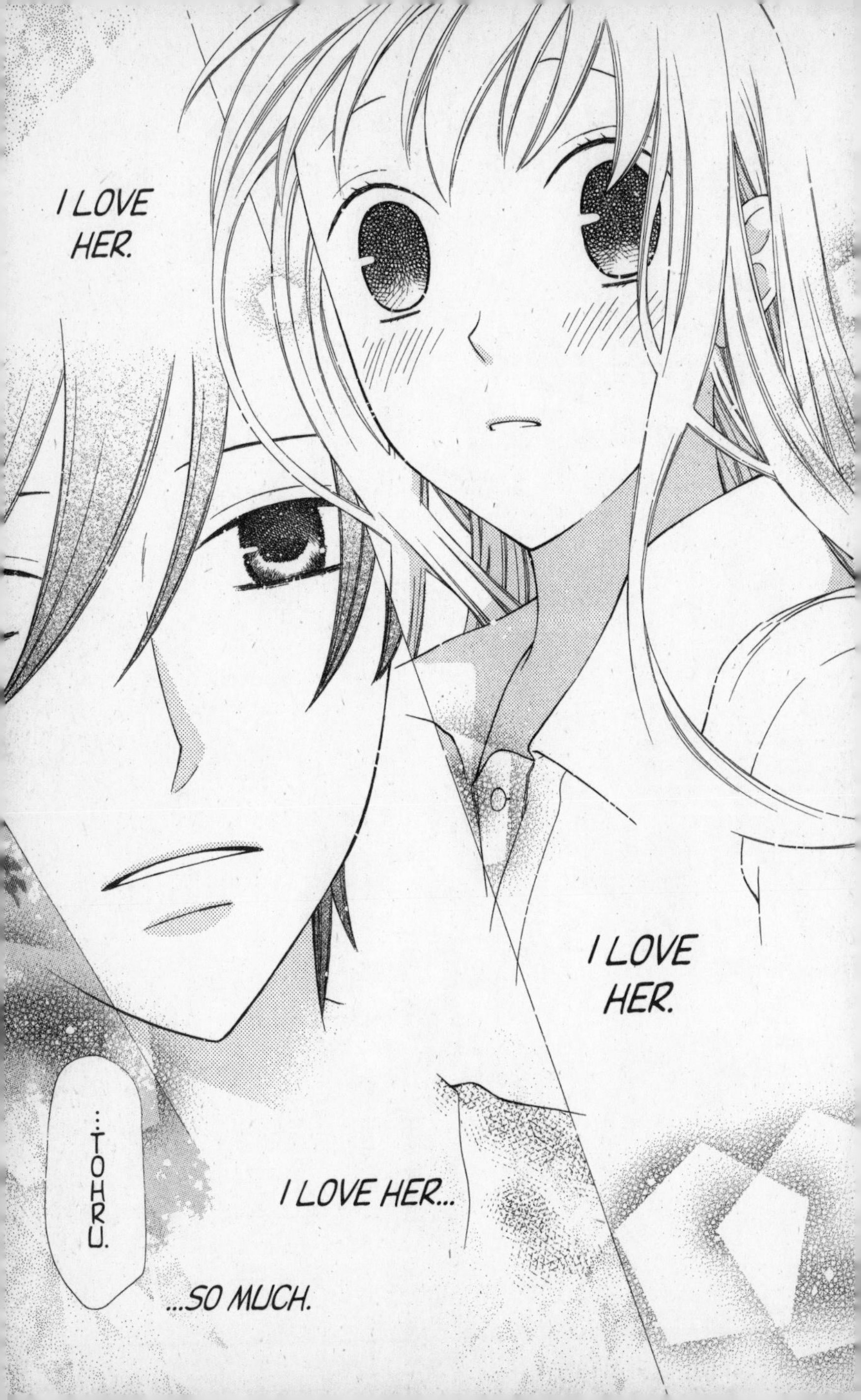
I LOVE HER.
I LOVE HER.
I LOVE HER...
...TOHRU.
...SO MUCH.

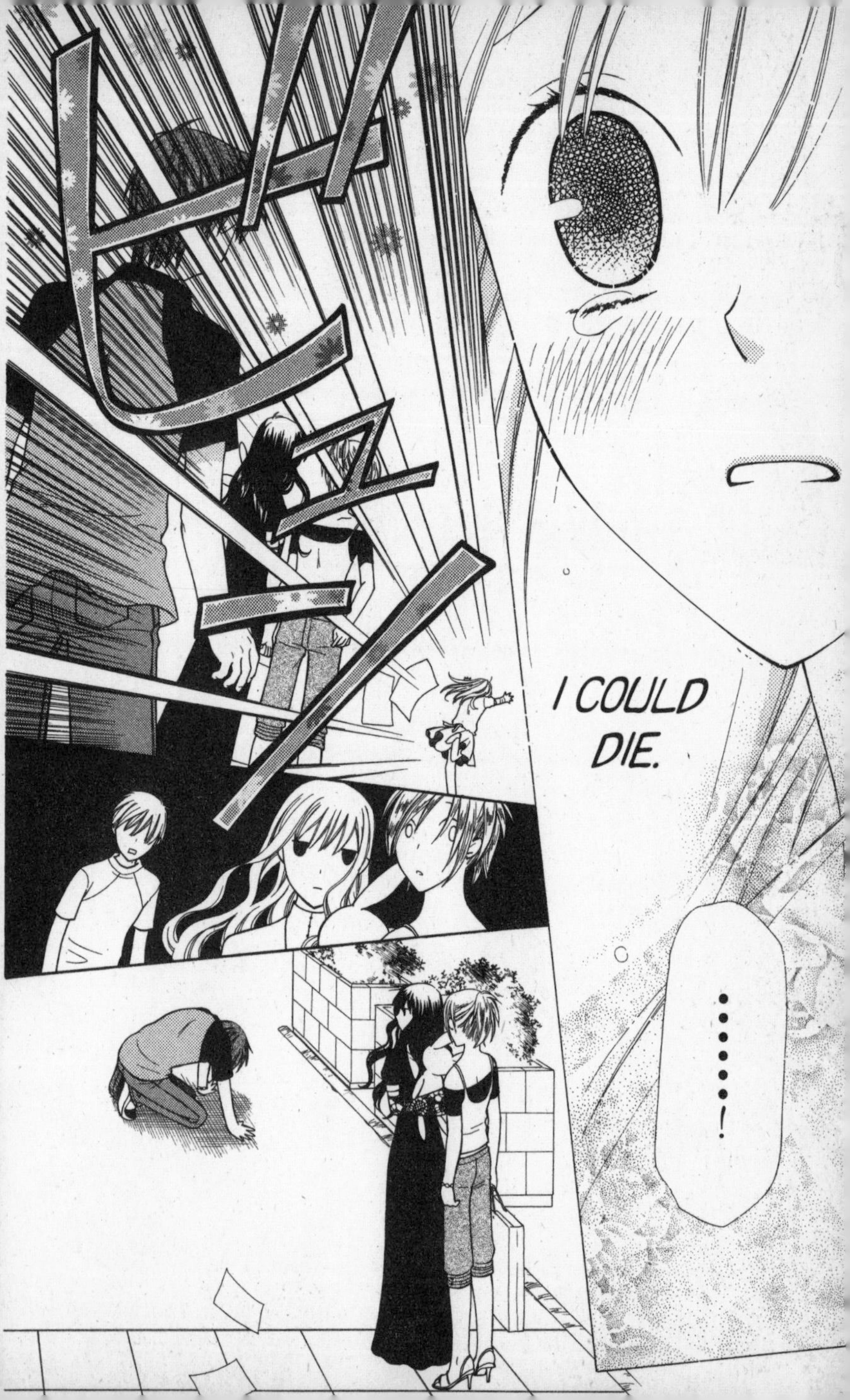
I COULD DIE.
......!

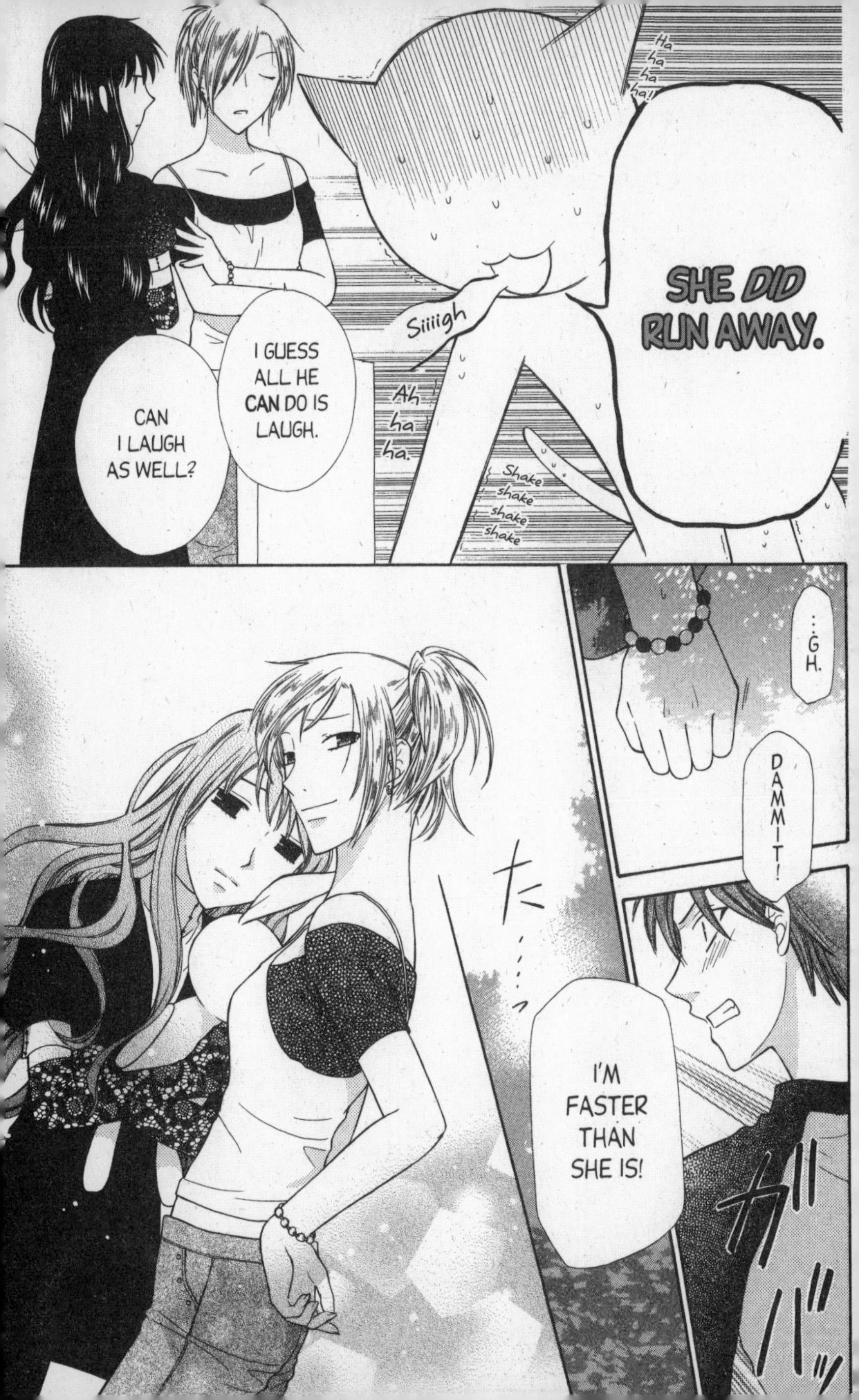
Ha ha ha ha!
SHE DID RUN AWAY.
Siiiigh
Ah ha ha.
Shake shake shake shake
I GUESS ALL HE CAN DO IS LAUGH.
CAN I LAUGH AS WELL?
...GH.
DAMMIT!
I'M FASTER THAN SHE IS!

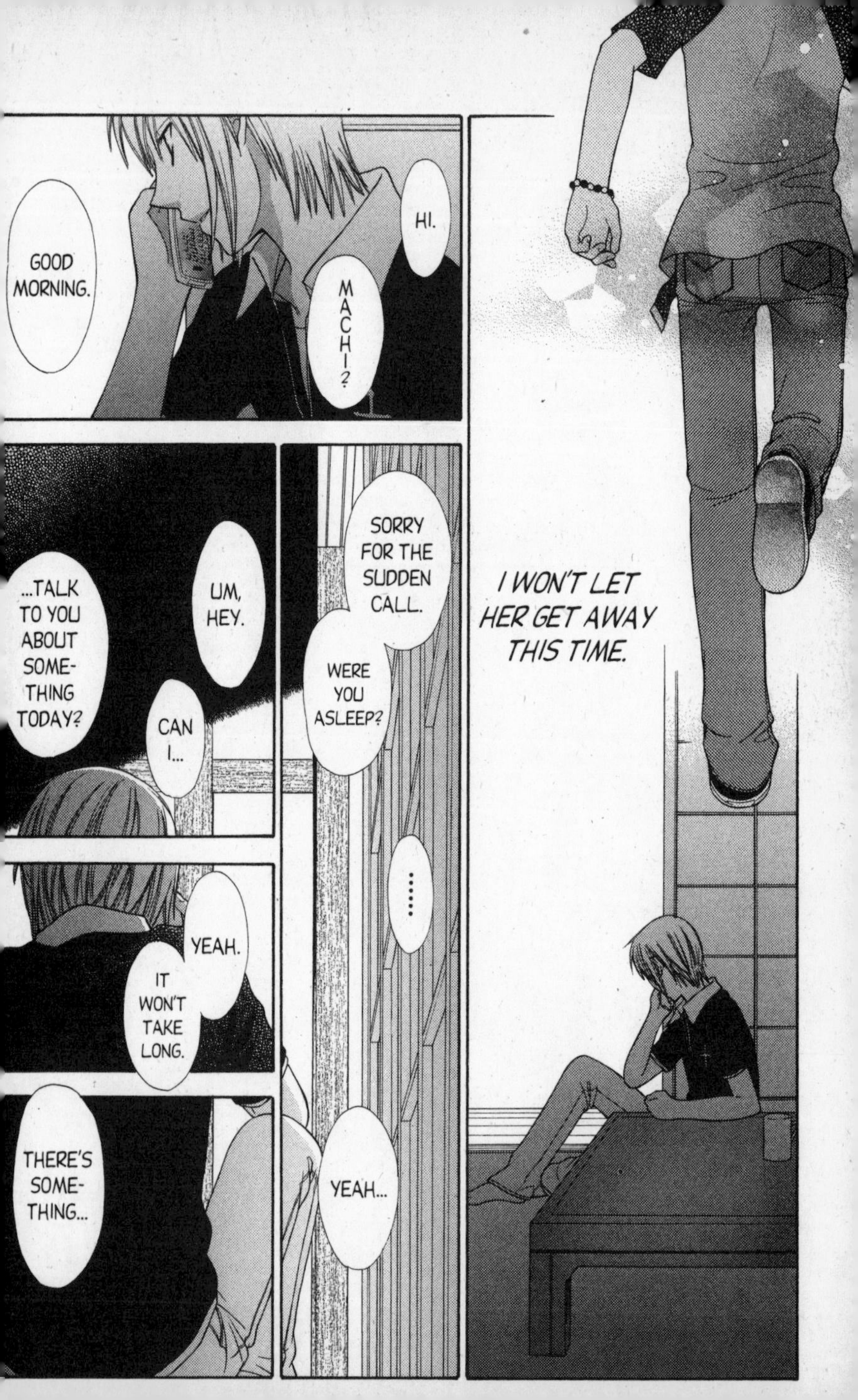
I WON'T LET HER GET AWAY THIS TIME.
HI.
MACHI?
GOOD MORNING.
SORRY FOR THE SUDDEN CALL.
WERE YOU ASLEEP?
......
YEAH...
UM, HEY.
CAN I...
...TALK TO YOU ABOUT SOME-THING TODAY?
YEAH.
IT WON'T TAKE LONG.
THERE'S SOME-THING...

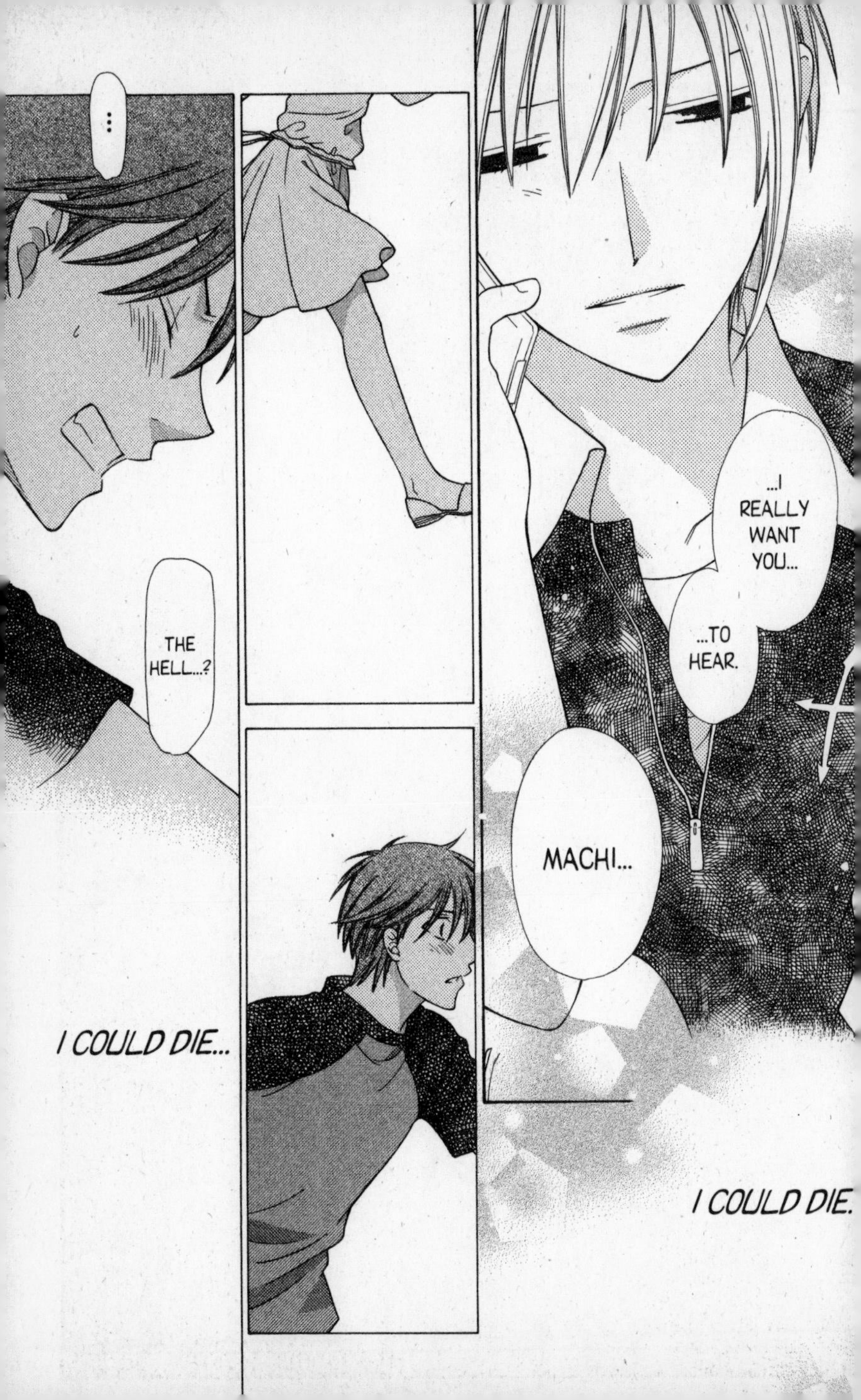
...I REALLY WANT YOU...
...TO HEAR.
MACHI...
I COULD DIE.
...
THE HELL...?
I COULD DIE...

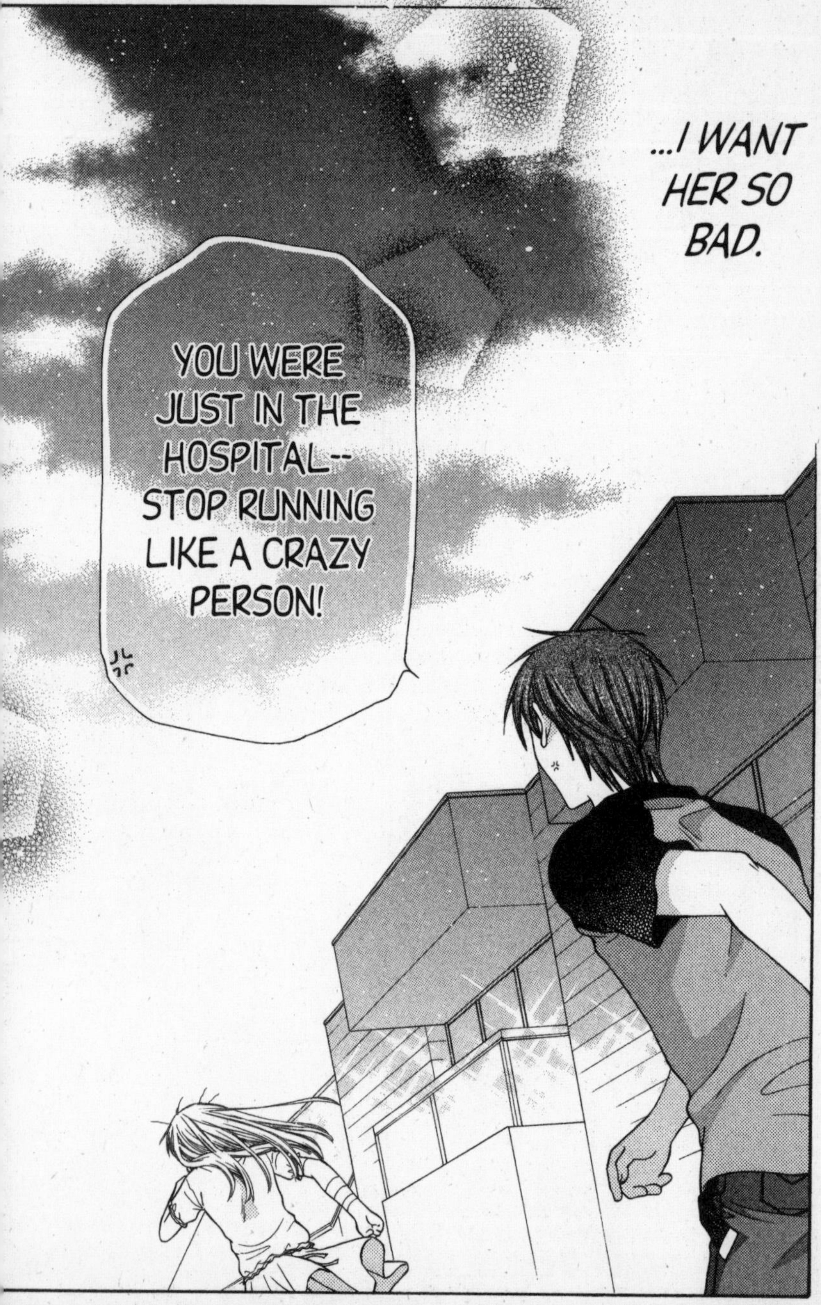
...I WANT HER SO BAD.
YOU WERE JUST IN THE HOSPITAL-- STOP RUNNING LIKE A CRAZY PERSON!

Chapter 129

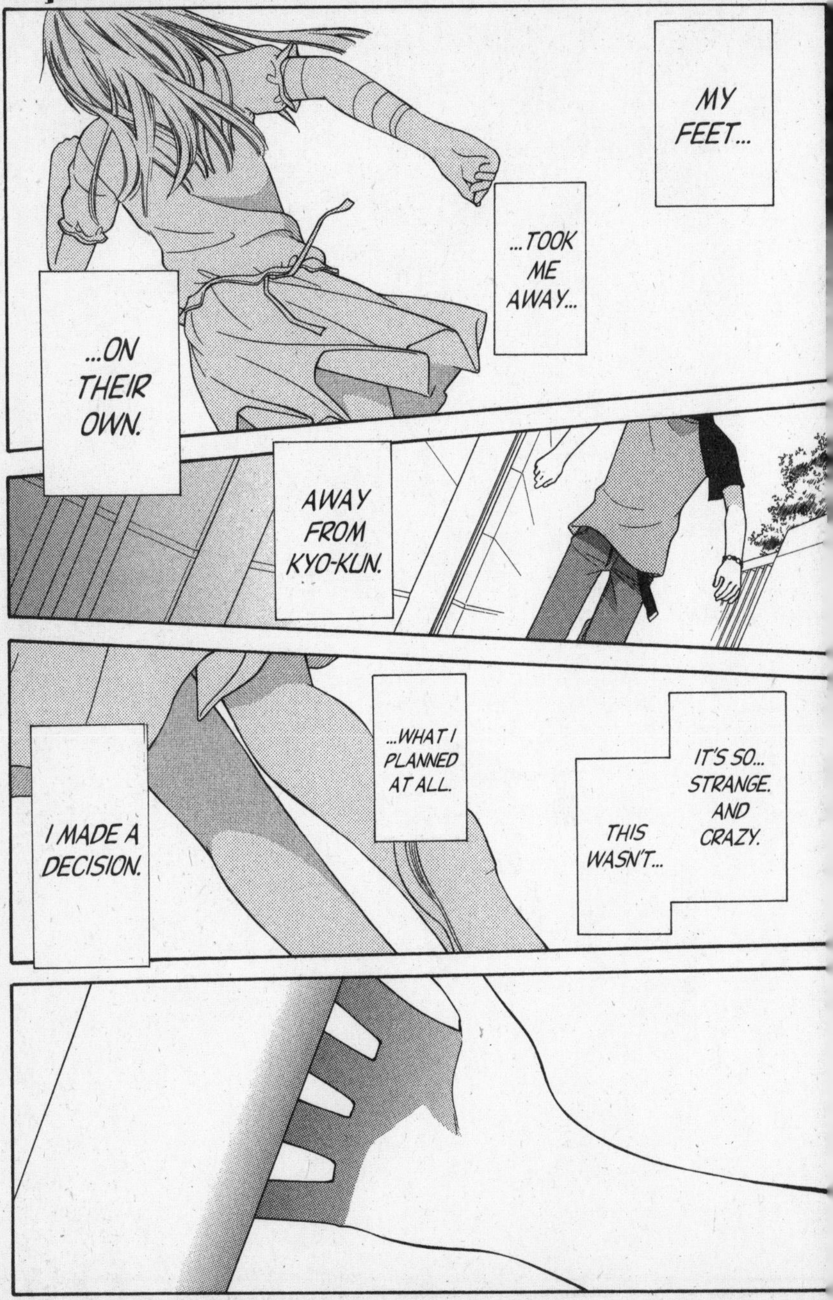
MY FEET...
...TOOK ME AWAY...
...ON THEIR OWN.
AWAY FROM KYO-KUN.
IT'S SO... STRANGE. AND CRAZY.
THIS WASN'T...
...WHAT I PLANNED AT ALL.
I MADE A DECISION.

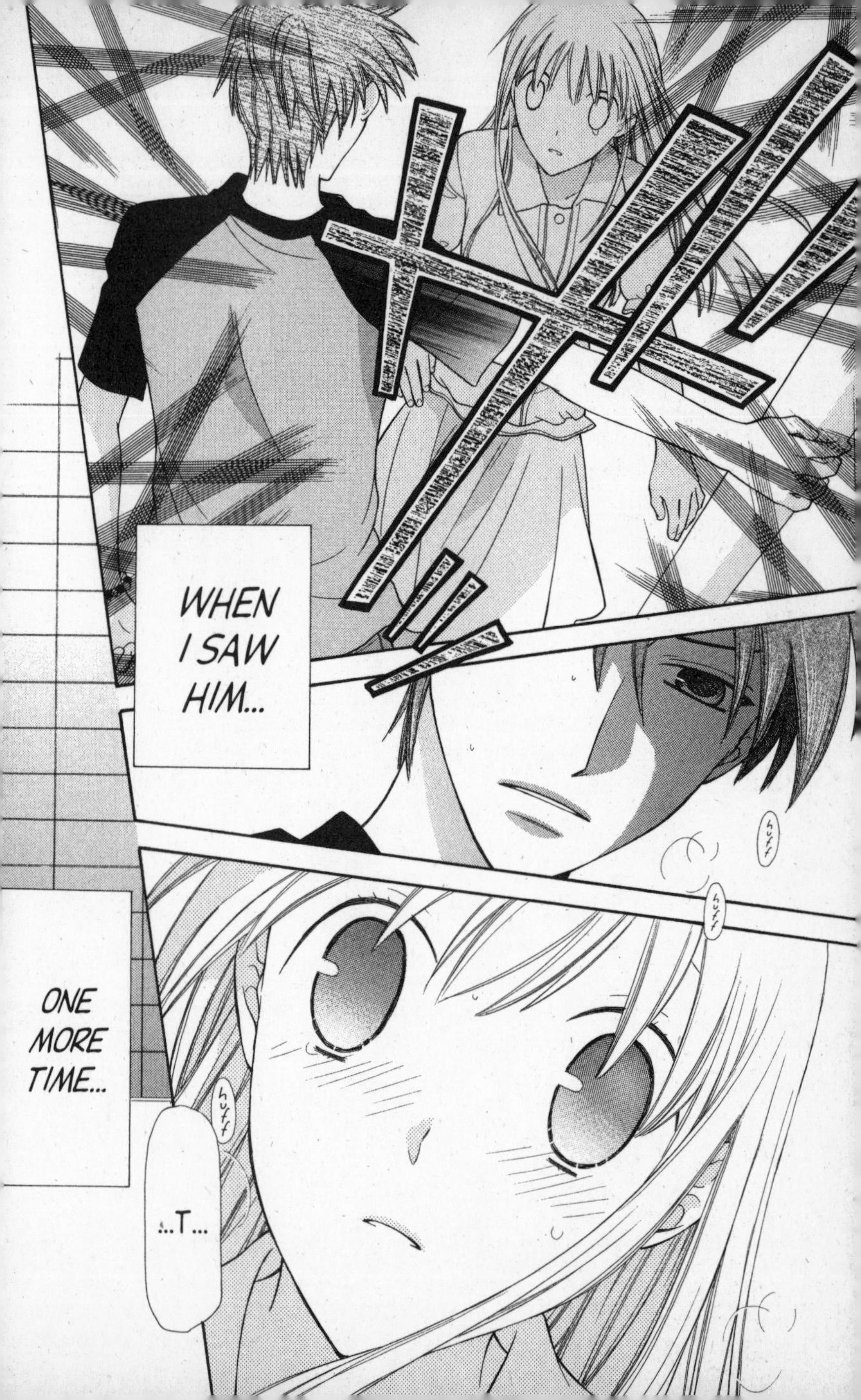
WHEN I SAW HIM...
huff
huff
ONE MORE TIME...
huff
...T...

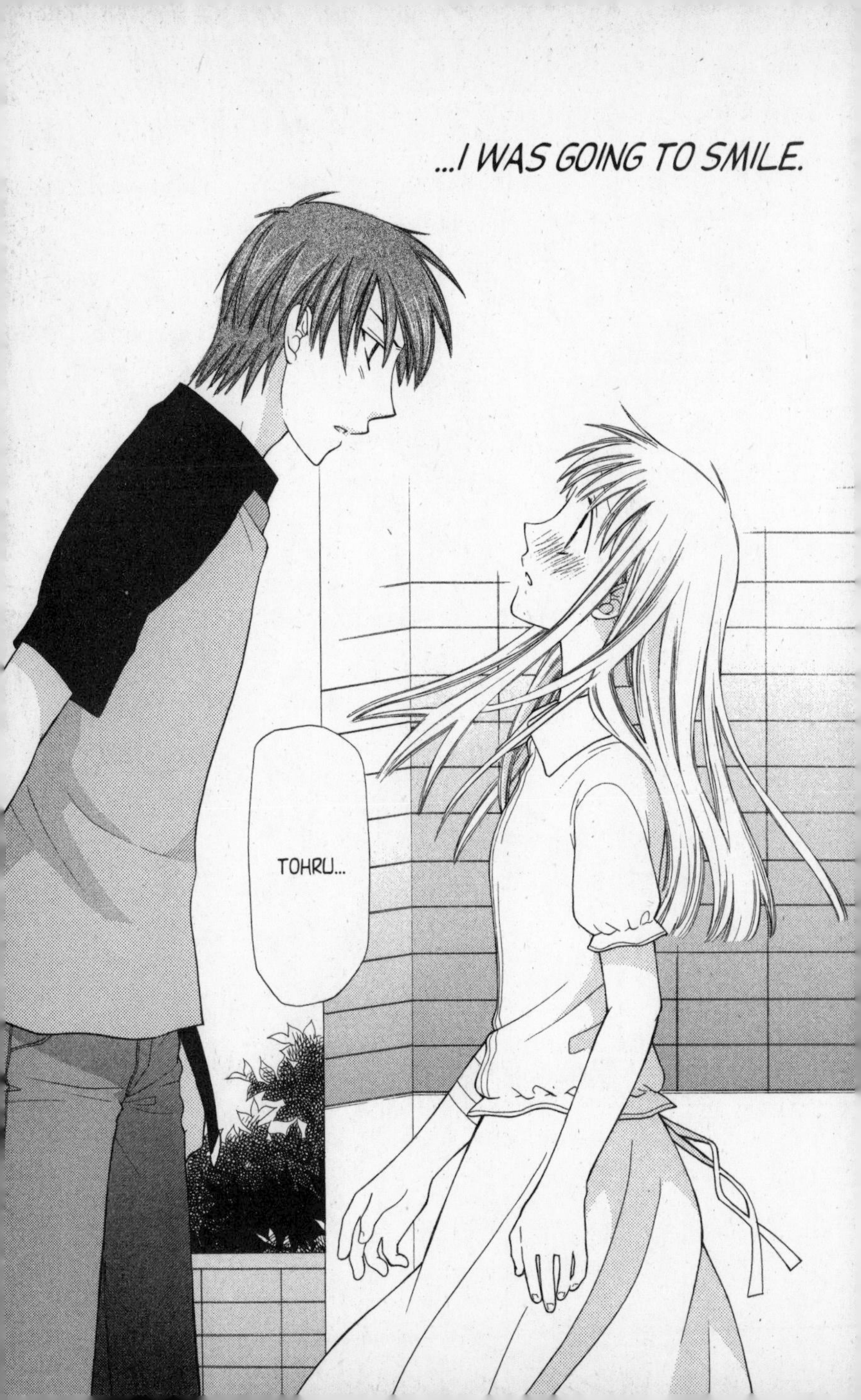
...I WAS GOING TO SMILE.
TOHRU...

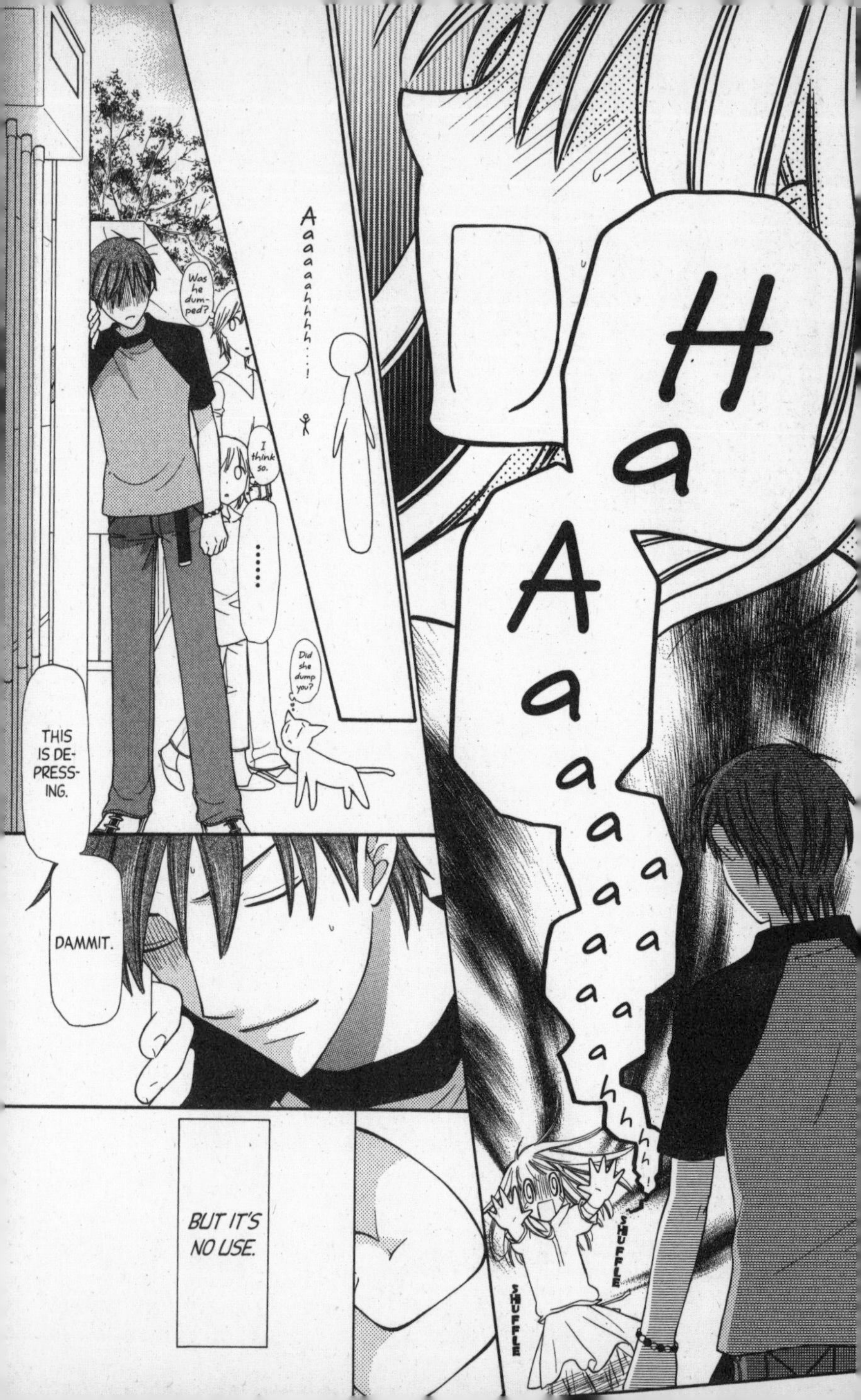
HaAaaaaaaaaaaaahhh!
SHUFFLE
SHUFFLE
Aaaaaaaahhhh...!
Was he dumped?
I think so.
......
Did she dump you?
THIS IS DE-PRESS-ING.
DAMMIT.
BUT IT'S NO USE.

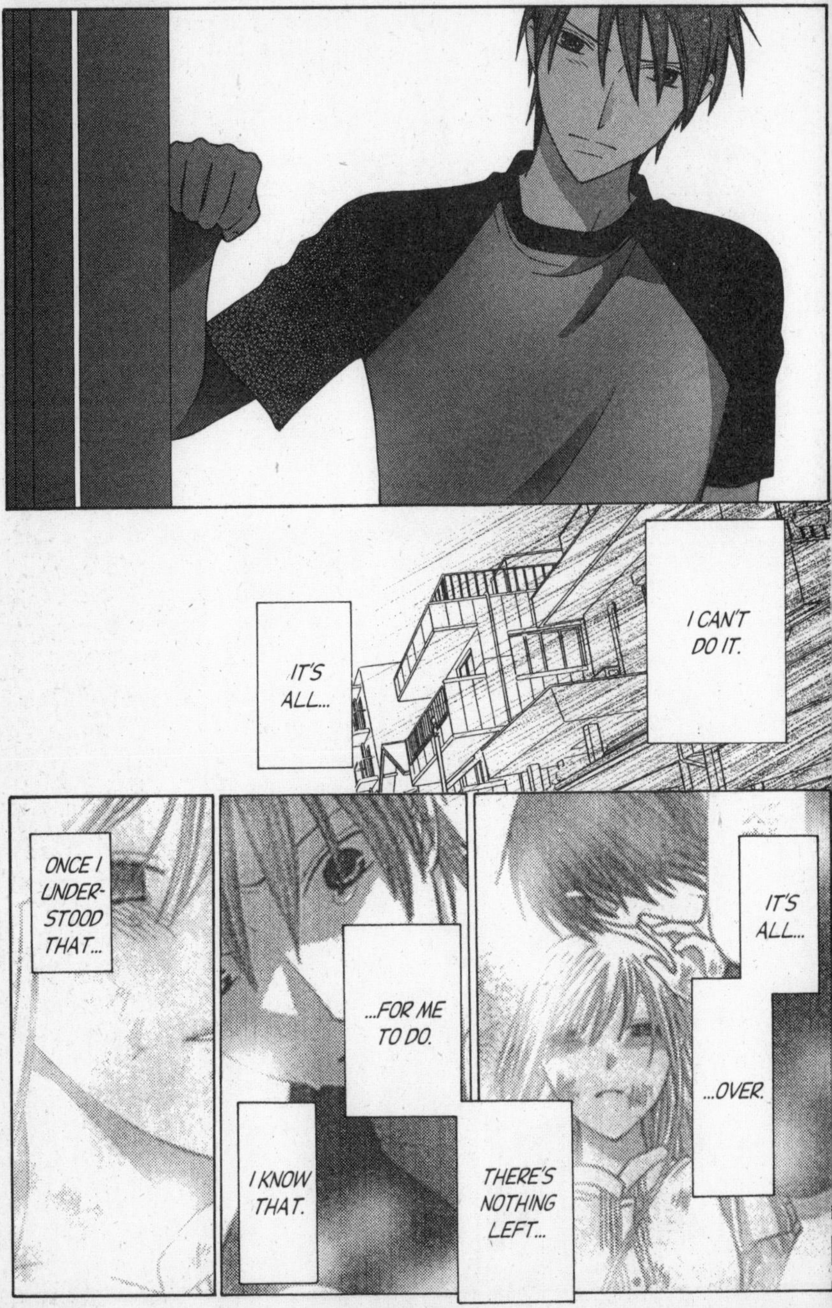
I CAN'T DO IT.
IT'S ALL...
IT'S ALL...
...OVER.
THERE'S NOTHING LEFT...
...FOR ME TO DO.
I KNOW THAT.
ONCE I UNDER-STOOD THAT...

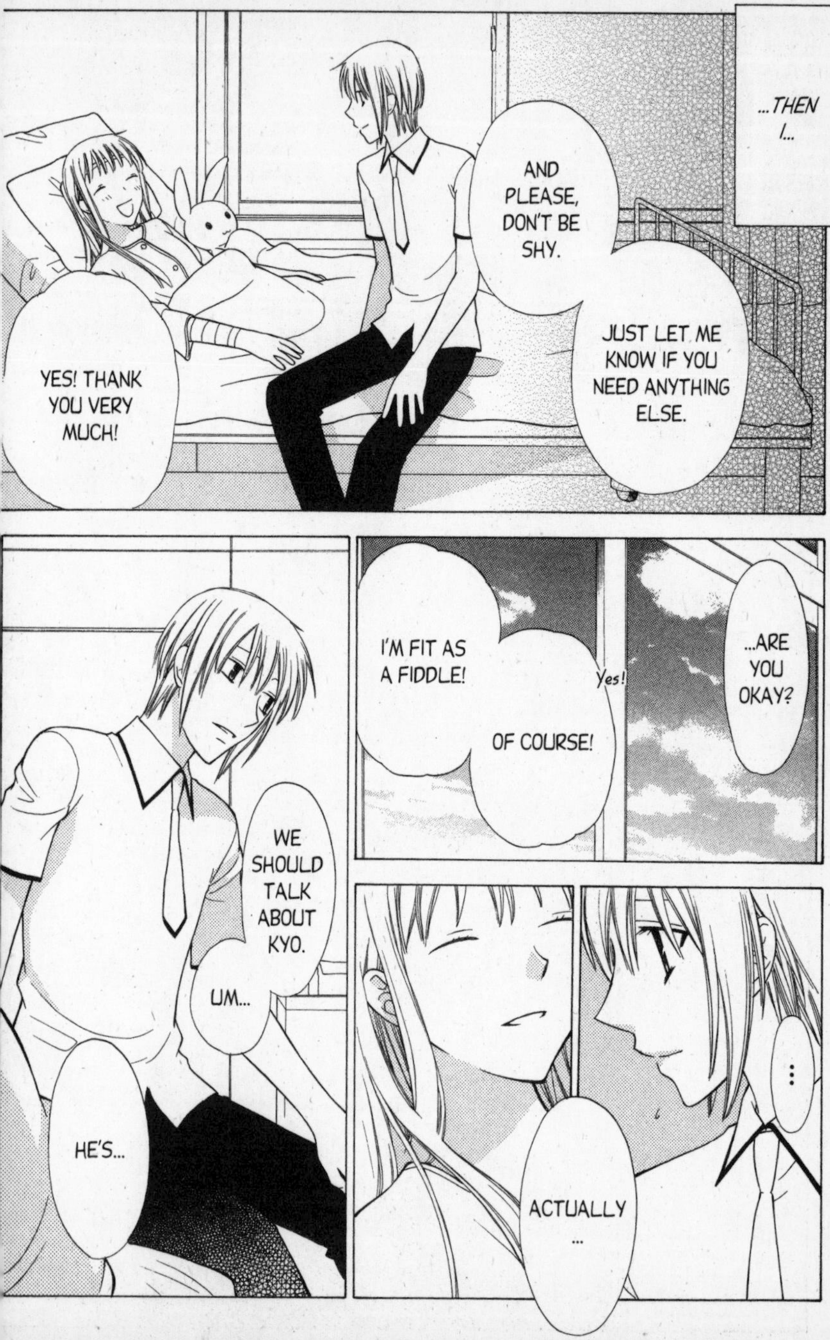
...THEN I...
AND PLEASE, DON'T BE SHY.
JUST LET ME KNOW IF YOU NEED ANYTHING ELSE.
YES! THANK YOU VERY MUCH!
...ARE YOU OKAY?
Yes!
I'M FIT AS A FIDDLE!
OF COURSE!
...
ACTUALLY ...
WE SHOULD TALK ABOUT KYO.
UM...
HE'S...

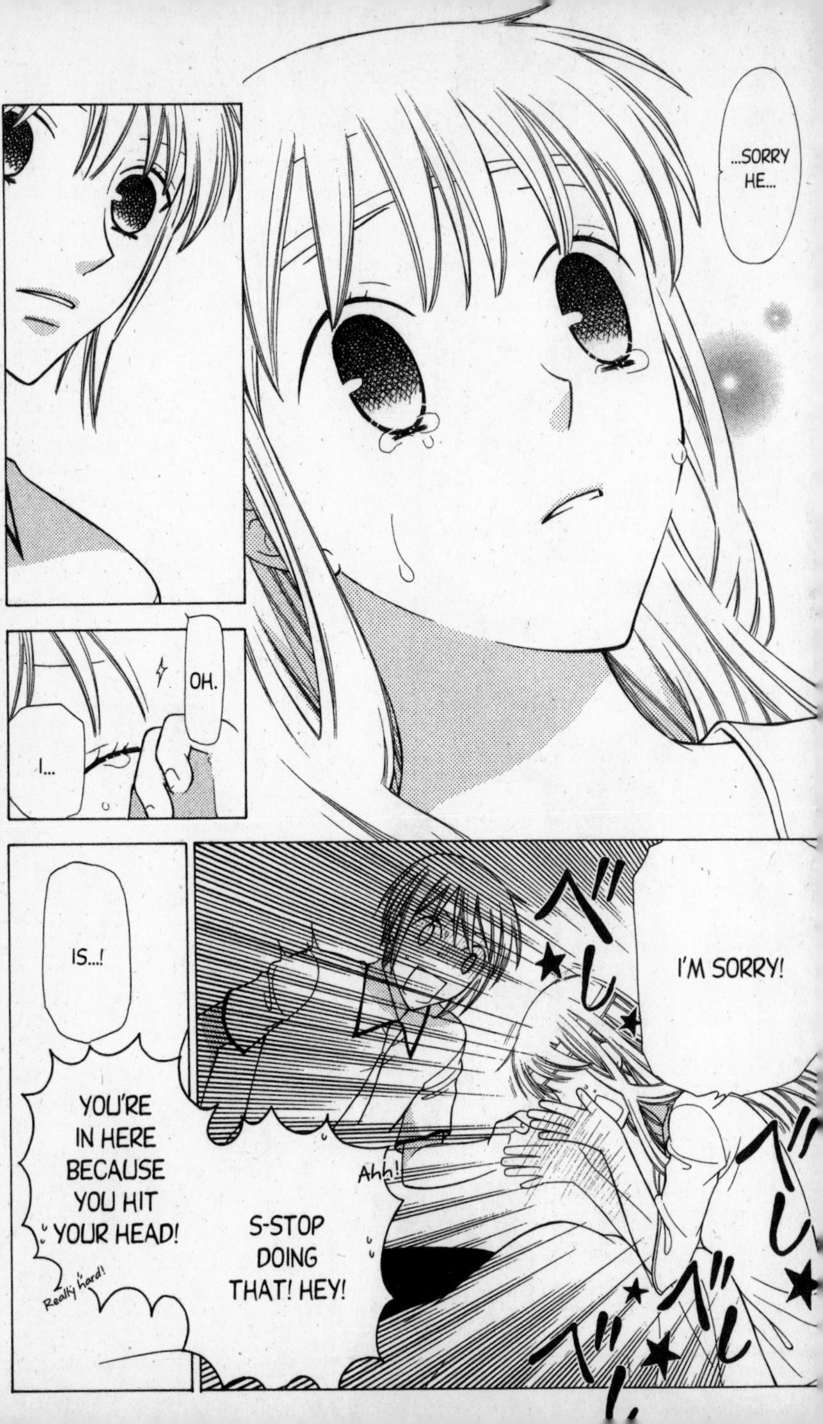
...SORRY HE...
OH.
I...
I'M SORRY!
Ahh!
S-STOP DOING THAT! HEY!
IS...!
YOU'RE IN HERE BECAUSE YOU HIT YOUR HEAD!
Really hard!

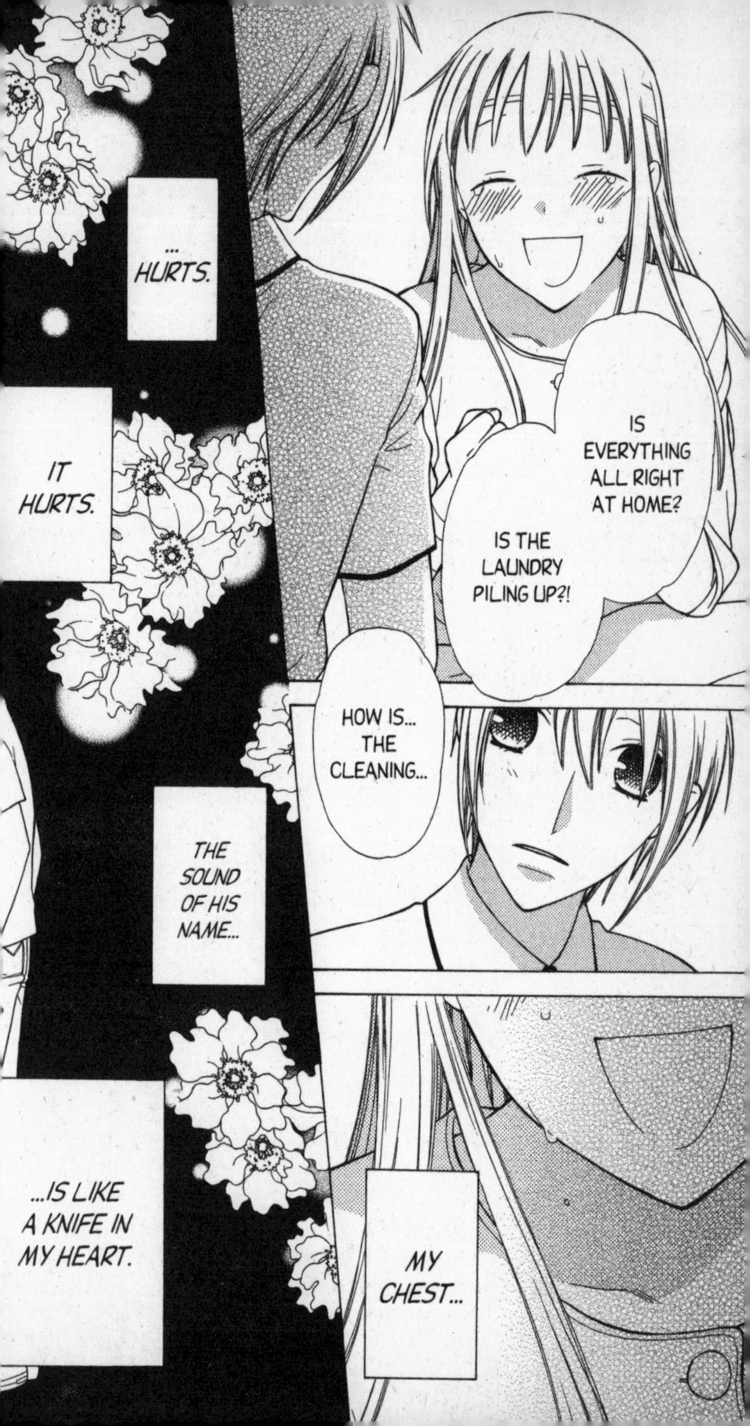
IS EVERYTHING ALL RIGHT AT HOME?
IS THE LAUNDRY PILING UP?!
HOW IS... THE CLEANING...
MY CHEST...
...HURTS.
IT HURTS.
THE SOUND OF HIS NAME...
...IS LIKE A KNIFE IN MY HEART.

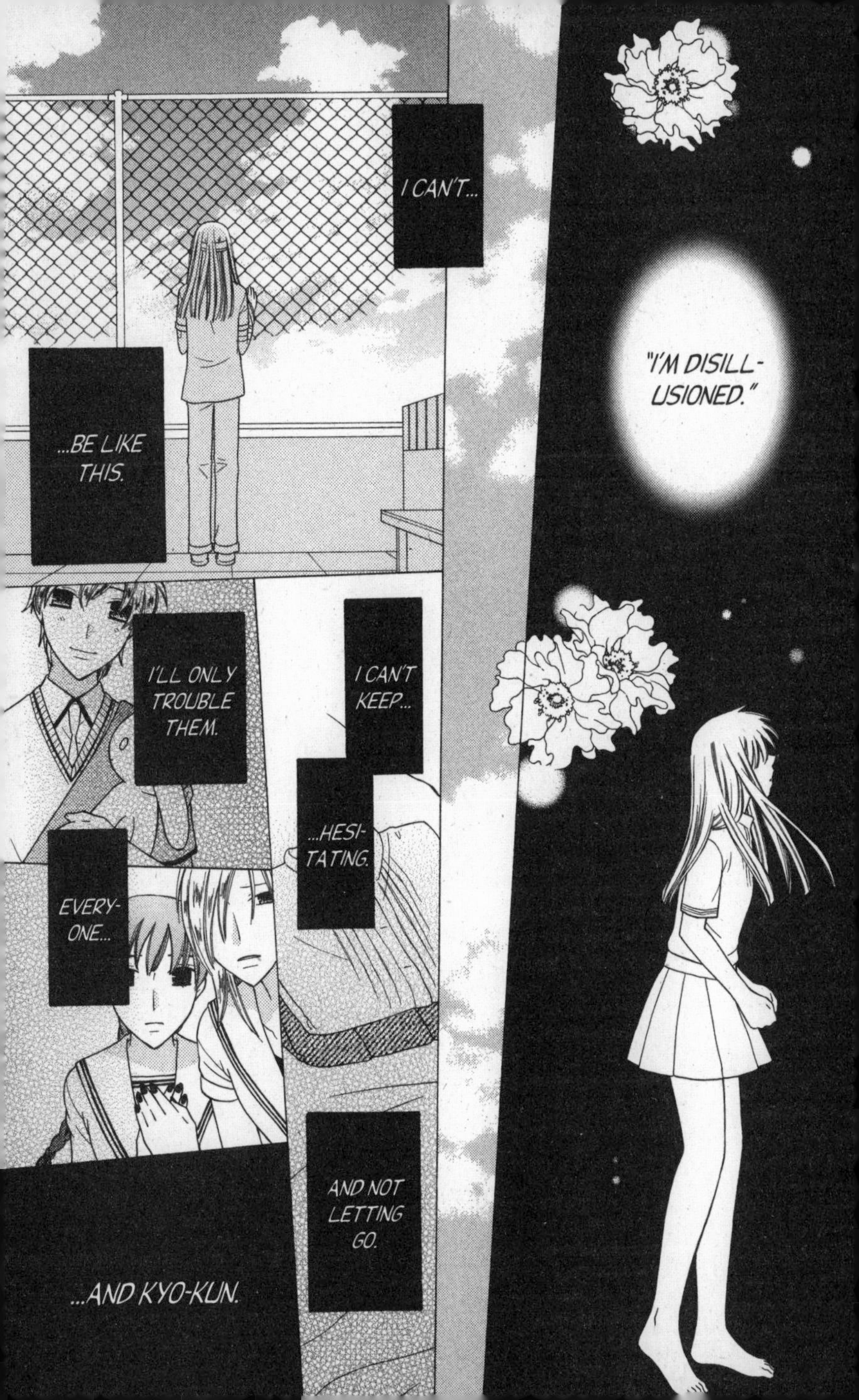
"I'M DISILL-USIONED."
I CAN'T...
...BE LIKE THIS.
I CAN'T KEEP...
...HESI-TATING.
AND NOT LETTING GO.
I'LL ONLY TROUBLE THEM.
EVERY-ONE...
...AND KYO-KUN.

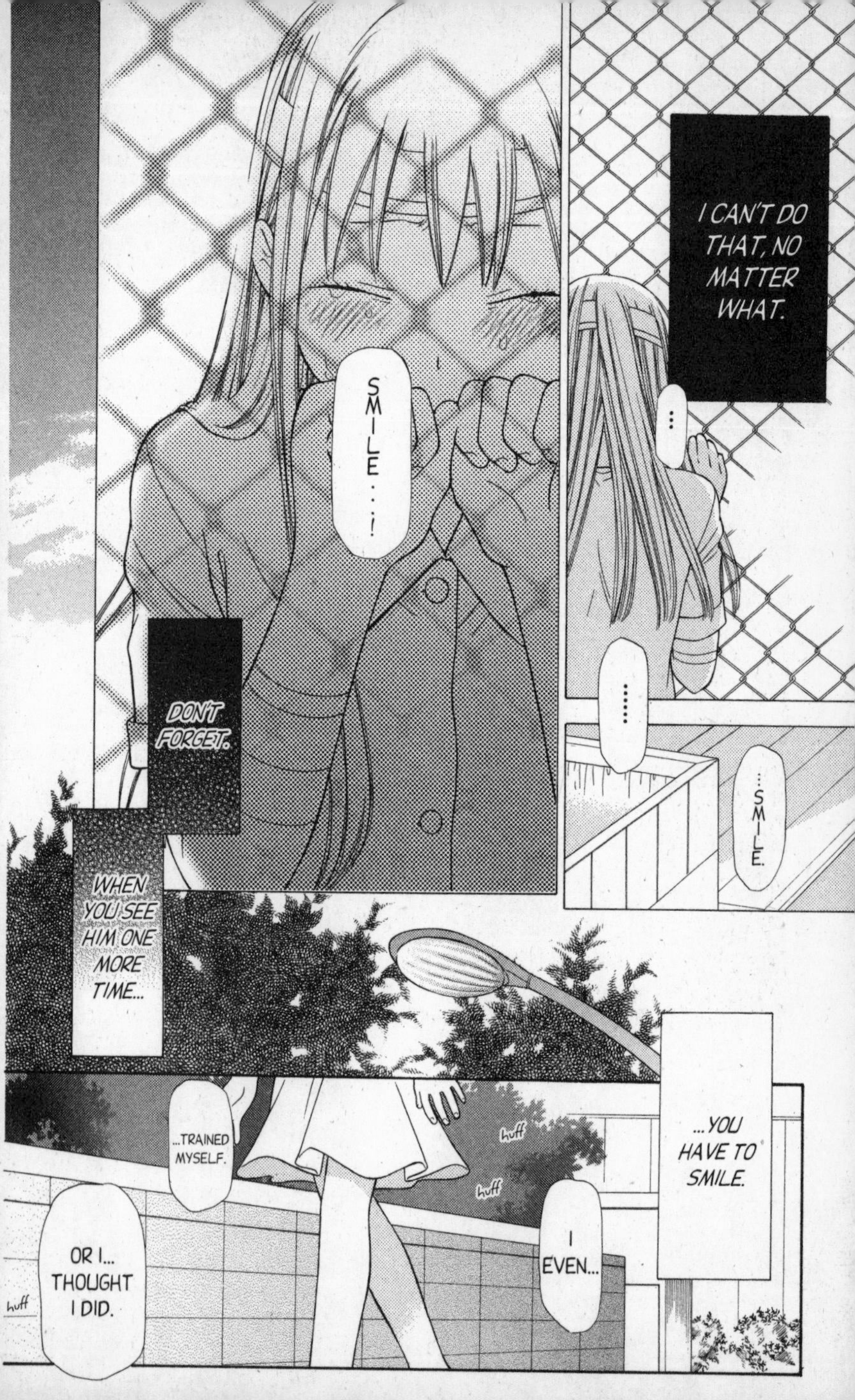
I CAN'T DO THAT, NO MATTER WHAT.
...
......
...SMILE.
SMILE...!
DON'T FORGET.
WHEN YOU SEE HIM ONE MORE TIME...
...YOU HAVE TO SMILE.
I EVEN...
huff
huff
...TRAINED MYSELF.
OR I... THOUGHT I DID.
huff

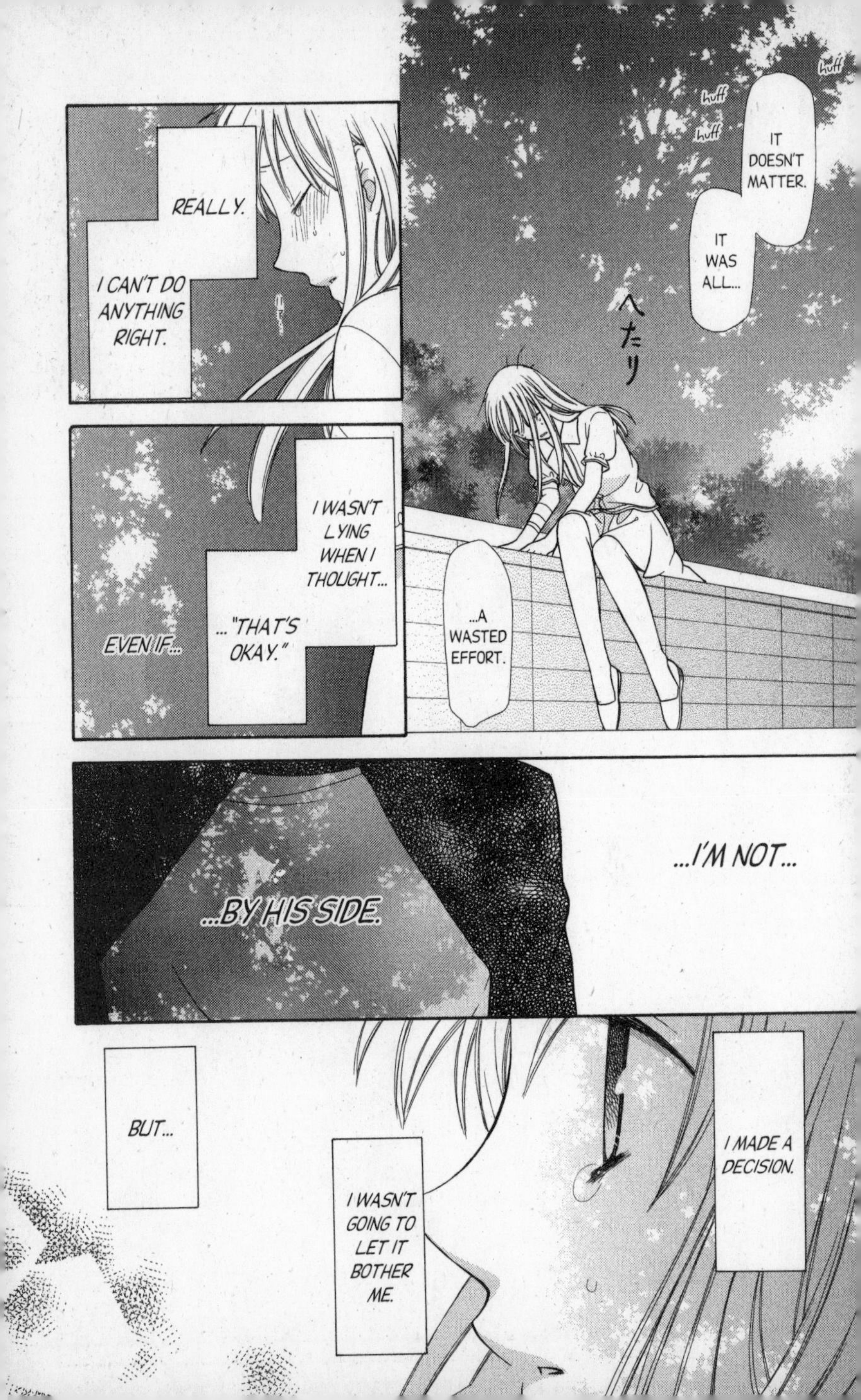
huff
huff
huff
IT DOESN'T MATTER.
IT WAS ALL...
へたり
...A WASTED EFFORT.
REALLY.
I CAN'T DO ANYTHING RIGHT.
I WASN'T LYING WHEN I THOUGHT...
... "THAT'S OKAY."
EVEN IF...
...I'M NOT...
...BY HIS SIDE.
I MADE A DECISION.
I WASN'T GOING TO LET IT BOTHER ME.
BUT...

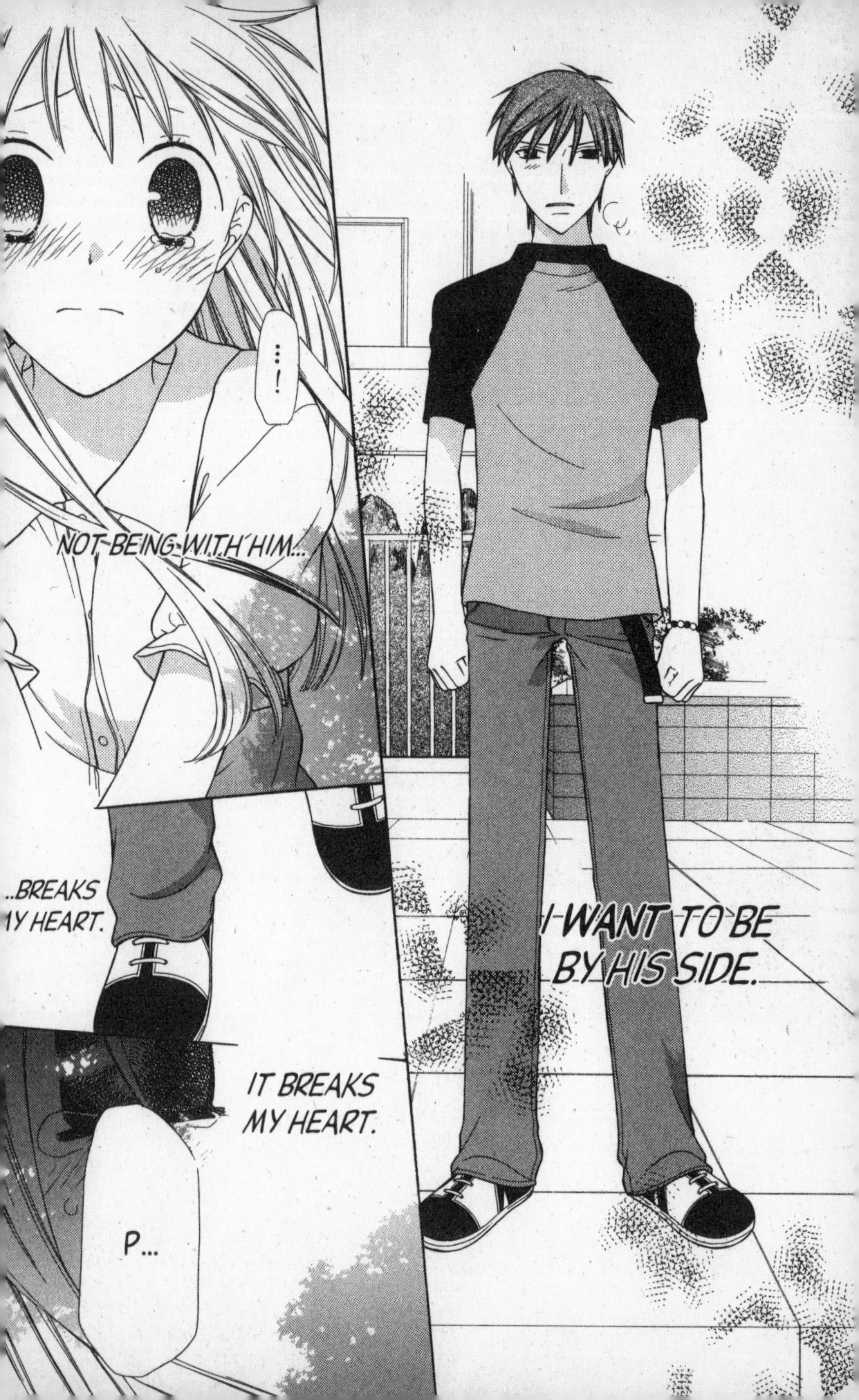

I WANT TO BE BY HIS SIDE.
...!
NOT BEING WITH HIM...
..BREAKS MY HEART.
IT BREAKS MY HEART.
P...

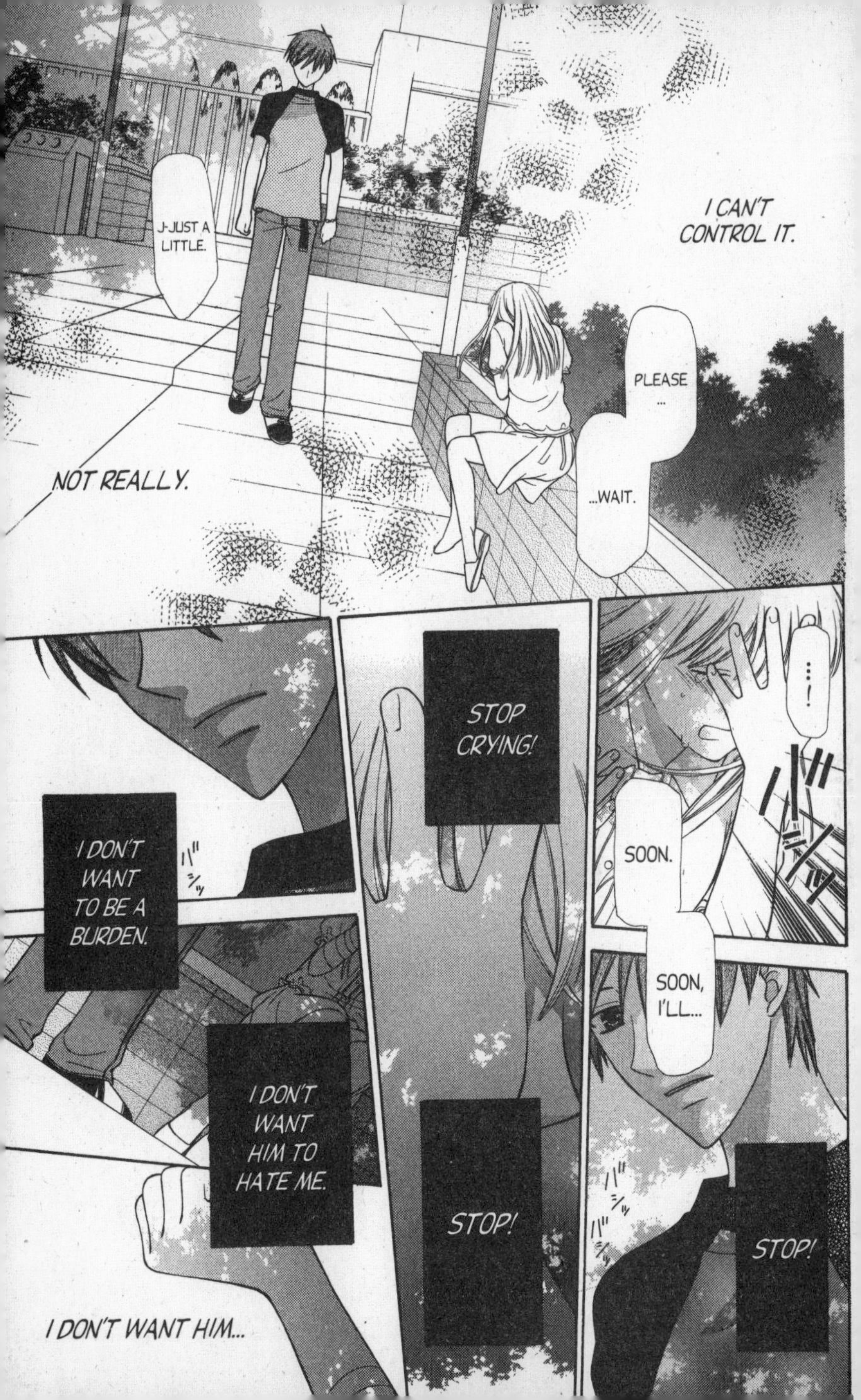
I CAN'T CONTROL IT.
PLEASE ...
...WAIT.
J-JUST A LITTLE.
NOT REALLY.
...!
SOON.
SOON, I'LL...
STOP!
STOP CRYING!
STOP!
I DON'T WANT TO BE A BURDEN.
I DON'T WANT HIM TO HATE ME.
I DON'T WANT HIM...

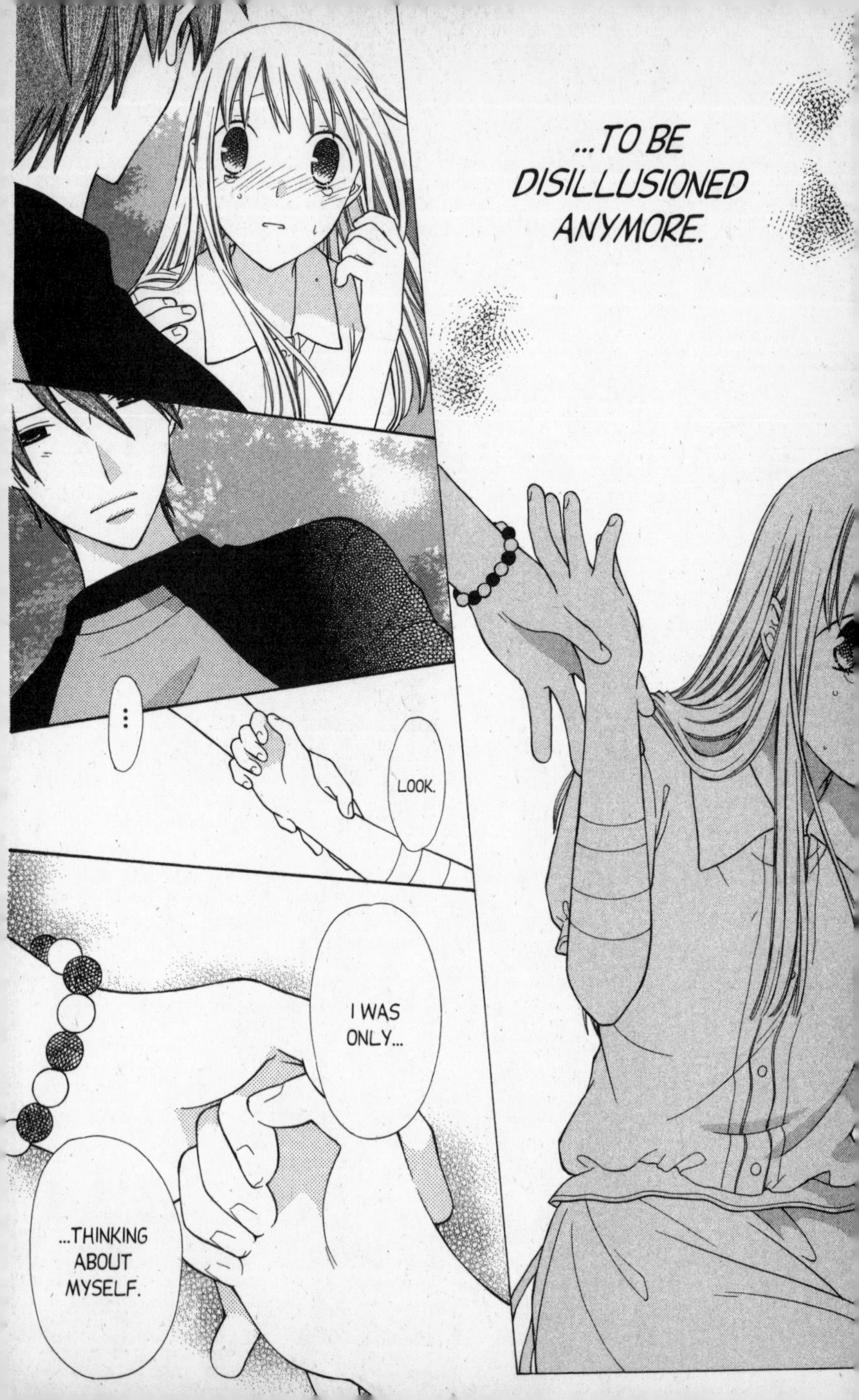
...TO BE DISILLUSIONED ANYMORE.
...
LOOK.
I WAS ONLY...
...THINKING ABOUT MYSELF.

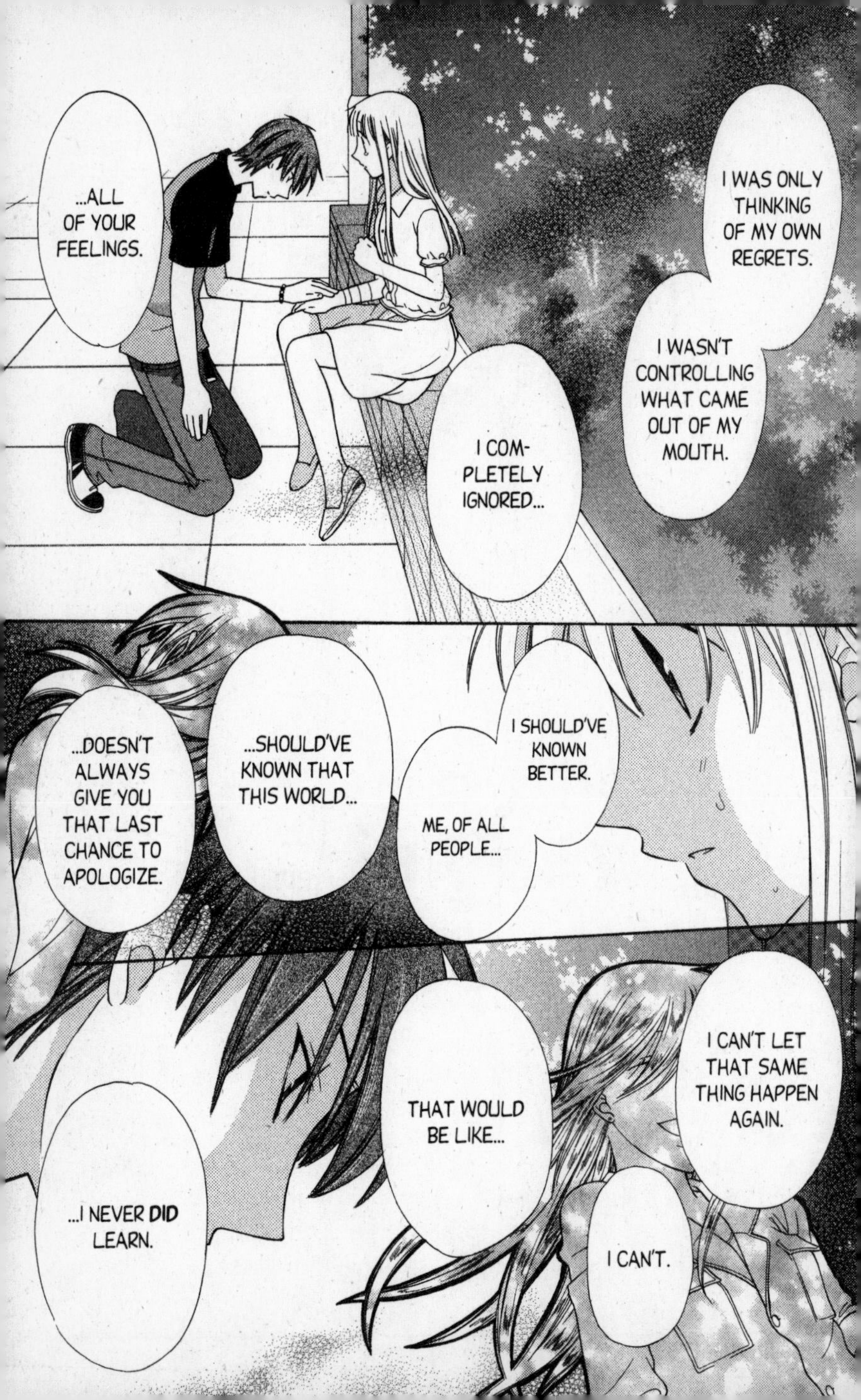
I WAS ONLY THINKING OF MY OWN REGRETS.
I WASN'T CONTROLLING WHAT CAME OUT OF MY MOUTH.
I COM-PLETELY IGNORED...
...ALL OF YOUR FEELINGS.
I SHOULD'VE KNOWN BETTER.
ME, OF ALL PEOPLE...
...SHOULD'VE KNOWN THAT THIS WORLD...
...DOESN'T ALWAYS GIVE YOU THAT LAST CHANCE TO APOLOGIZE.
I CAN'T LET THAT SAME THING HAPPEN AGAIN.
I CAN'T.
THAT WOULD BE LIKE...
...I NEVER DID LEARN.

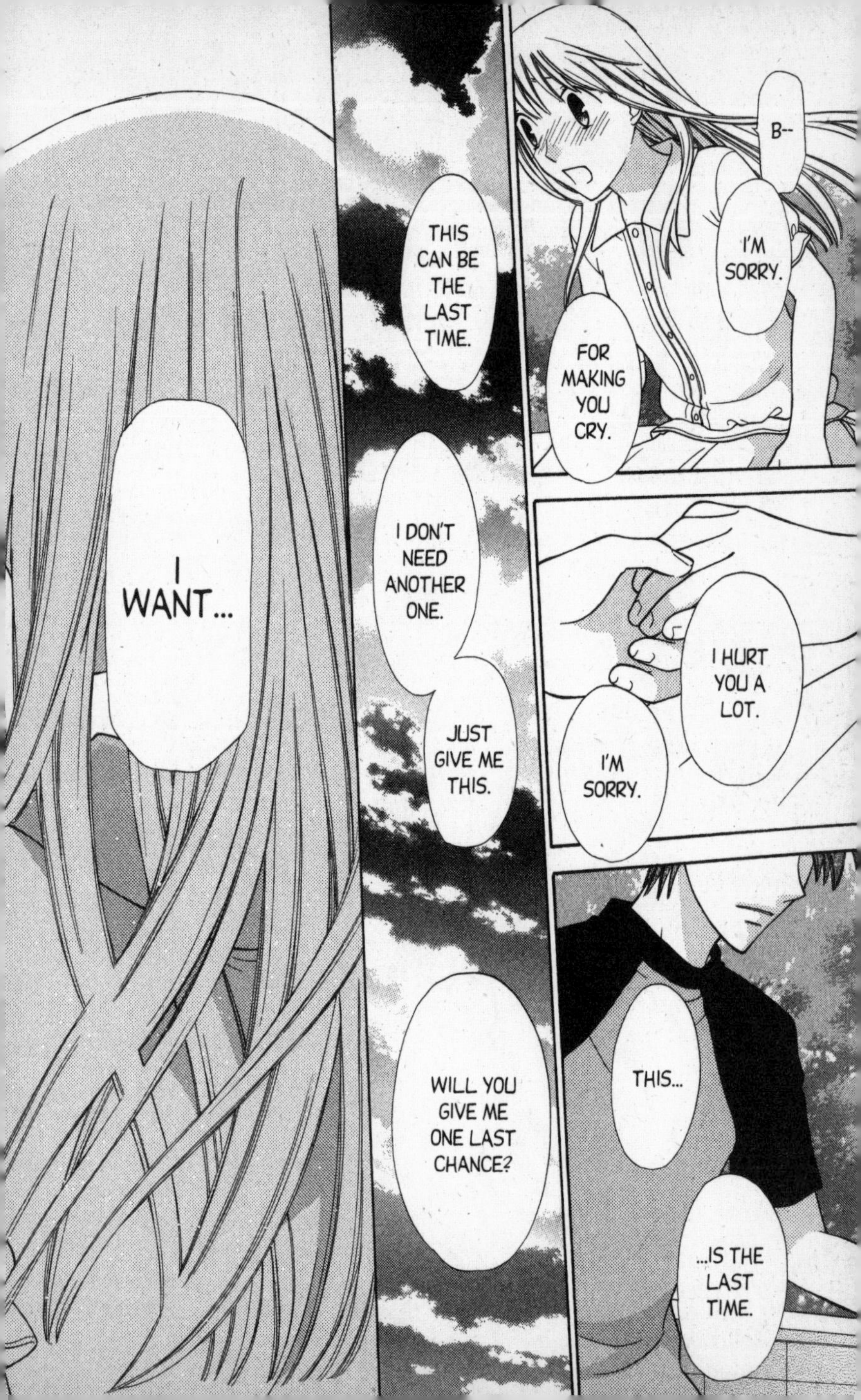
B--
I'M SORRY.
FOR MAKING YOU CRY.
I HURT YOU A LOT.
I'M SORRY.
THIS...
...IS THE LAST TIME.
THIS CAN BE THE LAST TIME.
I DON'T NEED ANOTHER ONE.
JUST GIVE ME THIS.
WILL YOU GIVE ME ONE LAST CHANCE?
I WANT...

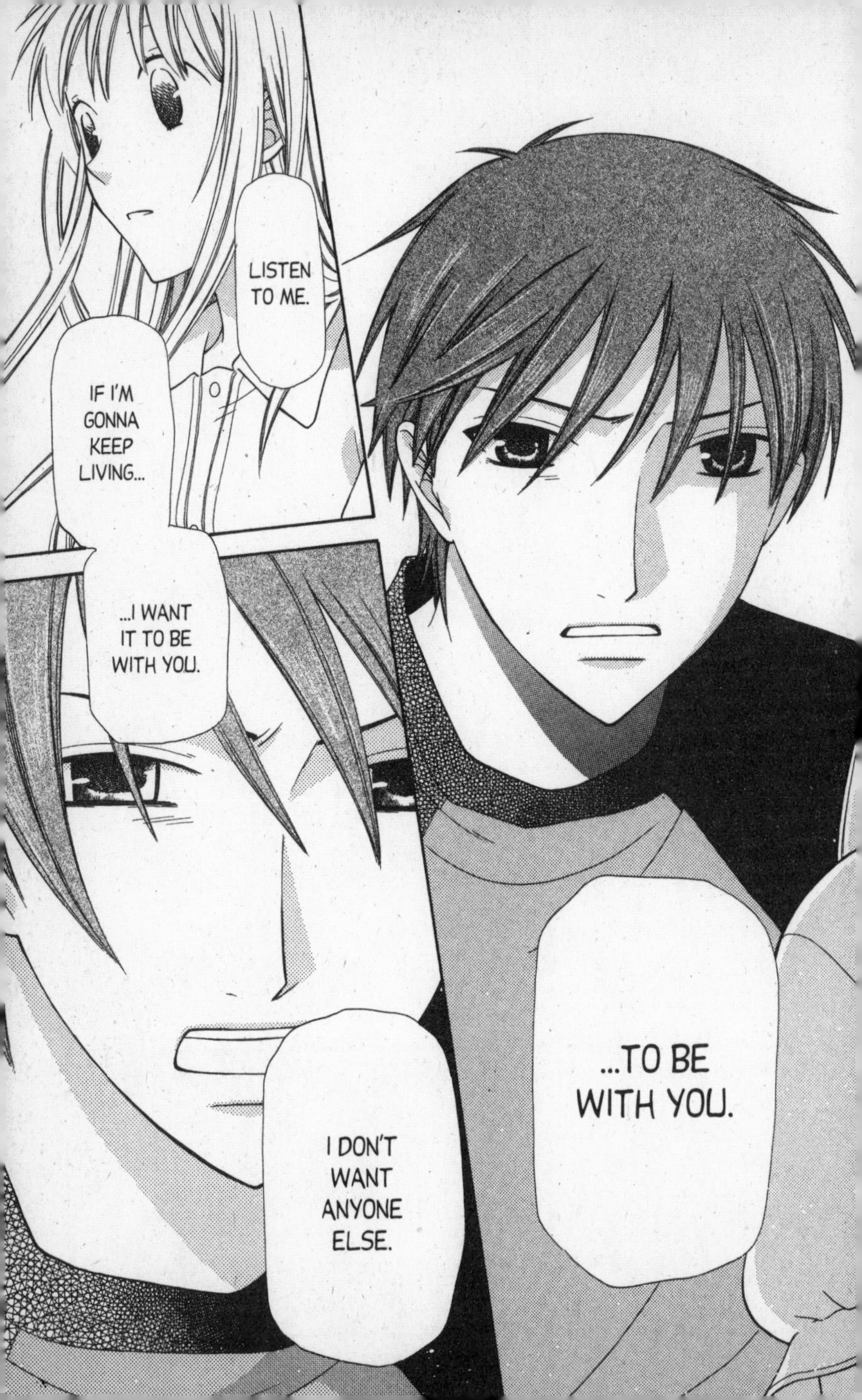
LISTEN TO ME.
IF I'M GONNA KEEP LIVING...
...I WANT IT TO BE WITH YOU.
I DON'T WANT ANYONE ELSE.
...TO BE WITH YOU.

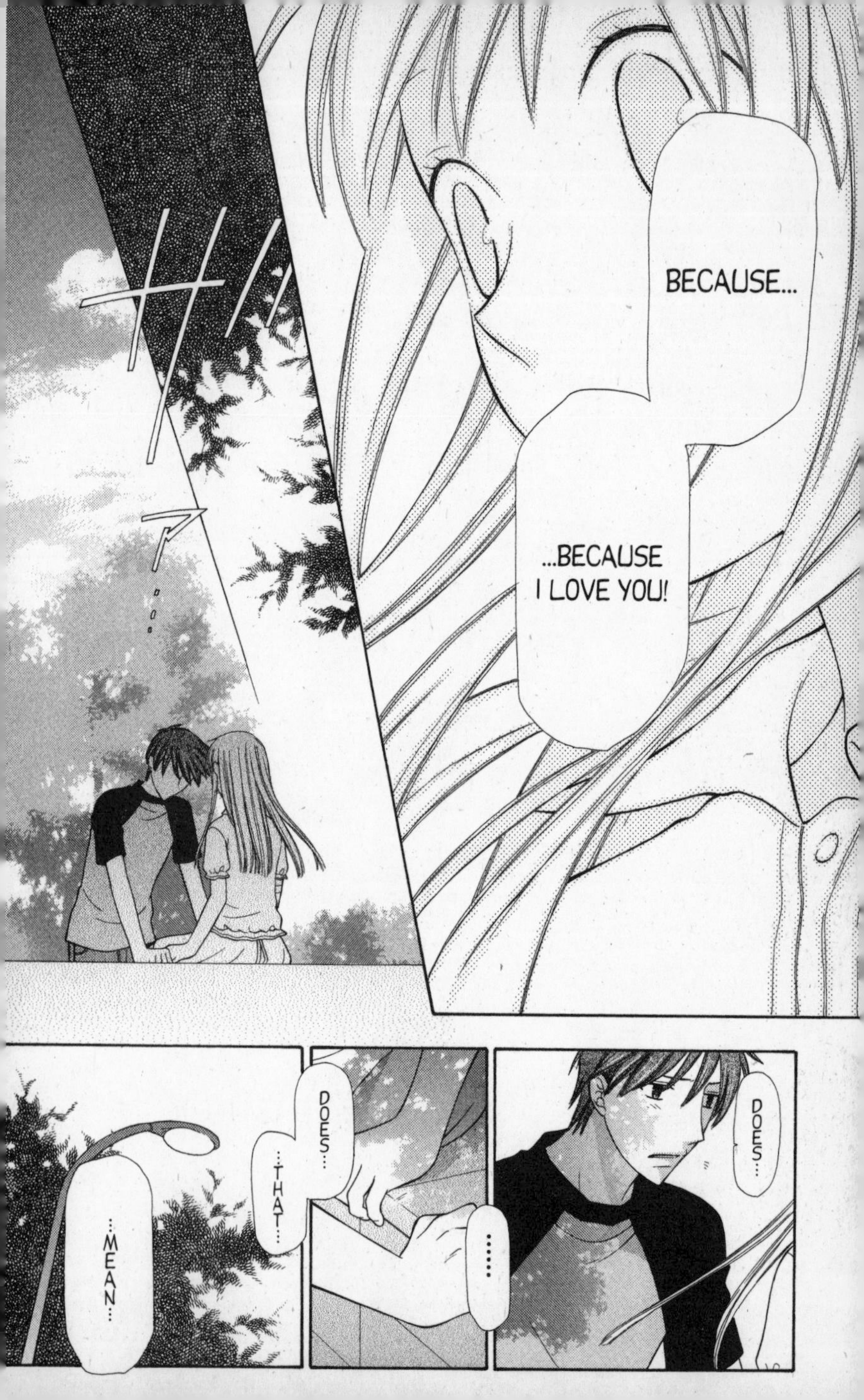
BECAUSE...
...BECAUSE I LOVE YOU!
DOES...
......
DOES...
...THAT...
...MEAN...

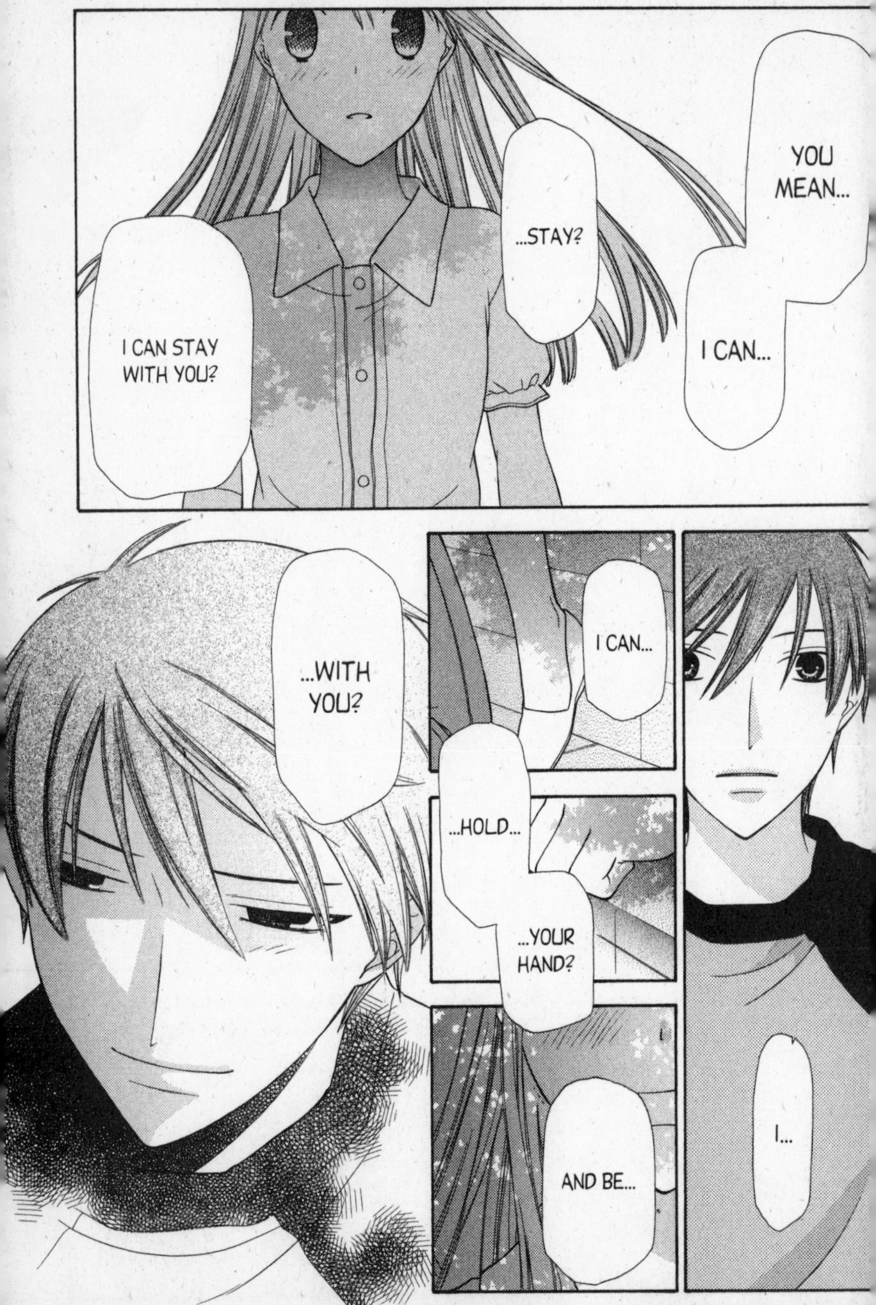
YOU MEAN...
I CAN...
...STAY?
I CAN STAY WITH YOU?
I...
I CAN...
...HOLD...
...YOUR HAND?
AND BE...
...WITH YOU?

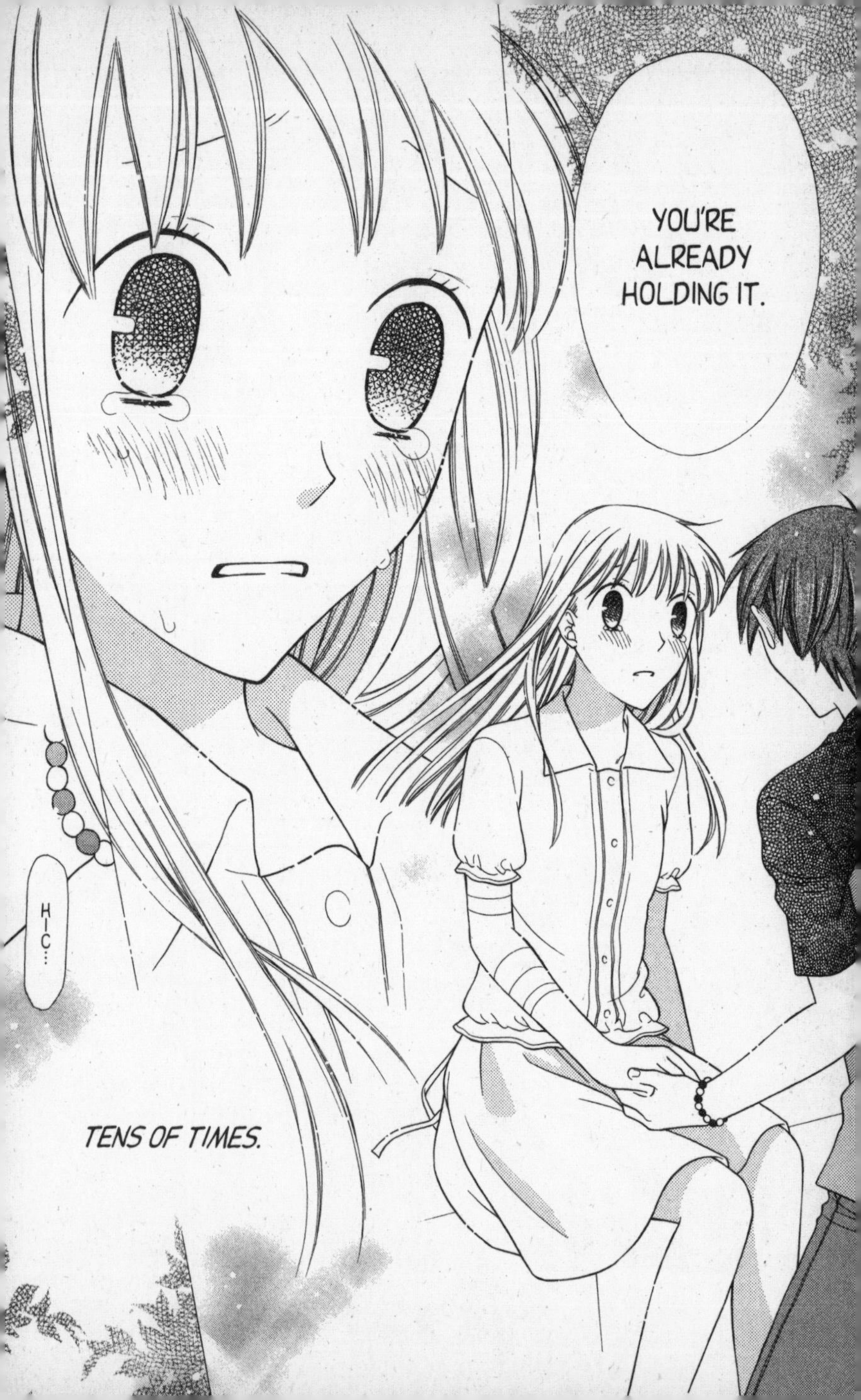
YOU'RE ALREADY HOLDING IT.
HIC...
TENS OF TIMES.

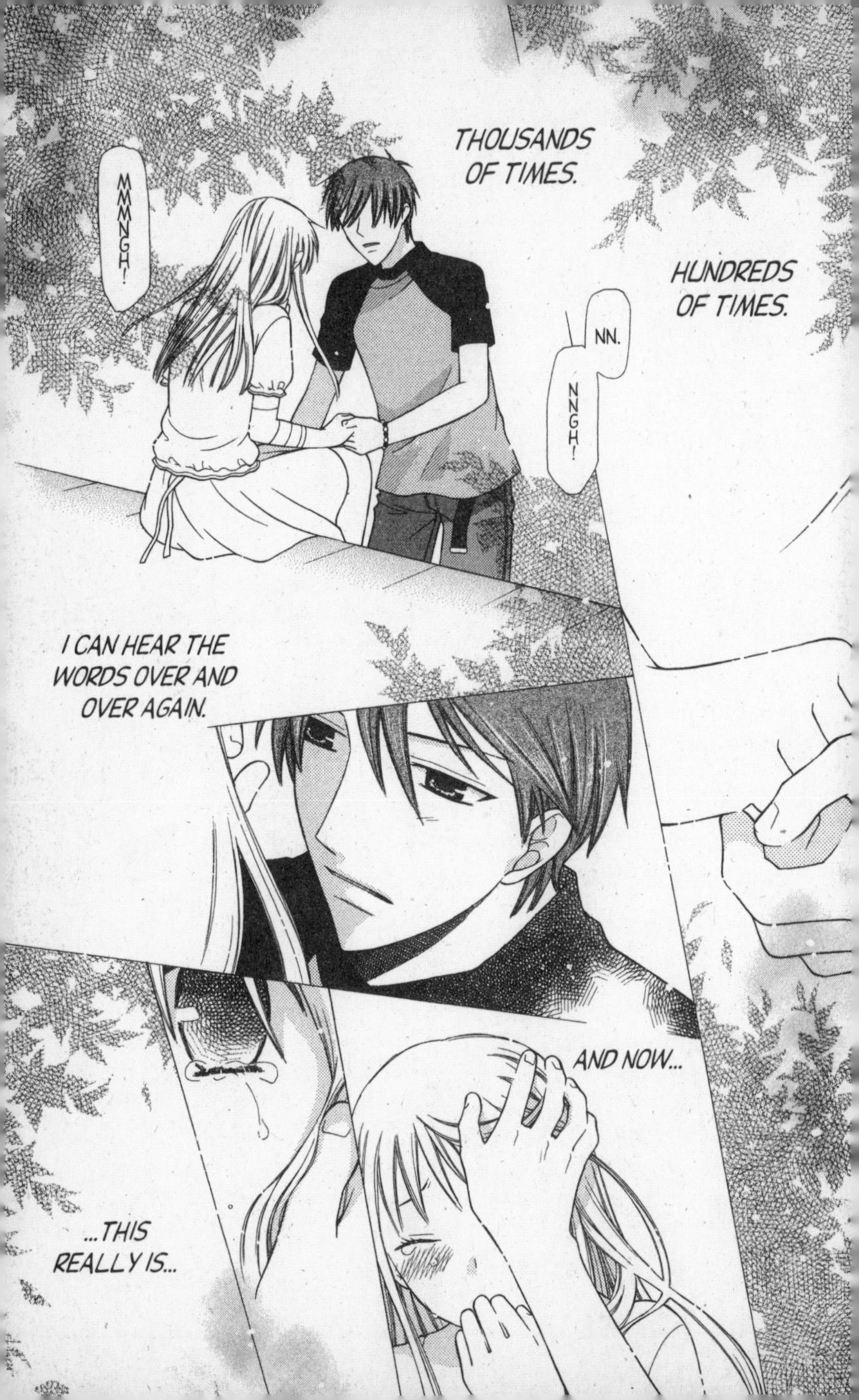
THOUSANDS OF TIMES.
HUNDREDS OF TIMES.
NN.
NNGH!
MMMNGH!
I CAN HEAR THE WORDS OVER AND OVER AGAIN.
AND NOW...
...THIS REALLY IS...

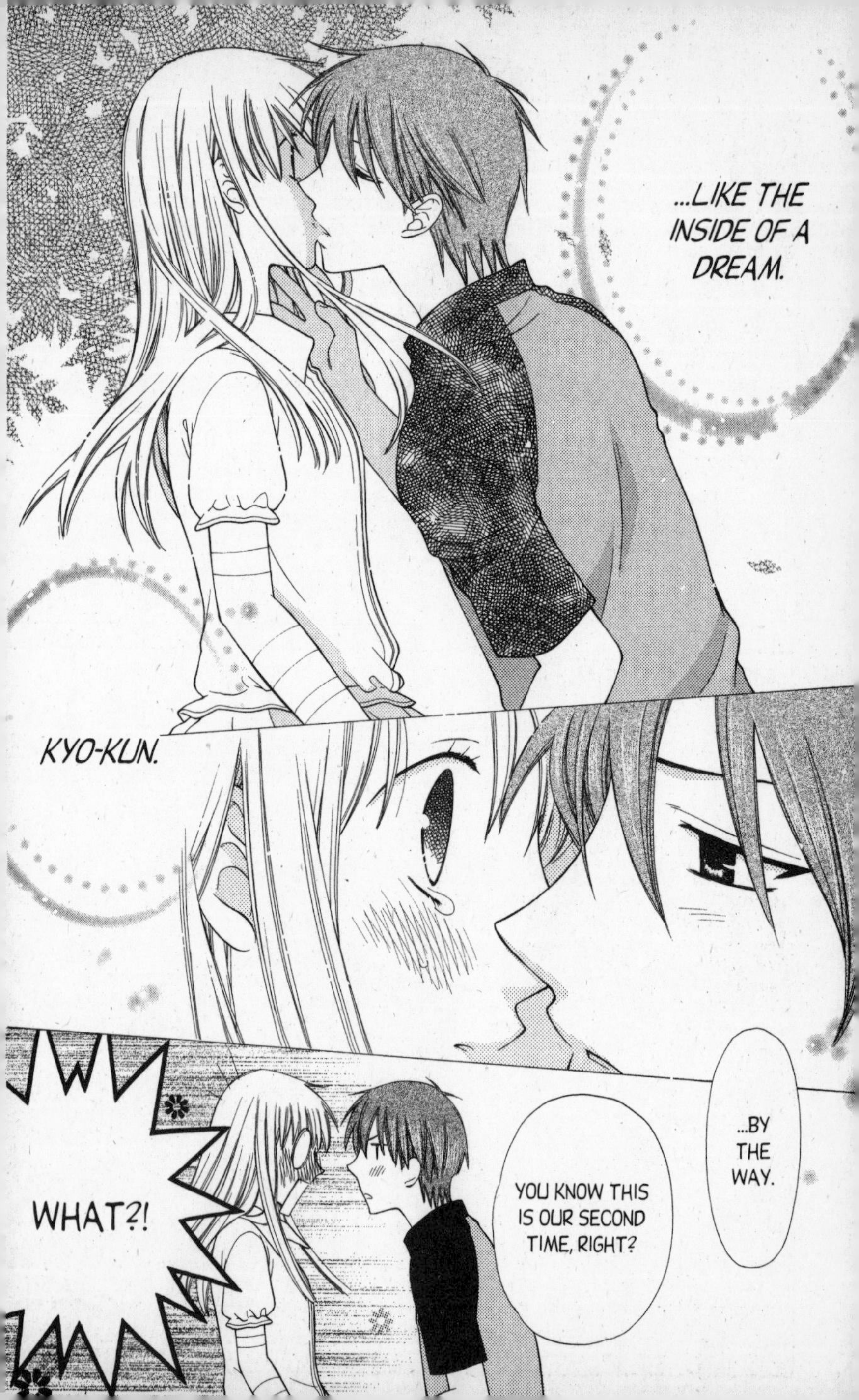
...LIKE THE INSIDE OF A DREAM.
KYO-KUN.
...BY THE WAY.
YOU KNOW THIS IS OUR SECOND TIME, RIGHT?
WHAT?!

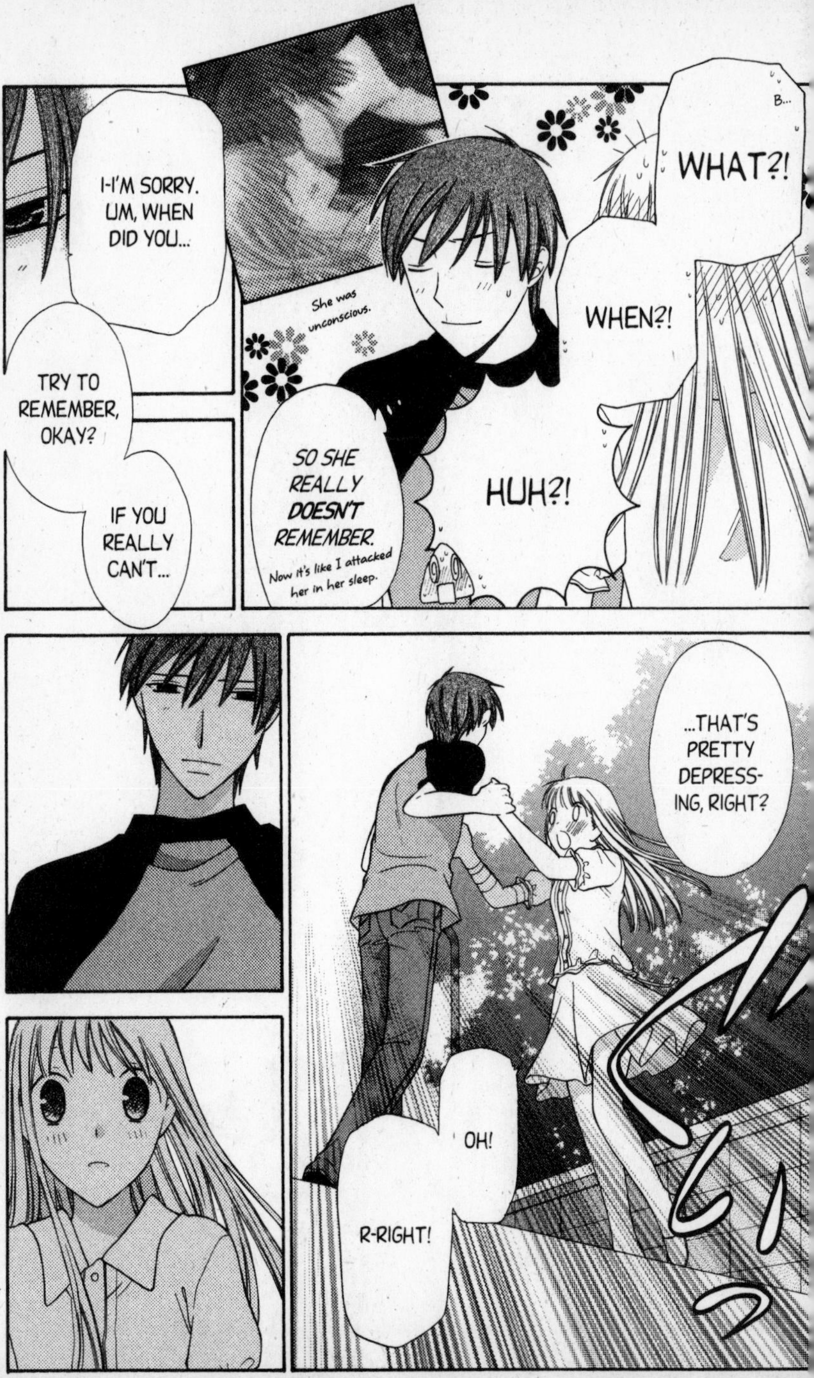
B...
WHAT?!
WHEN?!
She was unconscious.
HUH?!
SO SHE REALLY DOESN'T REMEMBER.
Now it's like I attacked her in her sleep.
I-I'M SORRY. UM, WHEN DID YOU...
TRY TO REMEMBER, OKAY?
IF YOU REALLY CAN'T...
...THAT'S PRETTY DEPRESSING, RIGHT?
OH!
R-RIGHT!

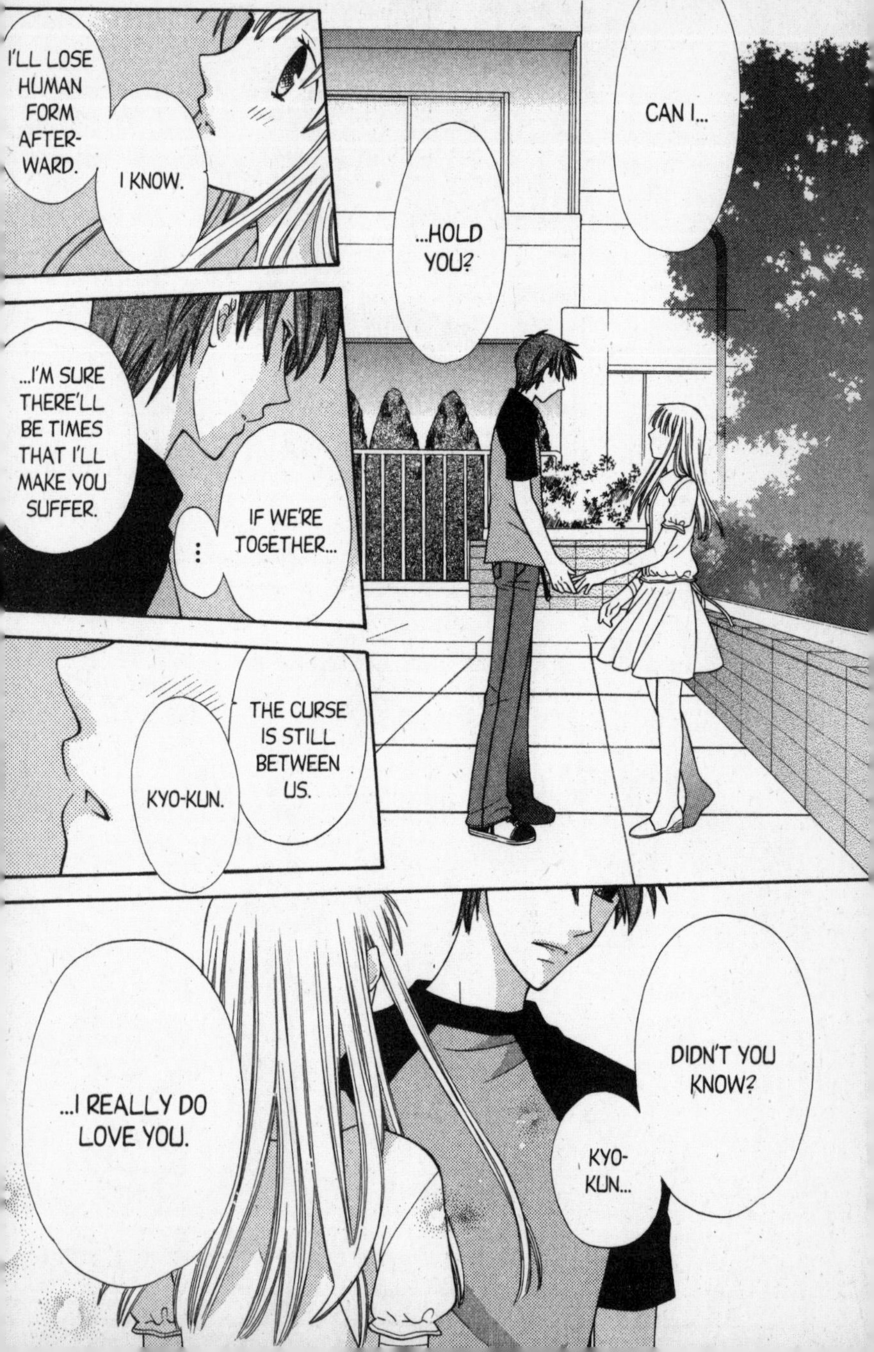
CAN I...
...HOLD YOU?
I'LL LOSE HUMAN FORM AFTER-WARD.
I KNOW.
IF WE'RE TOGETHER...
...
...I'M SURE THERE'LL BE TIMES THAT I'LL MAKE YOU SUFFER.
THE CURSE IS STILL BETWEEN US.
KYO-KUN.
DIDN'T YOU KNOW?
KYO-KUN...
...I REALLY DO LOVE YOU.

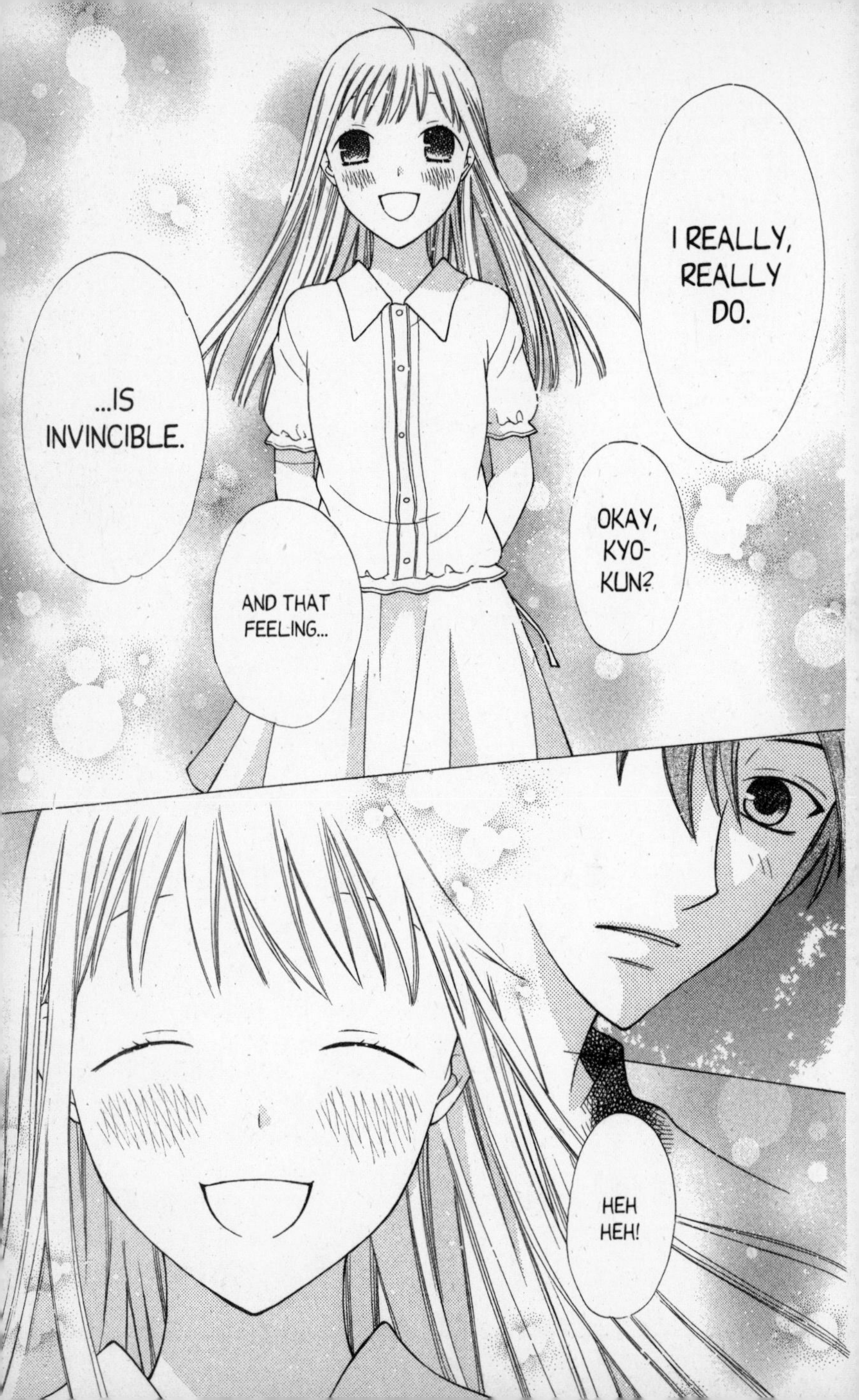
I REALLY, REALLY DO.
AND THAT FEELING...
...IS INVINCIBLE.
OKAY, KYO-KUN?
HEH HEH!

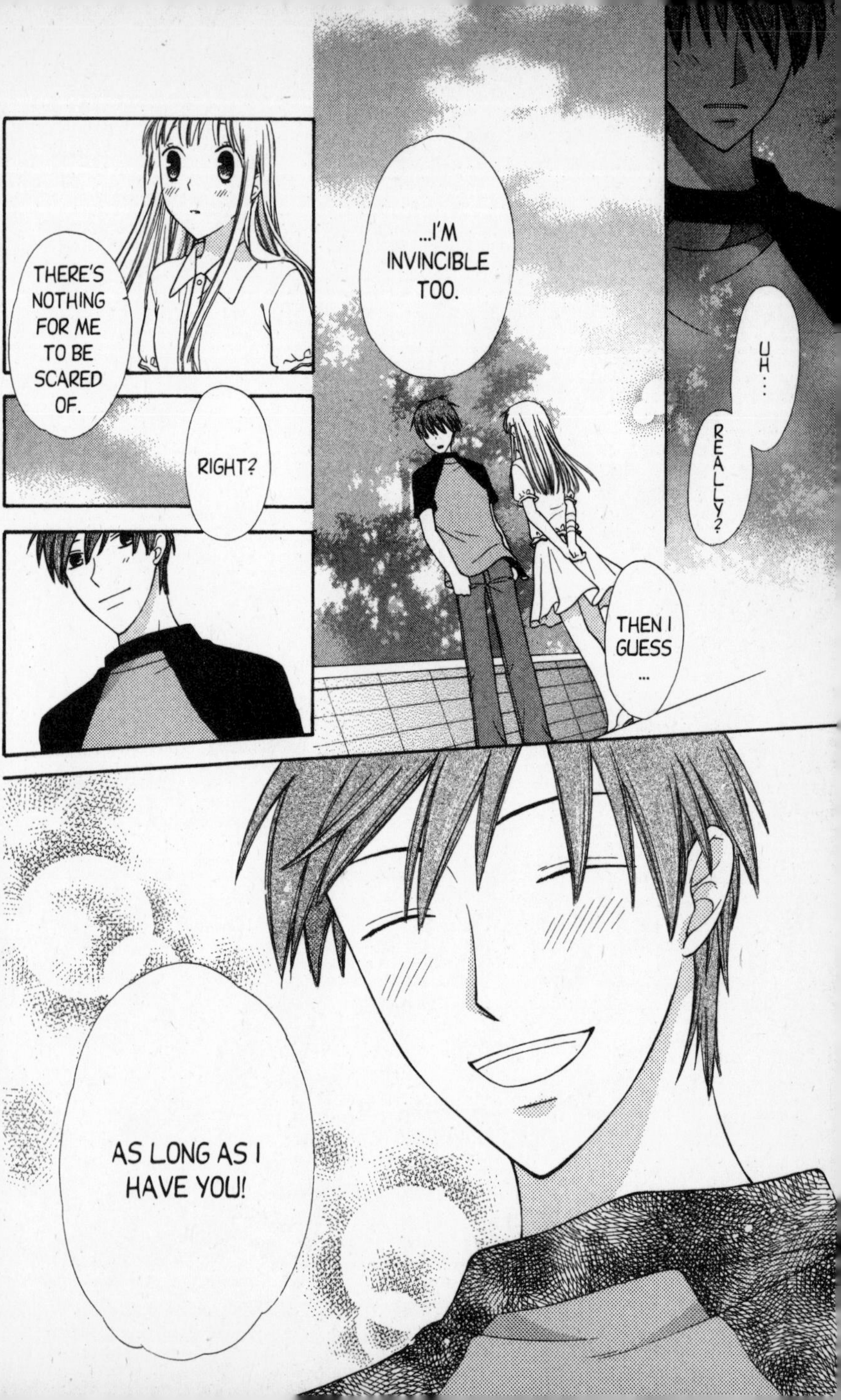
UH... REALLY?
...I'M INVINCIBLE TOO.
THERE'S NOTHING FOR ME TO BE SCARED OF.
RIGHT?
THEN I GUESS ...
AS LONG AS I HAVE YOU!

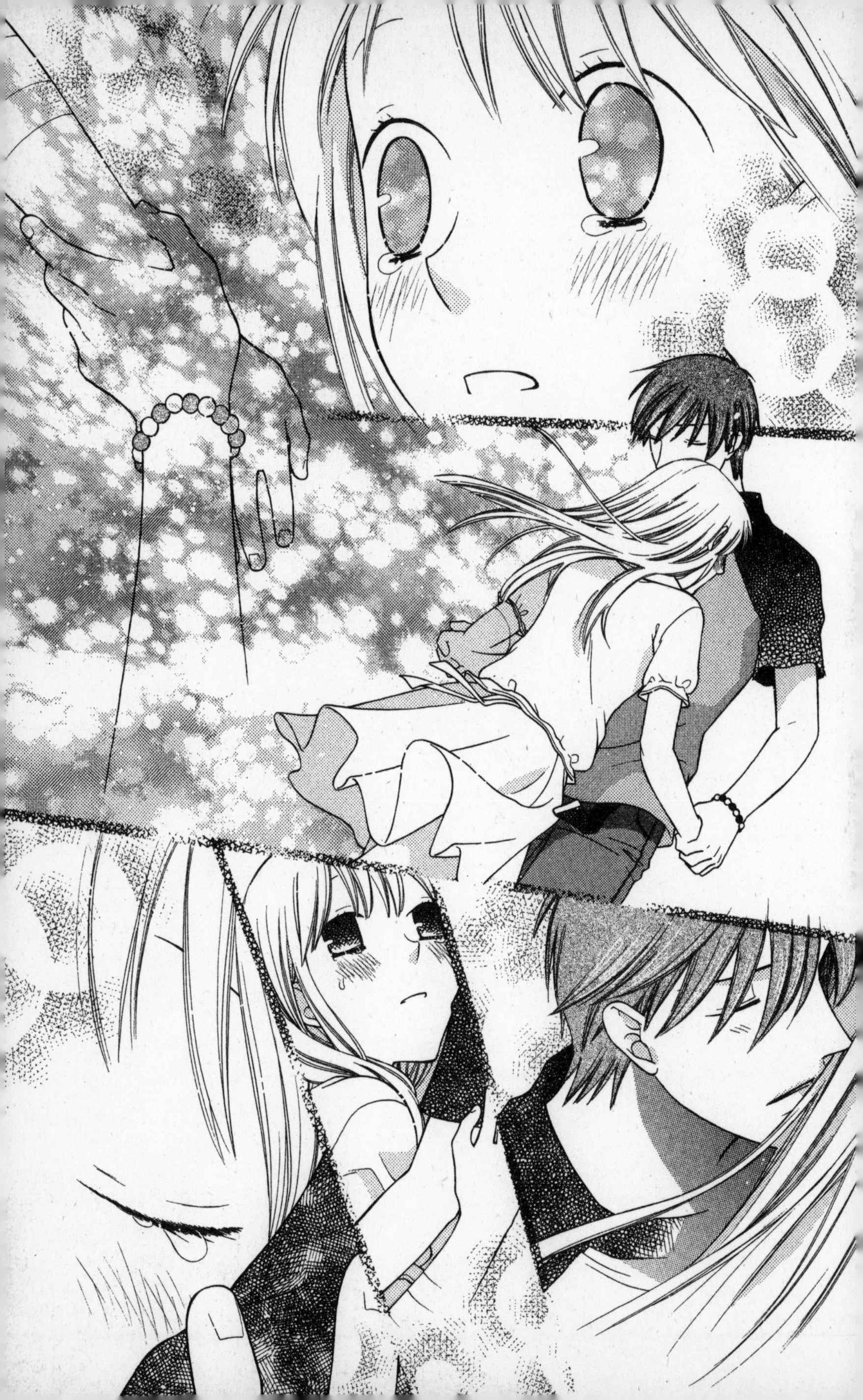

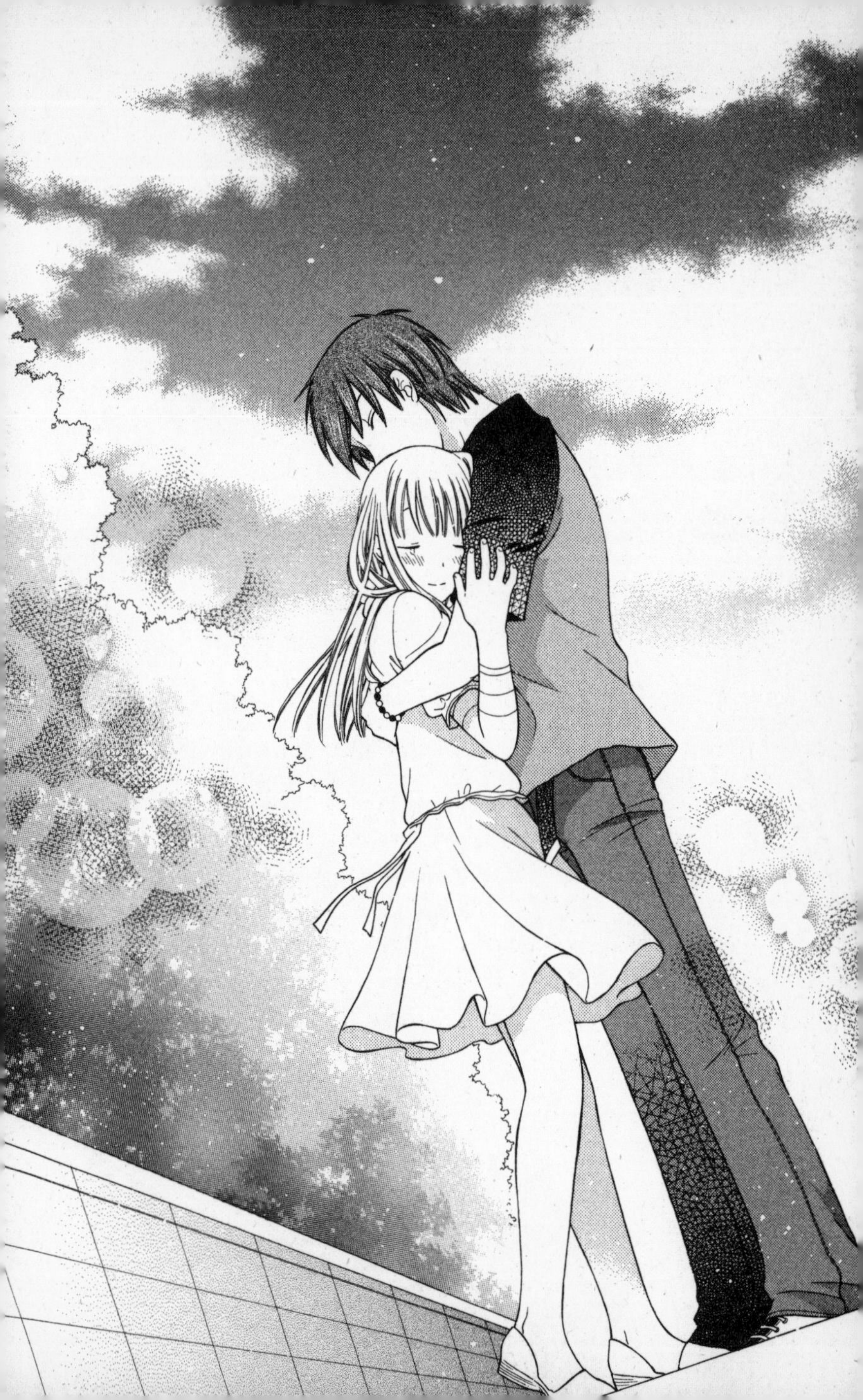

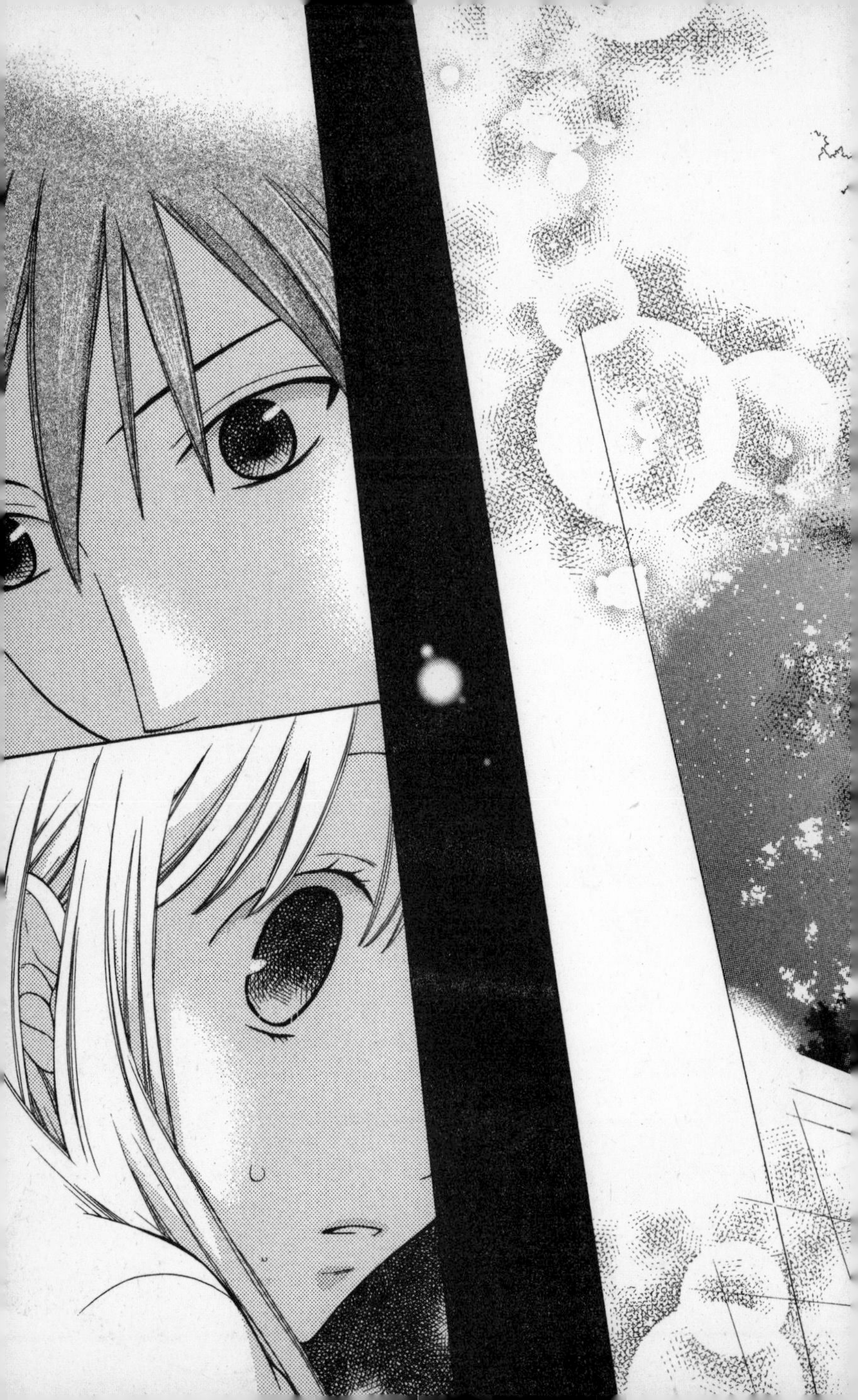

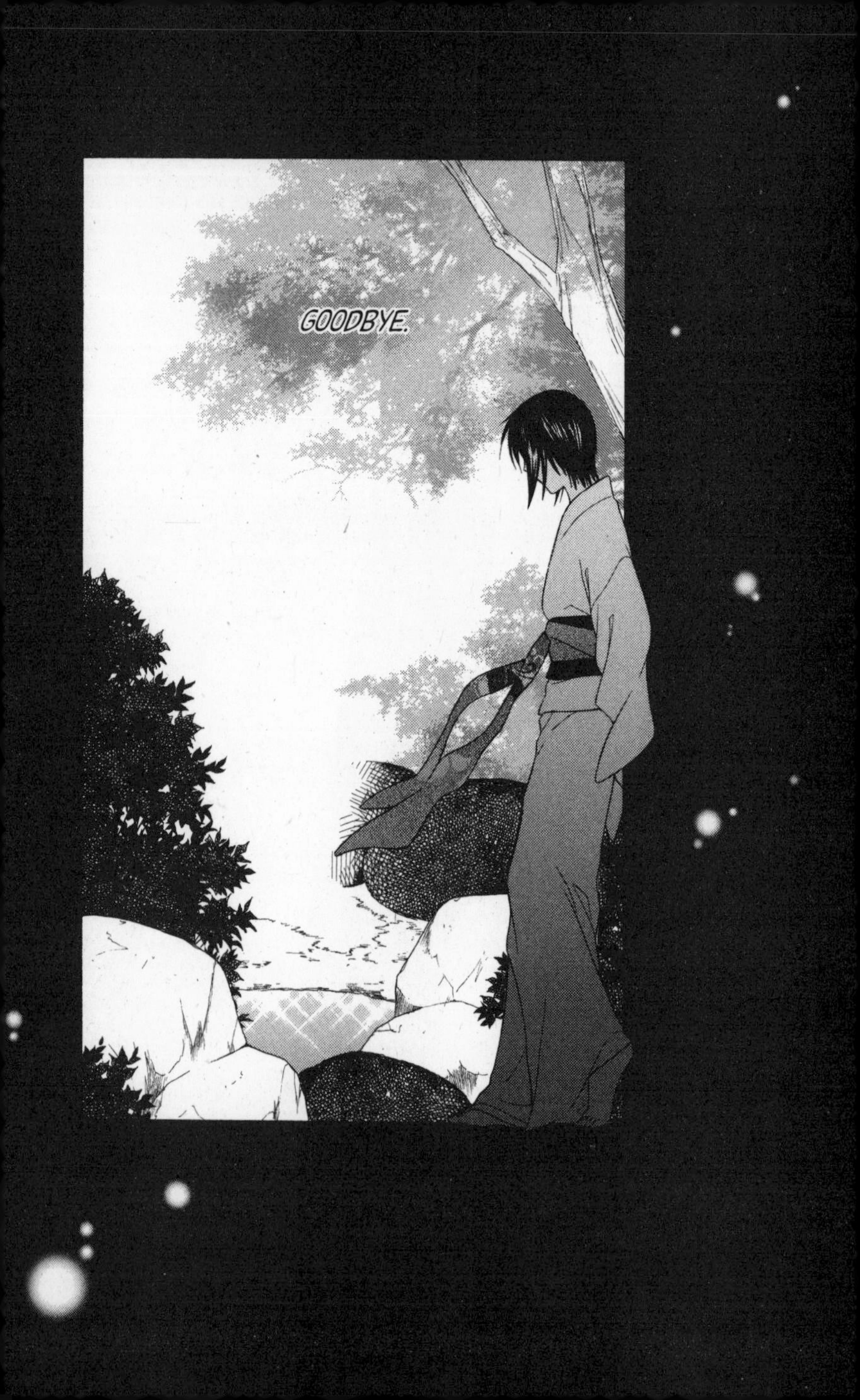
GOODBYE.

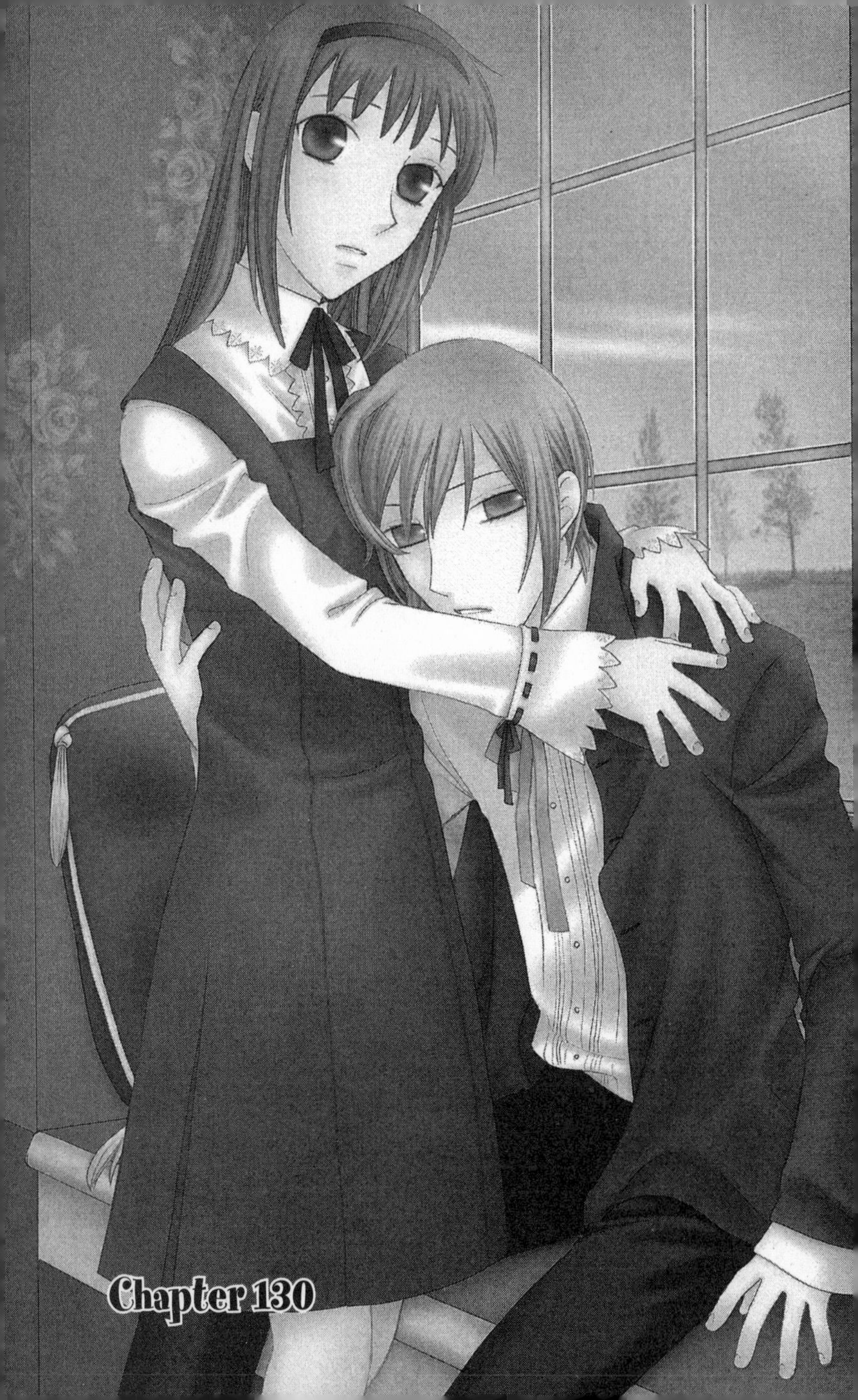
Chapter 130

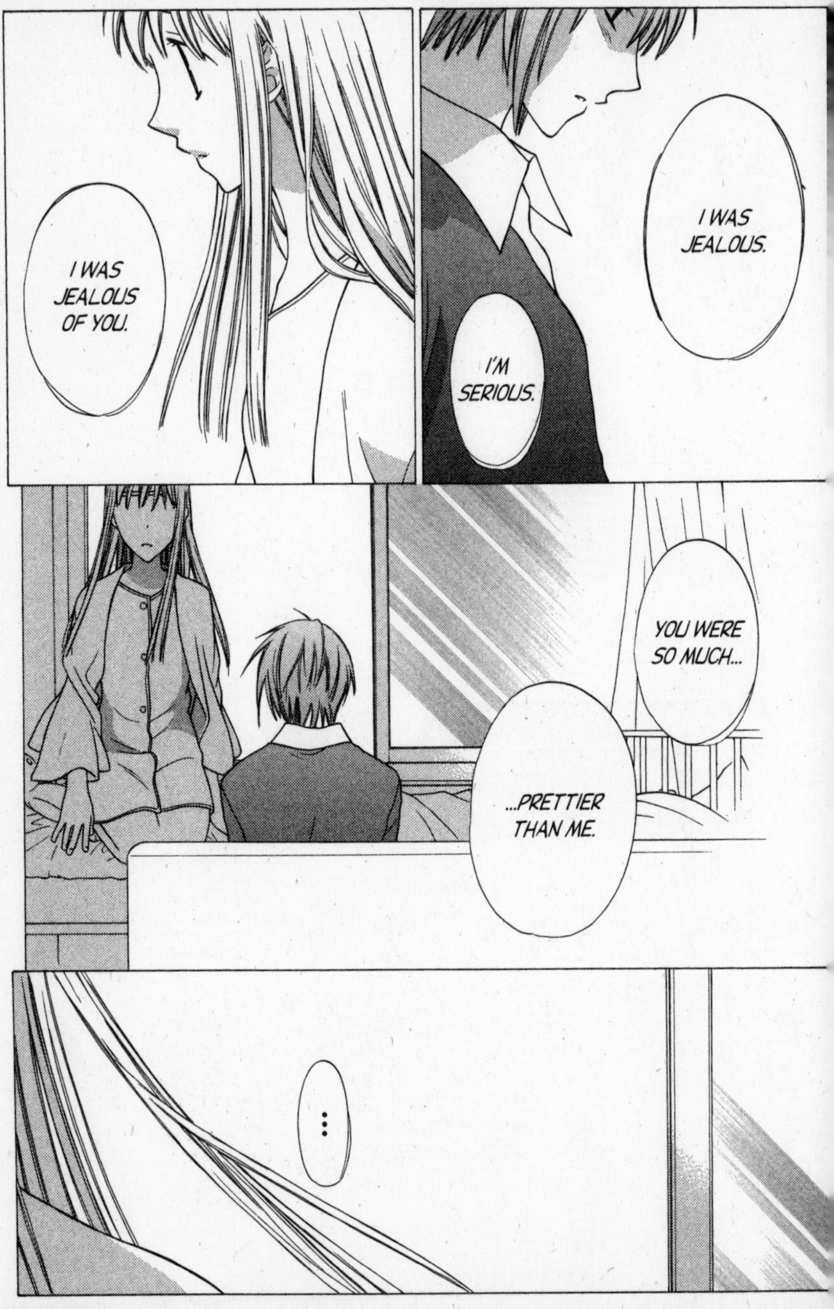
I WAS JEALOUS.
I'M SERIOUS.
I WAS JEALOUS OF YOU.
YOU WERE SO MUCH...
...PRETTIER THAN ME.
...

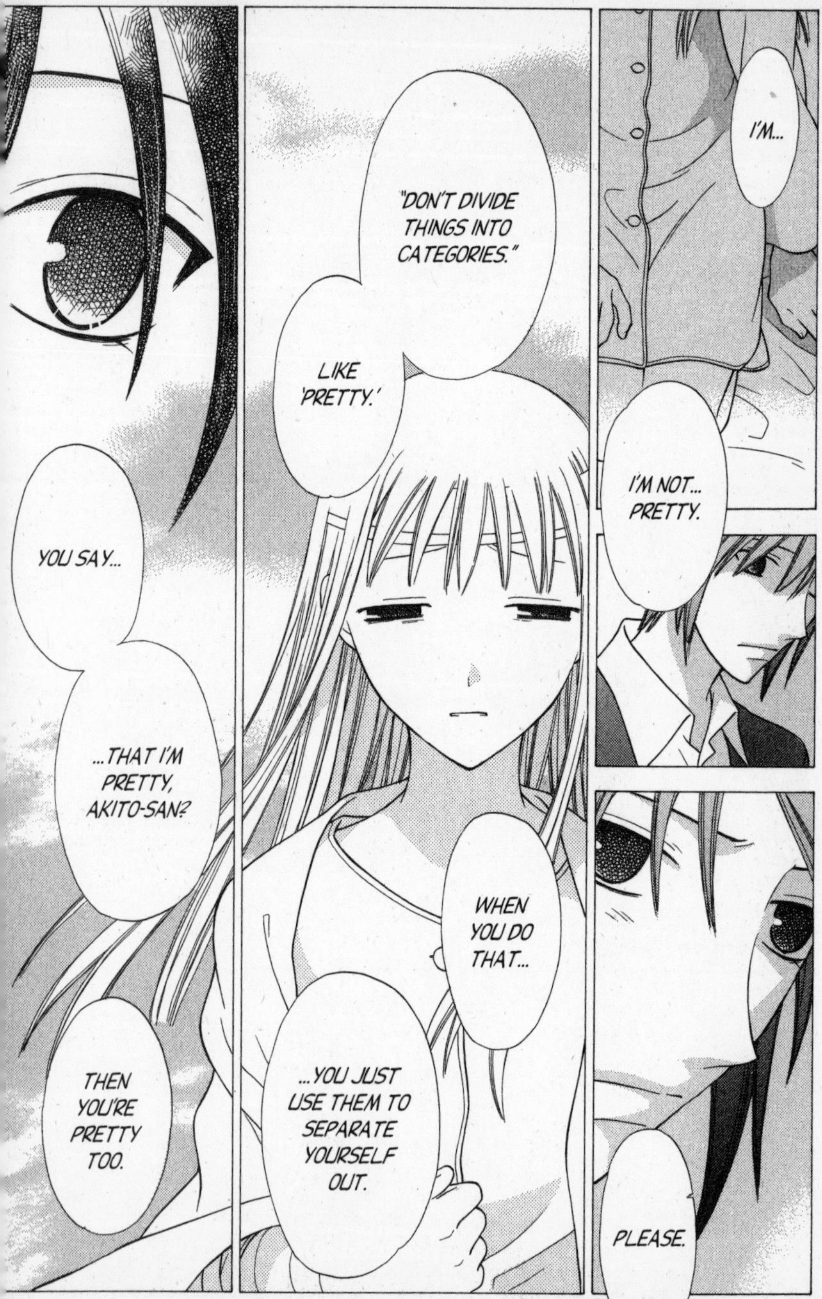
I'M...
I'M NOT... PRETTY.
PLEASE.
"DON'T DIVIDE THINGS INTO CATEGORIES."
LIKE 'PRETTY.'
WHEN YOU DO THAT...
...YOU JUST USE THEM TO SEPARATE YOURSELF OUT.
YOU SAY...
...THAT I'M PRETTY, AKITO-SAN?
THEN YOU'RE PRETTY TOO.

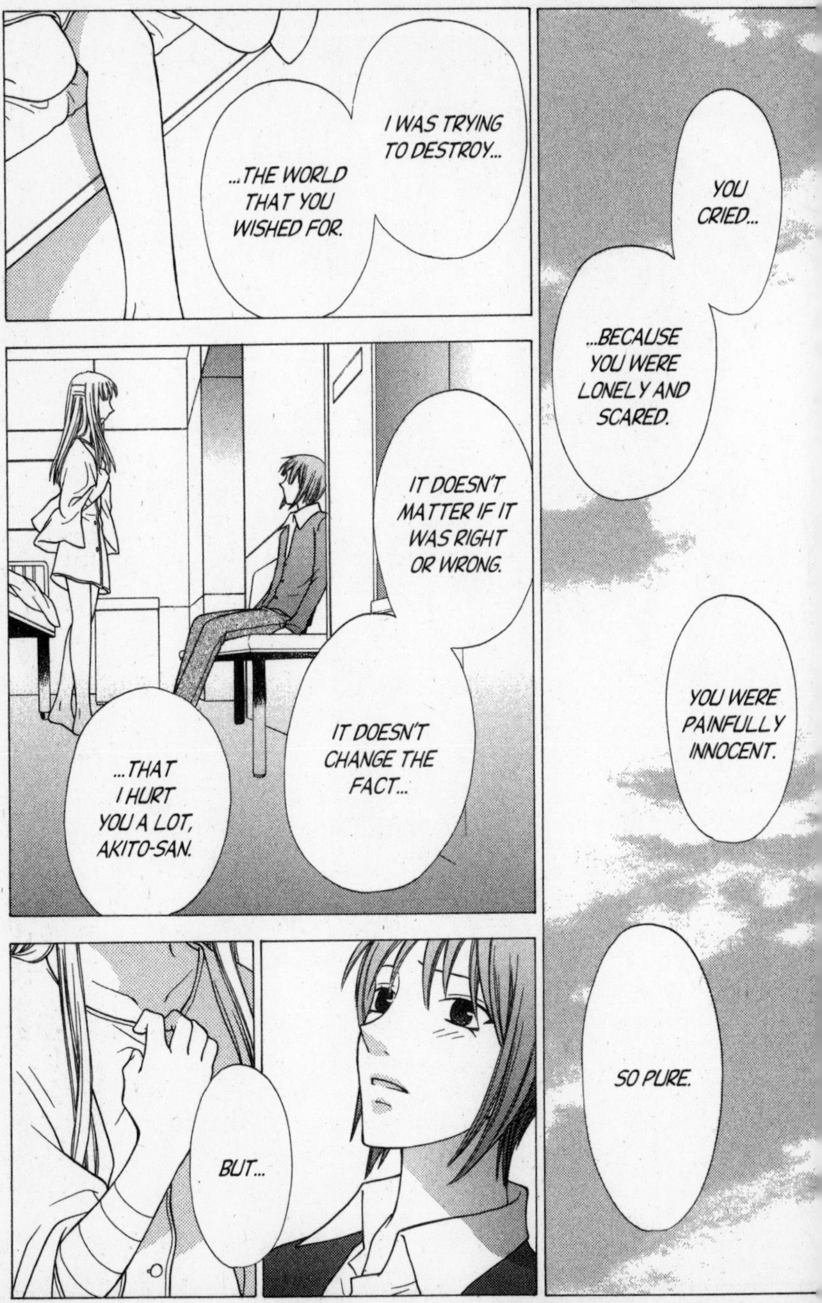
YOU CRIED...
...BECAUSE YOU WERE LONELY AND SCARED.
YOU WERE PAINFULLY INNOCENT.
SO PURE.
I WAS TRYING TO DESTROY...
...THE WORLD THAT YOU WISHED FOR.
IT DOESN'T MATTER IF IT WAS RIGHT OR WRONG.
IT DOESN'T CHANGE THE FACT...
...THAT I HURT YOU A LOT, AKITO-SAN.
BUT...

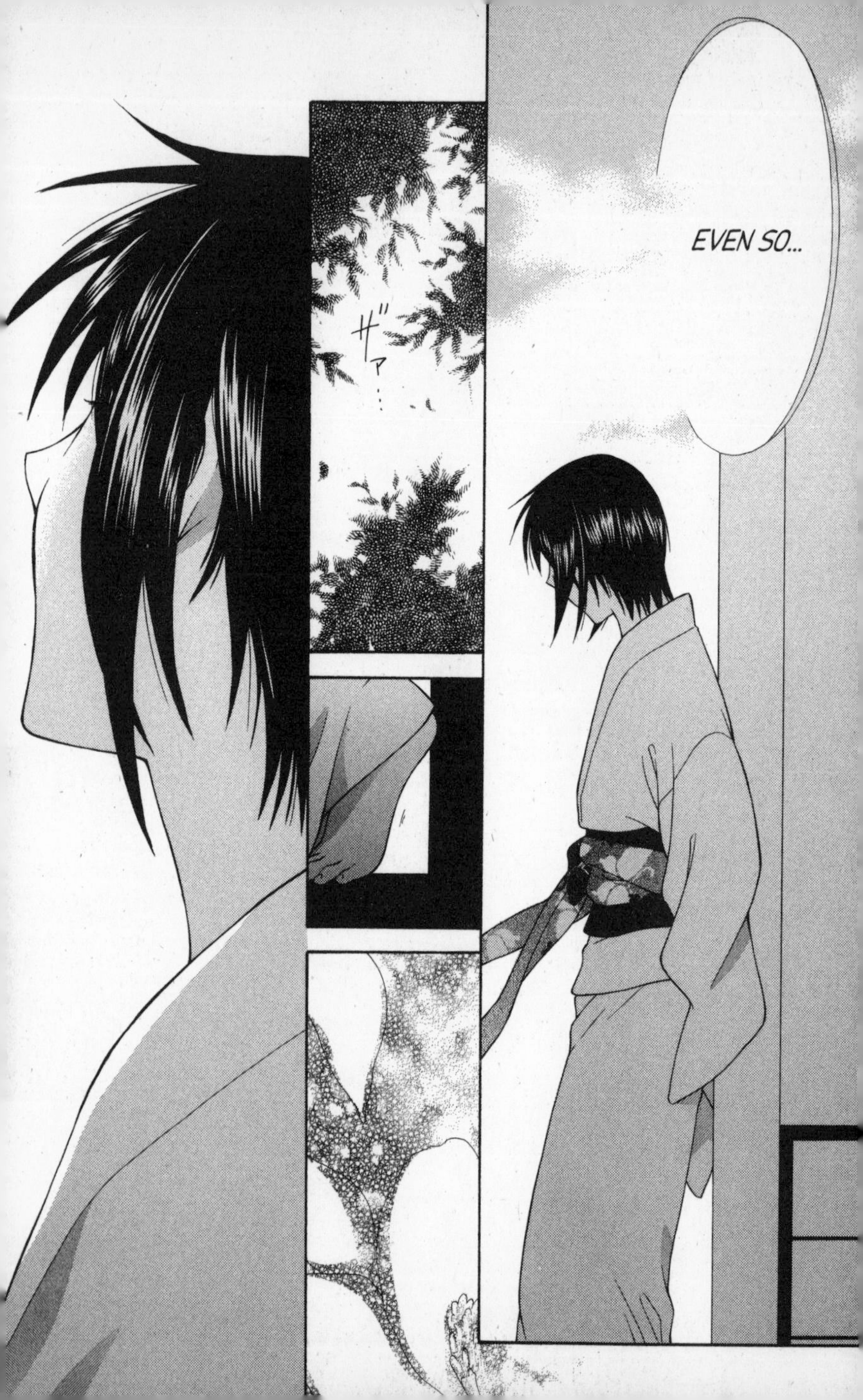
EVEN SO...
ザァ…

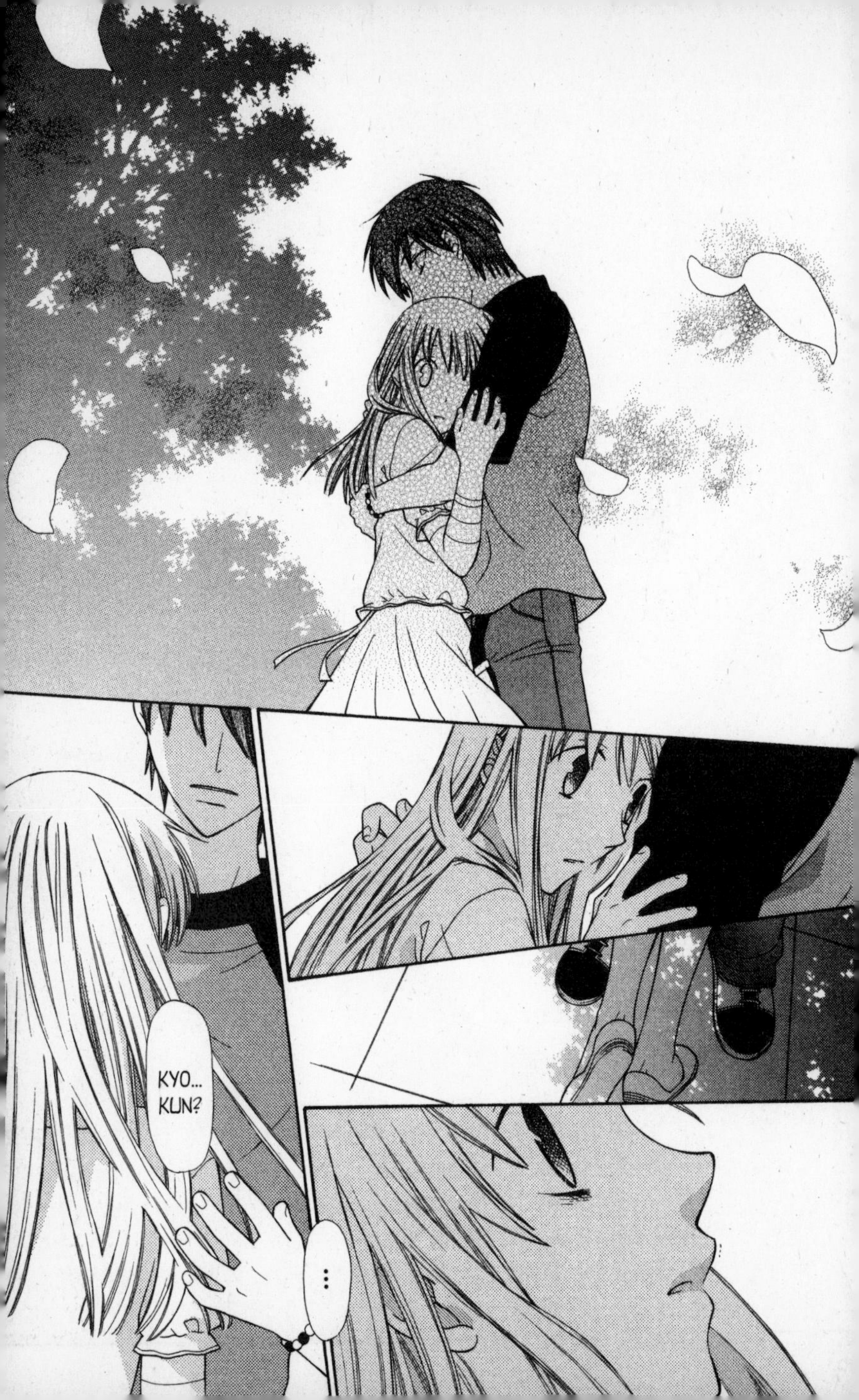
KYO... KUN?
...

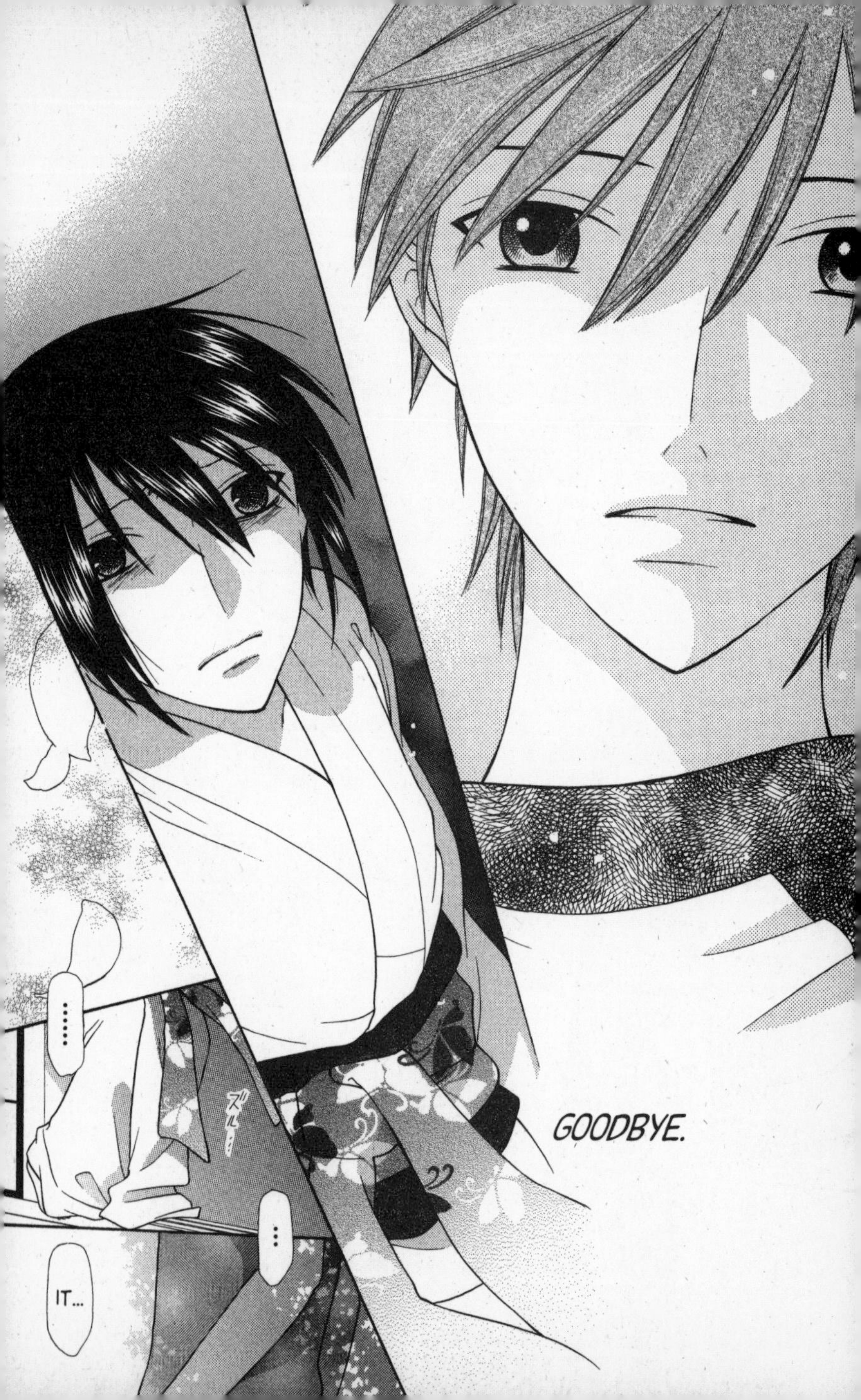
GOODBYE.
......
ズル…
...
IT...

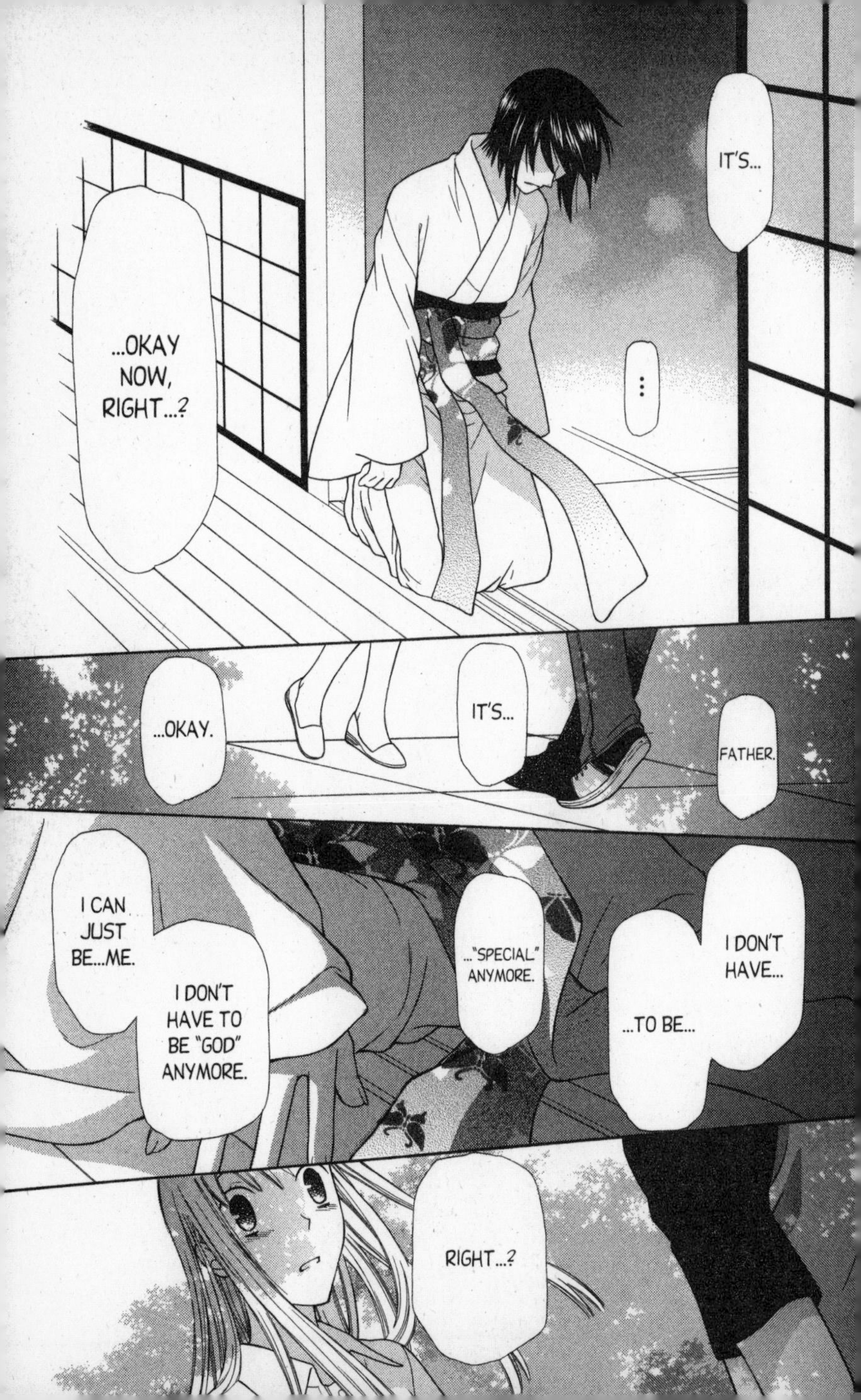
IT'S...
...
...OKAY NOW, RIGHT...?
FATHER.
IT'S...
...OKAY.
I DON'T HAVE...
...TO BE...
..."SPECIAL" ANYMORE.
I DON'T HAVE TO BE "GOD" ANYMORE.
I CAN JUST BE...ME.
RIGHT...?

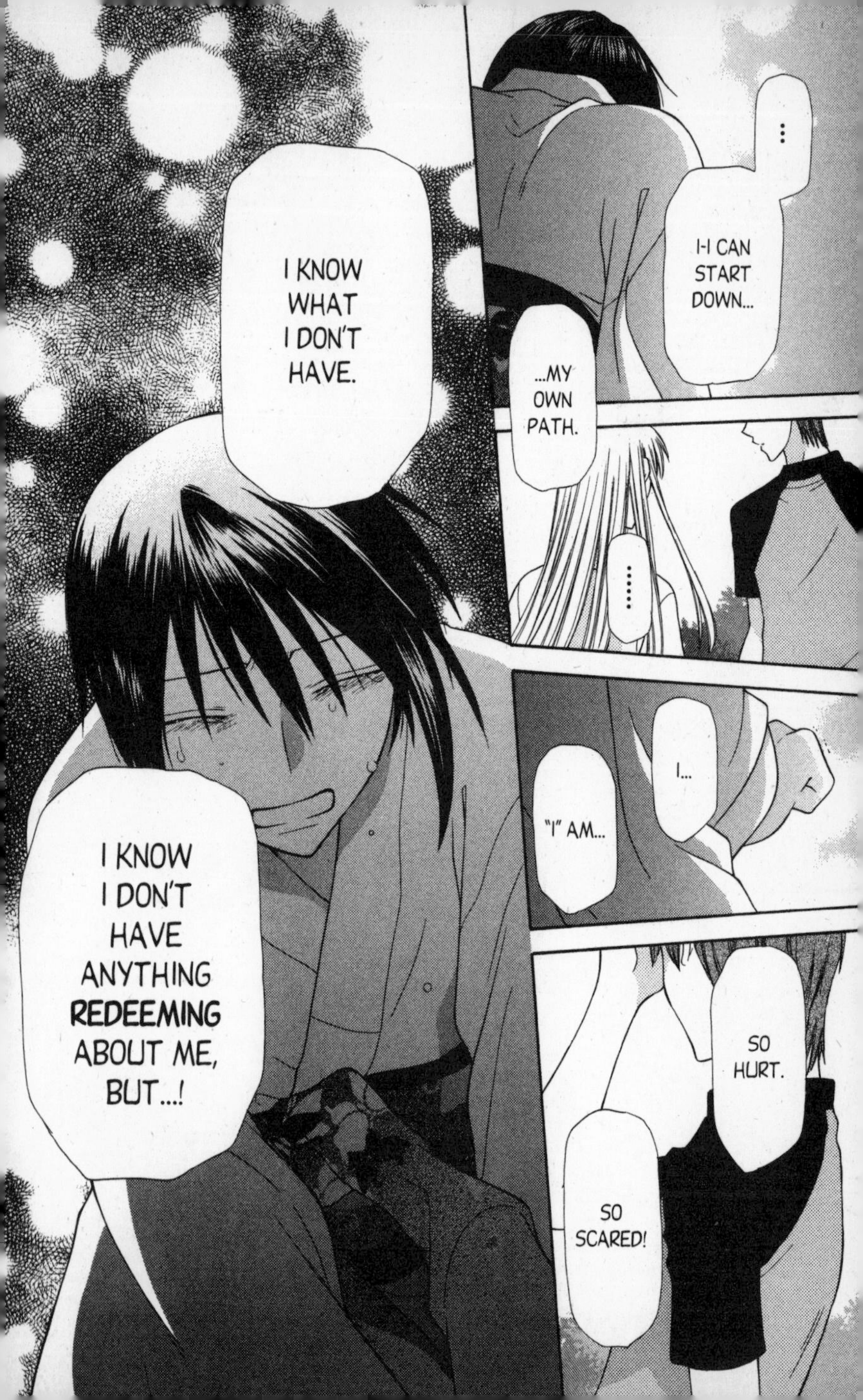
...
I-I CAN START DOWN...
...MY OWN PATH.
......
I...
"I" AM...
SO HURT.
SO SCARED!
I KNOW WHAT I DON'T HAVE.
I KNOW I DON'T HAVE ANYTHING **REDEEMING** ABOUT ME, BUT...!

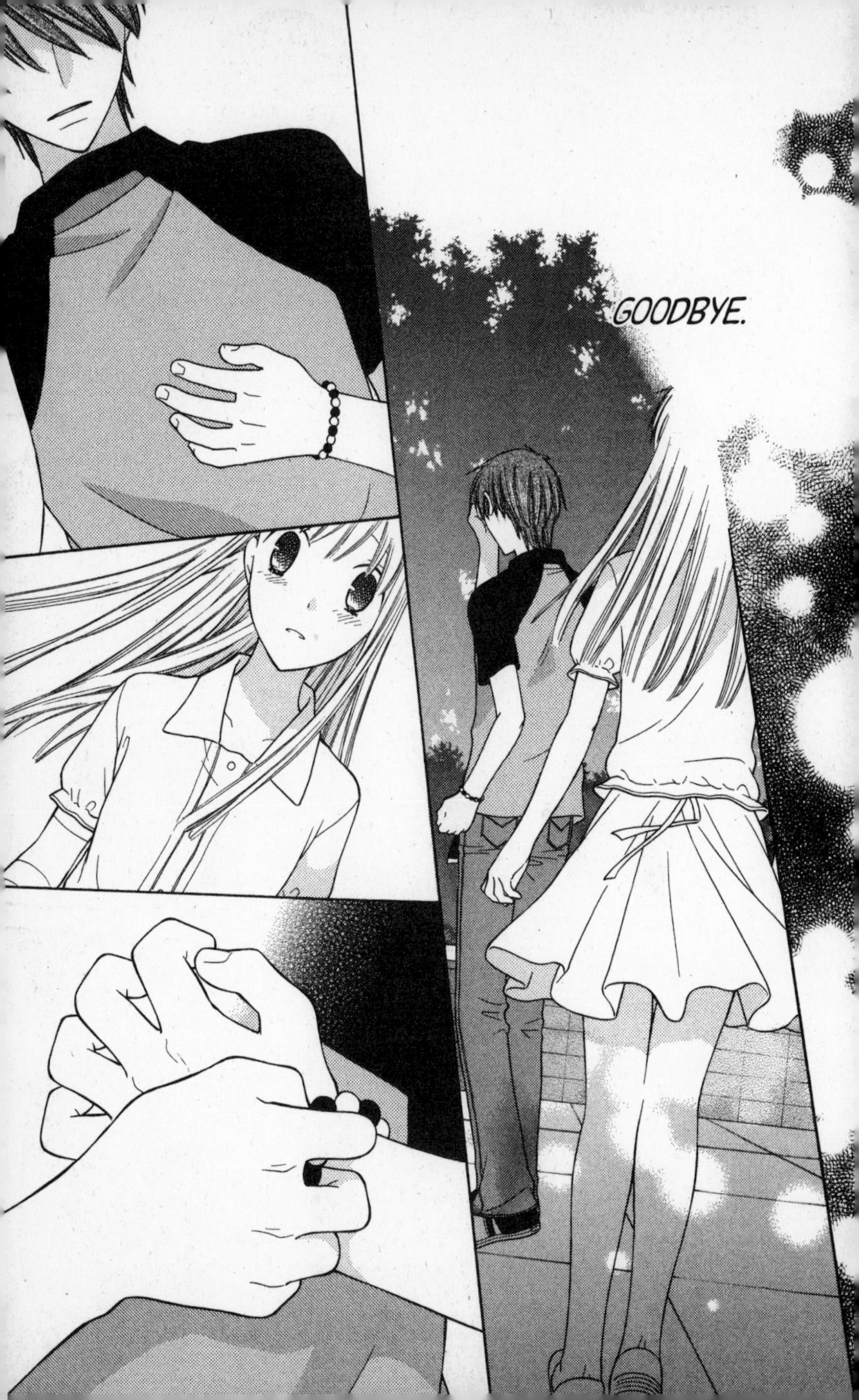
GOODBYE.

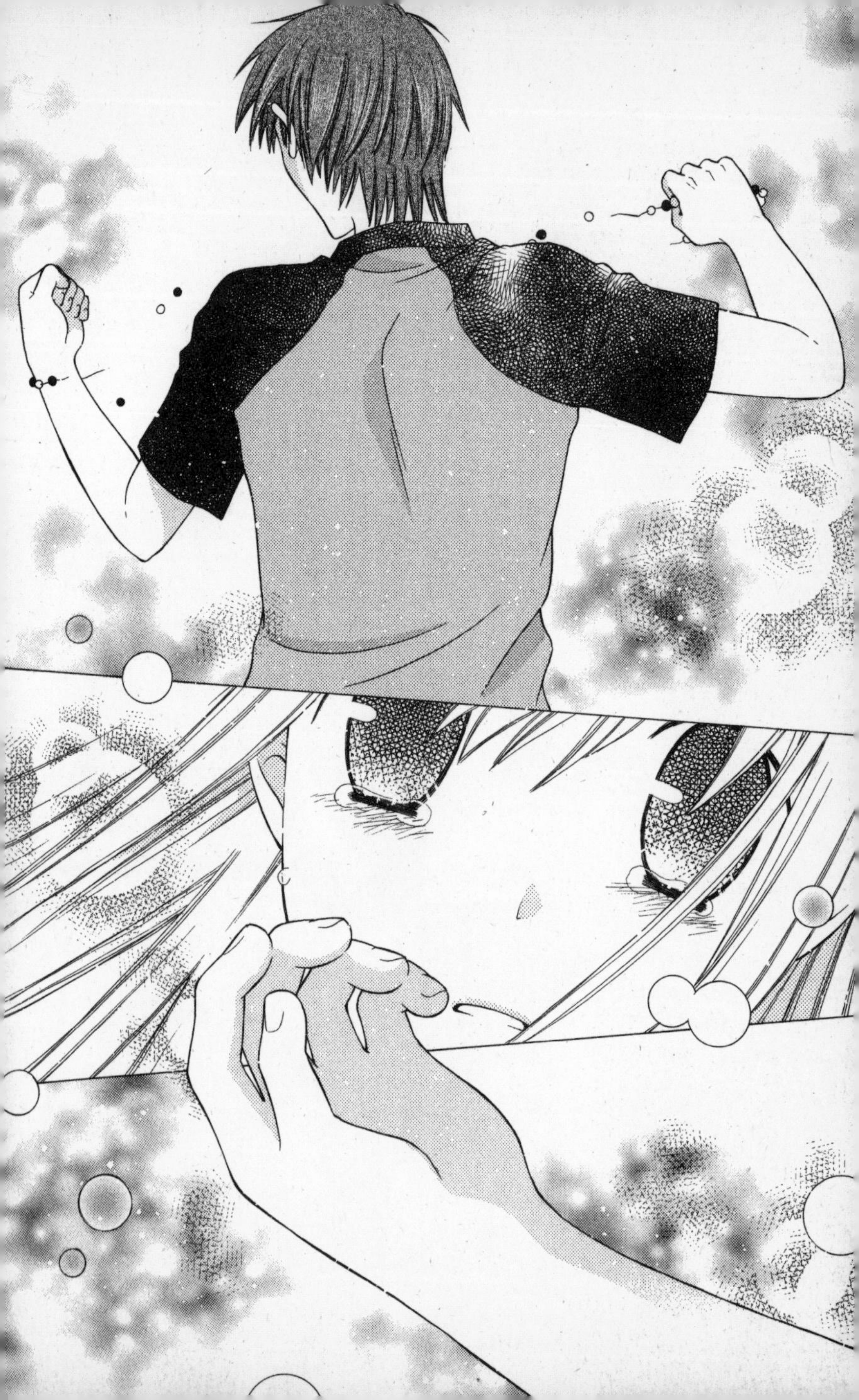

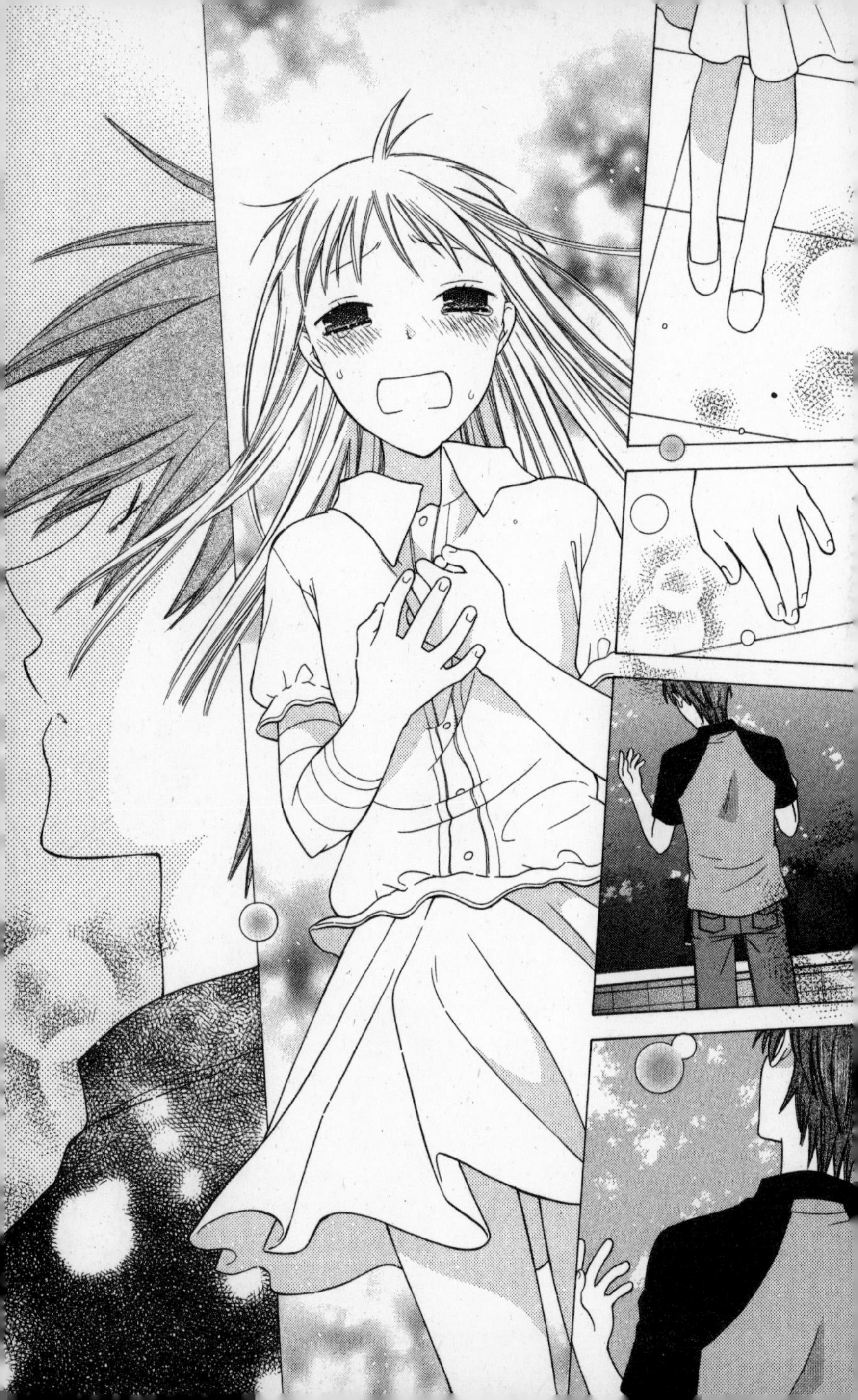

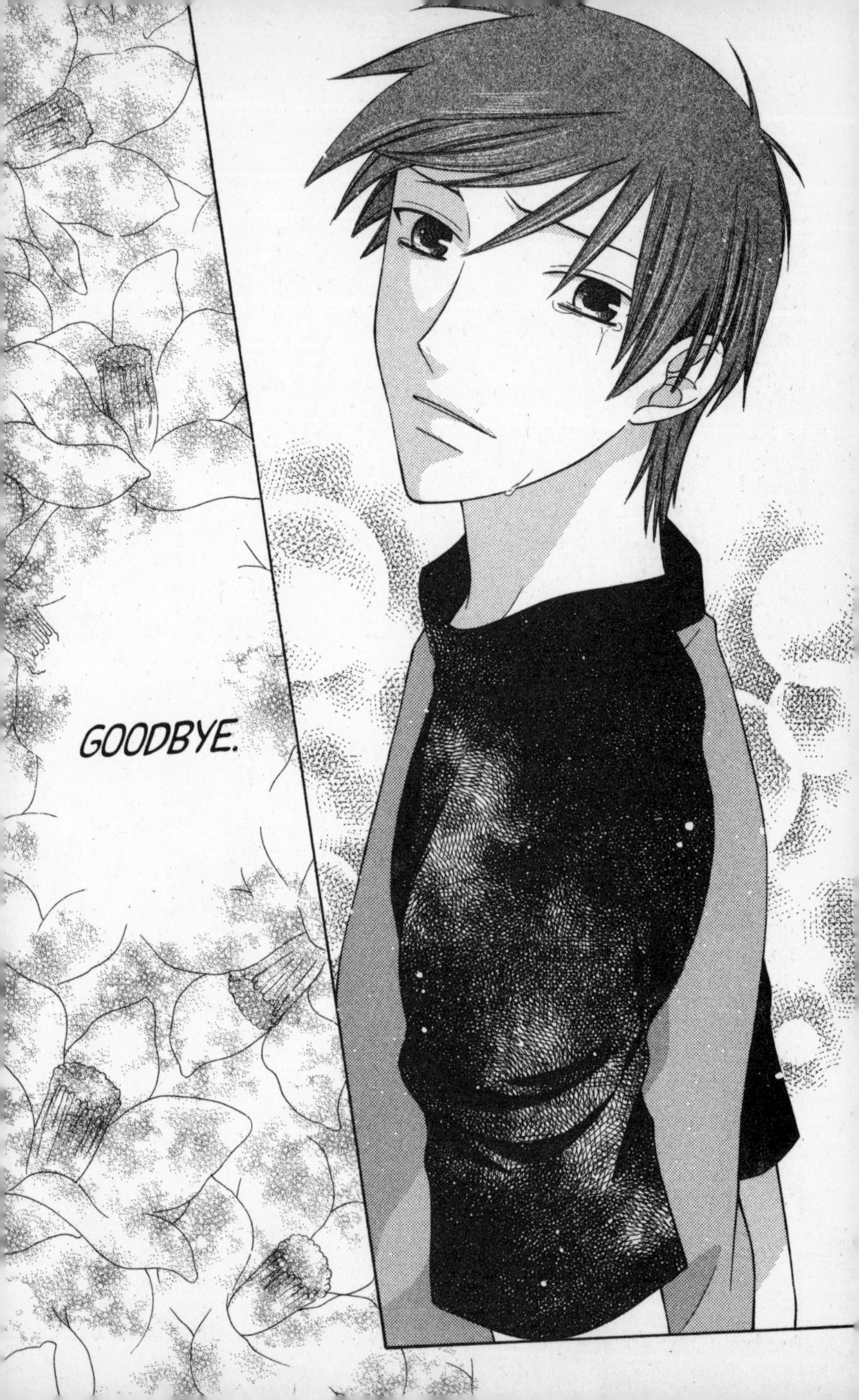
GOODBYE.

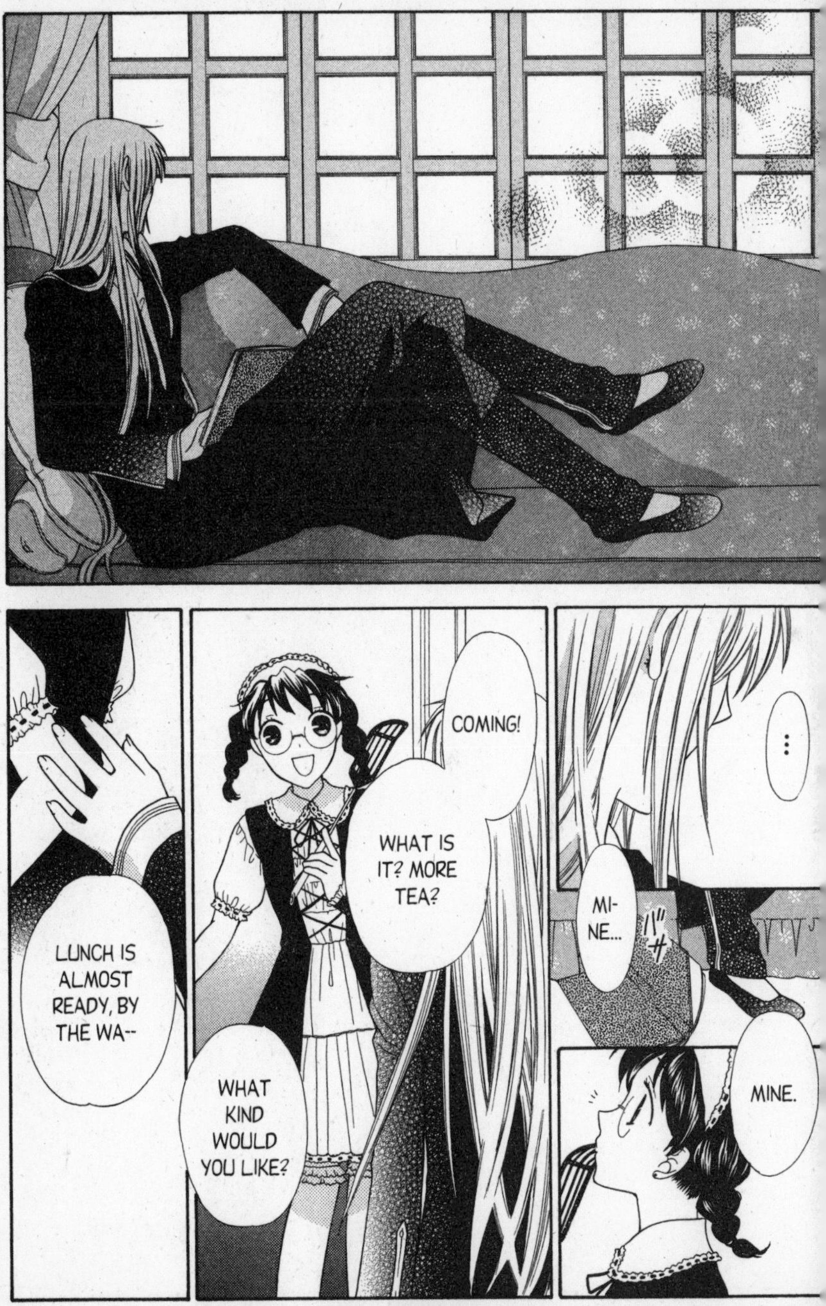
...
MI- NE...
バサ
MINE.
COMING!
WHAT IS IT? MORE TEA?
WHAT KIND WOULD YOU LIKE?
LUNCH IS ALMOST READY, BY THE WA--

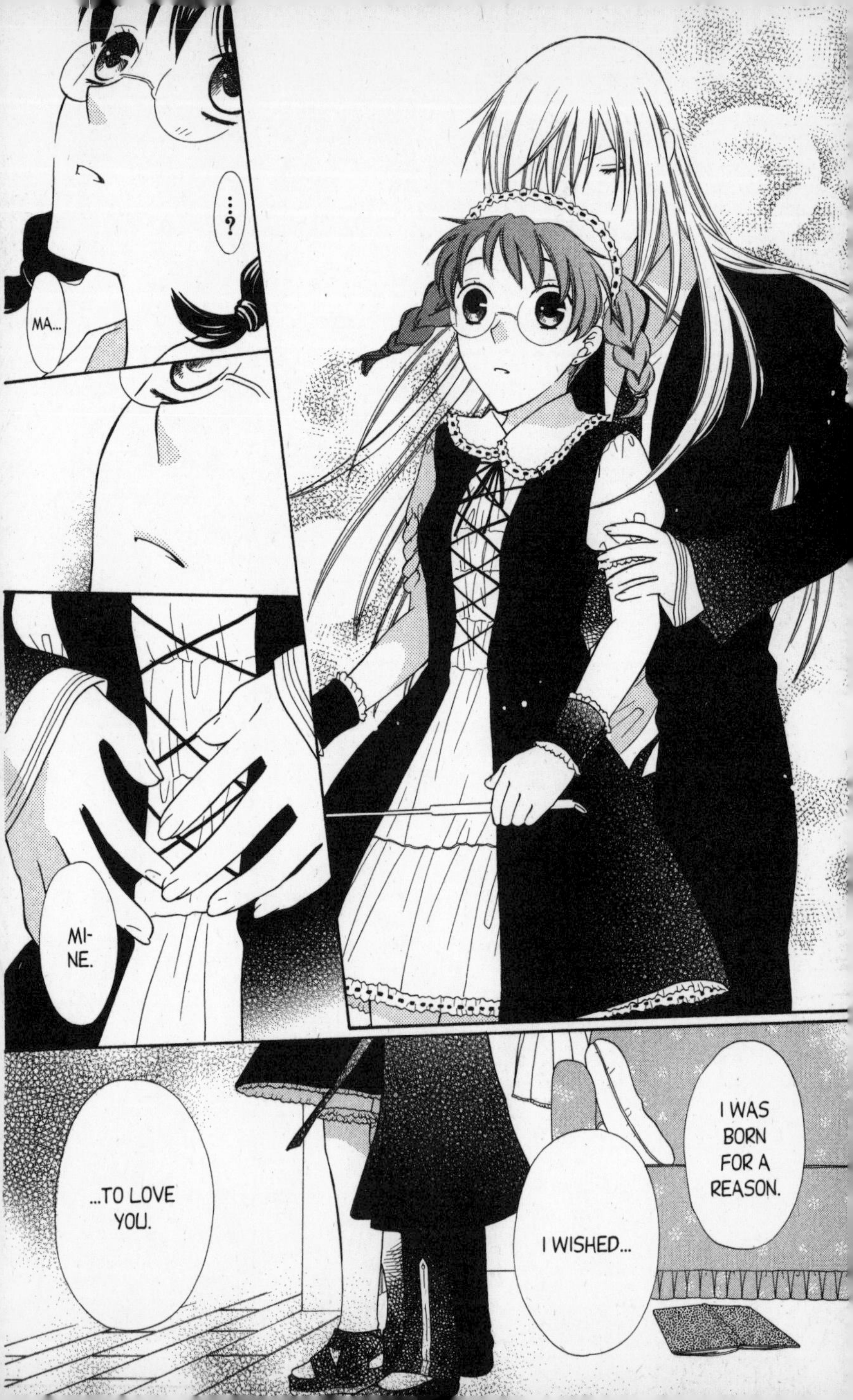
...?
MA...
MI-NE.
I WAS BORN FOR A REASON.
I WISHED...
...TO LOVE YOU.

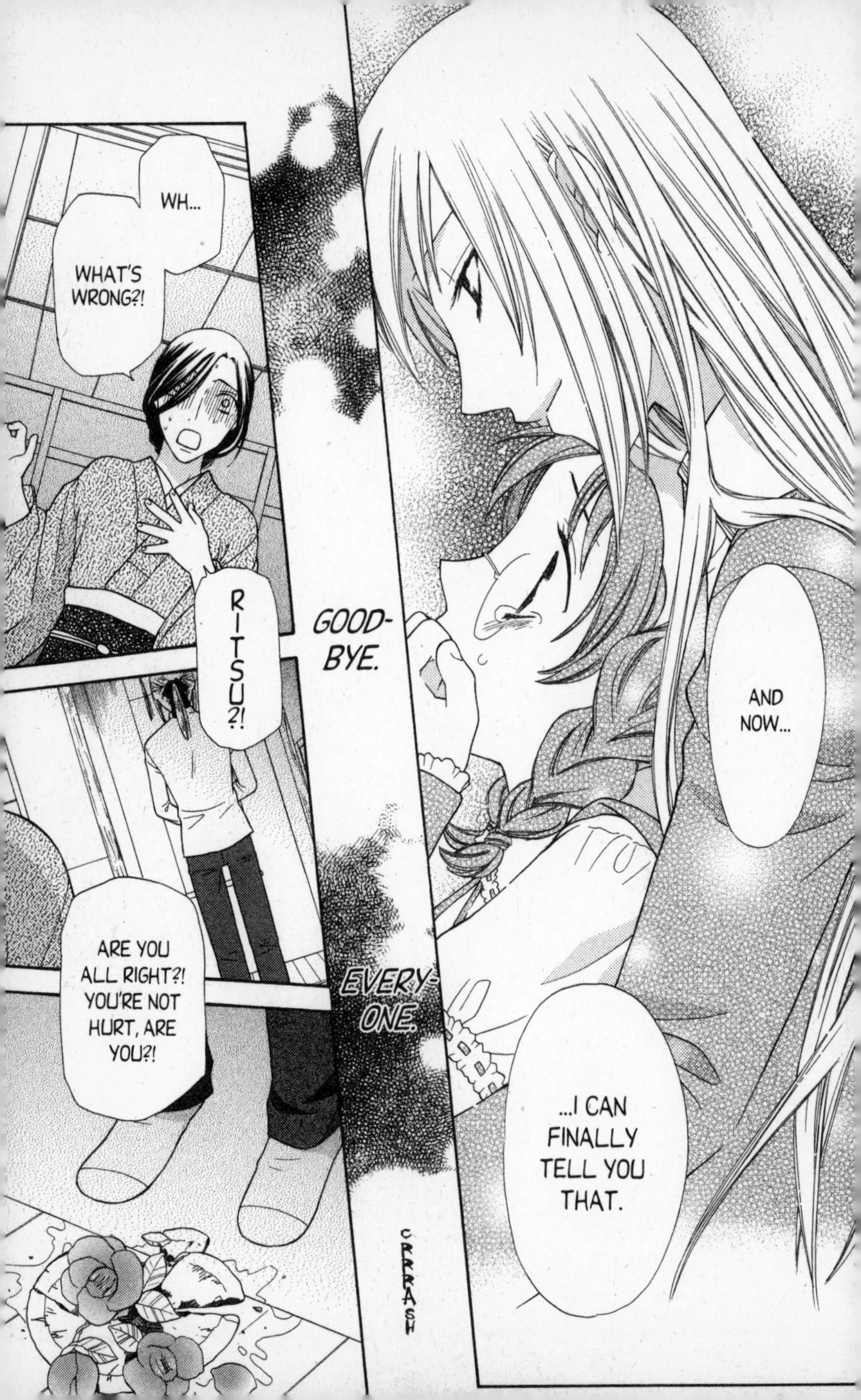
AND NOW...
...I CAN FINALLY TELL YOU THAT.
GOOD-BYE.
EVERY-ONE.
CRRRASH
WH...
WHAT'S WRONG?!
RITSU?!
ARE YOU ALL RIGHT?! YOU'RE NOT HURT, ARE YOU?!

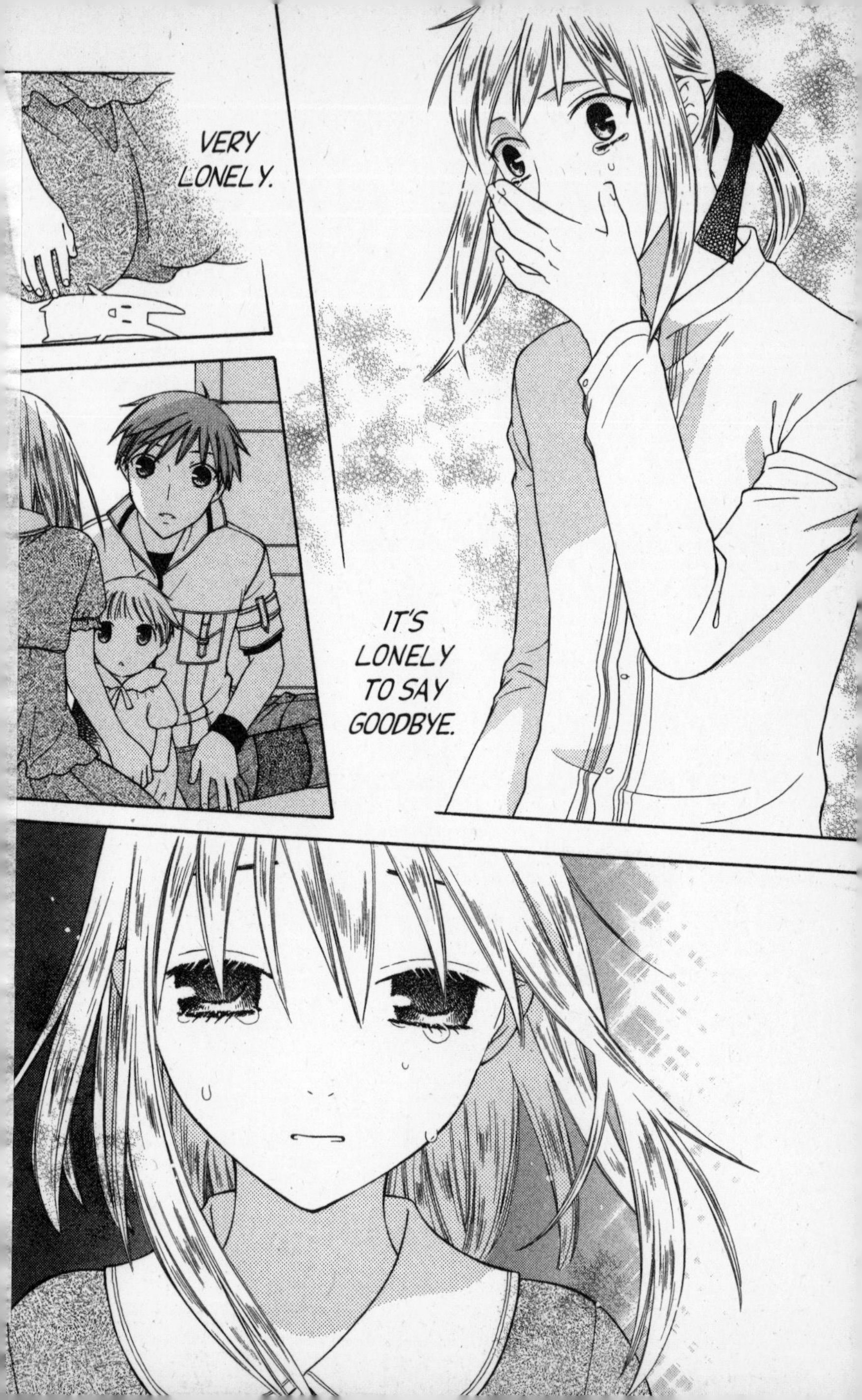
IT'S LONELY TO SAY GOODBYE.
VERY LONELY.

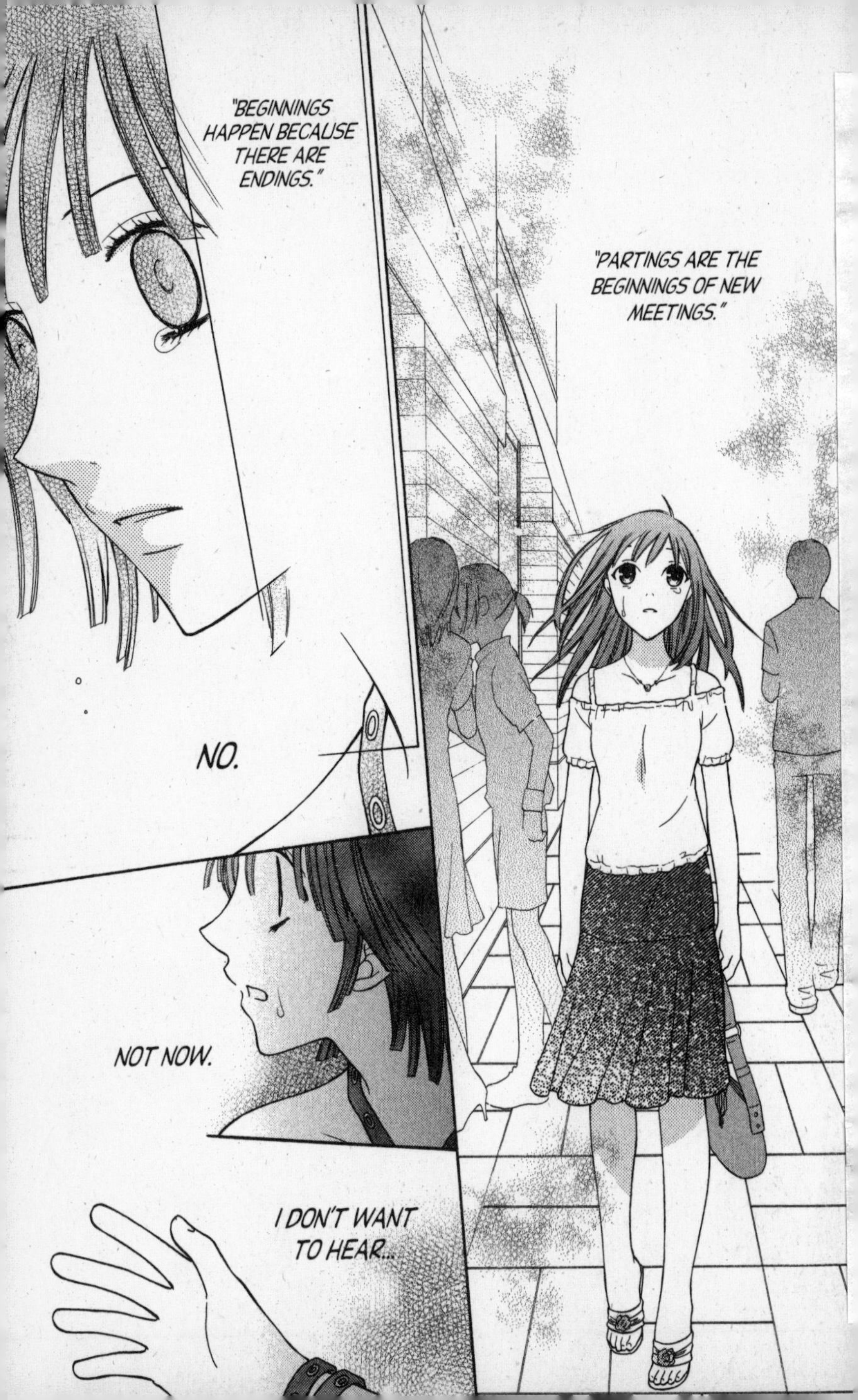
"PARTINGS ARE THE BEGINNINGS OF NEW MEETINGS."
"BEGINNINGS HAPPEN BECAUSE THERE ARE ENDINGS."
NO.
NOT NOW.
I DON'T WANT TO HEAR...

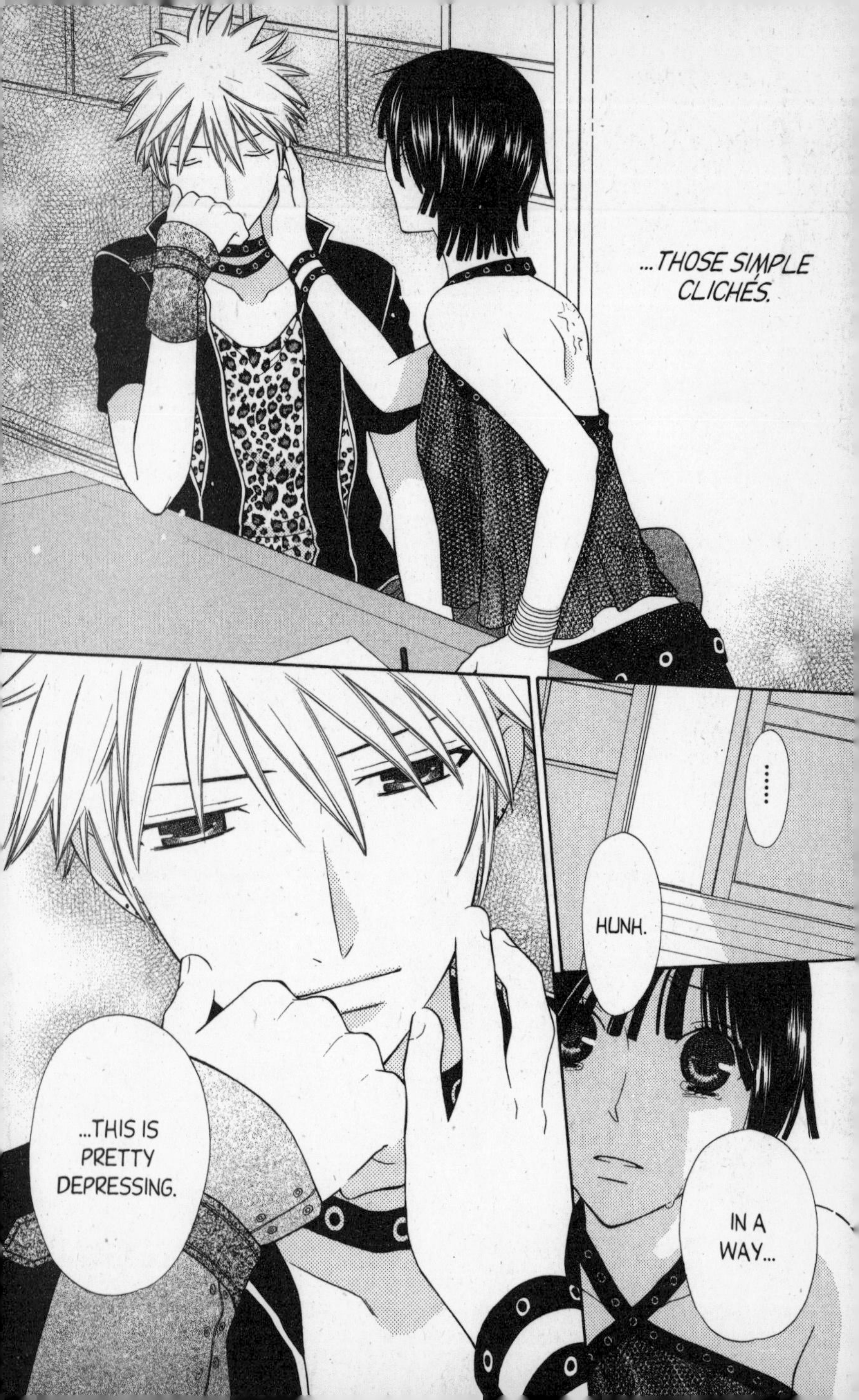

...THOSE SIMPLE CLICHÉS.
......
HUNH.
IN A WAY...
...THIS IS PRETTY DEPRESSING.

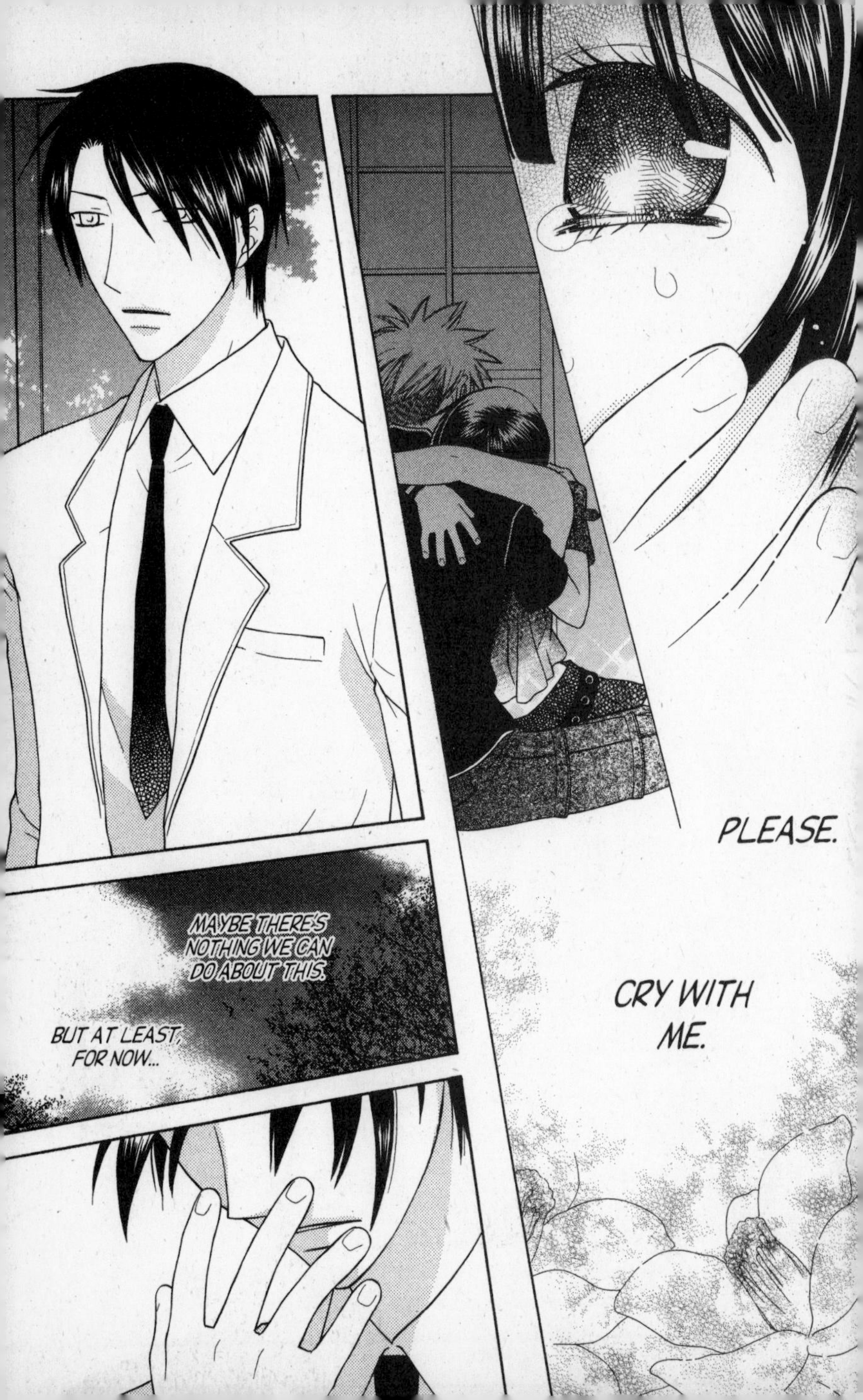
MAYBE THERE'S NOTHING WE CAN DO ABOUT THIS.
BUT AT LEAST, FOR NOW...
PLEASE.
CRY WITH ME.

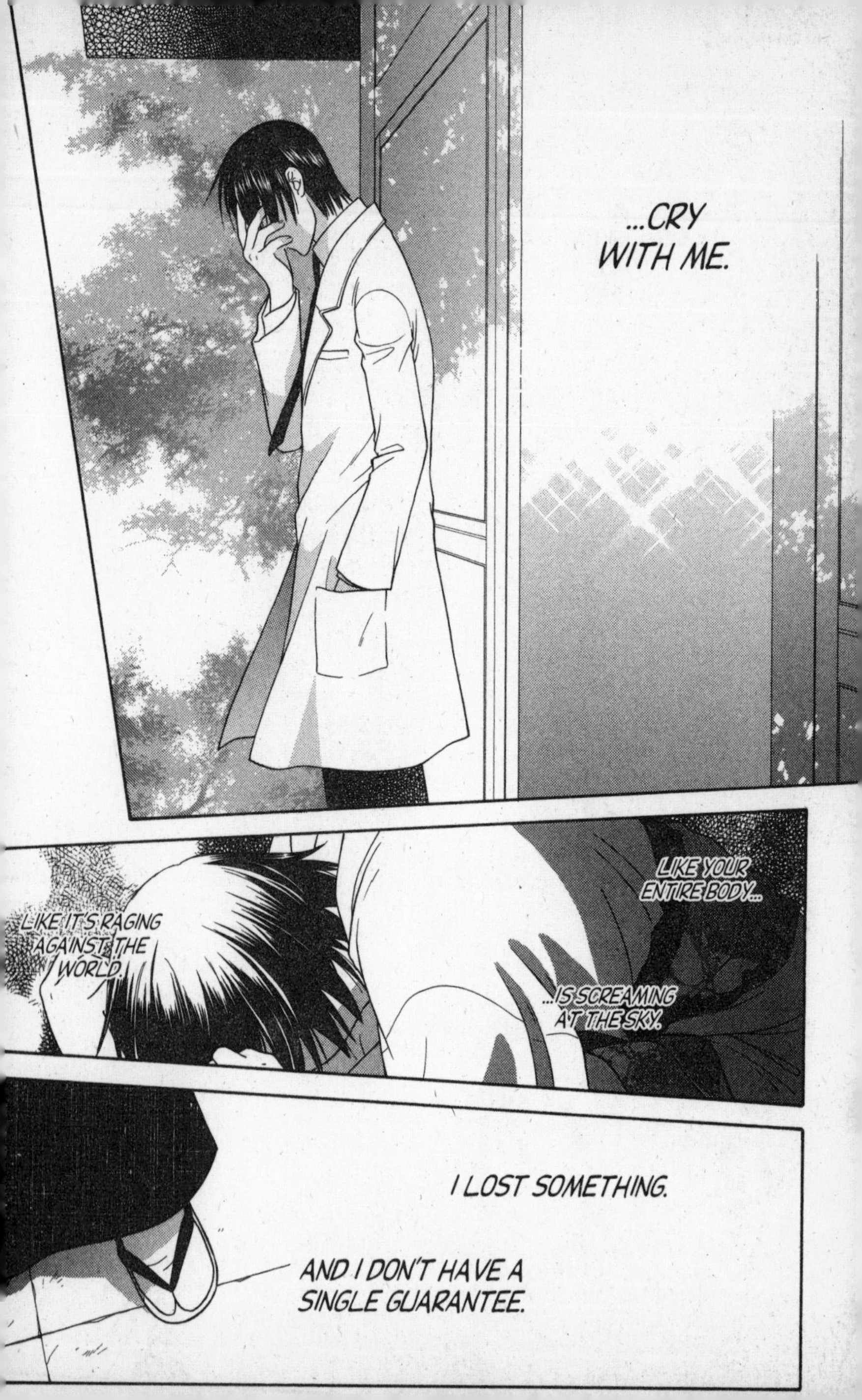
...CRY WITH ME.
LIKE YOUR ENTIRE BODY...
...IS SCREAMING AT THE SKY.
LIKE IT'S RAGING AGAINST THE WORLD.
I LOST SOMETHING.
AND I DON'T HAVE A SINGLE GUARANTEE.

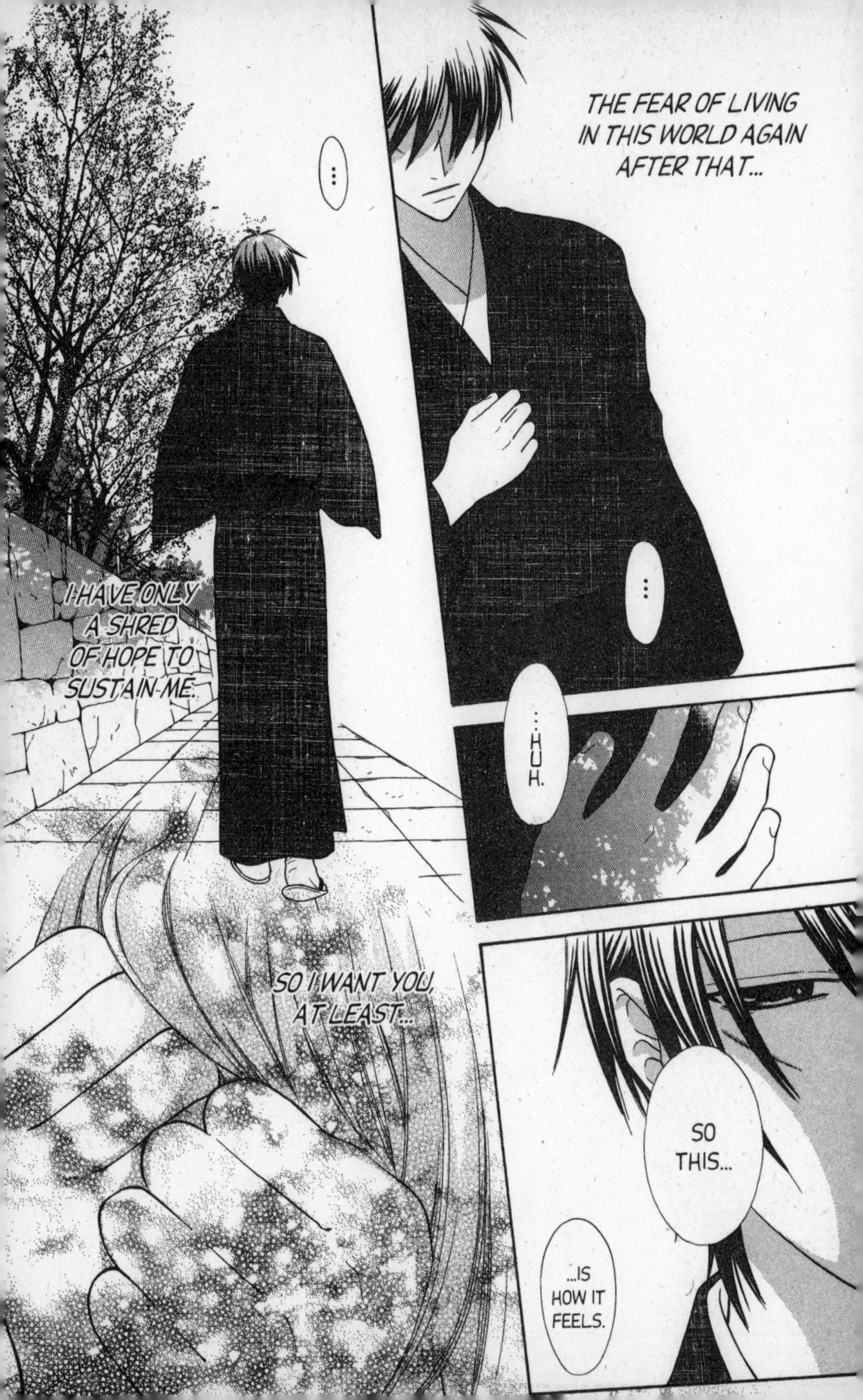
THE FEAR OF LIVING IN THIS WORLD AGAIN AFTER THAT...
...
...HUH.
SO THIS...
...IS HOW IT FEELS.
...
I HAVE ONLY A SHRED OF HOPE TO SUSTAIN ME.
SO I WANT YOU, AT LEAST...

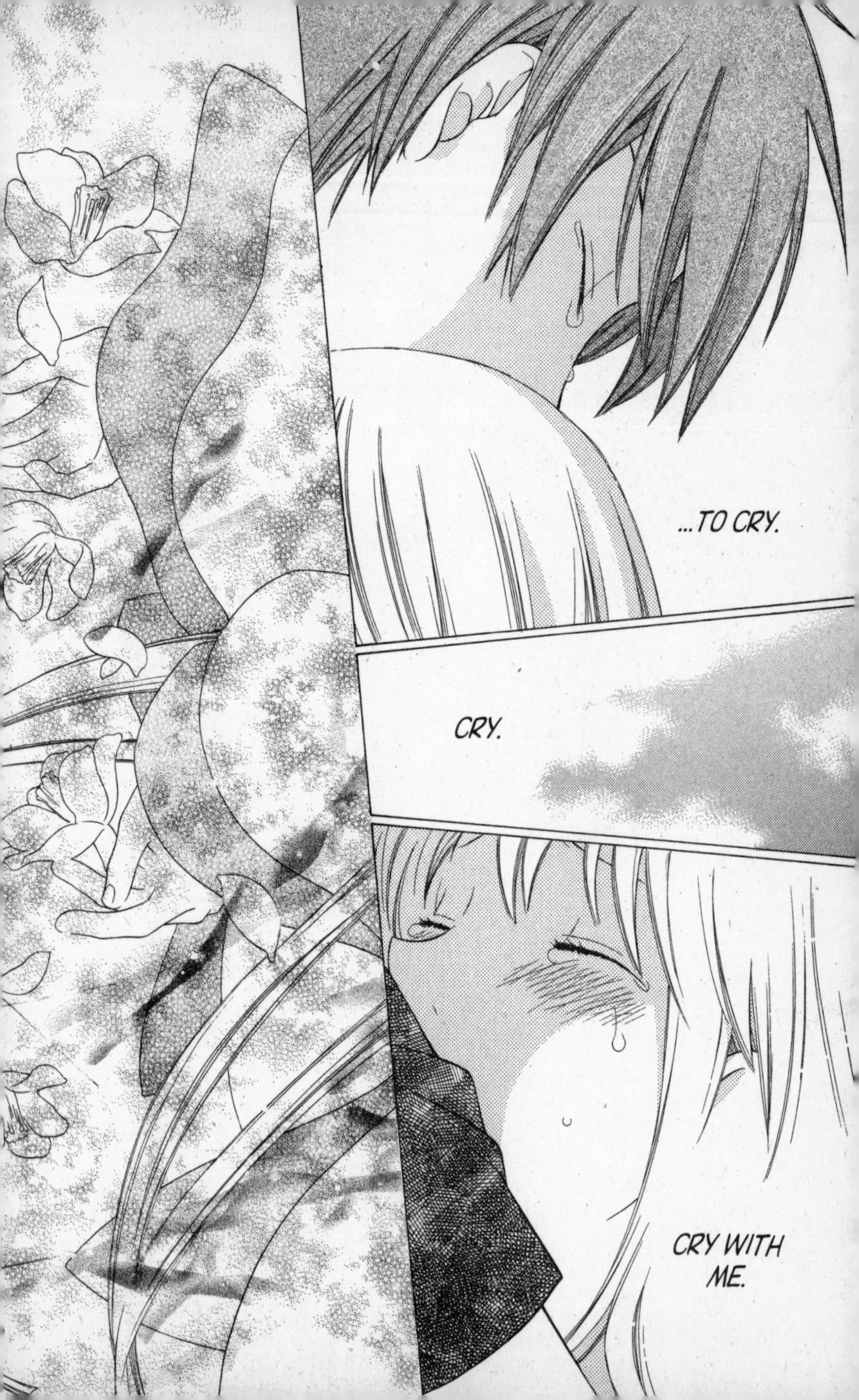
...TO CRY.
CRY.
CRY WITH ME.

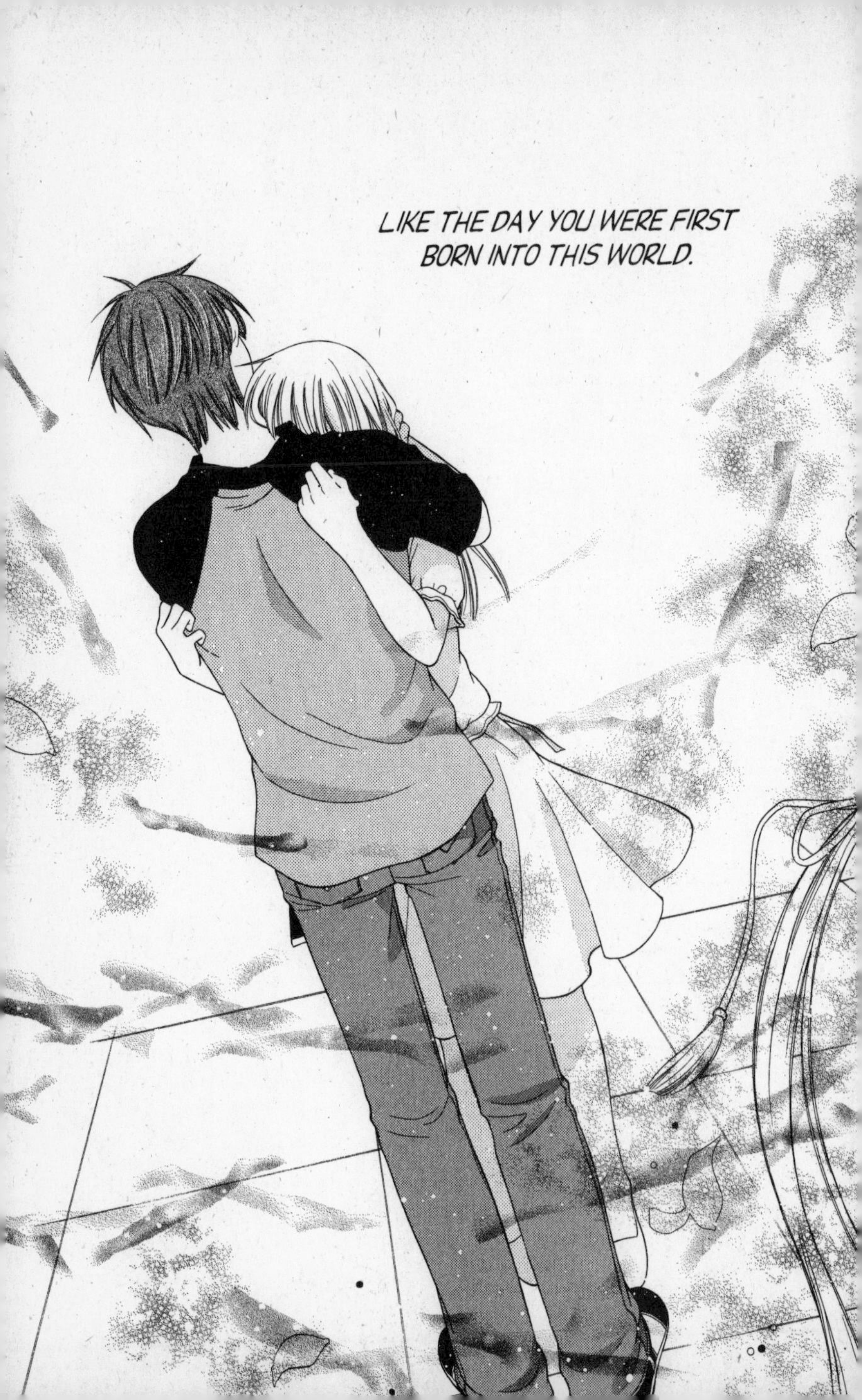
LIKE THE DAY YOU WERE FIRST BORN INTO THIS WORLD.

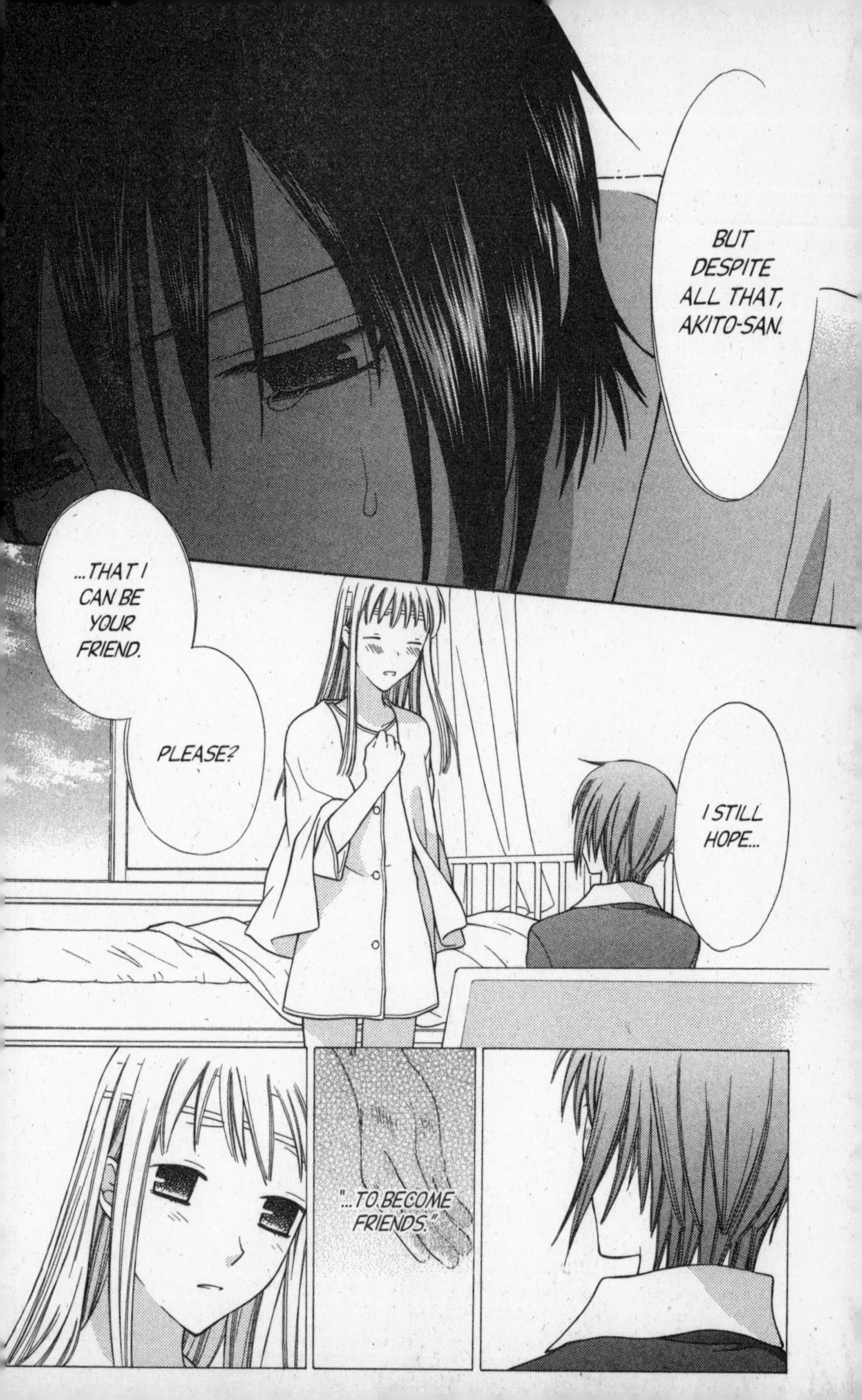
BUT DESPITE ALL THAT, AKITO-SAN.
I STILL HOPE...
...THAT I CAN BE YOUR FRIEND.
PLEASE?
"...TO BECOME FRIENDS."

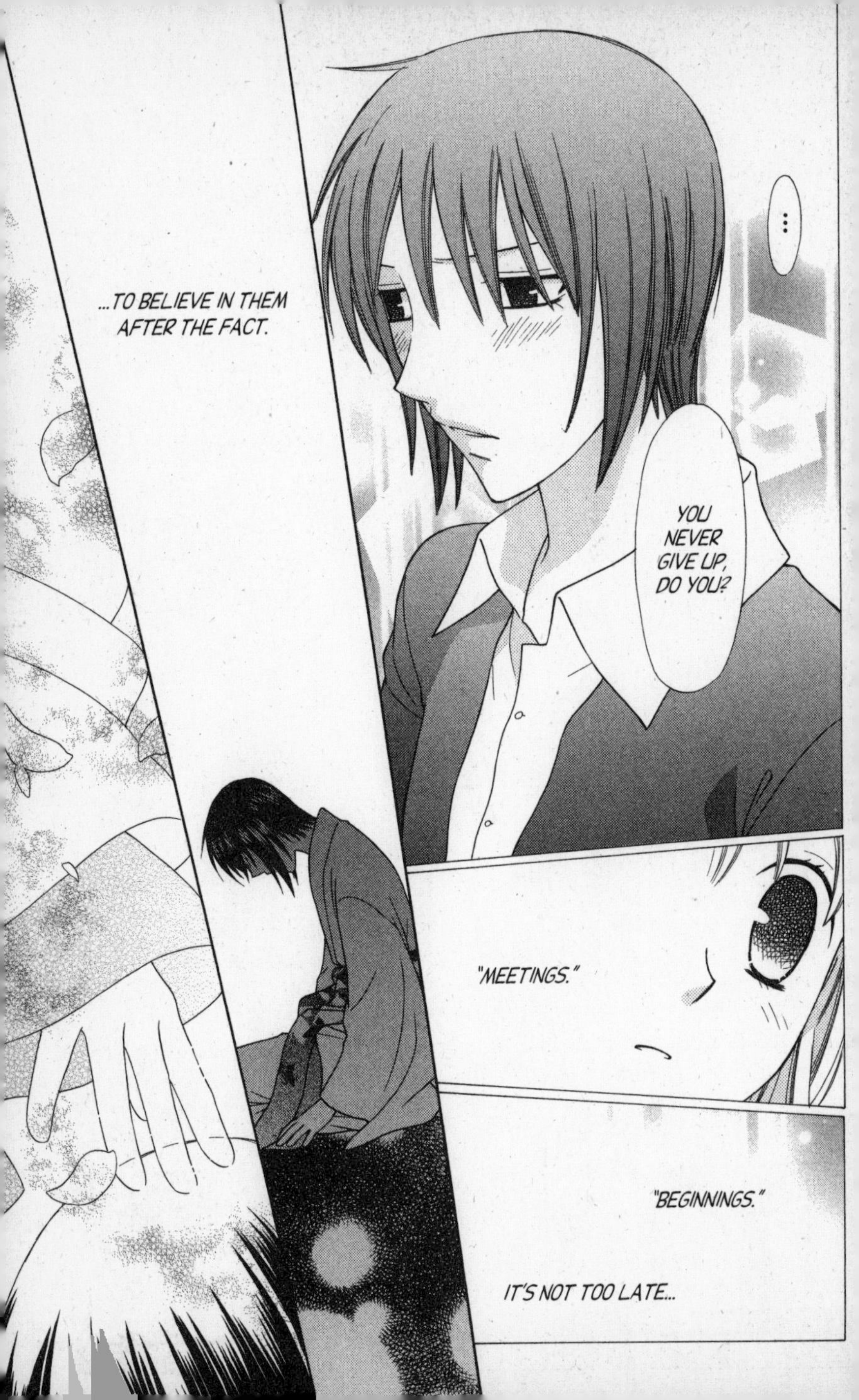
...
YOU NEVER GIVE UP, DO YOU?
"MEETINGS."
"BEGINNINGS."
IT'S NOT TOO LATE...
...TO BELIEVE IN THEM AFTER THE FACT.

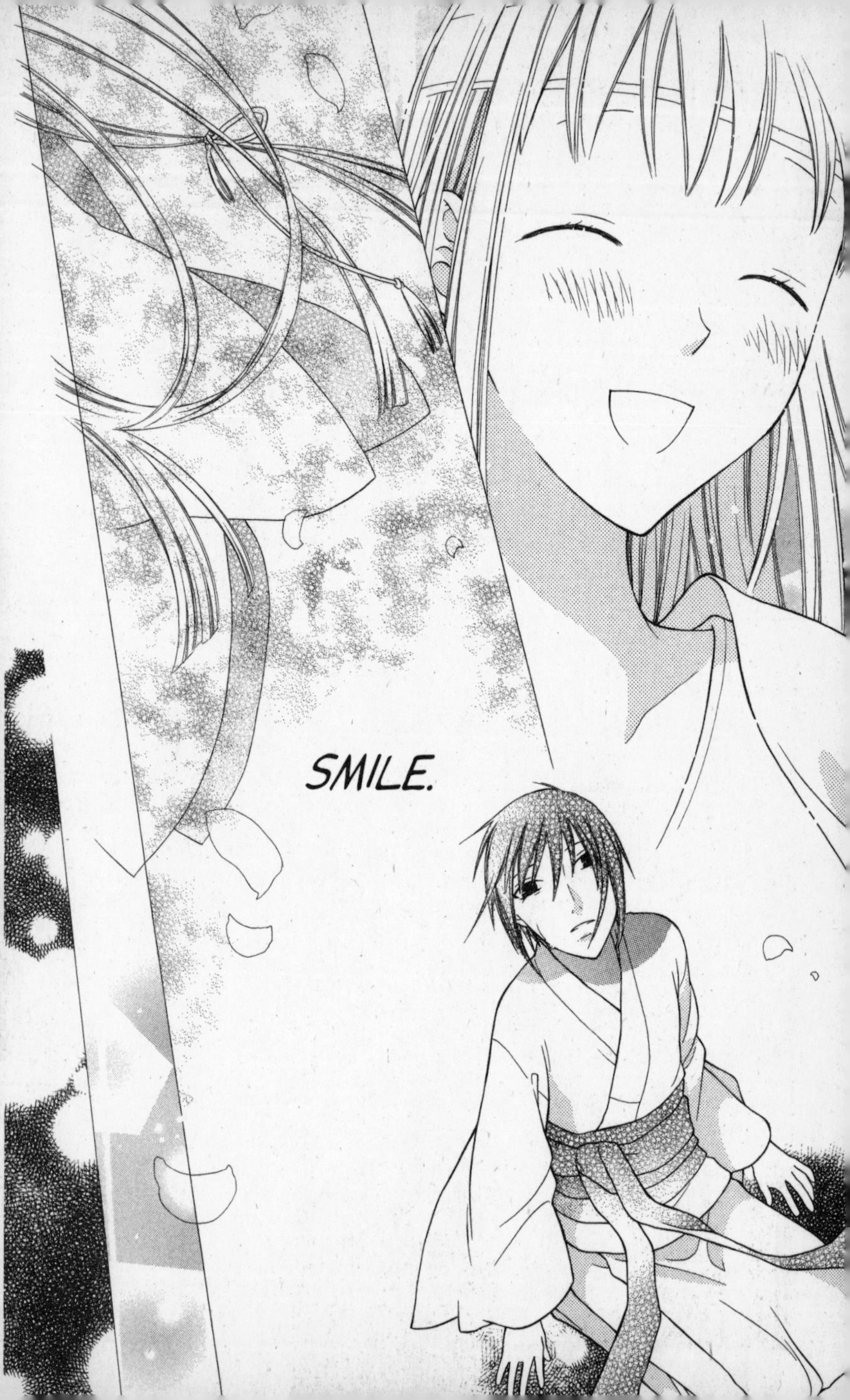
SMILE.

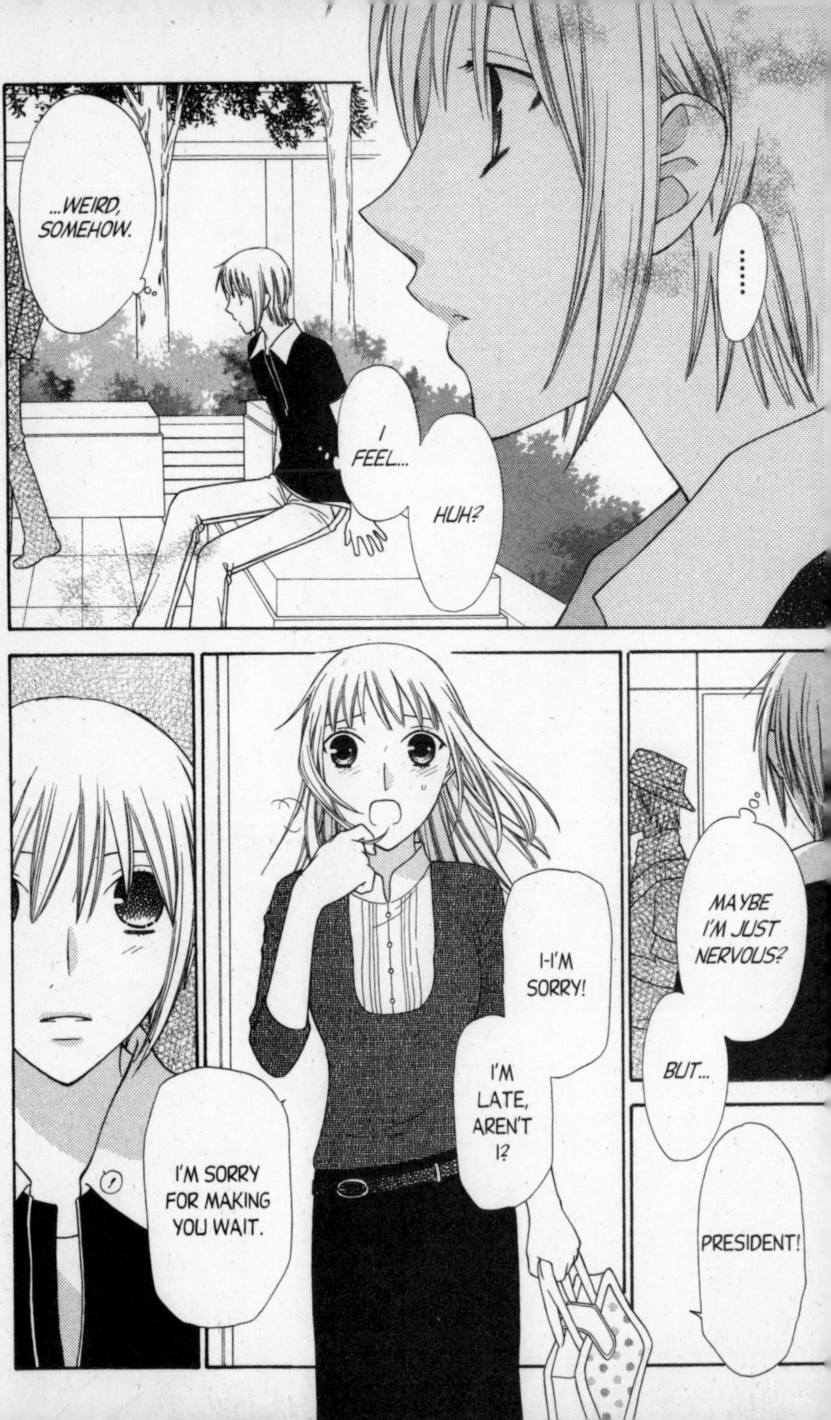
......
I FEEL...
HUH?
...WEIRD, SOMEHOW.
MAYBE I'M JUST NERVOUS?
BUT...
PRESIDENT!
I-I'M SORRY!
I'M LATE, AREN'T I!?
I'M SORRY FOR MAKING YOU WAIT.

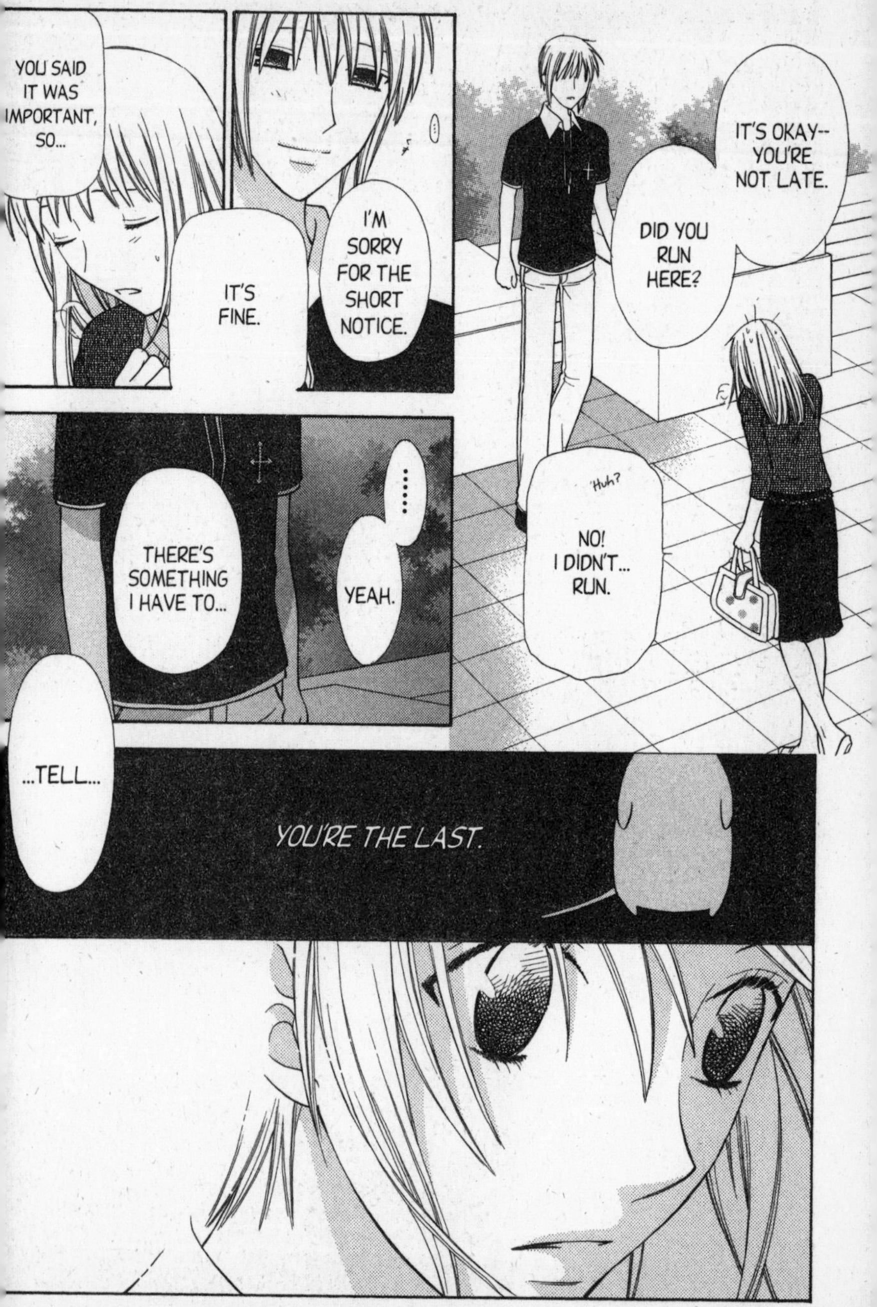
IT'S OKAY-- YOU'RE NOT LATE.
DID YOU RUN HERE?
Huh?
NO! I DIDN'T... RUN.
...
I'M SORRY FOR THE SHORT NOTICE.
IT'S FINE.
YOU SAID IT WAS IMPORTANT, SO...
......
YEAH.
THERE'S SOMETHING I HAVE TO...
...TELL...
YOU'RE THE LAST.

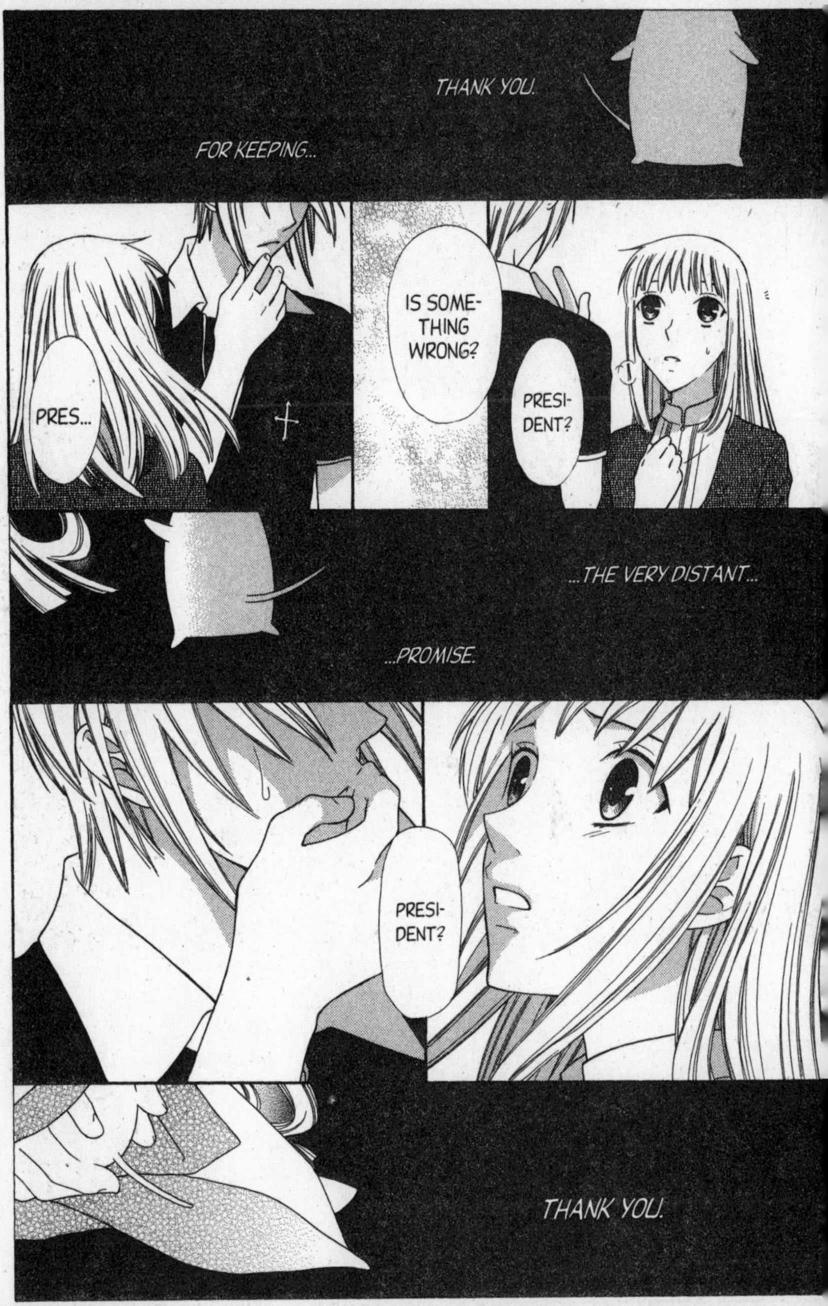
THANK YOU.
FOR KEEPING...
PRESI-DENT?
IS SOME-THING WRONG?
PRES...
...THE VERY DISTANT...
...PROMISE.
PRESI-DENT?
THANK YOU.

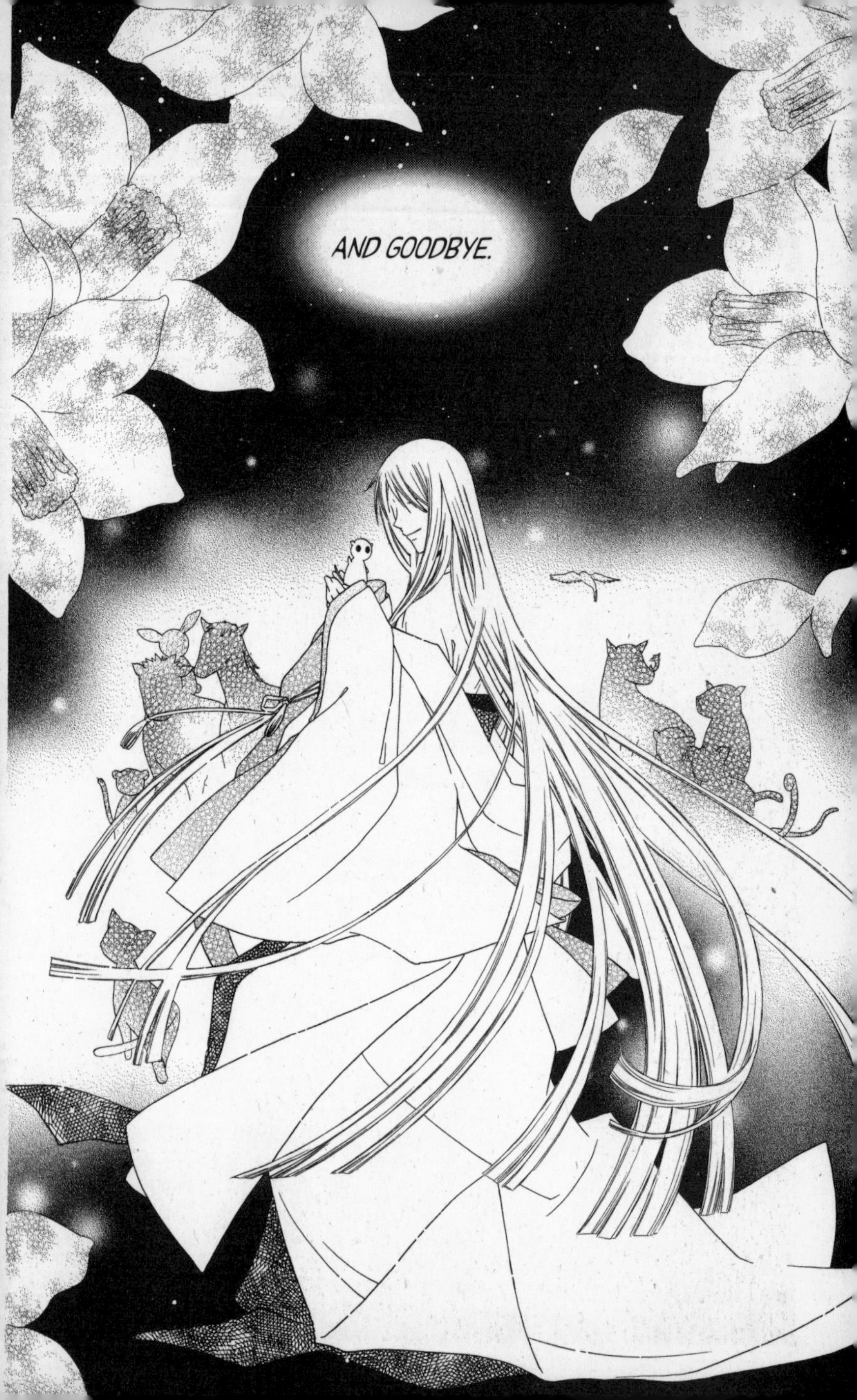
AND GOODBYE.

Chapter 131

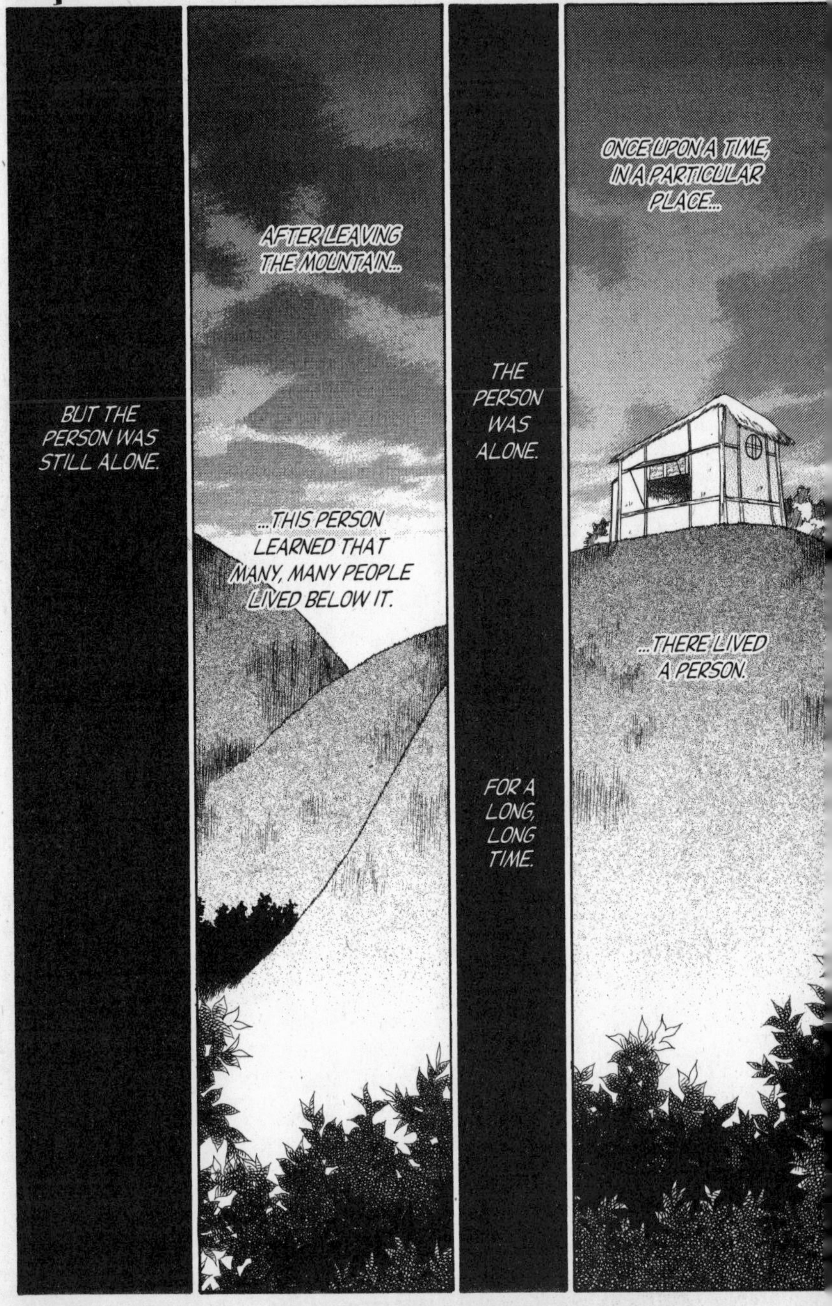
ONCE UPON A TIME, IN A PARTICULAR PLACE...
...THERE LIVED A PERSON.
THE PERSON WAS ALONE.
FOR A LONG, LONG TIME.
AFTER LEAVING THE MOUNTAIN...
...THIS PERSON LEARNED THAT MANY, MANY PEOPLE LIVED BELOW IT.
BUT THE PERSON WAS STILL ALONE.

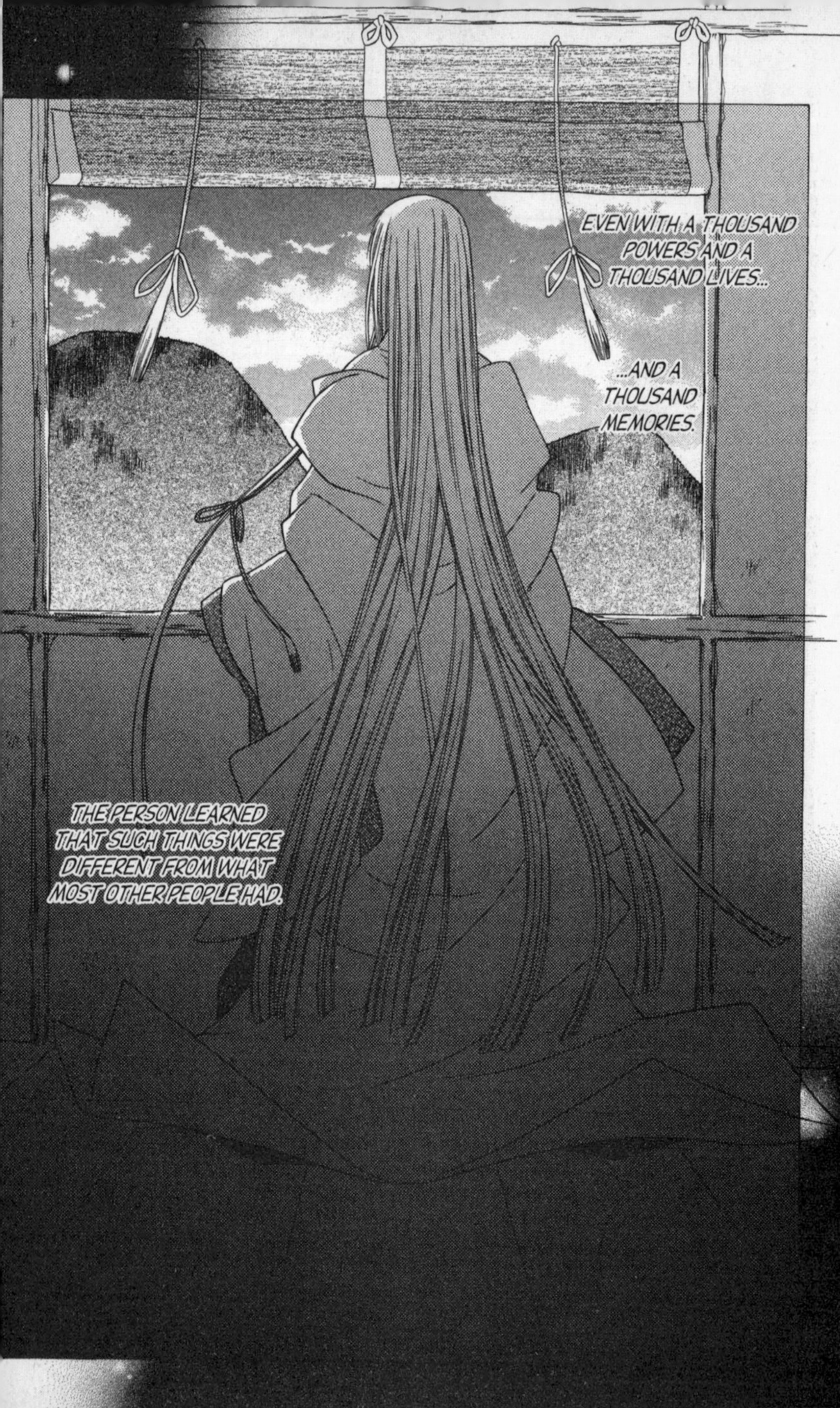
EVEN WITH A THOUSAND POWERS AND A THOUSAND LIVES...
...AND A THOUSAND MEMORIES.
THE PERSON LEARNED THAT SUCH THINGS WERE DIFFERENT FROM WHAT MOST OTHER PEOPLE HAD.

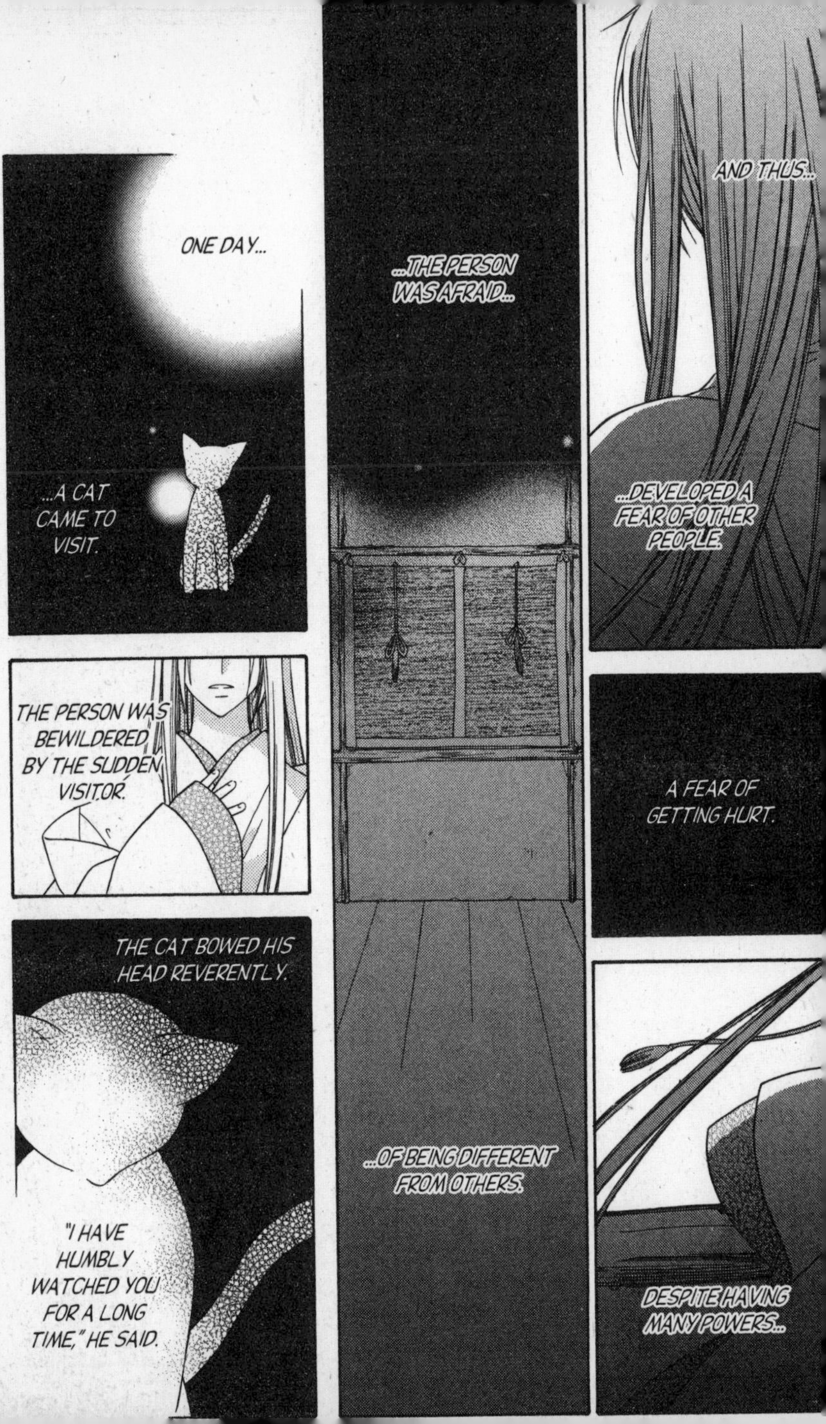
AND THUS...
...DEVELOPED A FEAR OF OTHER PEOPLE.
A FEAR OF GETTING HURT.
DESPITE HAVING MANY POWERS...
...THE PERSON WAS AFRAID...
...OF BEING DIFFERENT FROM OTHERS.
ONE DAY...
...A CAT CAME TO VISIT.
THE PERSON WAS BEWILDERED BY THE SUDDEN VISITOR.
THE CAT BOWED HIS HEAD REVERENTLY.
"I HAVE HUMBLY WATCHED YOU FOR A LONG TIME," HE SAID.

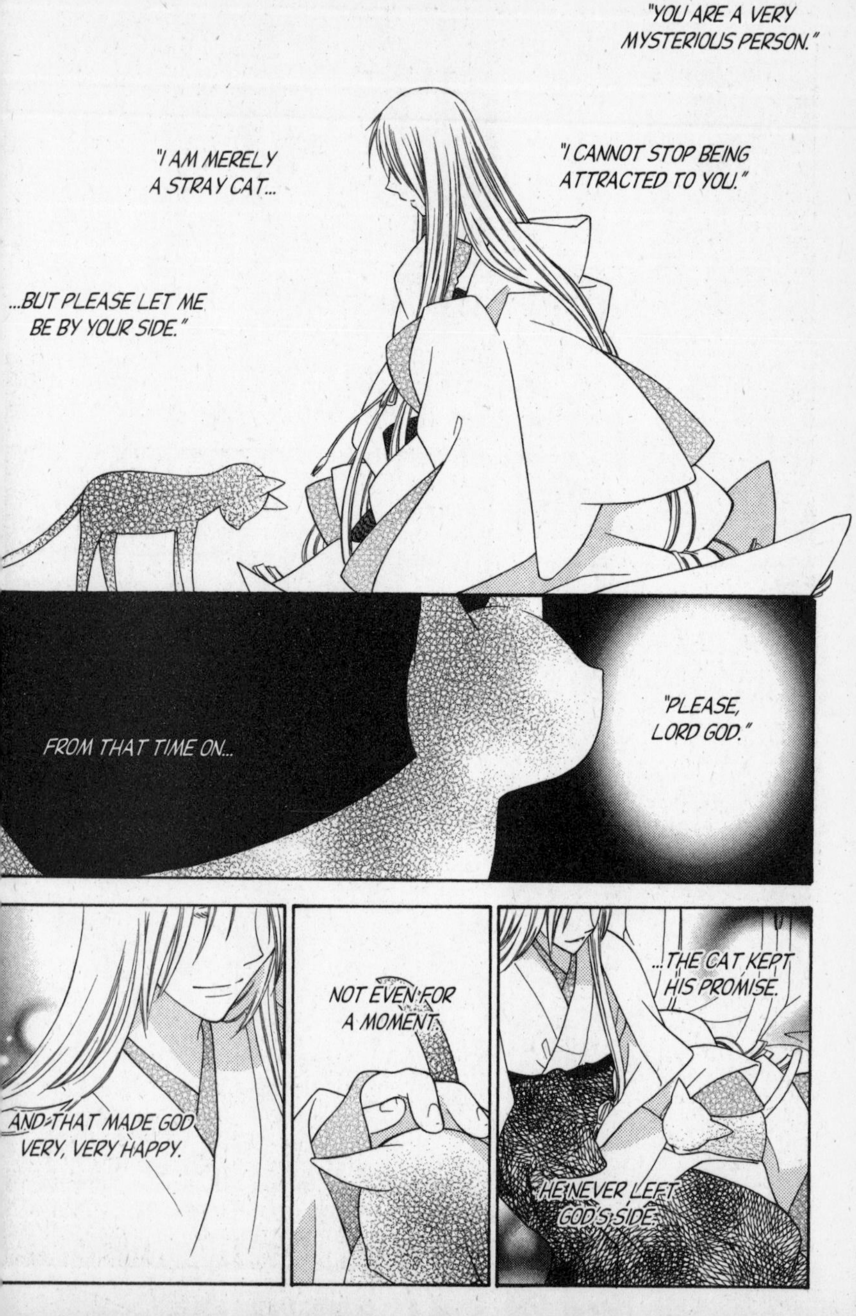
"YOU ARE A VERY MYSTERIOUS PERSON."
"I CANNOT STOP BEING ATTRACTED TO YOU."
"I AM MERELY A STRAY CAT...
...BUT PLEASE LET ME BE BY YOUR SIDE."
"PLEASE, LORD GOD."
FROM THAT TIME ON...
...THE CAT KEPT HIS PROMISE.
HE NEVER LEFT GOD'S SIDE.
NOT EVEN FOR A MOMENT.
AND THAT MADE GOD VERY, VERY HAPPY.

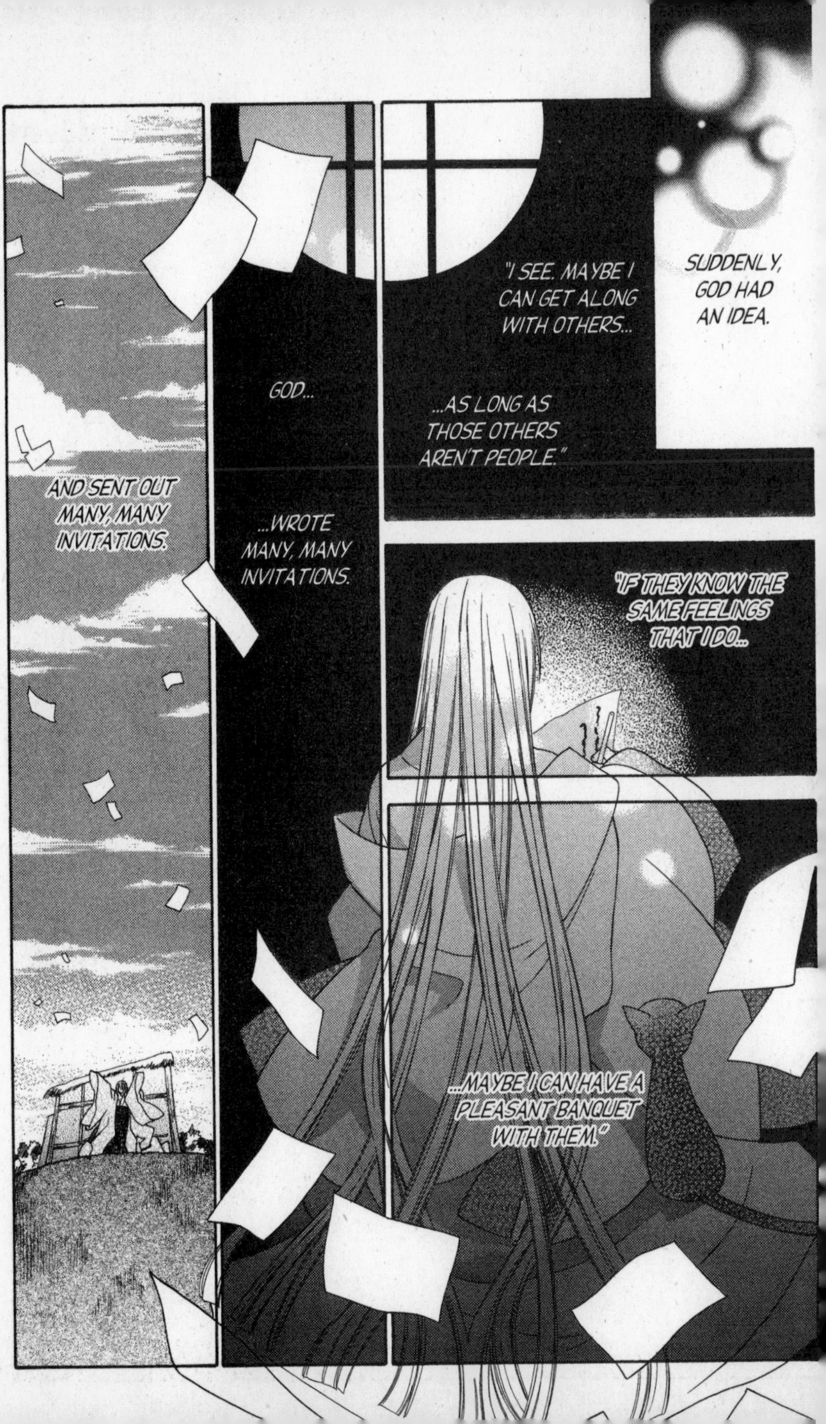
SUDDENLY, GOD HAD AN IDEA.
"I SEE. MAYBE I CAN GET ALONG WITH OTHERS...
...AS LONG AS THOSE OTHERS AREN'T PEOPLE."
"IF THEY KNOW THE SAME FEELINGS THAT I DO...
...MAYBE I CAN HAVE A PLEASANT BANQUET WITH THEM."
GOD...
...WROTE MANY, MANY INVITATIONS.
AND SENT OUT MANY, MANY INVITATIONS.

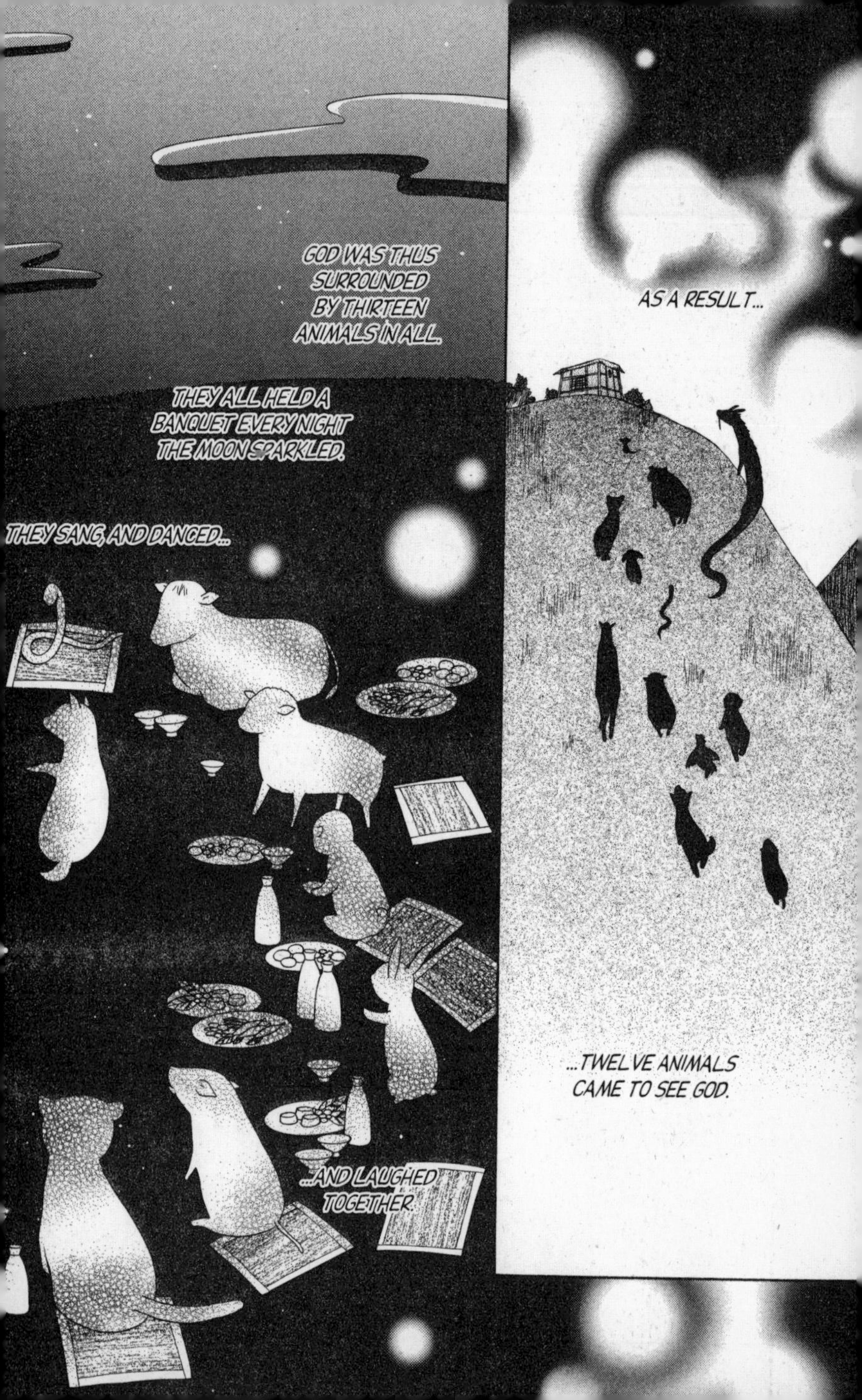
AS A RESULT...
...TWELVE ANIMALS CAME TO SEE GOD.
GOD WAS THUS SURROUNDED BY THIRTEEN ANIMALS IN ALL.
THEY ALL HELD A BANQUET EVERY NIGHT THE MOON SPARKLED.
THEY SANG, AND DANCED...
...AND LAUGHED TOGETHER.

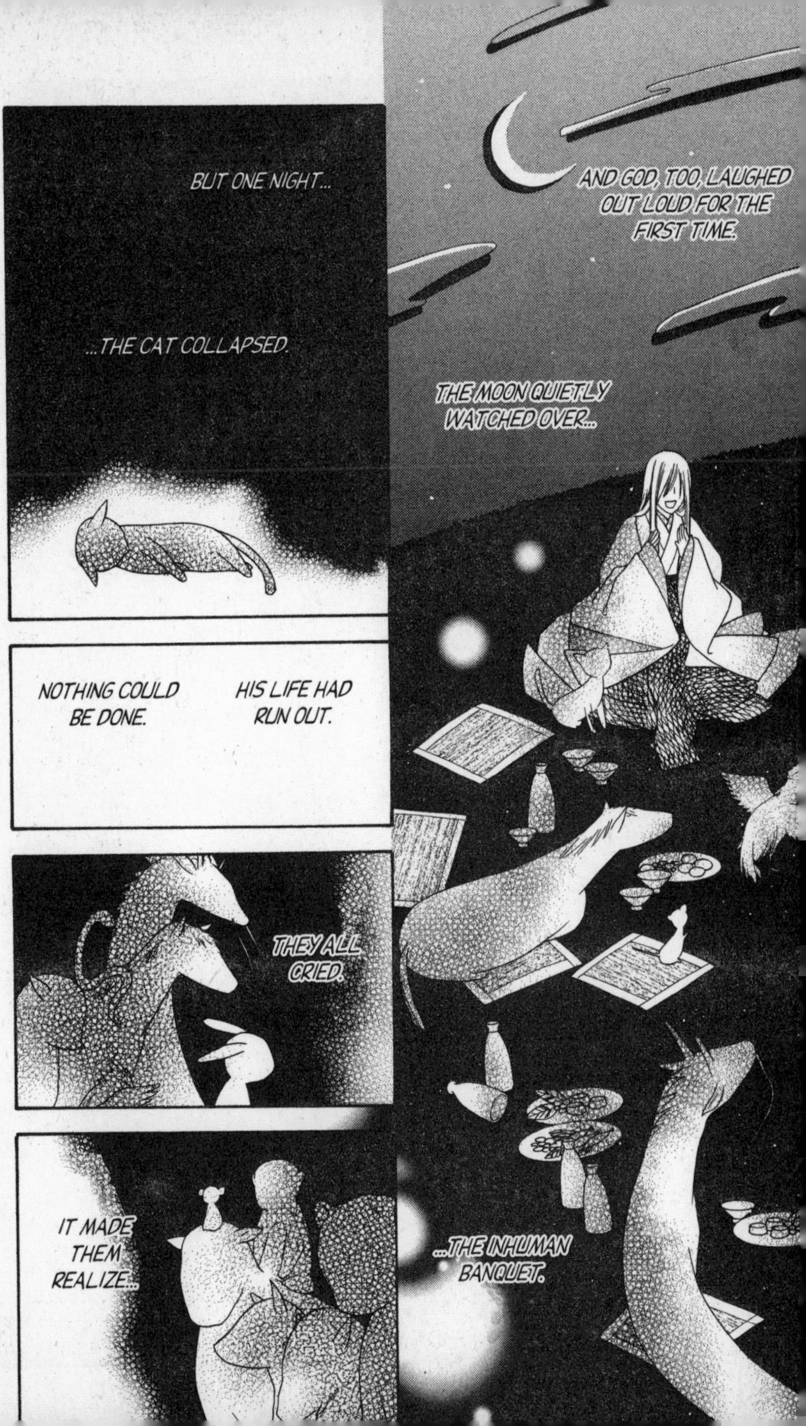
AND GOD, TOO, LAUGHED OUT LOUD FOR THE FIRST TIME.
THE MOON QUIETLY WATCHED OVER...
...THE INHUMAN BANQUET.
BUT ONE NIGHT...
...THE CAT COLLAPSED.
HIS LIFE HAD RUN OUT.
NOTHING COULD BE DONE.
THEY ALL CRIED.
IT MADE THEM REALIZE...

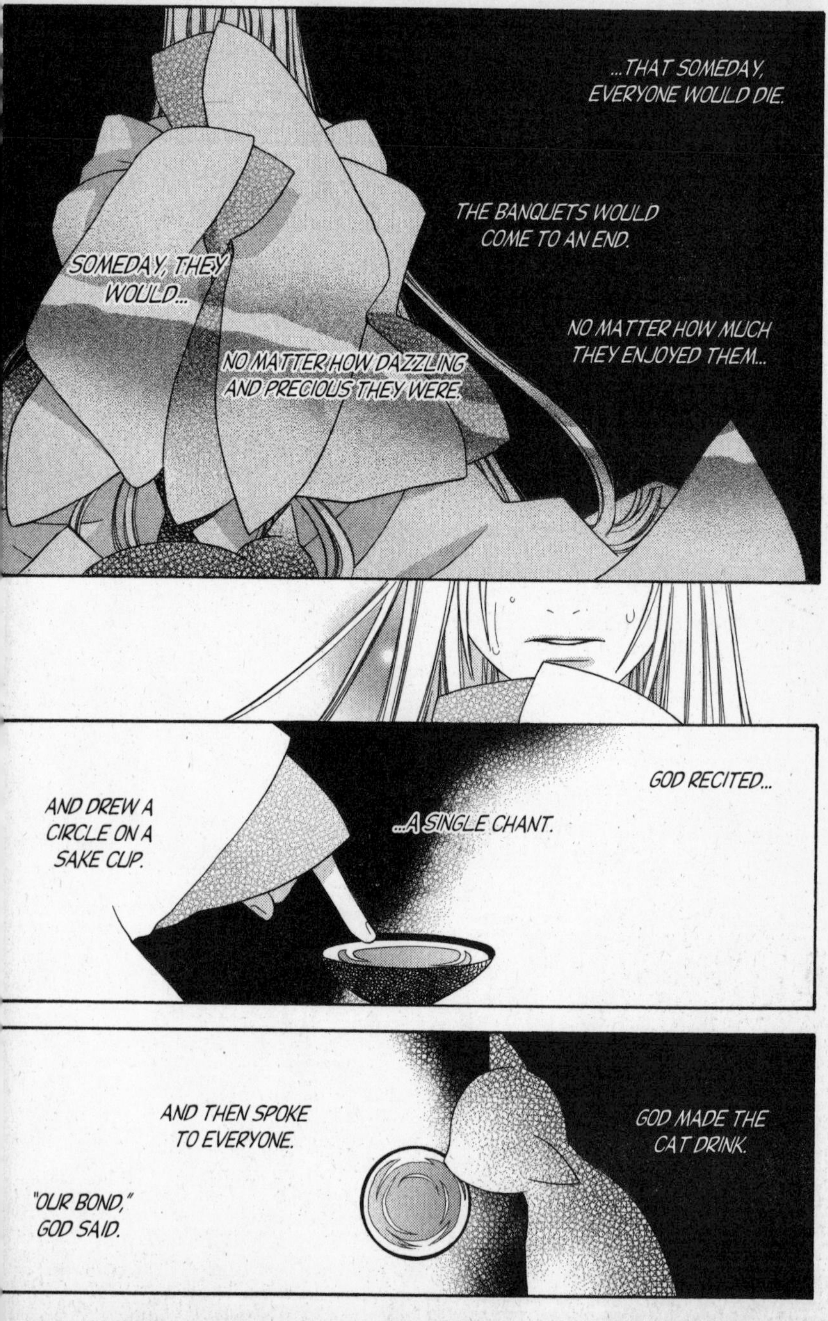
...THAT SOMEDAY, EVERYONE WOULD DIE.
THE BANQUETS WOULD COME TO AN END.
NO MATTER HOW MUCH THEY ENJOYED THEM...
SOMEDAY, THEY WOULD...
NO MATTER HOW DAZZLING AND PRECIOUS THEY WERE.
GOD RECITED...
...A SINGLE CHANT.
AND DREW A CIRCLE ON A SAKE CUP.
GOD MADE THE CAT DRINK.
AND THEN SPOKE TO EVERYONE.
"OUR BOND," GOD SAID.

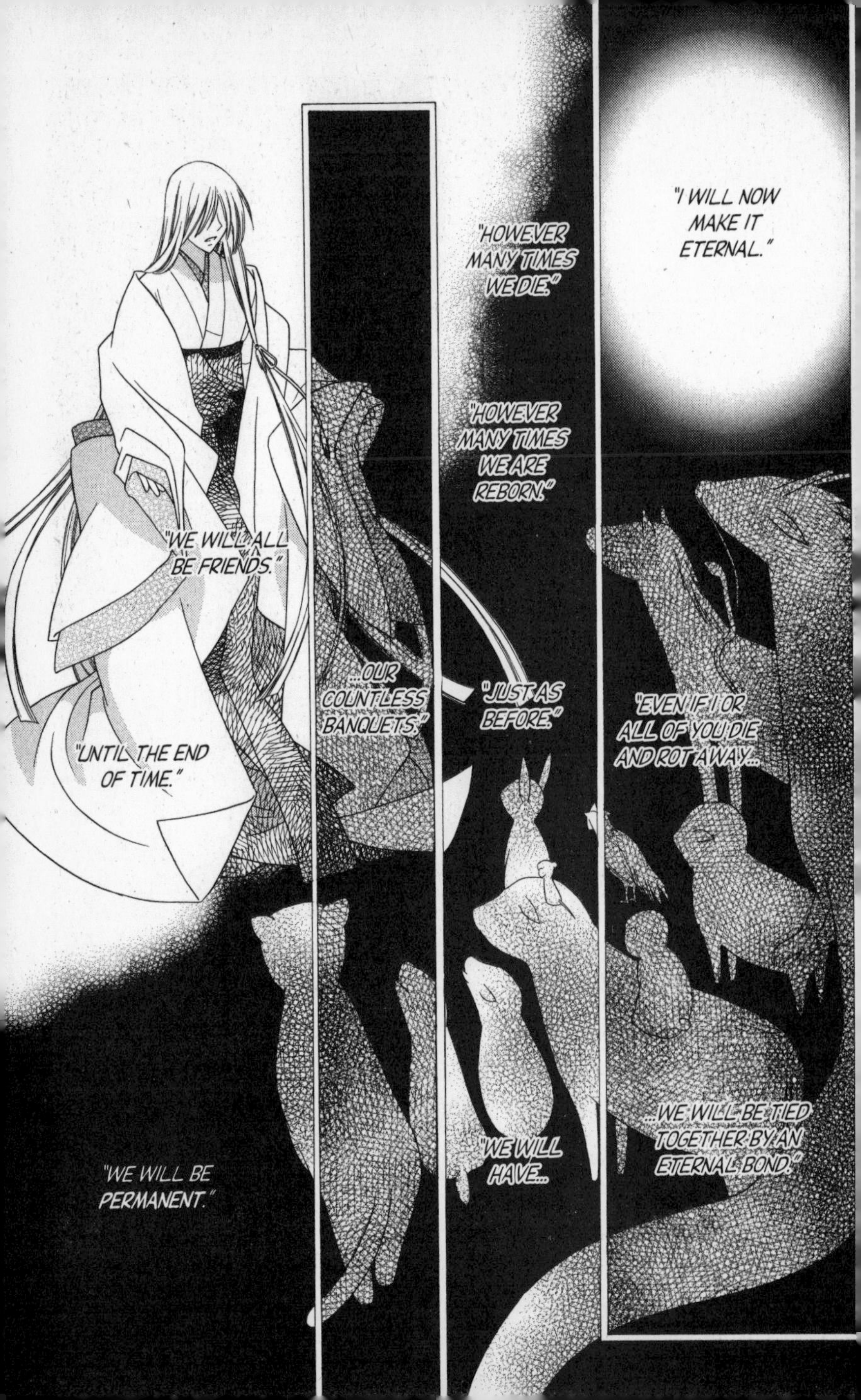
"I WILL NOW MAKE IT ETERNAL."
"EVEN IF I OR ALL OF YOU DIE AND ROT AWAY...
...WE WILL BE TIED TOGETHER BY AN ETERNAL BOND."
"HOWEVER MANY TIMES WE DIE."
"HOWEVER MANY TIMES WE ARE REBORN."
"JUST AS BEFORE."
"WE WILL HAVE...
...OUR COUNTLESS BANQUETS."
"WE WILL ALL BE FRIENDS."
"UNTIL THE END OF TIME."
"WE WILL BE PERMANENT."

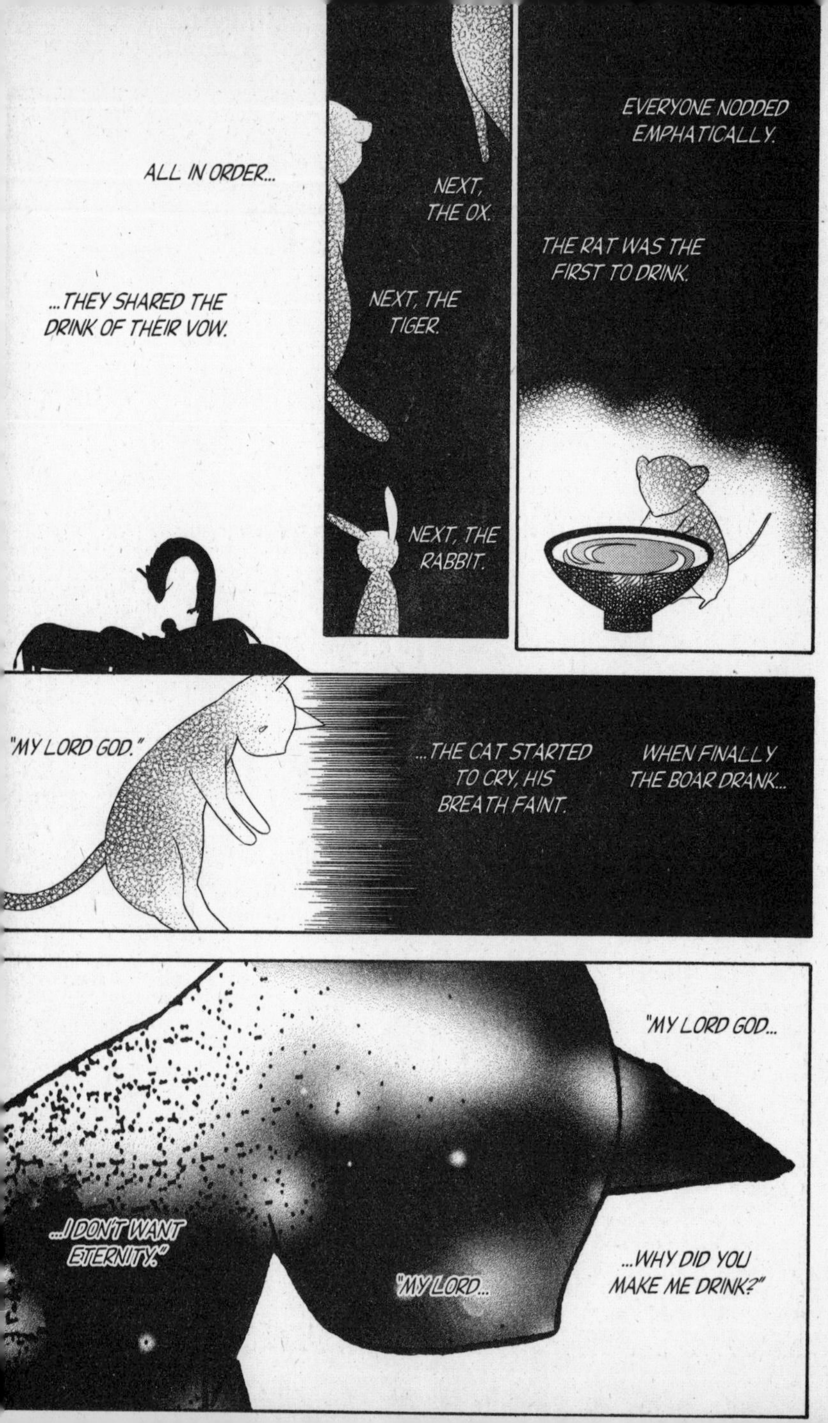
EVERYONE NODDED EMPHATICALLY.
THE RAT WAS THE FIRST TO DRINK.
NEXT, THE OX.
NEXT, THE TIGER.
NEXT, THE RABBIT.
ALL IN ORDER...
...THEY SHARED THE DRINK OF THEIR VOW.
WHEN FINALLY THE BOAR DRANK...
...THE CAT STARTED TO CRY, HIS BREATH FAINT.
"MY LORD GOD."
"MY LORD GOD...
...WHY DID YOU MAKE ME DRINK?"
"MY LORD...
...I DON'T WANT ETERNITY."

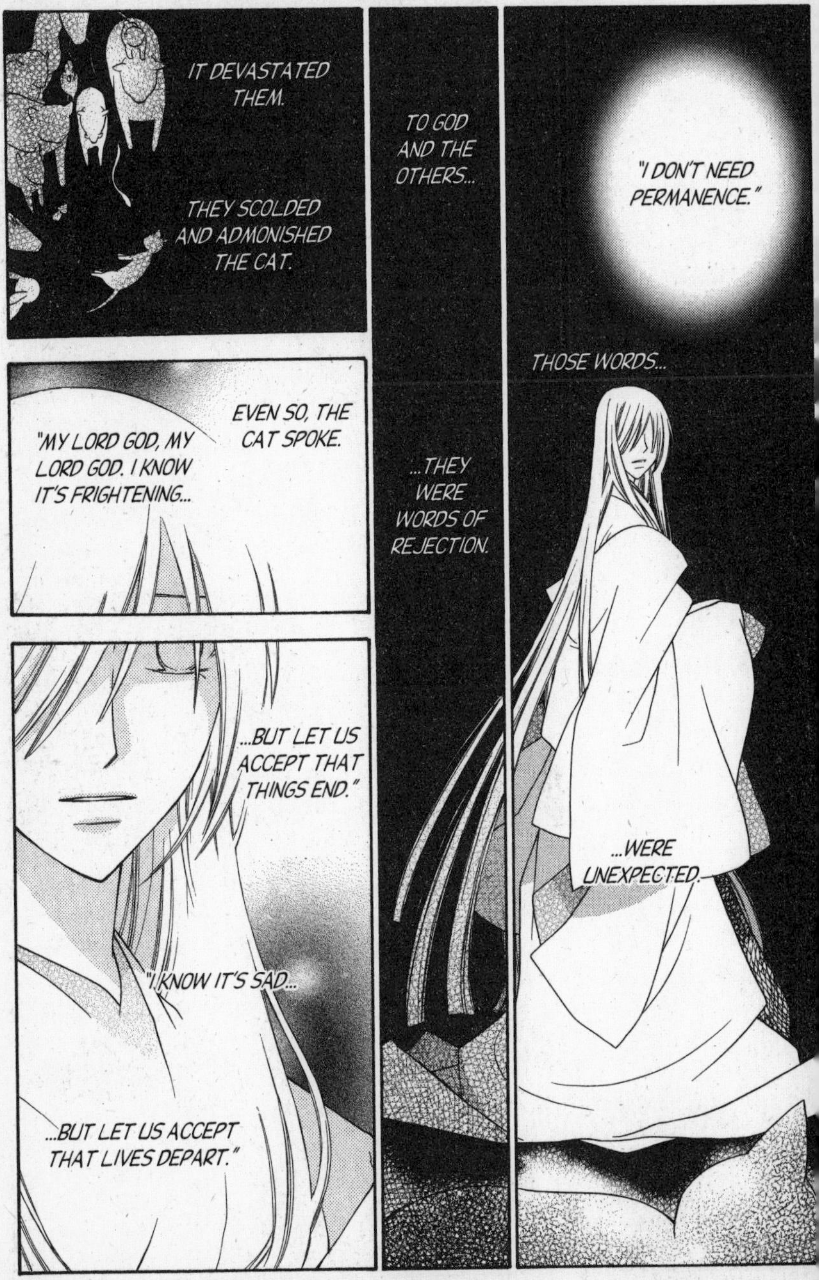
"I DON'T NEED PERMANENCE."
THOSE WORDS...
...WERE UNEXPECTED.
TO GOD AND THE OTHERS...
...THEY WERE WORDS OF REJECTION.
IT DEVASTATED THEM.
THEY SCOLDED AND ADMONISHED THE CAT.
EVEN SO, THE CAT SPOKE.
"MY LORD GOD, MY LORD GOD. I KNOW IT'S FRIGHTENING...
...BUT LET US ACCEPT THAT THINGS END."
"I KNOW IT'S SAD...
...BUT LET US ACCEPT THAT LIVES DEPART."

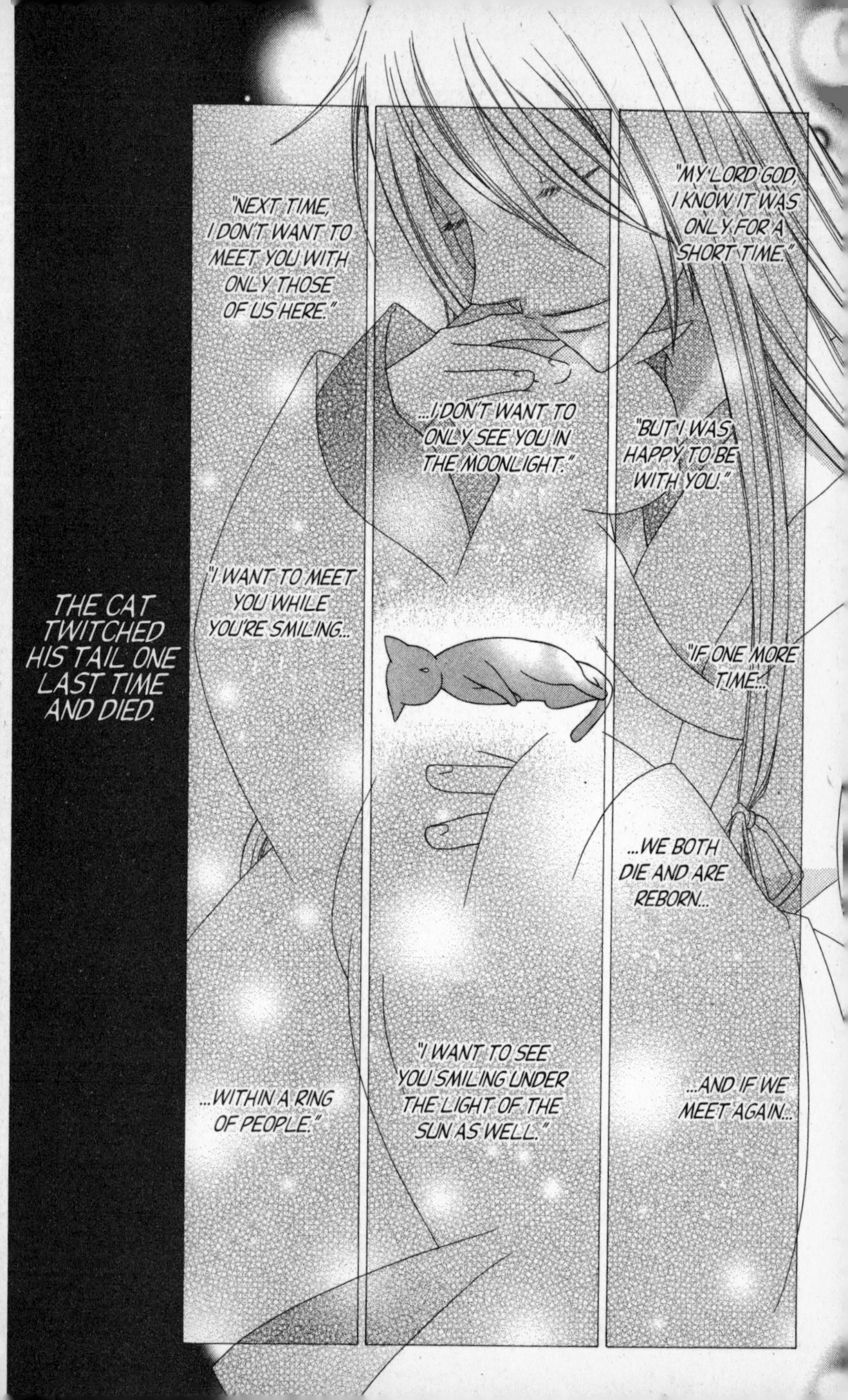
"MY LORD GOD, I KNOW IT WAS ONLY FOR A SHORT TIME."
"BUT I WAS HAPPY TO BE WITH YOU."
"IF ONE MORE TIME...
...WE BOTH DIE AND ARE REBORN...
...AND IF WE MEET AGAIN...
...I DON'T WANT TO ONLY SEE YOU IN THE MOONLIGHT."
"I WANT TO SEE YOU SMILING UNDER THE LIGHT OF THE SUN AS WELL."
"NEXT TIME, I DON'T WANT TO MEET YOU WITH ONLY THOSE OF US HERE."
"I WANT TO MEET YOU WHILE YOU'RE SMILING...
...WITHIN A RING OF PEOPLE."
THE CAT TWITCHED HIS TAIL ONE LAST TIME AND DIED.

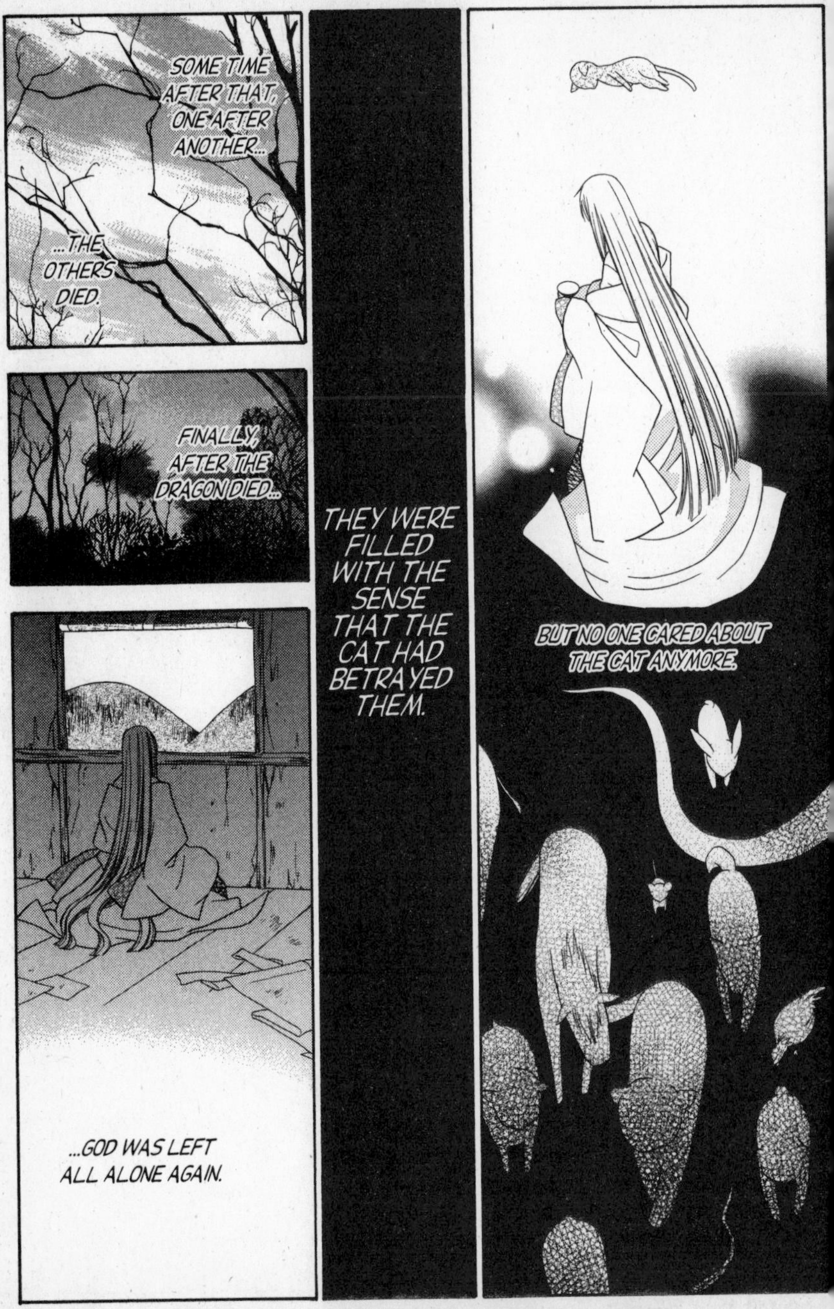
BUT NO ONE CARED ABOUT THE CAT ANYMORE.
THEY WERE FILLED WITH THE SENSE THAT THE CAT HAD BETRAYED THEM.
SOME TIME AFTER THAT, ONE AFTER ANOTHER...
...THE OTHERS DIED.
FINALLY, AFTER THE DRAGON DIED...
...GOD WAS LEFT ALL ALONE AGAIN.

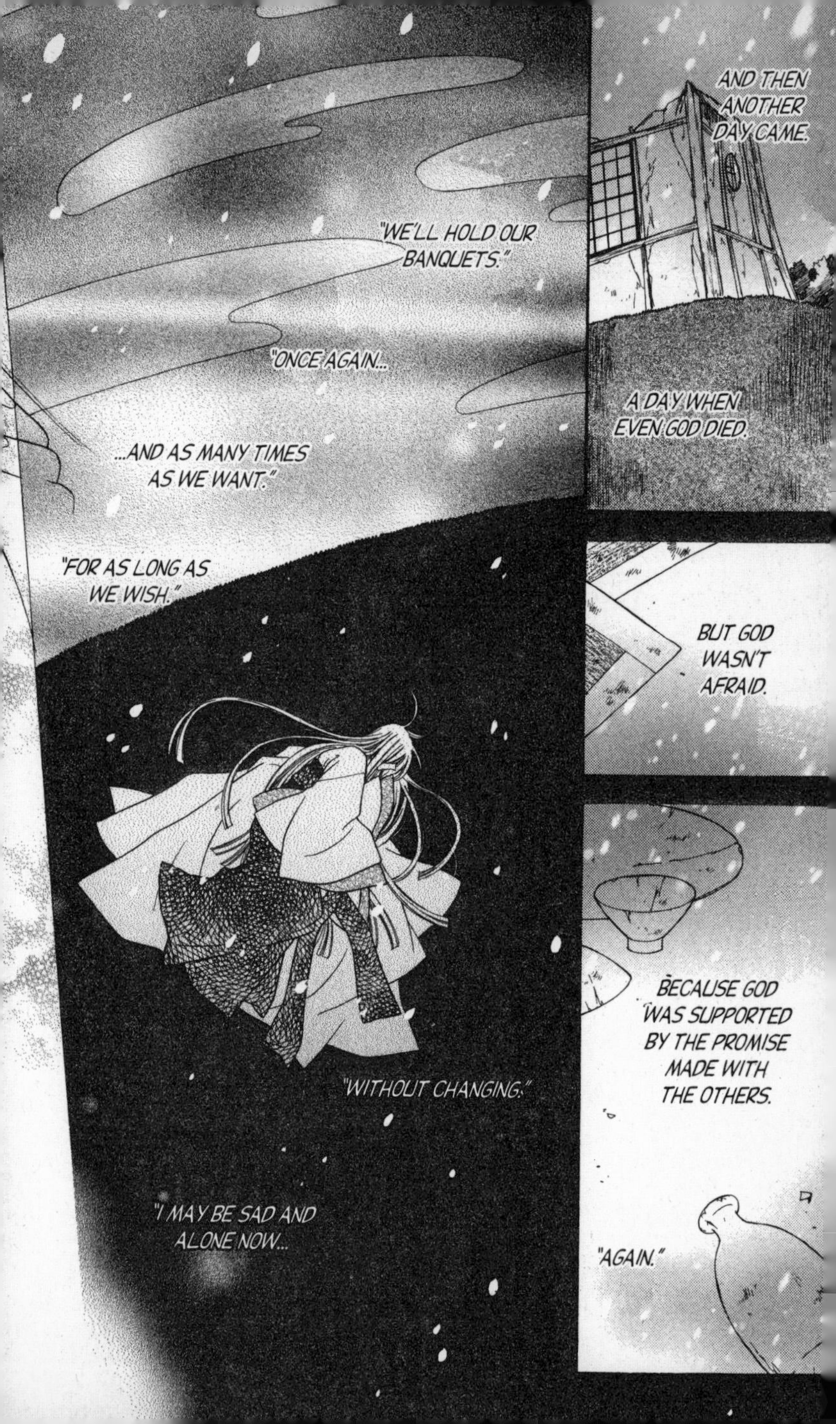
AND THEN ANOTHER DAY CAME.
A DAY WHEN EVEN GOD DIED.
BUT GOD WASN'T AFRAID.
BECAUSE GOD WAS SUPPORTED BY THE PROMISE MADE WITH THE OTHERS.
"AGAIN."
"WE'LL HOLD OUR BANQUETS."
"ONCE AGAIN...
...AND AS MANY TIMES AS WE WANT."
"FOR AS LONG AS WE WISH."
"WITHOUT CHANGING."
"I MAY BE SAD AND ALONE NOW...

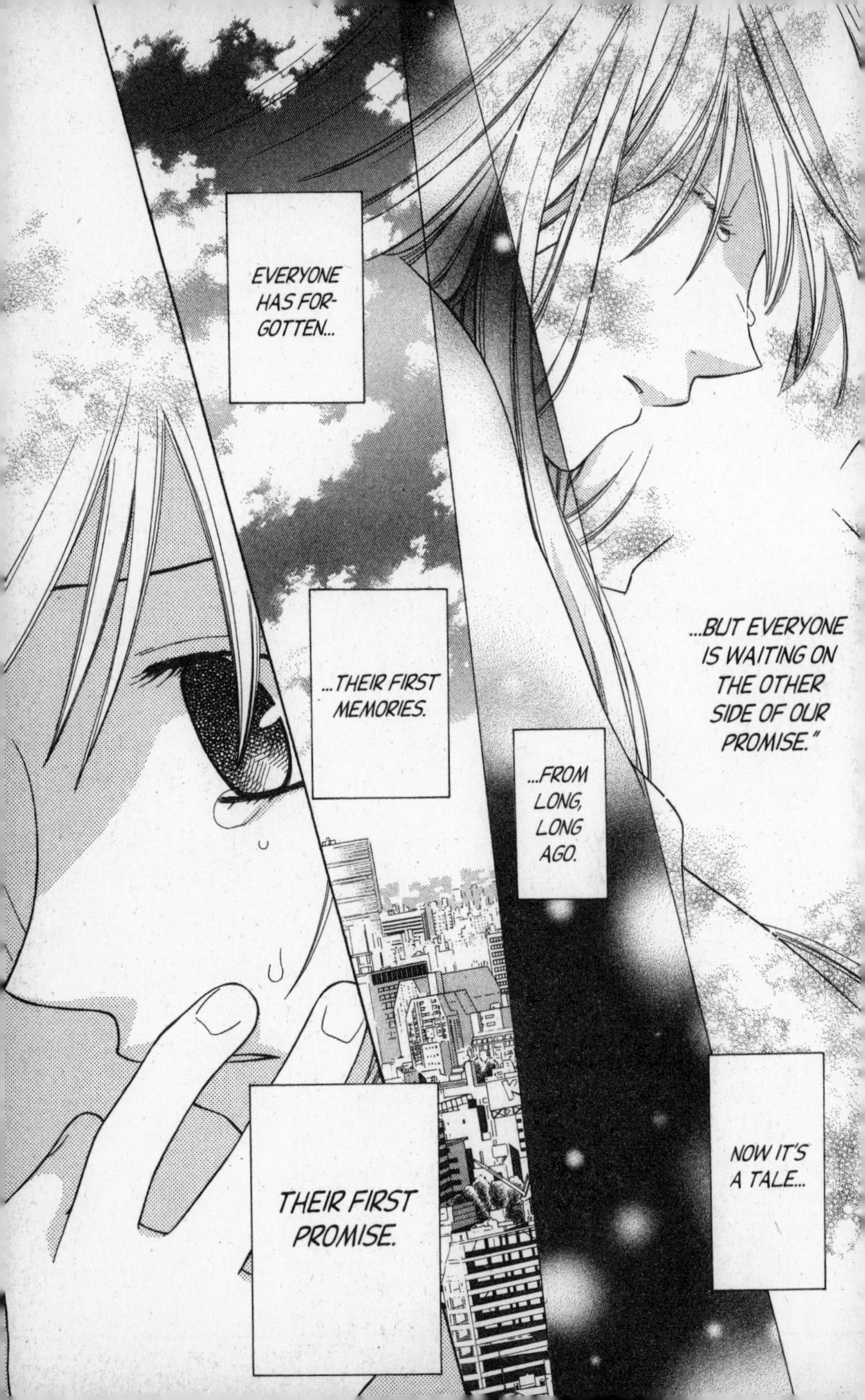
NOW IT'S A TALE...
...FROM LONG, LONG AGO.
EVERYONE HAS FOR-GOTTEN...
...THEIR FIRST MEMORIES.
THEIR FIRST PROMISE.
...BUT EVERYONE IS WAITING ON THE OTHER SIDE OF OUR PROMISE."

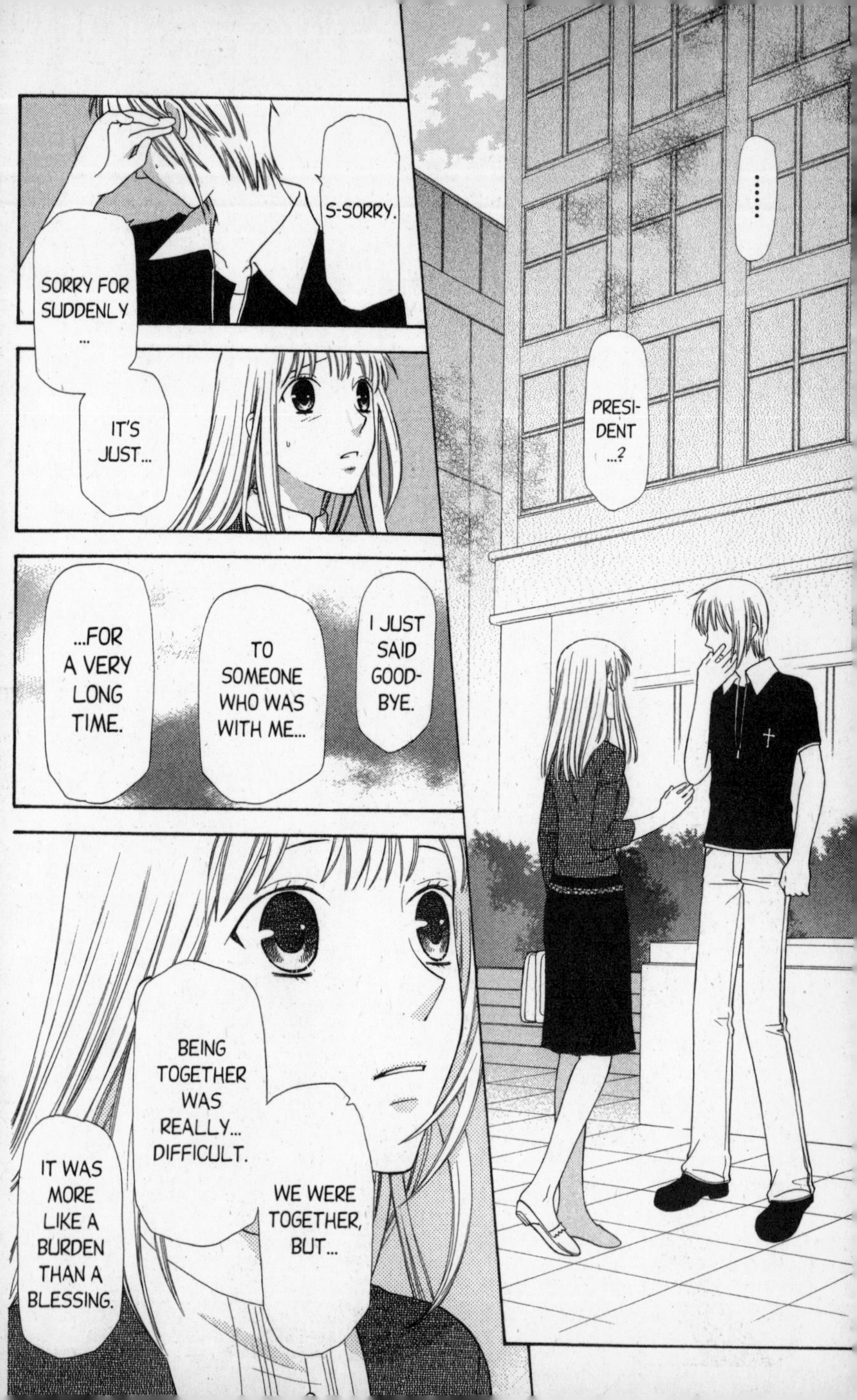
......
PRESI-DENT ...?
S-SORRY.
SORRY FOR SUDDENLY ...
IT'S JUST...
I JUST SAID GOOD-BYE.
TO SOMEONE WHO WAS WITH ME...
...FOR A VERY LONG TIME.
WE WERE TOGETHER, BUT...
BEING TOGETHER WAS REALLY... DIFFICULT.
IT WAS MORE LIKE A BURDEN THAN A BLESSING.

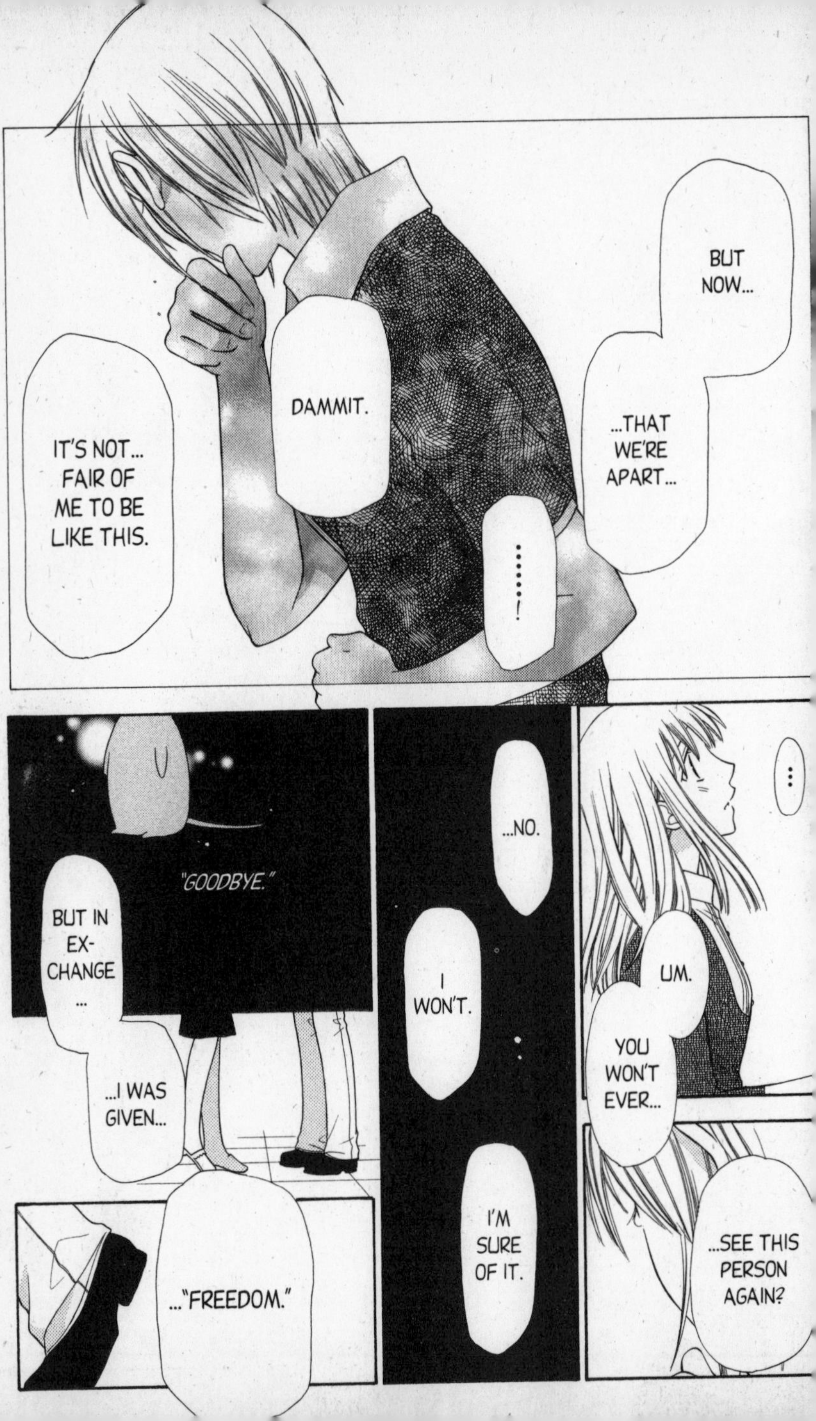
BUT NOW...
...THAT WE'RE APART...
......!
DAMMIT.
IT'S NOT... FAIR OF ME TO BE LIKE THIS.
...
UM.
YOU WON'T EVER...
...SEE THIS PERSON AGAIN?
...NO.
I WON'T.
I'M SURE OF IT.
"GOODBYE."
BUT IN EX-CHANGE...
...I WAS GIVEN...
..."FREEDOM."

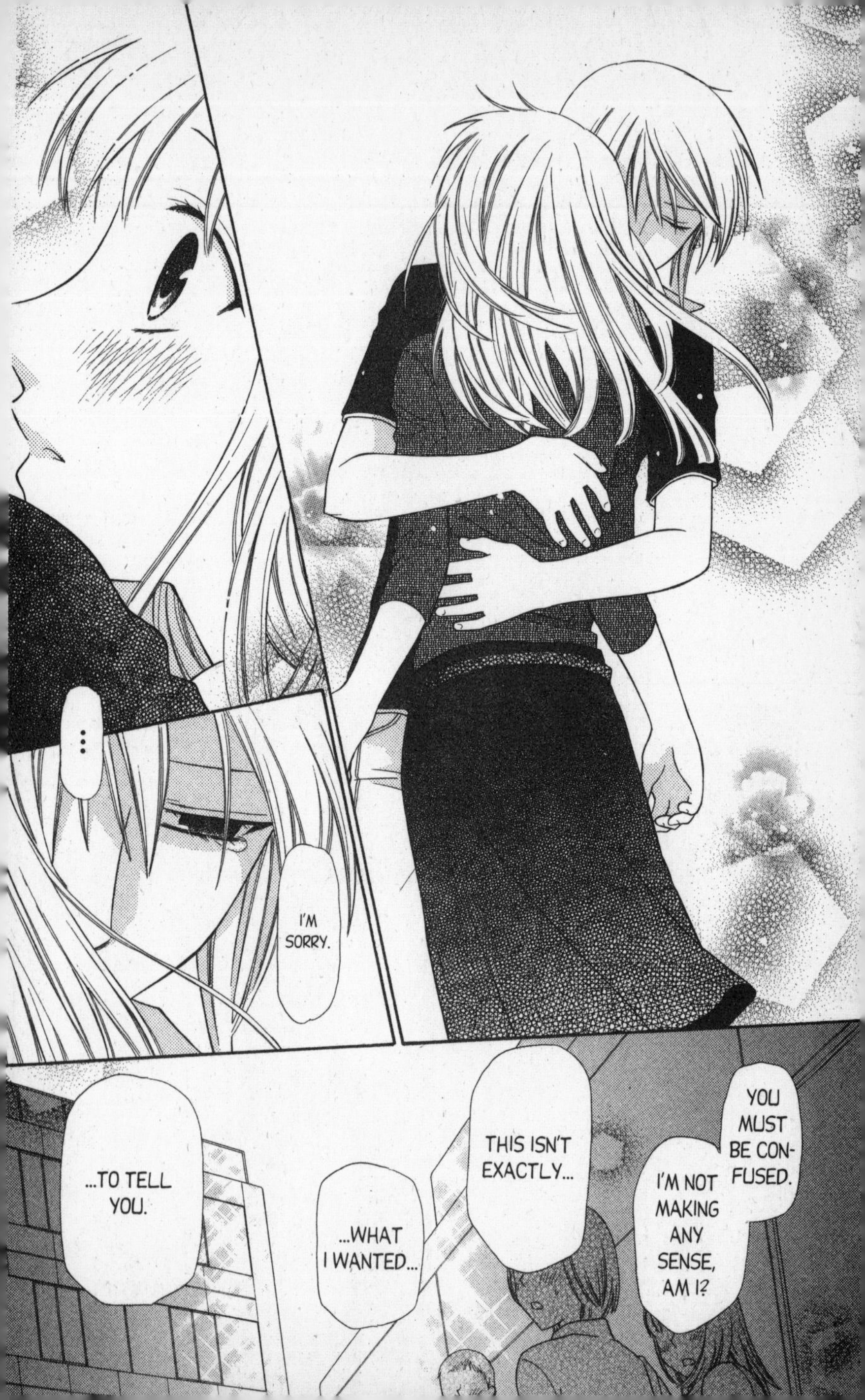
...
I'M SORRY.
YOU MUST BE CON-FUSED.
I'M NOT MAKING ANY SENSE, AM I?
THIS ISN'T EXACTLY...
...WHAT I WANTED...
...TO TELL YOU.

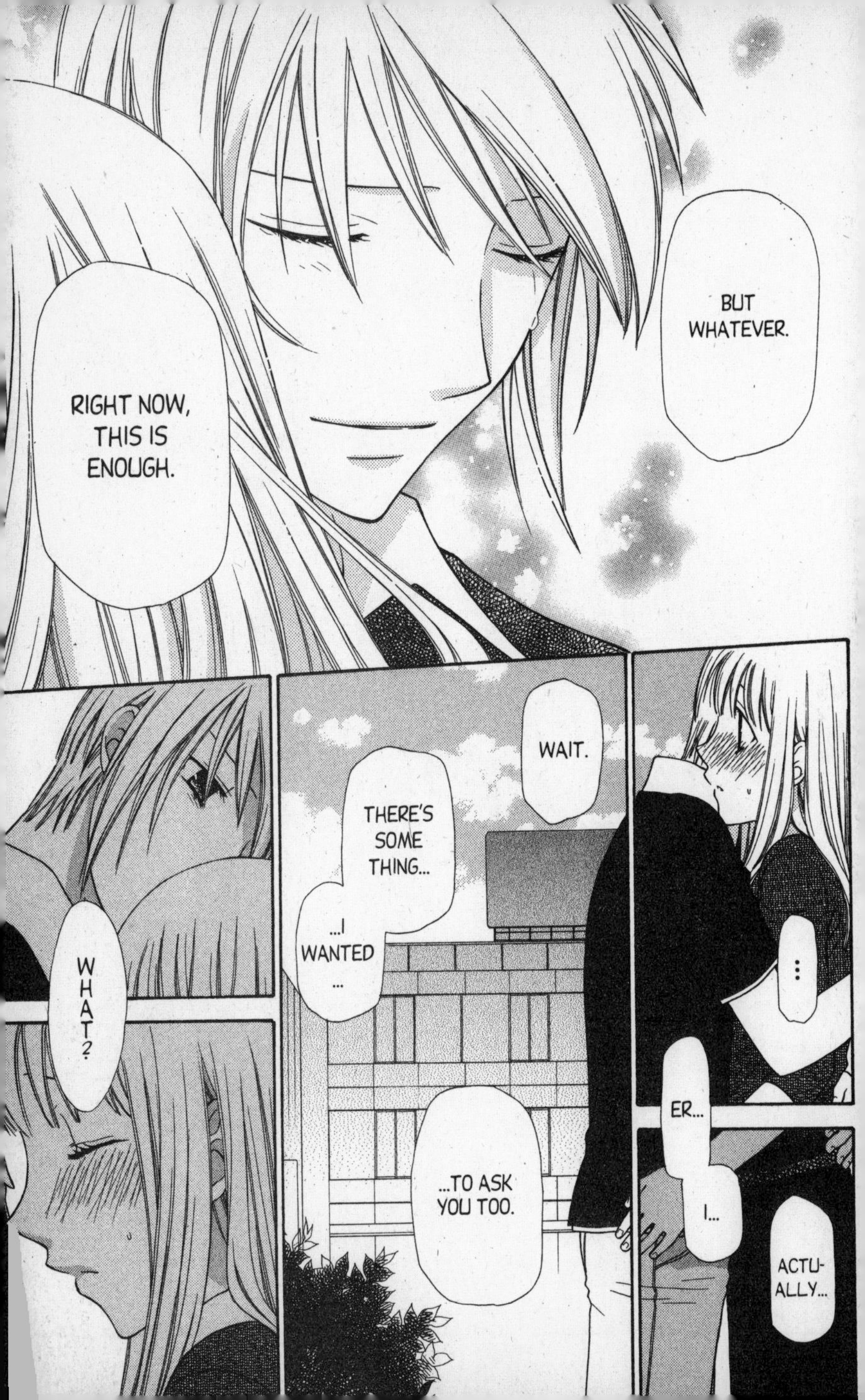
BUT WHATEVER.
RIGHT NOW, THIS IS ENOUGH.
...
ER...
I...
ACTUALLY...
WAIT.
THERE'S SOME THING...
...I WANTED ...
...TO ASK YOU TOO.
WHAT?

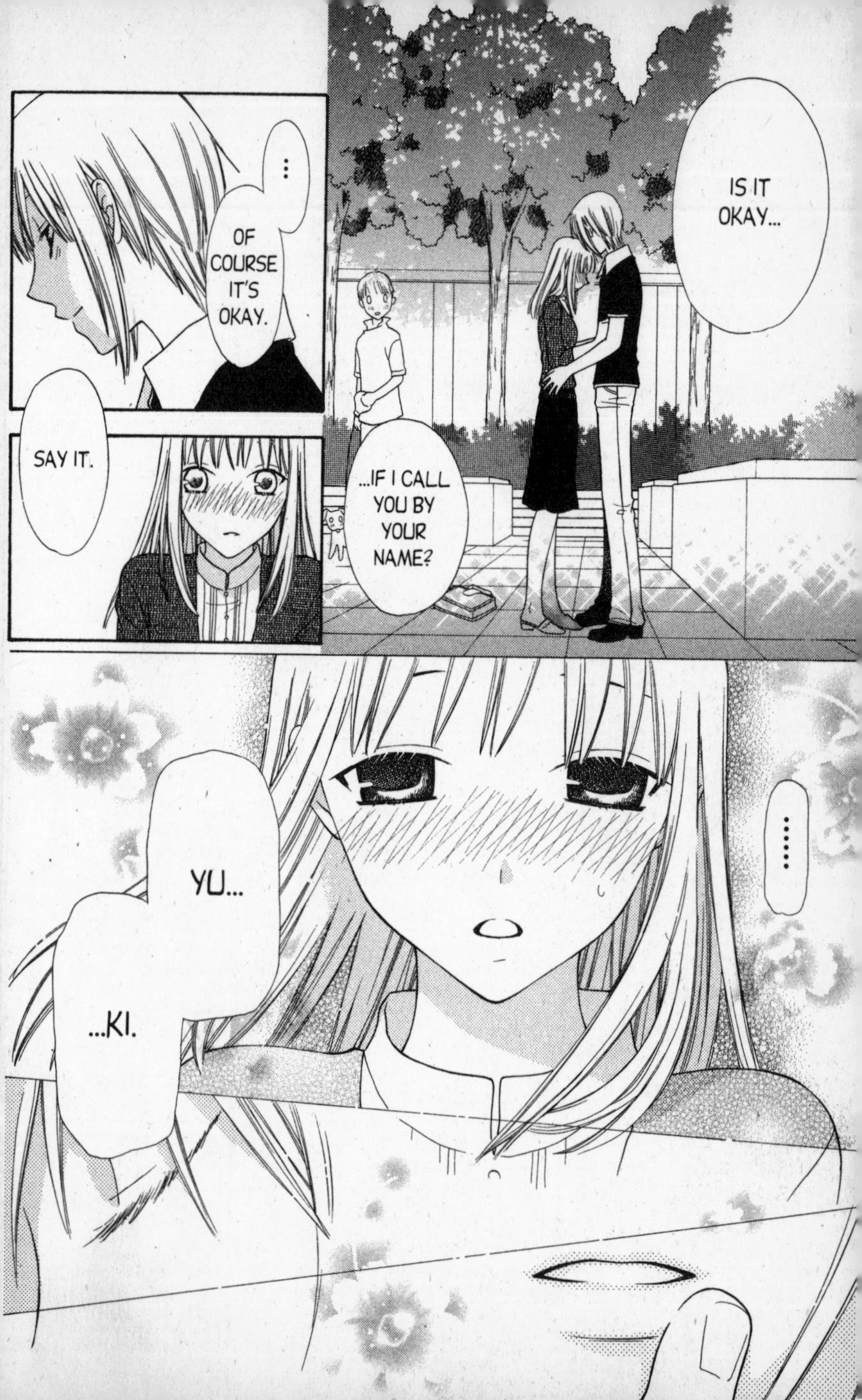

IS IT OKAY...
...IF I CALL YOU BY YOUR NAME?
...
OF COURSE IT'S OKAY.
SAY IT.
......
YU...
...KI.

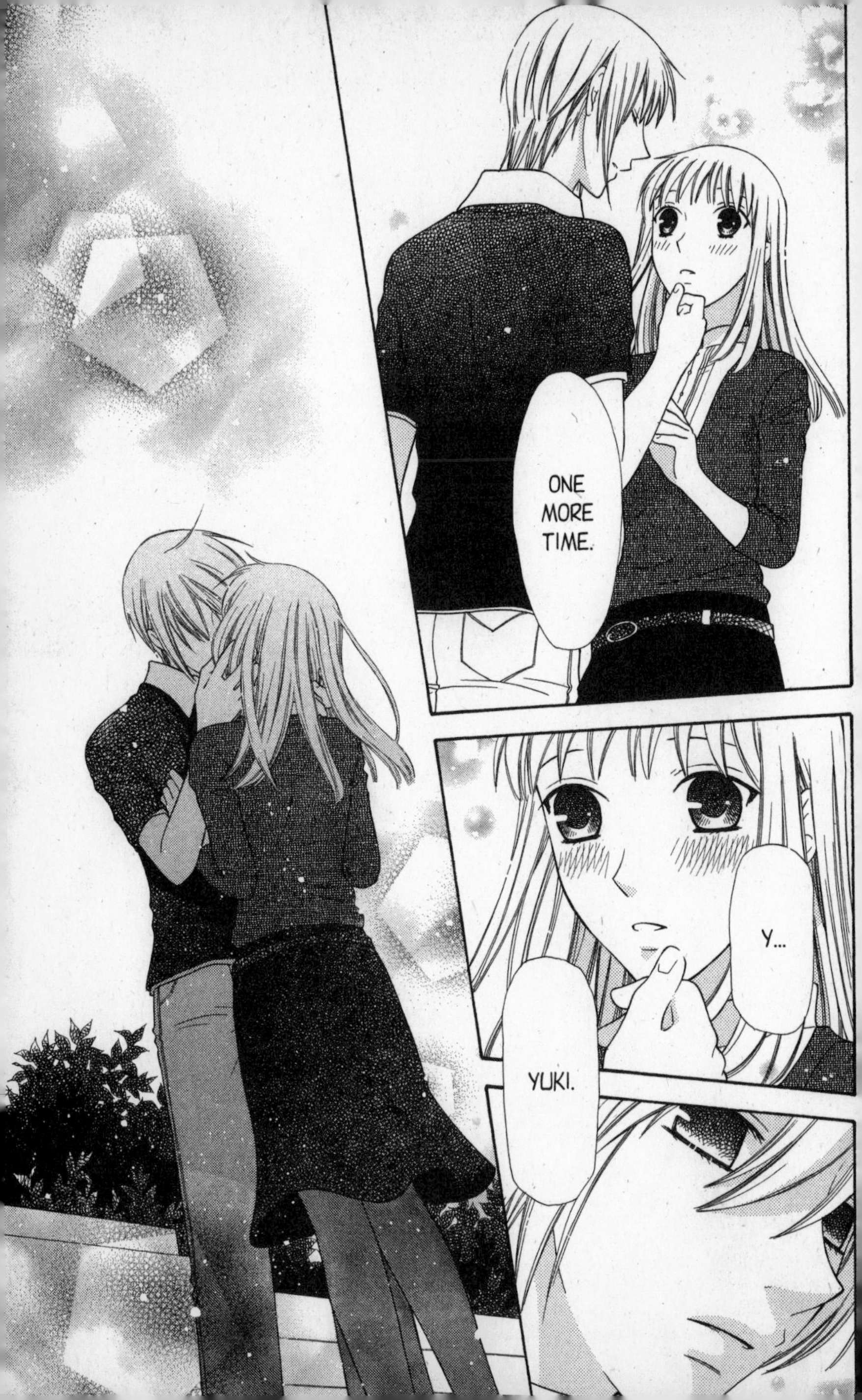
ONE MORE TIME.
Y...
YUKI.

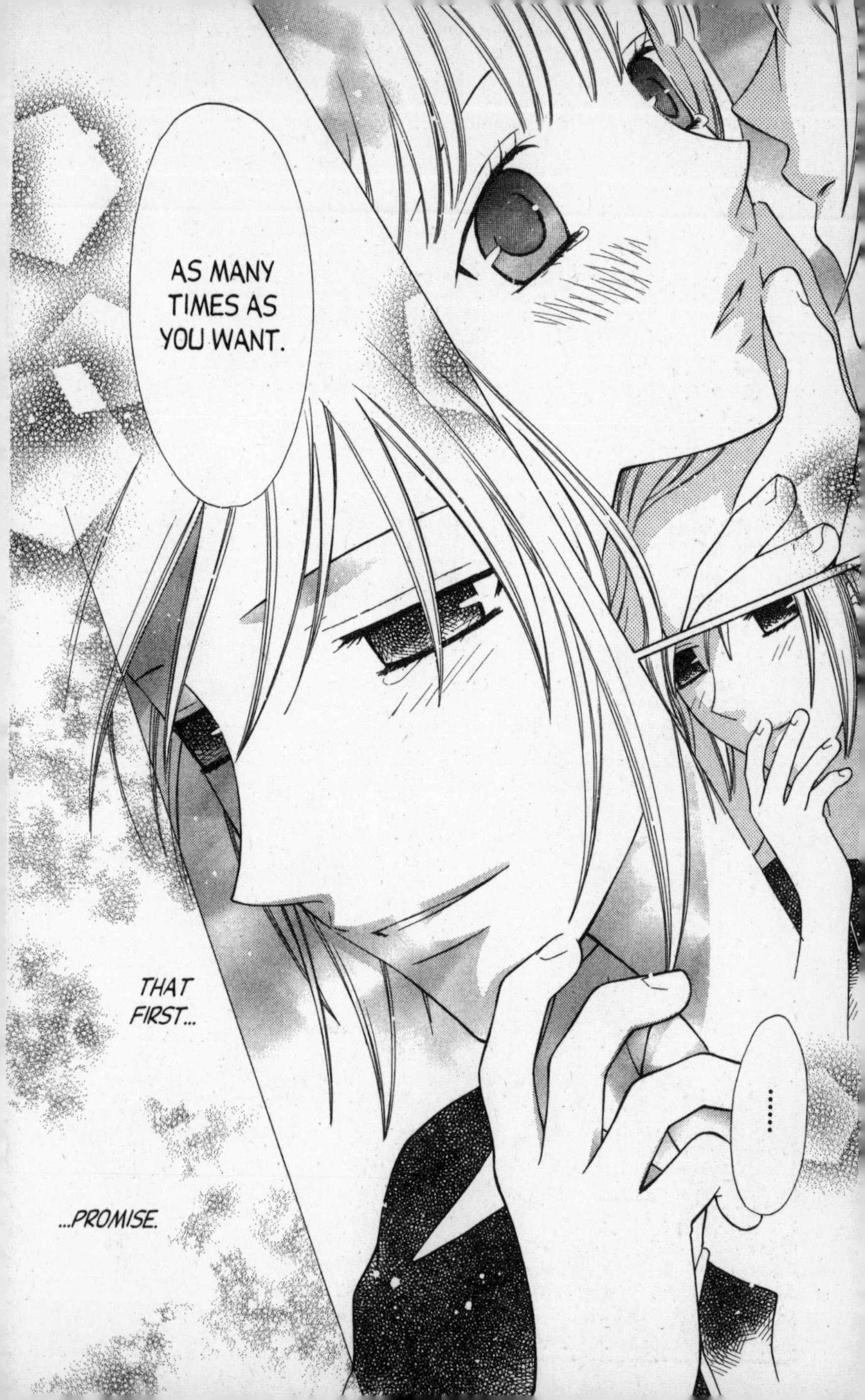
AS MANY TIMES AS YOU WANT.
......
THAT FIRST...
...PROMISE.

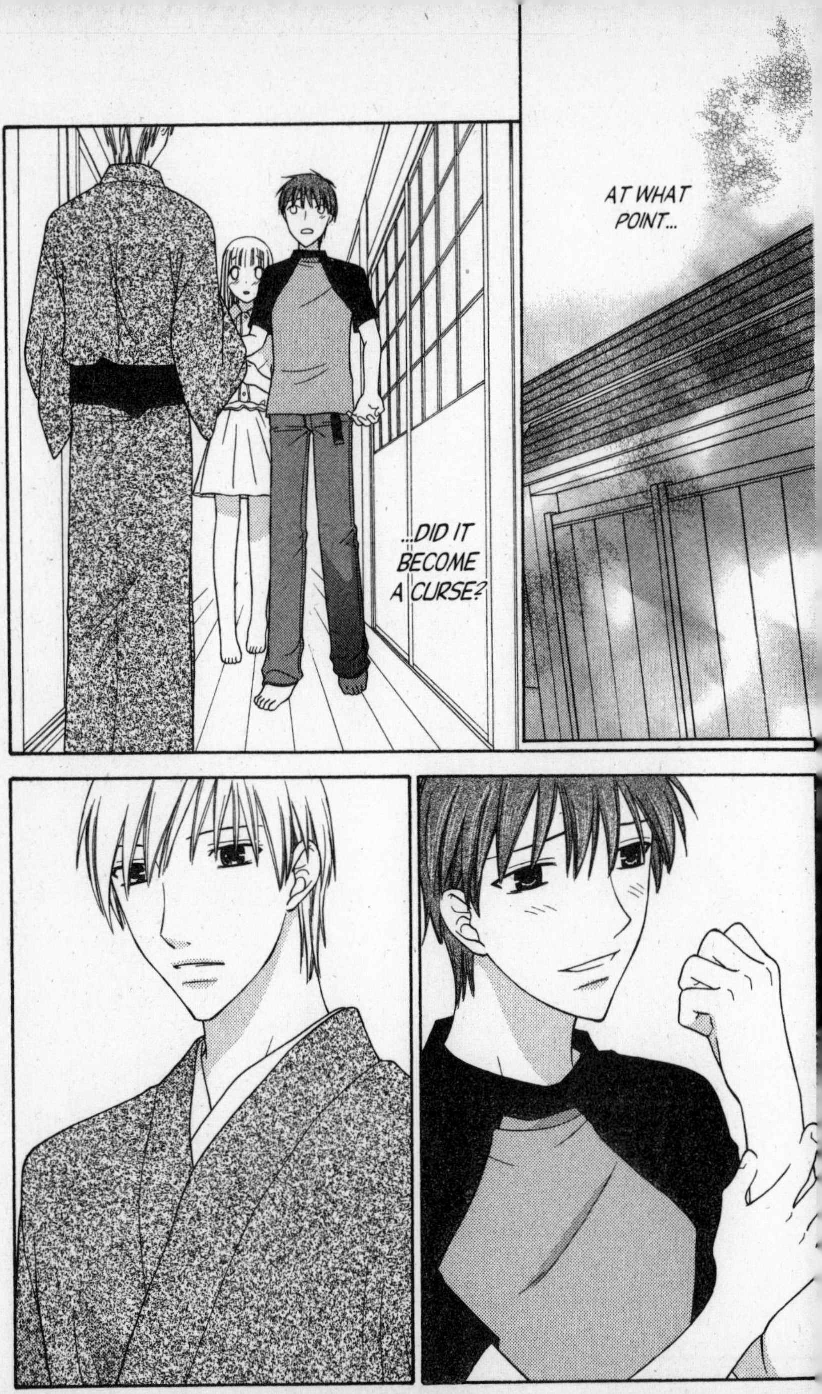
AT WHAT POINT...
...DID IT BECOME A CURSE?

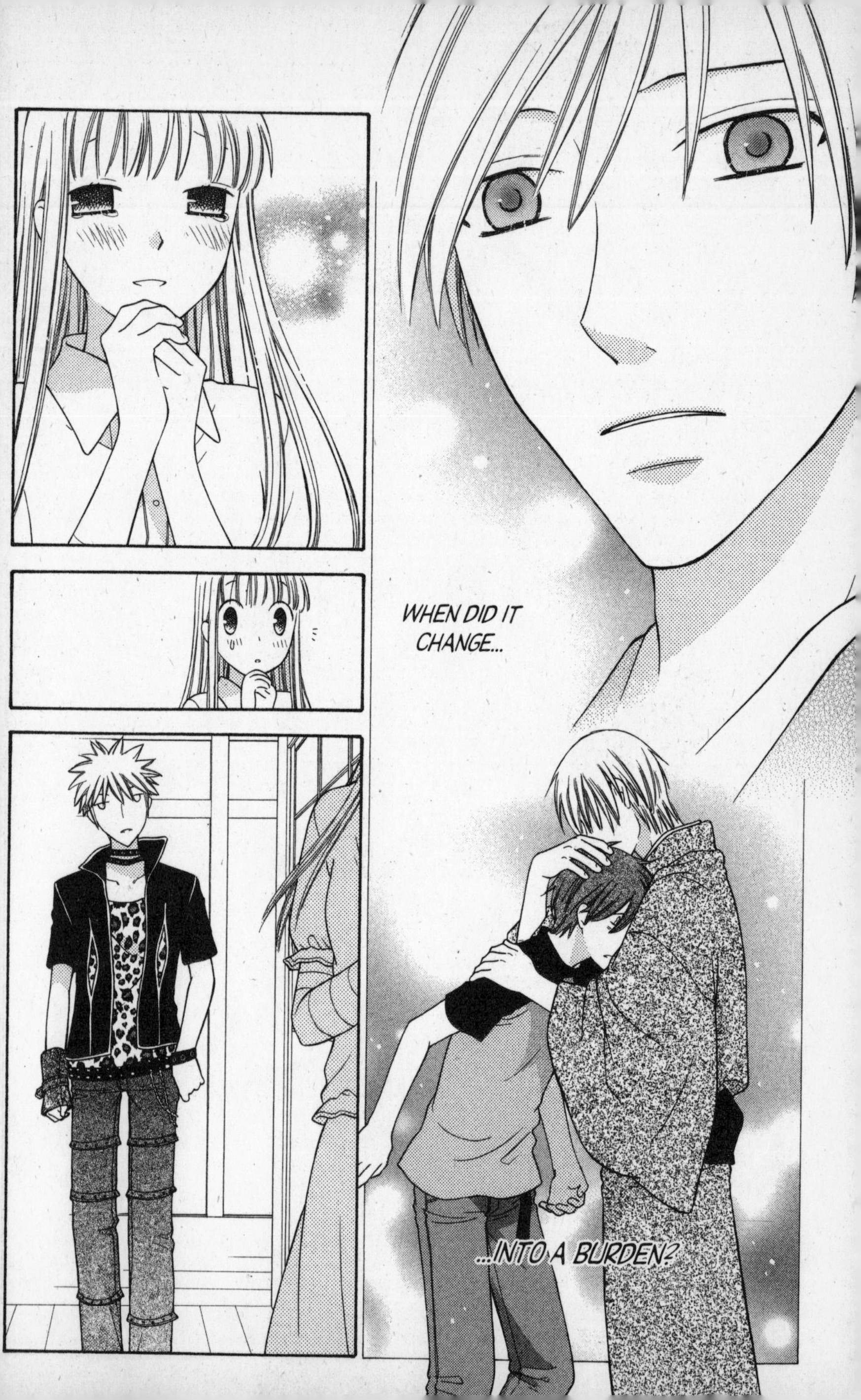
WHEN DID IT CHANGE...
...INTO A BURDEN?

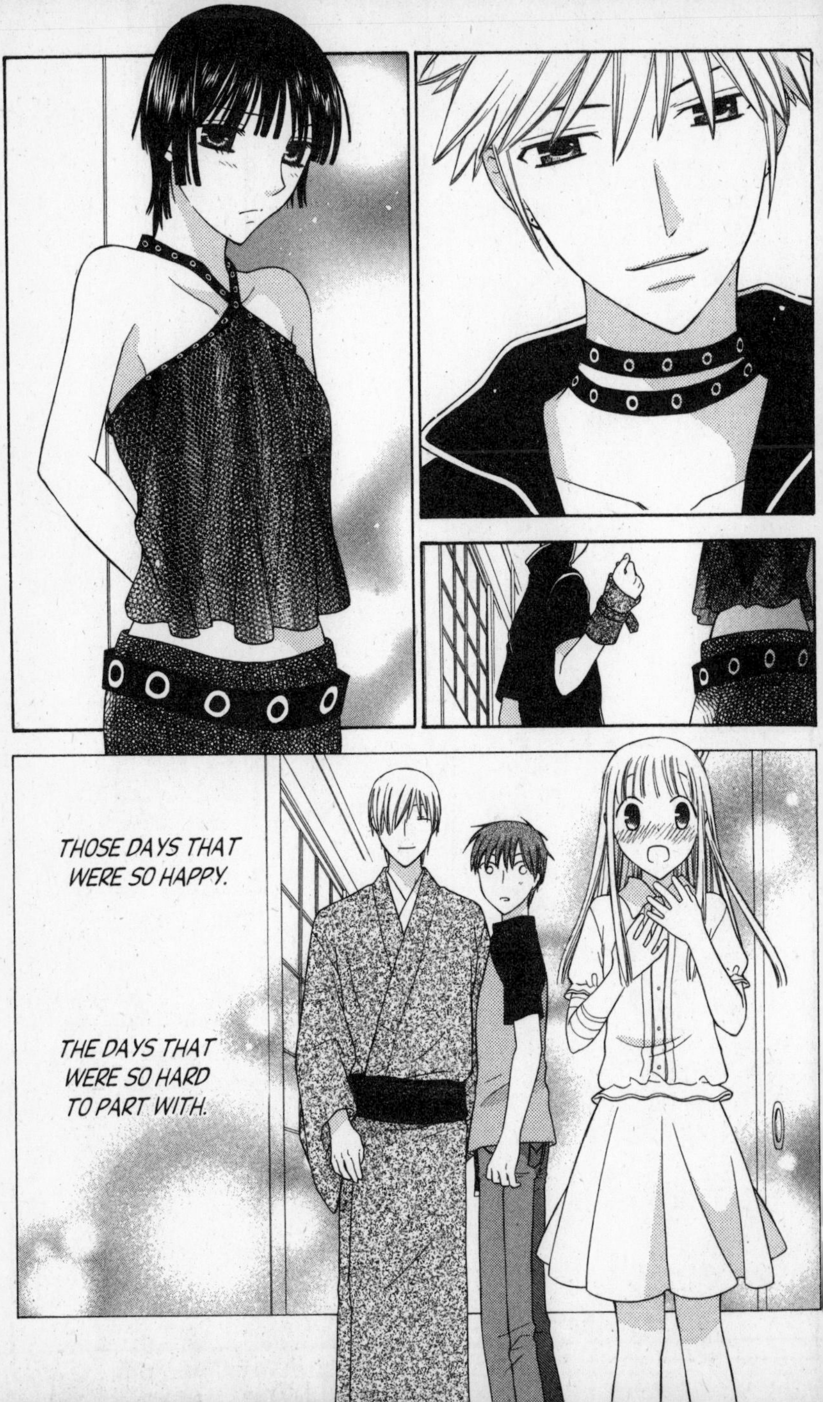
THOSE DAYS THAT WERE SO HAPPY.
THE DAYS THAT WERE SO HARD TO PART WITH.

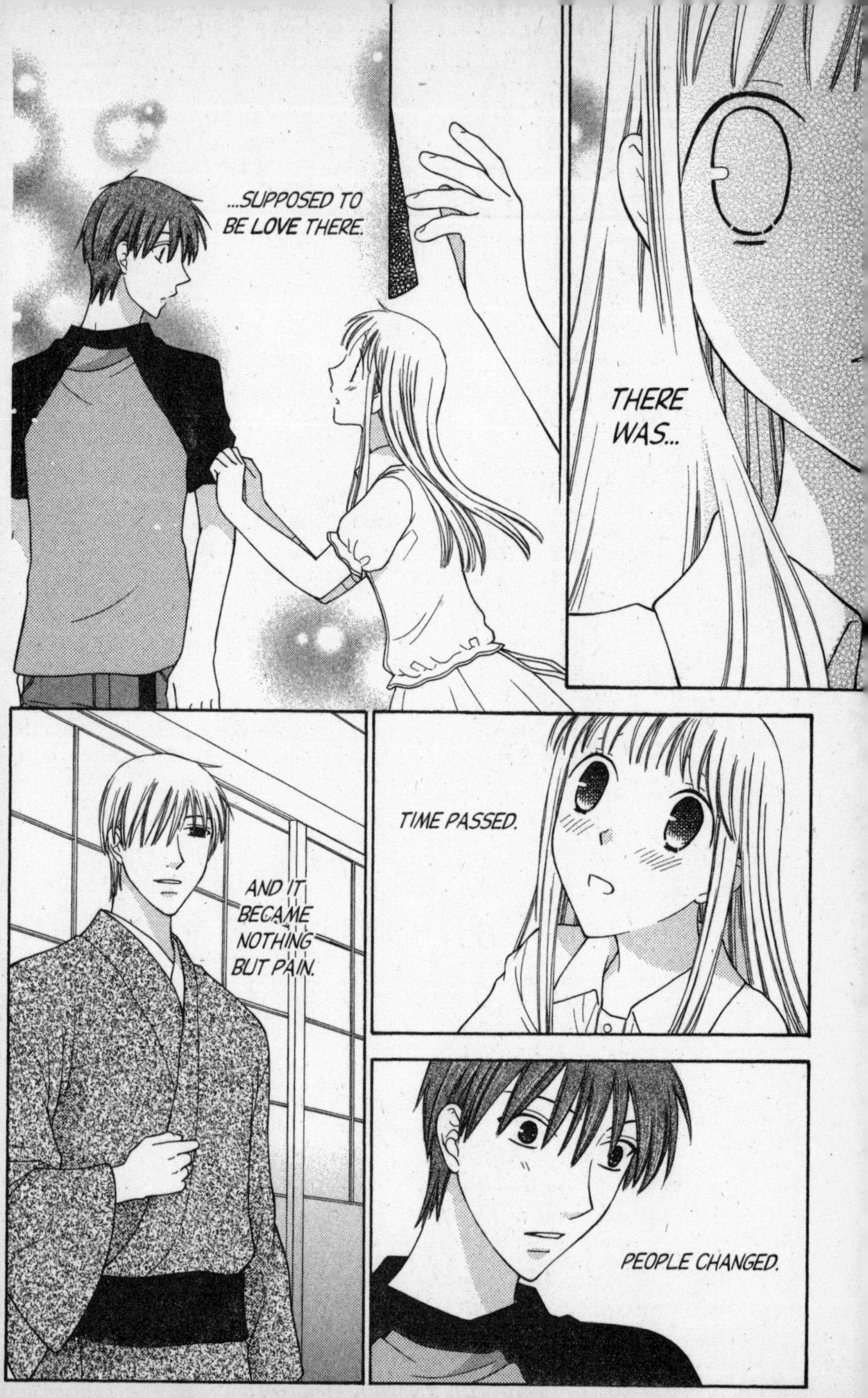
THERE WAS...
...SUPPOSED TO BE LOVE THERE.
TIME PASSED.
PEOPLE CHANGED.
AND IT BECAME NOTHING BUT PAIN.

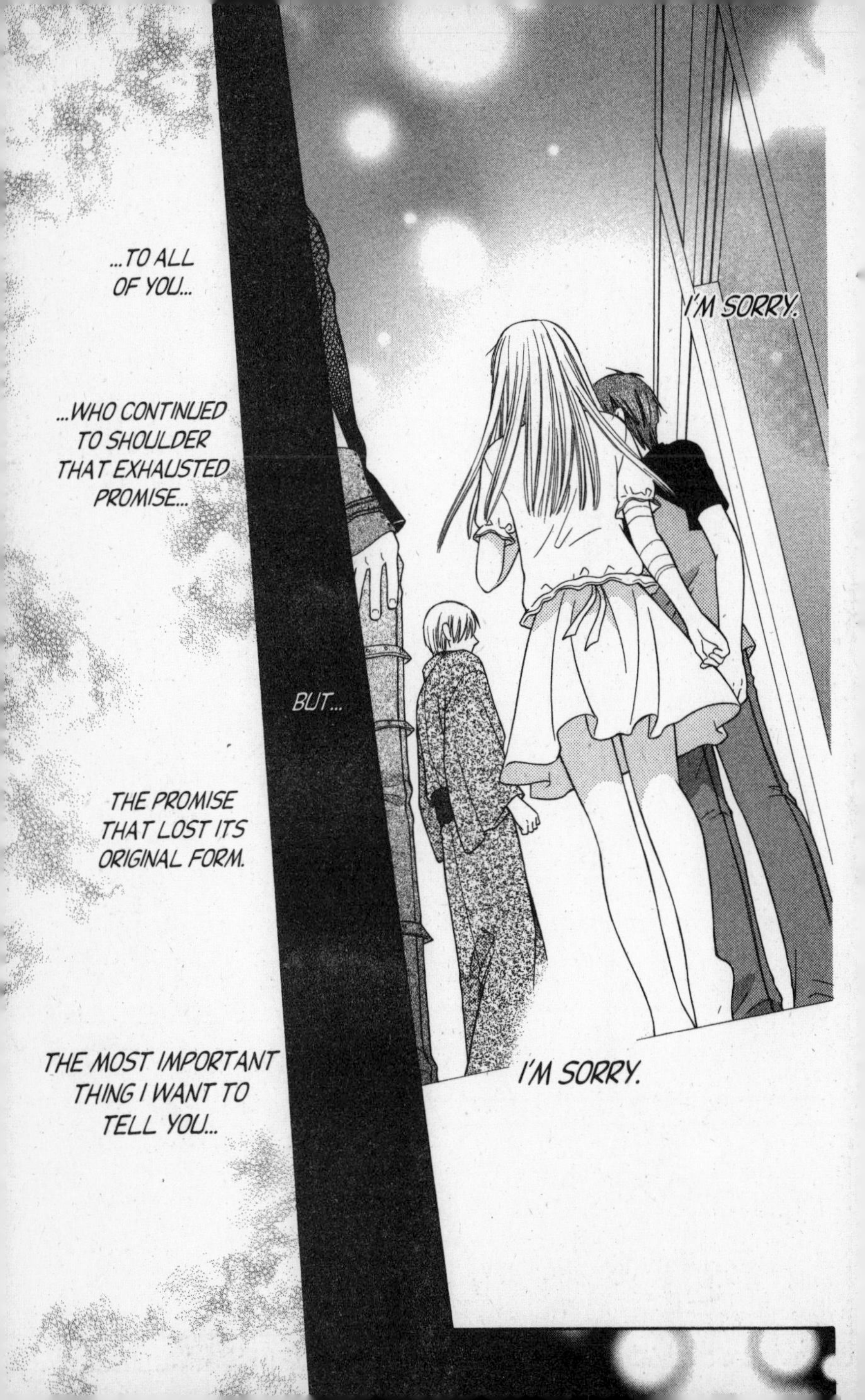
I'M SORRY.
I'M SORRY.
...TO ALL OF YOU...
...WHO CONTINUED TO SHOULDER THAT EXHAUSTED PROMISE...
BUT...
THE PROMISE THAT LOST ITS ORIGINAL FORM.
THE MOST IMPORTANT THING I WANT TO TELL YOU...

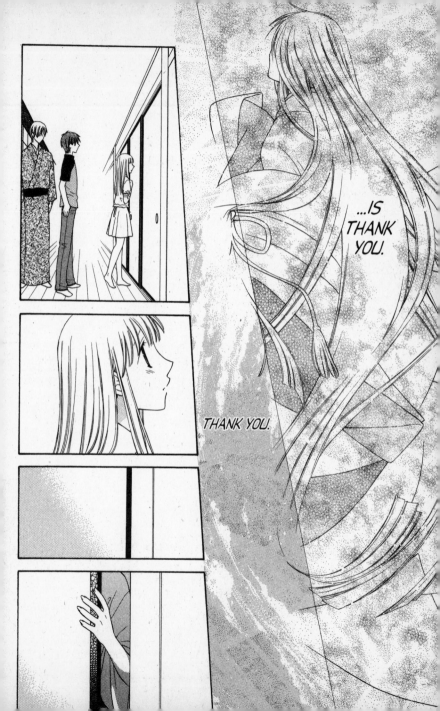

...IS THANK YOU.

THANK YOU.

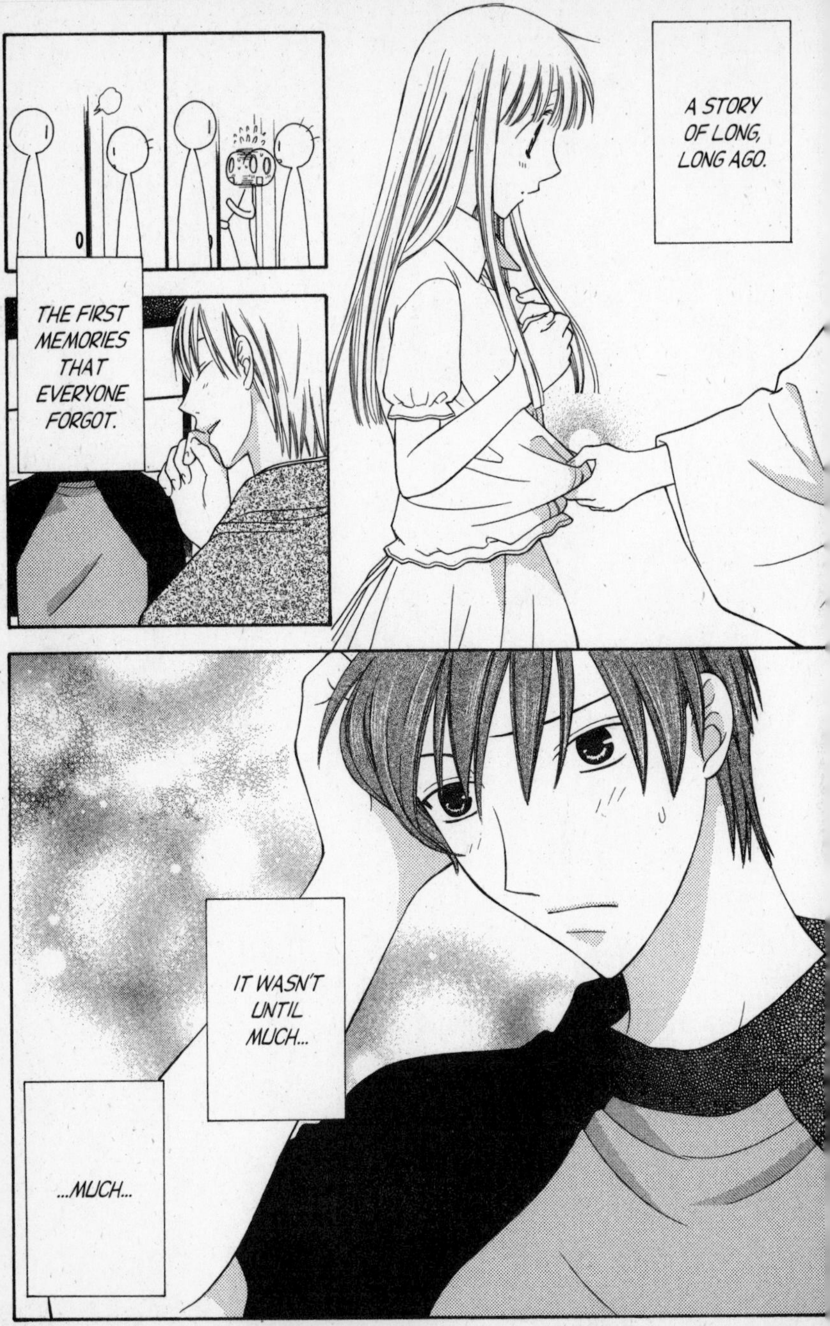
A STORY OF LONG, LONG AGO.
THE FIRST MEMORIES THAT EVERYONE FORGOT.
IT WASN'T UNTIL MUCH...
...MUCH...

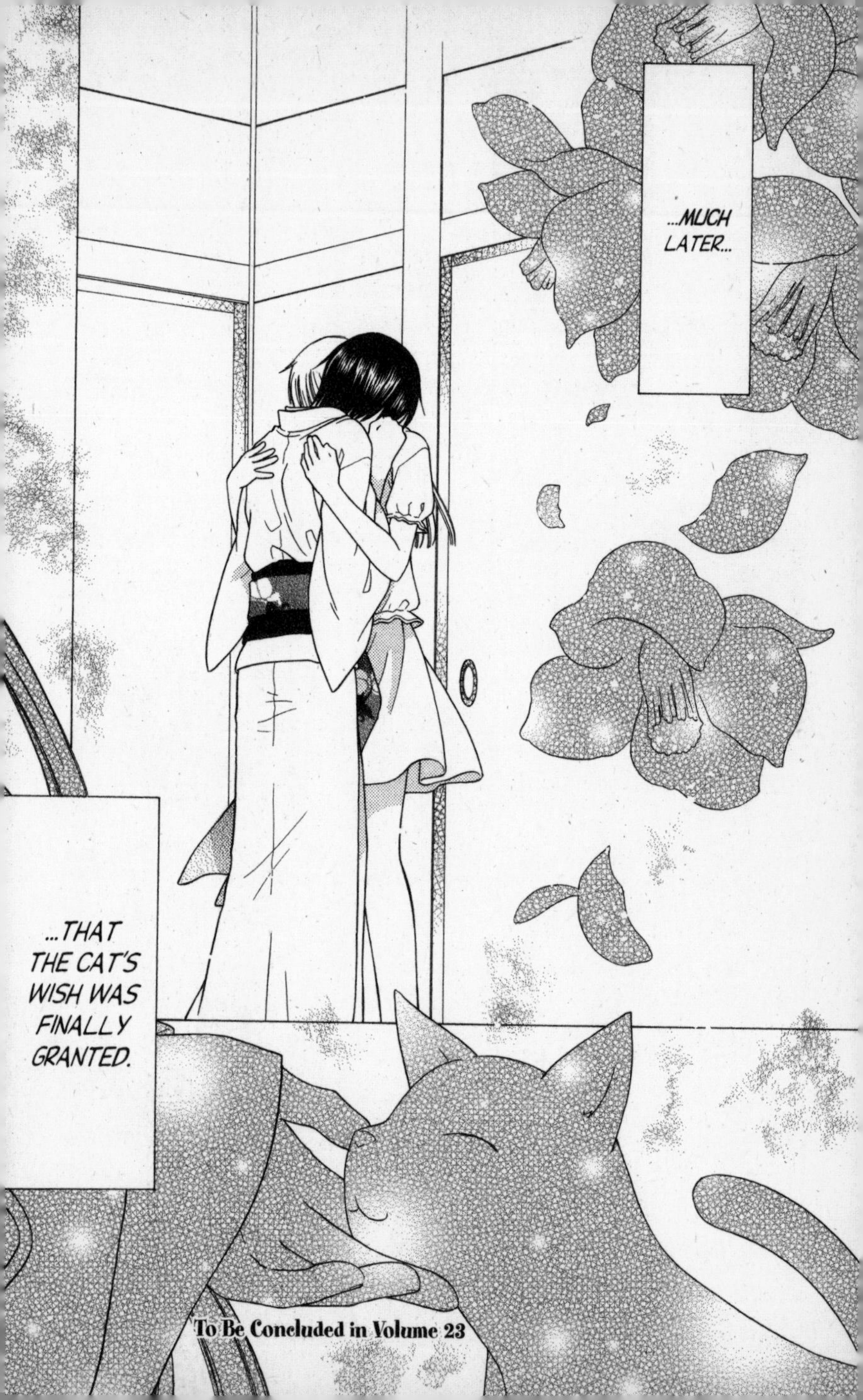
...MUCH LATER...
...THAT THE CAT'S WISH WAS FINALLY GRANTED.
To Be Concluded in Volume 23

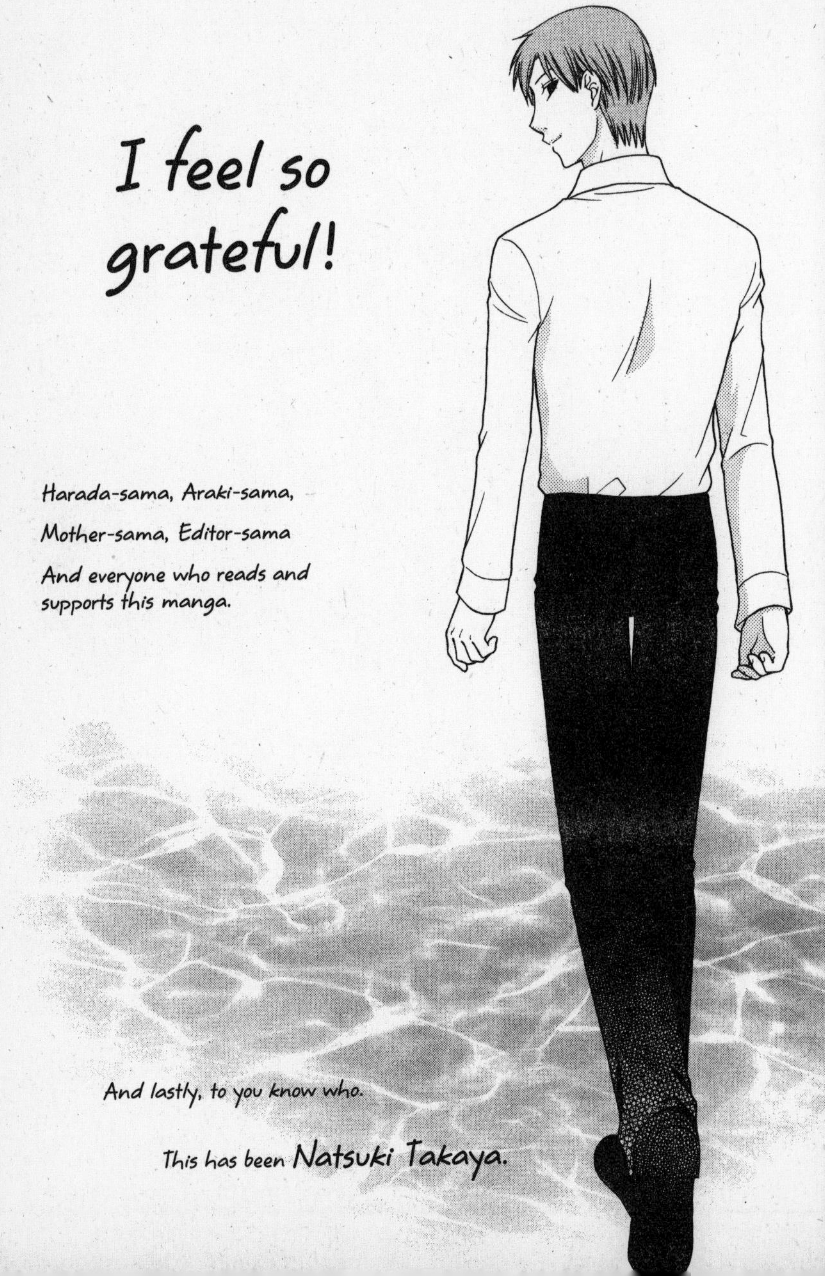
I feel so grateful!
Harada-sama, Araki-sama,
Mother-sama, Editor-sama
And everyone who reads and supports this manga.
And lastly, to you know who.
This has been Natsuki Takaya.

Next time in...

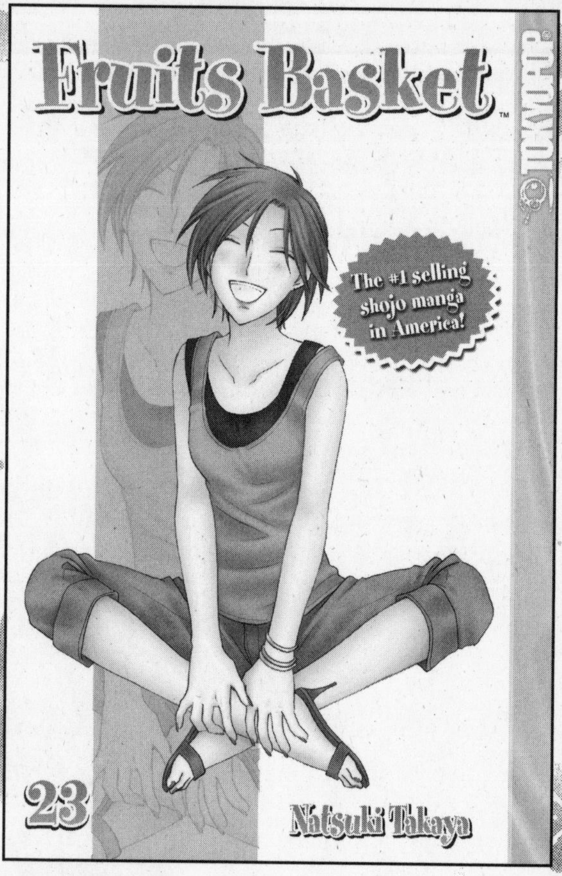
Fruits Basket™
TOKYOPOP
The #1 selling shojo manga in America!
23
Natsuki Takaya

The Journey's End...

Curses have broken and the eternal banquet has finally come to a close. But there are still some loose ends to be wrapped up before the last page of Fruits Basket arrives! How will each of the members of the Zodiac deal with their newfound freedom? Can forgiveness come in the wake of Akito's past actions, and a new surprising revelation?

Fruits Basket Volume 23
Available July 2009

Fans Basket

Fans Basket is back thanks to awesome intern Stephanie Trautwein from Los Angeles. She picked out a great batch of art to highlight and wrote some inspired comments. Thanks for all your help, Stephanie! And of course, thanks to all the fans who keep sending us their wonderful work. To properly thank you all, we are sending out postcards to all of you who provided addresses. And to those who we couldn't reach, please know that we appreciate you so much. Thank you for helping make Fruits Basket the phenomenon that it is!

And so we can continue to appreciate all the great fan art you guys provide, TOKYOPOP is starting something new. From now on, please do NOT send any more fan art to our office. Huh? What? Relax! What we want instead is for you to upload the images to our website! This way, everyone can appreciate your work even after volume 23 is published. Check the end of this section for exactly what to do. Fruits Basket Forever!

- Alexis Kirsch, Editor

Love
or
Hate

**Jessica Lin
Age 13
Lexington, MA**

I have to tell you, I wish I could draw this well when I was thirteen–or even now, for that matter! This artwork is so darling; Akito and Yuki's hair is shaped with great grace and the eyes, especially Yuki's, show great emotion. The question on Yuki's right side begs to be thought about. Is it love or is it hate? I do not think I understand the answer yet–do you?

Alexander Oriordan
Age 16
St. Paul, IN

I was amazed by this artwork from the first moment I saw it! The zodiac animals look so real. (Alexander, do you visit the zoo often?) Hiro is my favorite here—he looks so cute and yet so proud at the same time. But Tohru also looks very darling; happy to be with the ones she loves. And as for how to improve, just keep practicing!

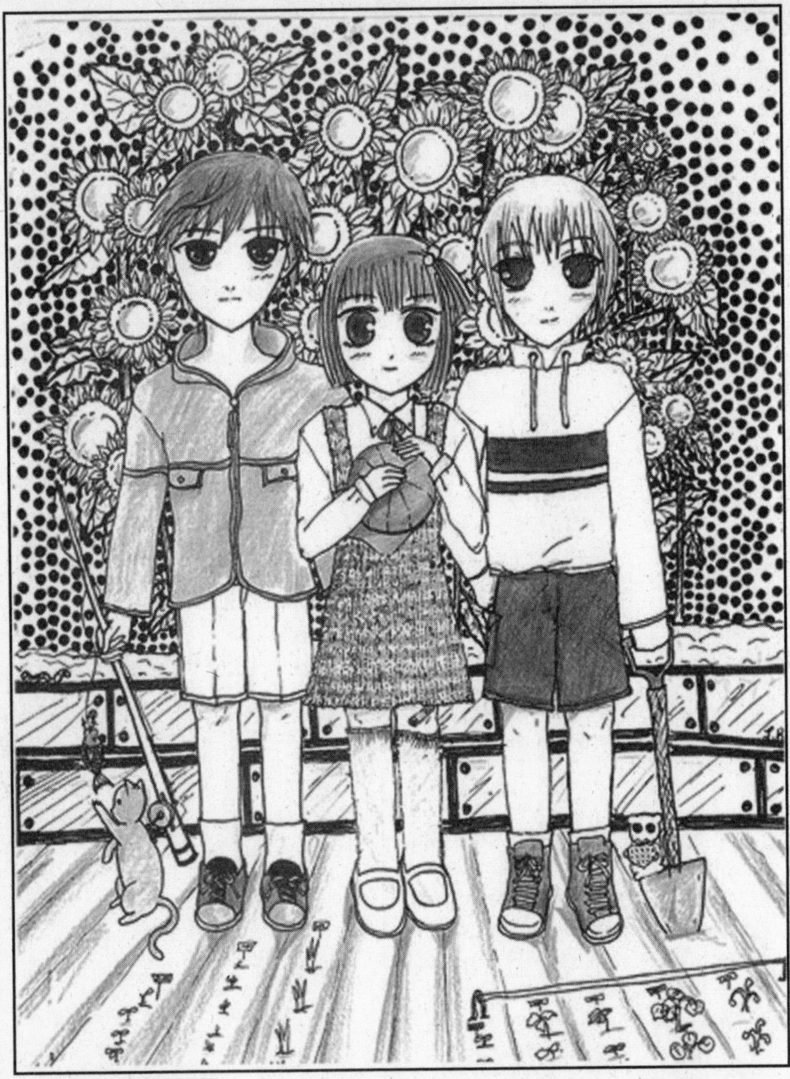

Lauralirio Rodriguez
Age 23
Seaside, CA

The detail on this artwork can be explained with no other word but "stunning." Look at all the little details; the little band-aid on Tohru's knee, the plants at their feet, the exquisite pattern on Tohru's dress or the dead little fishy being swatted at by the kitty underneath. It looks like a wonderful place to be a young Kyo, Tohru and Yuki!

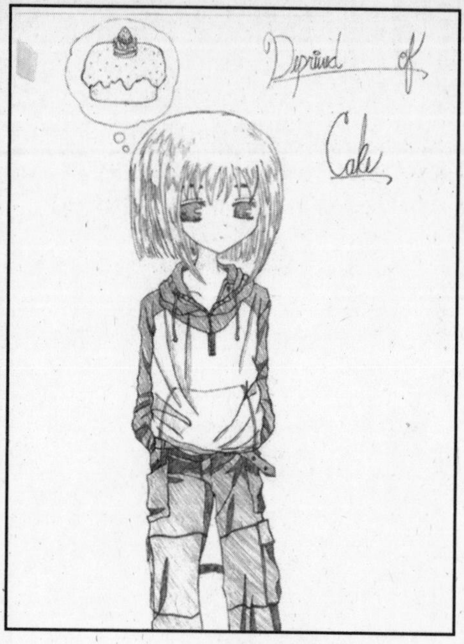
Deprived of Cake

Elizabeth Dobak
Age 12
Manassas, VA

Well Elizabeth, your dream has come true! Why did you take three long years to send this awesome work of art to us? The detail on the clothes is absolutely amazing! Kisa-chan looks so very cute in her sad state of cake-less-ness, and the yummy looking cake is making me hungry. Please continue to draw! I want to see more of your talent published in the future!

Linh Truang
Age 13
Rochester, NY

Of all the talented artwork Ling submitted (four in total!) this one was my favorite. Kisa-chan looks so cute in her loli outfit holding a very cuddly-looking tiger. The details are great—I love the shading and her cute little socks. She looks so happy and excited, like she is seeing something wonderful just beyond the page! What are you so happy about Kisa-chan? Please let us know soon!

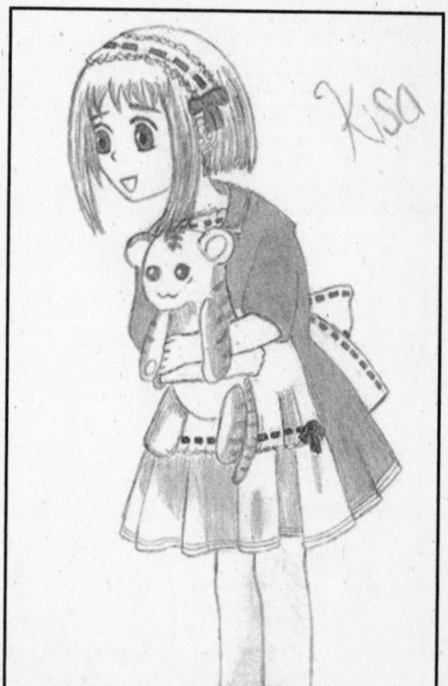
Kisa

Jenna Barnes
Age 13
Spencer, IA

Jesse Barnes
Age 13
Spencer, IA

Check out these pictures from twins Jenna and Jesse! Yuki must be very hungry in this picture! Is that drool I see? I guess you can say that his cute little chibi eyes are in fact bigger than his stomach! Will he be able to eat the entire rice ball? Only time will tell. These are some of the cutest chibis I've ever seen.

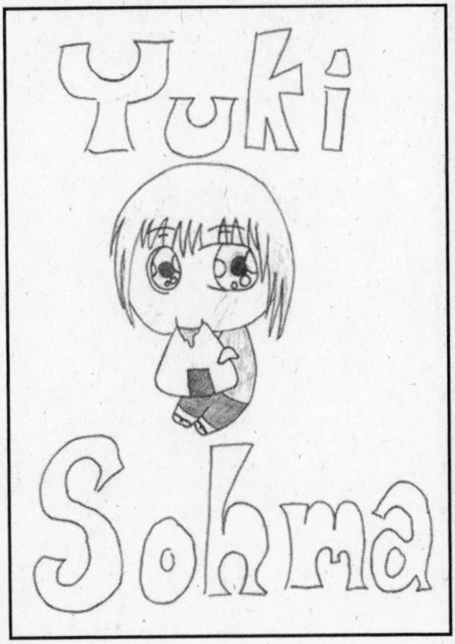
Yuki
Sohma

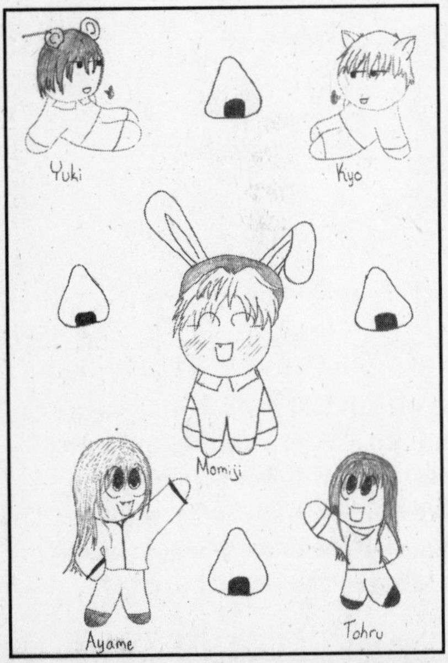
Yuki
Kyo
Momiji
Ayame
Tohru

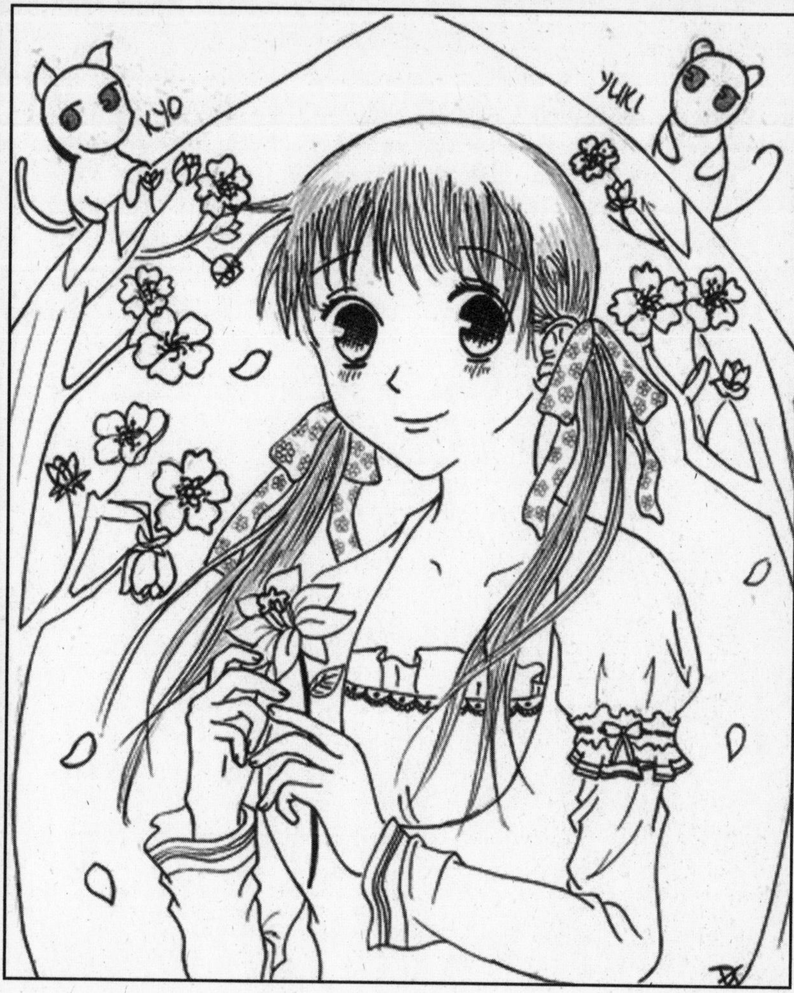
KYO
YUKI

Danah Macaraig
Age 17
Pomona, NY

Wouldn't it be so nice to take a stroll underneath the cherry blossoms on a breezy spring day? Tohru looks so peaceful here, with her cute hair ties blowing in the breeze. She is holding a daffodil's petal–perhaps to ask if the one she loves, loves her back. "He loves me, he loves me not..."

Angele Salanga
Age 17
Na'alehu, Hawaii

Hana, Tohru and Uo look so sophisticated and beautiful in these original pieces by Angele. I love especially the details in Hana's skirt and Tohru's neckpiece. Tohru's face is also very sweet as well, and I enjoy the fact that this is not the quintessential Furuba style.

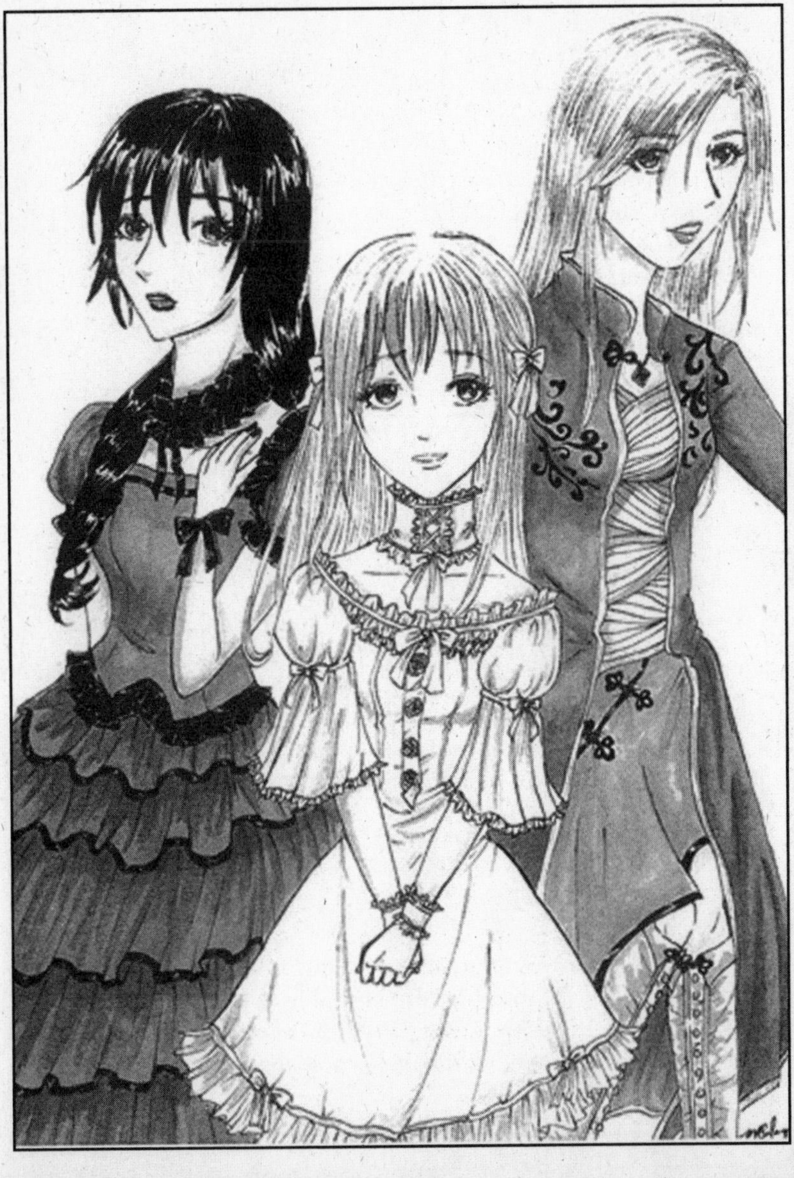

Andrea Parra
Age 17
Beaufort, SC

Everyone looks so happy in this picture it is hard not to become happy as well! It looks as even the stoic Kyo is trying hard to resist a cheerful smile. I love the position of the kitty Kyo, and the shading on the colored version is really great! I am sorry you cannot see it here!

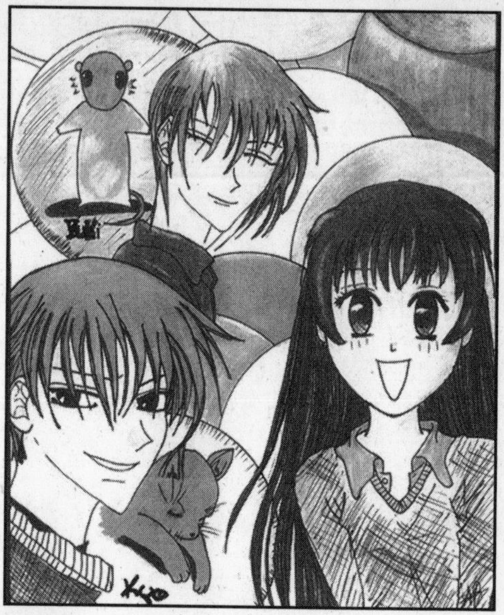
Kyo

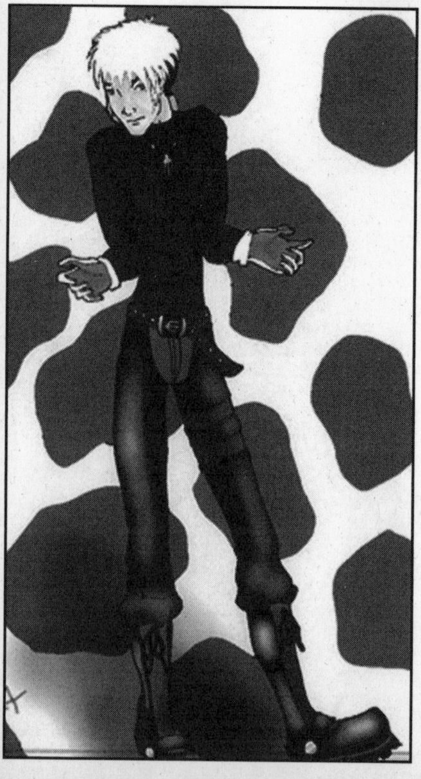

Katie Lin Bishop
Age 19
Payson, UT

Hatsuharu looks quite cool in this artwork–letting the dark Hatsu seep through, am I right? His shrugging expression really brings the attitude he is known for to the surface. But how will Rin react to his new fashion choices?

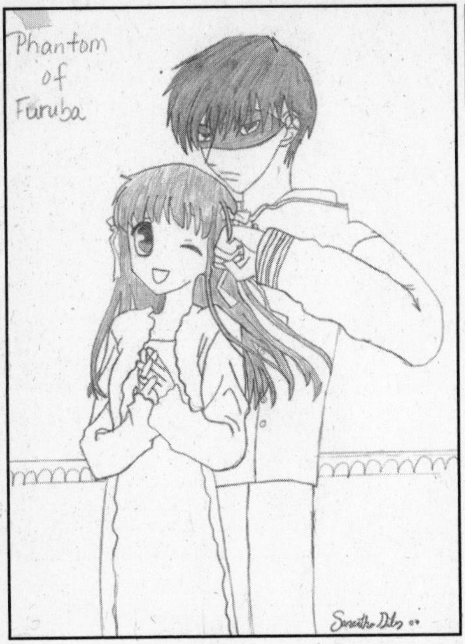
Phantom of Furuba

Samantha Giles
Age 13
Duarte, CA

Kyo looks so dashing in this picture with this mysterious mask on! Tohru doesn't seem to mind either, and she looks quite happy at his teasing. But will this "Phantom of Furuba" get the girl in the end of the story? You will have to keep reading to find out!

Jennifer Sawyer
Age 19
Bakersfield, CA

Aww! I want a free kitty! Kisa-chan looks so cute in that cardboard box with all those fuzzy balls of joy. Great job on her little legs and tail–it makes her look all the cuter! They are all so precious, but if I had to choose, I'd have to pick the kitty with the sign. I have wanted to take Kisa-chan home since the first day I saw her!

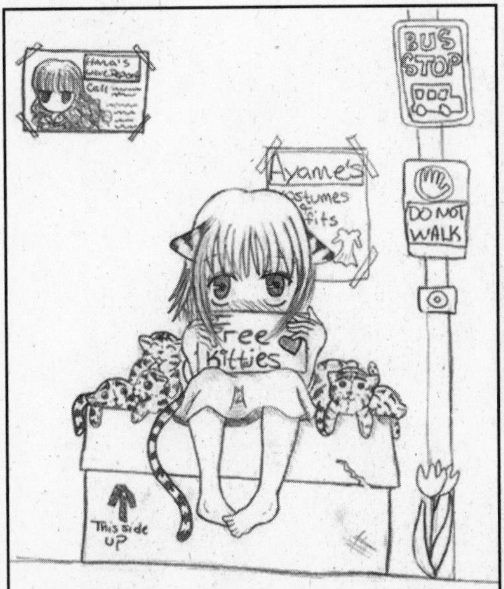
BUS STOP
DO NOT WALK
Ayame's
Free Kitties
This side up

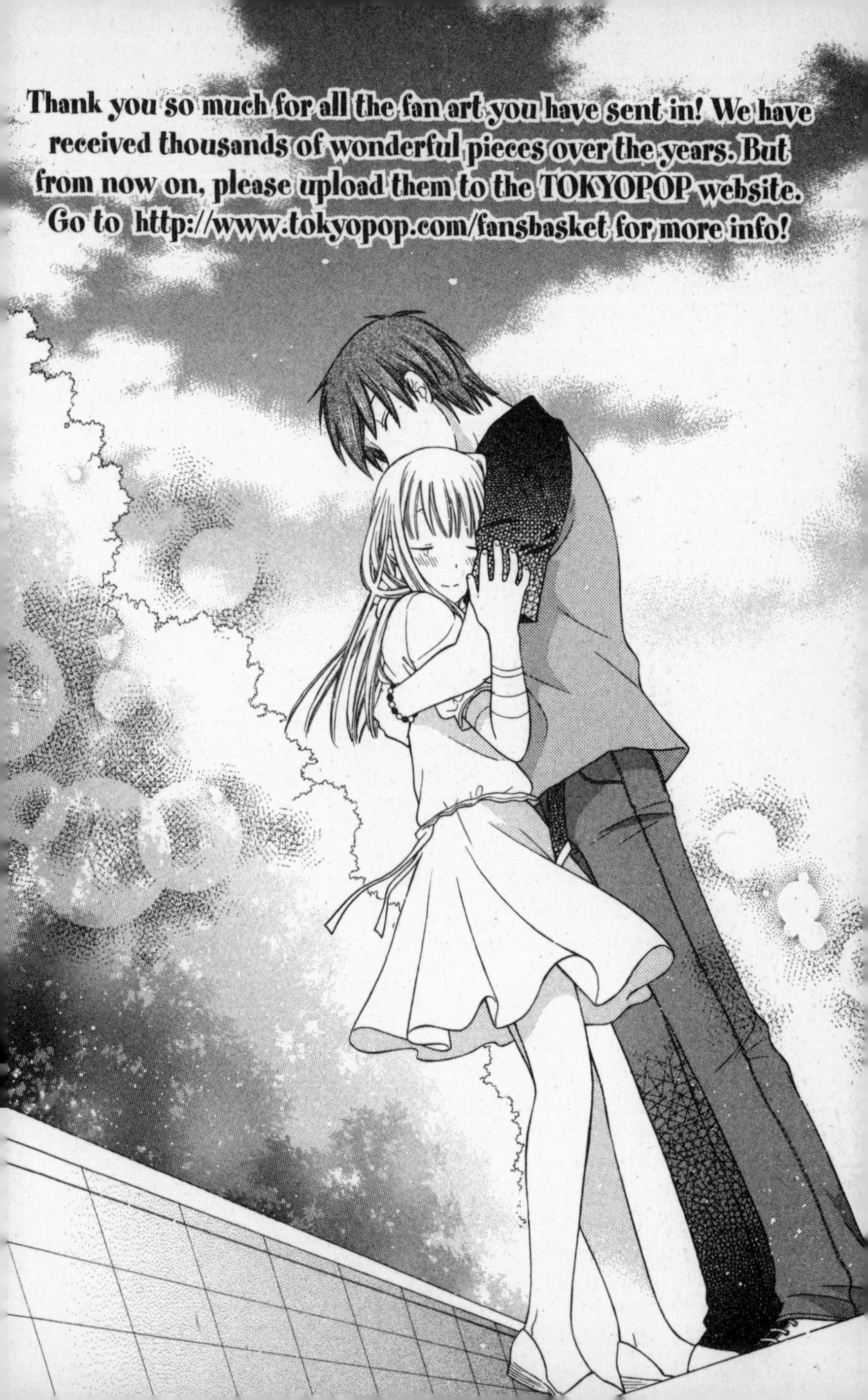
Thank you so much for all the fan art you have sent in! We have received thousands of wonderful pieces over the years. But from now on, please upload them to the TOKYOPOP website.
Go to http://www.tokyopop.com/fansbasket for more info!

TOKYOPOP MANGA SUPPLEMENT

TSUBASA™
THOSE WITH WINGS

FROM THE CREATOR OF
FRUITS BASKET!

All ex-thief Kotobuki and her ex-military commander boyfriend Raimon want is a quiet, peaceful life together. But if those seeking a legendary wish-granting wing have anything to say about it, they won't be in retirement for long!

Available wherever books are sold!

FANTASY

OT OLDER TEEN AGE 16+

TSUBASA WO MOTSU MONO © 1995 Natsuki Takaya // HAKUSENSHA, Inc.

FOR MORE INFORMATION VISIT: WWW.TOKYOPOP.COM

TOKYOPOP MANGA SUPPLEMENT

Phantom Dream™
volume 1

new manga from fruits basket creator natsuki takaya!

Tamaki Otoya, the last in an ancient line of summoners, is tasked to battle evil forces that threaten mankind. But when this fight turns against the love of his life, will he choose his passion or his destiny?

ON SALE NOW!

Read *Phantom Dream* online at
TOKYOPOP.com/PhantomDream

ROMANCE

T
TEEN
AGE 13+

GENEI-MUSOU: © 1994 Natsuki Takaya / HAKUSENSHA, INC.

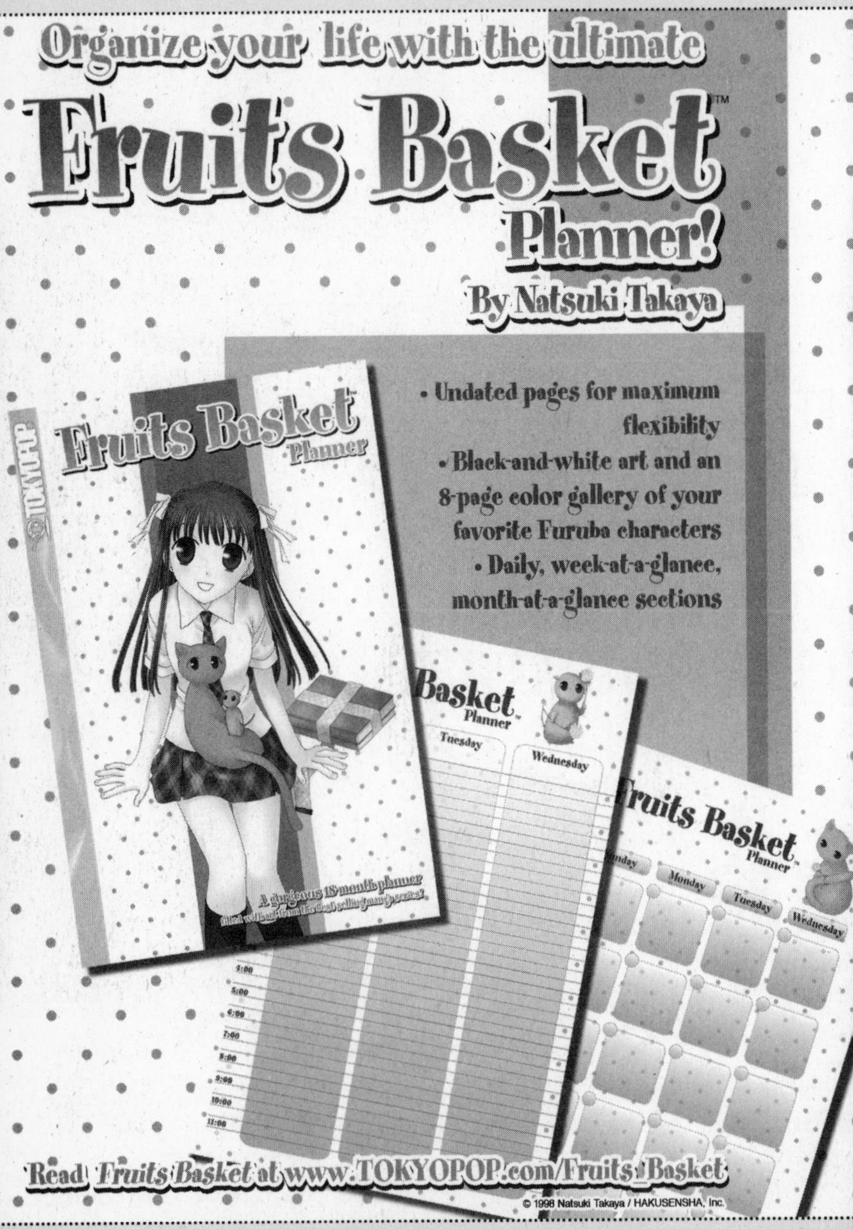

BUY IT AT WWW.TOKYOPOP.COM/SHOP

Fruits Basket™
sticker collection
stickers, pinups, and temporary tattoos!!

BEAUTIFY YOUR SURROUNDINGS —AND YOURSELF!— WITH GORGEOUS ART FROM *FRUITS BASKET!*

Fruits Basket
sticker collection

The #1 selling shojo manga in America!

Natsuki Takaya

includes pinups, stickers and temporary tattoos!

Pinup Sample Page

Pinup Sample Page

Temp. Tattoo Sample Page

Winner of the American Anime Award for Best Manga

This limited edition art book includes:
- Pinup art of all your favorite *Fruits Basket* characters
- Stickers
- Temporary Tattoos

© 1998 Natsuki Takaya / HAKUSENSHA, Inc

FOR MORE INFORMATION VISIT: WWW.TOKYOPOP.COM

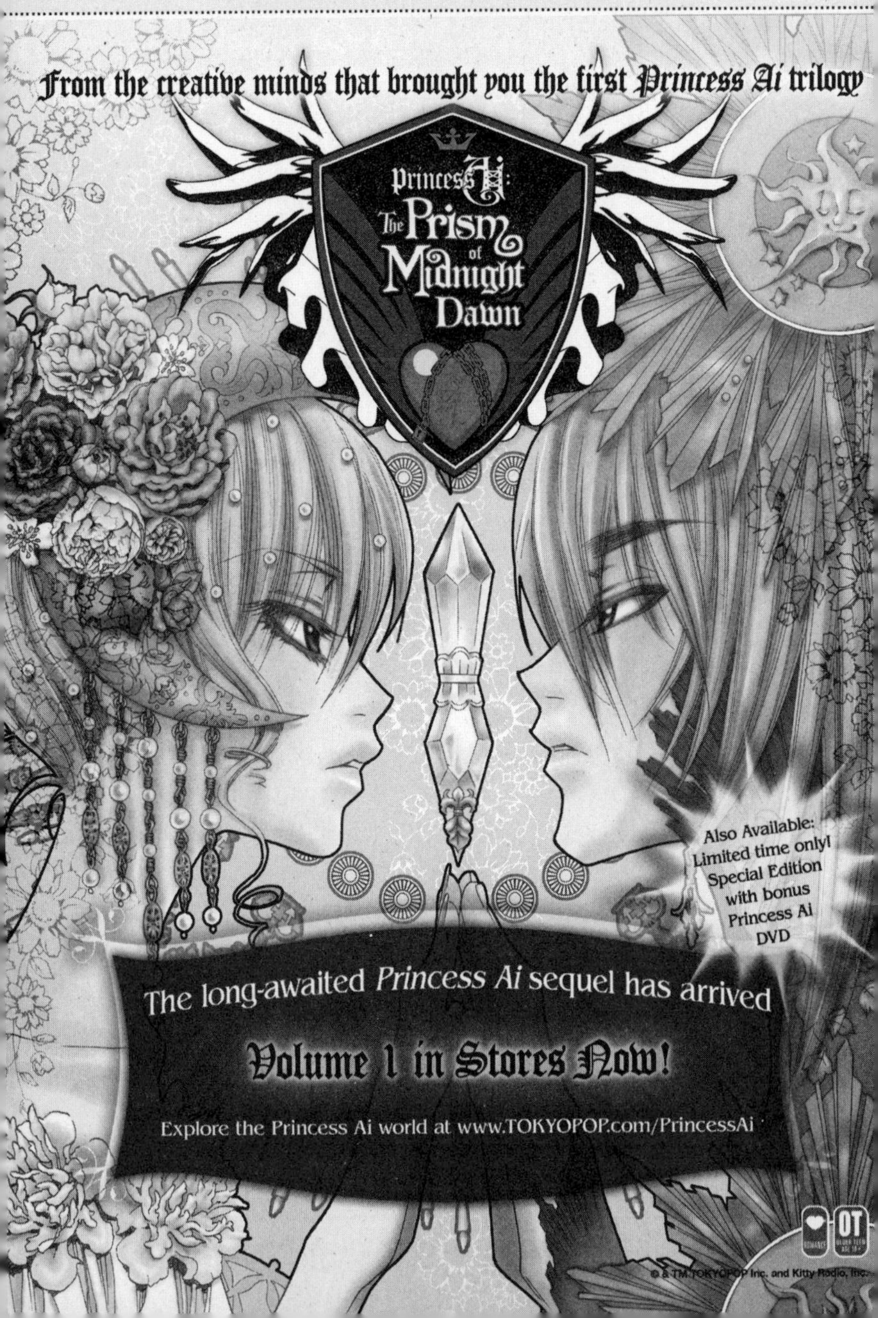
From the creative minds that brought you the first Princess Ai trilogy
Princess Ai: The Prism of Midnight Dawn
Also Available: Limited time only! Special Edition with bonus Princess Ai DVD
The long-awaited Princess Ai sequel has arrived
Volume 1 in Stores Now!
Explore the Princess Ai world at www.TOKYOPOP.com/PrincessAi
OT
© & TM TOKYOPOP Inc. and Kitty Radio, Inc.

LOVELESS™

Volume 8

LOVELESS
by Yun Kouga

ART NOT FINAL

HOW DO YOU FIND HAPPINESS WHEN YOUR NAME IS LOVELESS?

Ritsuka will have to decide once and for all what his true feelings are about his mysterious (and malevolent) older brother, not to mention where his loyalties lie!

FANTASY

OT
OLDER TEEN
AGE 15+

© Yun Kouga

Rated "Must Have" —IGN.com

ON SALE NOW!

Read *LOVELESS* at www.TOKYOPOP.com/onlinemanga

FOR MORE INFORMATION VISIT: WWW.TOKYOPOP.COM

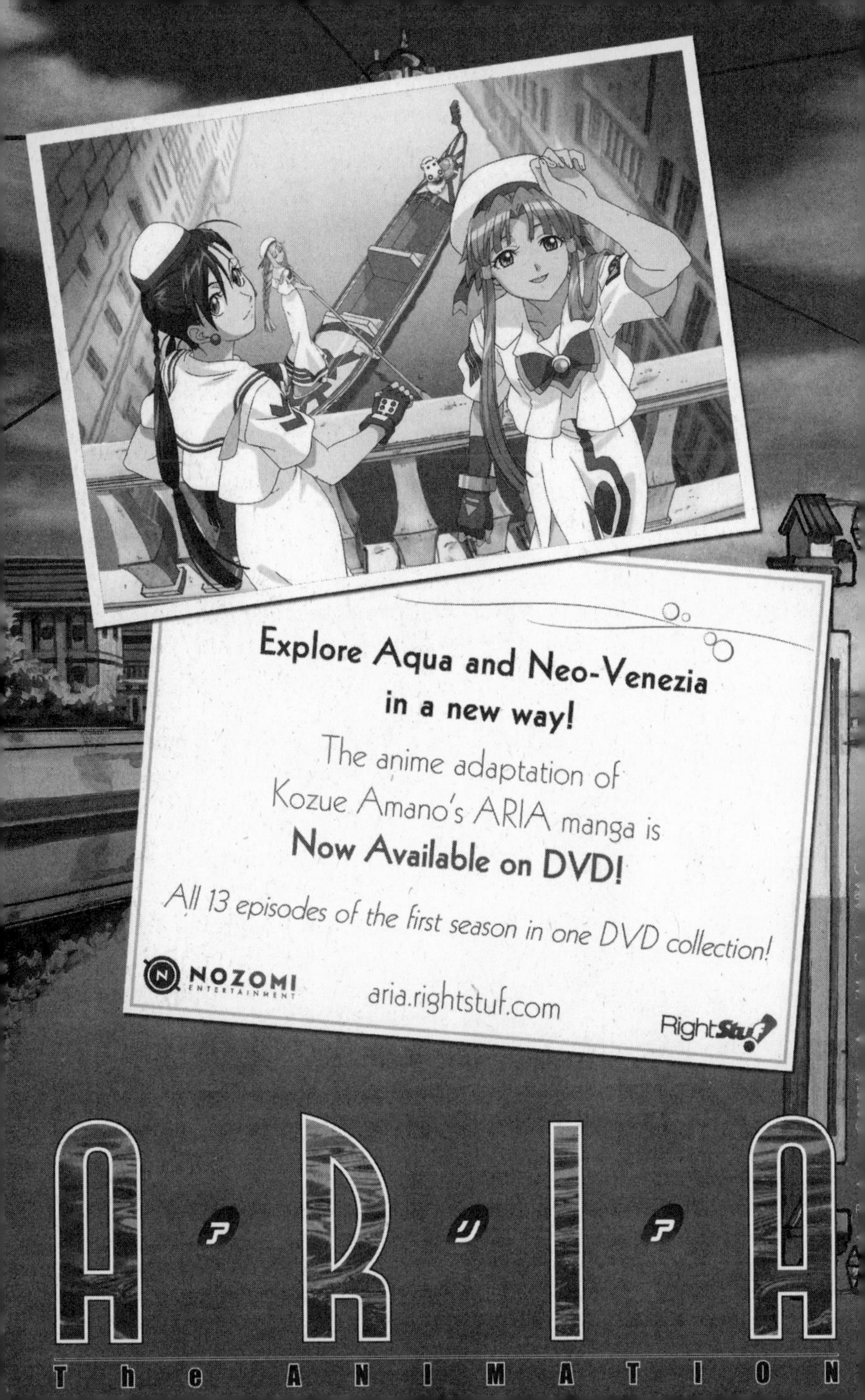
Explore Aqua and Neo-Venezia
in a new way!
The anime adaptation of
Kozue Amano's ARIA manga is
Now Available on DVD!
All 13 episodes of the first season in one DVD collection!
NOZOMI ENTERTAINMENT
aria.rightstuf.com
RightStuf!
ARIA
アリア
The ANIMATION

STOP!

This is the back of the book.
You wouldn't want to spoil a great ending!

This book is printed "manga-style," in the authentic Japanese right-to-left format. Since none of the artwork has been flipped or altered, readers get to experience the story just as the creator intended. You've been asking for it, so TOKYOPOP® delivered: authentic, hot-off-the-press, and far more fun!

DIRECTIONS

If this is your first time reading manga-style, here's a quick guide to help you understand how it works.

It's easy... just start in the top right panel and follow the numbers. Have fun, and look for more 100% authentic manga from TOKYOPOP®!